Management Across Cultures

The third edition of this popular textbook has been revised and updated throughout to explore the latest approaches to cross-cultural management, presenting strategies and tactics for managing international assignments and global teams. With a clear emphasis on learning and development, this new edition introduces a global management model, along with enhanced "Applications" and "Manager's Notebooks," to encourage students to acquire skills in multicultural competence that will be highly valued by their future employers. These skills have never been as important as now, in a world where, increasingly, all managers are global managers and where management practices and processes can differ significantly across national and regional boundaries. This book is suitable for students taking courses on international management, as well as those on executive training programs.

Richard M. Steers is Professor Emeritus of Organization and Management at the Lundquist College of Business, University of Oregon, USA.

Luciara Nardon is an Associate Professor of International Business at the Sprott School of Business, Carleton University, Canada.

Carlos J. Sanchez-Runde is Professor and Director in the Department of Managing People in Organizations at IESE Business School, University of Navarra, Spain.

Management Across Cultures

Developing Global Competencies

THIRD EDITION

Richard M. Steers

Luciara Nardon

Carlos J. Sanchez-Runde

CAMBRIDGE
UNIVERSITY PRESS

University Printing House, Cambridge CB2 8BS, United Kingdom

Cambridge University Press is part of the University of Cambridge.

It furthers the University's mission by disseminating knowledge in the pursuit of education, learning and research at the highest international levels of excellence.

www.cambridge.org
Information on this title: www.cambridge.org/9781107150799

First published 2016

Printed in the United Kingdom by Clays, St Ives plc

A catalogue record for this publication is available from the British Library

Library of Congress Cataloging in Publication data
Names: Steers, Richard M., author. | Nardon, Luciara, 1972- author. | Sanchez-Runde, Carlos, author.
Title: Management across cultures : developing global competencies / Richard M. Steers, Luciara Nardon, Carlos J. Sanchez-Runde.
Description: Third edition. | Cambridge, United Kingdom : Cambridge University Press, 2016.
Identifiers: LCCN 2016001615| ISBN 9781107150799 (Hardback) | ISBN 9781316604038 (Paperback)
Subjects: LCSH: Management–Cross-cultural studies. | International business enterprises–Management.
Classification: LCC HD62.4 .S735 2016 | DDC 658/.049–dc23 LC record available at http://lccn.loc.gov/2016001615

ISBN 978-1-107-15079-9 Hardback
ISBN 978-1-316-60403-8 Paperback

Contents

List of exhibits   *page* ix
Guided tour   xii
Preface   xv

1 Management across cultures: an introduction   1
Management challenge   1
The changing global landscape   3
Multicultural competence and managerial success   8
Manager's Notebook: Developing multicultural competence   9
Plan of book   12
Key terms   13
Discussion questions   13
Case: Global training at Google   14

2 Global managers: challenges and responsibilities   17
Management challenge   17
Traditional management models   19
Context of global management   21
Rethinking management models   25
Diversity in global assignments   30
Manager's Notebook: A model for global managers   38
Key terms   41
Discussion questions   41
Case: Two expatriates   42

3 Cultural environments   46
Management challenge   46
Culture, socialization, and normative behavior   48
Descriptive models of culture   52
Culture and institutional environments   59
Cultural complexities and contradictions   63
Cultural diversity and multiculturalism   70
Manager's Notebook: Working across cultures   72
Key terms   77
Discussion questions   77
Case: Anna Håkansson – from Sweden to Bahrain   78

4 Organizational environments   83
Management challenge   83
Organizations and environments   84
Stakeholders and global strategies   86
Organizing for global business   88
Regional organizing models   92
Control, participation, and decision-making   105
Corporate culture   109
Manager's Notebook: Working with global organizations   114
Key terms   119
Discussion questions   119
Case: Co-determination at Volkswagen   121

5 Communicating across cultures   126
Management challenge   126
Interpersonal communication   128
Cultural screens on interpersonal communication   130
Culture, cognition, and communication   132
Culture and communication protocols   141
Manager's Notebook: Communicating across cultures   149
Key terms   155
Discussion questions   155
Case: Roos Dekker, Global Healthcare   156

6 Leading global organizations   160
Management challenge   160
Dimensions of organizational leadership   162
Contemporary approaches to cross-cultural leadership   164
Limitations on contemporary approaches   171
GLOBE leadership study   174
Women leaders: challenges and opportunities   179
Leadership in China and the West   182
Manager's Notebook: Leading global organizations   185
Key terms   188
Discussion questions   188
Case: Emerson Electric – Suzhou   190

7 Negotiating global partnerships   194
Management challenge   194
Negotiations and global partnerships   196
Preparing for cross-cultural negotiations   201
Negotiating strategies and processes   207

Managing conflicts and compromise   211
Managing agreements and contracts   214
Manager's Notebook: Negotiating global partnerships   218
Key terms   221
Discussion questions   221
Case: Perils of being a junior manager   222

8   **Managing ethical conflicts**   228
Management challenge   228
Conflicts over beliefs and values   230
Conflicts between beliefs and institutional requirements   233
The ethical global leader   236
Ethical guidelines for global managers   239
Manager's Notebook: Managing ethical conflicts   252
Key terms   257
Discussion questions   257
Case: Energy contracts in Nigeria   258

9   **Managing work and motivation**   262
Management challenge   262
The world of work   264
Culture and the psychology of work   269
Managing incentives and rewards   275
Gender, compensation, and opportunities   280
Manager's Notebook: Managing work and motivation   283
Key terms   286
Discussion questions   286
Case: Samsung's *maquiladora* plant   287

10 **Managing global teams**   292
Management challenge   292
Global teams   294
Co-located and dispersed global teams   299
Special challenges of dispersed global teams   300
Managing dispersed global teams   306
Managing tasks and team processes   308
Leadership and global team-building   312
Manager's Notebook: Managing global teams   317
Key terms   321
Discussion questions   321
Case: IBM Cloud Labs   322

11 Managing global assignments   326
Management challenge   326
Global assignments   329
Challenges of living and working globally   336
Finding your way: coping with culture shock   341
Finding your place: acculturation strategies   350
Managing repatriation   353
Manager's Notebook: Managing global assignments   356
Key terms   361
Discussion questions   361
Case: Global assignment, Myanmar   362

12 Lessons learned   365
Management challenge   365
What have we learned?   366
Where do we go from here?   372

Appendix: Models of national cultures   378
Name index   393
Subject index   396

Exhibits

1.1	The changing global landscape	*page* 4
1.2	Building global management skills	10
1.3	Stages in developing multicultural competence	11
2.1	Traditional "logic" of organization and management	20
2.2	Managerial roles	21
2.3	Context of global management	23
2.4	Supervisory roles across cultures	25
2.5	Perceptions of managerial roles	26
2.6	Perceptions of managerial practices	27
2.7	Cultural influences on managerial roles	29
2.8	Challenges of global assignments	32
2.9	A model for global managers	39
3.1	The cultural environment of global management	48
3.2	Culture, personality, and human nature	51
3.3	Popular models of national cultures	54
3.4	Core cultural dimensions	58
3.5	Normative beliefs, institutional requirements, and social control	61
3.6	Cultural complexities and contradictions	67
3.7	Strategies for working across cultures	73
3.8	Hofstede's cultural dimensions for Bahrain and Sweden	80
4.1	The organizational environment of global management	85
4.2	Global organization designs	90
4.3	Regional models of organization	93
4.4	Example of US investor model of organization	95
4.5	Example of Chinese family model of organization (*gong-si*)	99
4.6	Example of Japanese network model of organization (Kirin Holdings *kaisha*, Mitsubishi *keiretsu*)	102
4.7	Example of German mutual benefit organization (*konzern*)	104
4.8	Employee participation in organizational decision-making	106
4.9	Decision analysis and implementation speed	107
4.10	Influences on corporate culture	111
4.11	Strategies for working with global organizations	116
4.12	Learning from different organizational models	118
5.1	AIA model of interpersonal communication	129
5.2	Cultural screens on interpersonal communication	131

5.3	Culturally mediated cognitions in communication	132
5.4	Native and non-native speakers	136
5.5	Culturally mandated communication protocols	141
5.6	Communication in low- and high-context cultures	145
5.7	Strategies for communicating across cultures	152
6.1	Dimensions of organizational leadership	163
6.2	Contemporary approaches to cross-cultural leadership	165
6.3	Global mindset of effective leaders	168
6.4	GLOBE cultural perspectives on leadership effectiveness	175
6.5	GLOBE leadership dimensions	176
6.6	Cultural beliefs about leadership styles	177
6.7	Percentage of women in senior leadership positions (rank order)	179
6.8	Percentage of board of director's seats held by women	180
6.9	Leadership patterns in China and the West	183
6.10	Strategies for leading global organizations	187
7.1	Benefits and challenges of global partnerships	197
7.2	Preparing for cross-cultural negotiations	202
7.3	Key success factors in cross-cultural partnerships	202
7.4	Competitive and problem-solving negotiation strategies	209
7.5	Examples of competitive and problem-solving negotiation strategies	210
7.6	Sequential and holistic bargaining strategies	211
7.7	Conflict resolution strategies	212
7.8	Contracts and the doctrine of changed circumstances	216
7.9	Strategies for negotiating global partnerships	219
8.1	Sources of ethical conflicts across cultures	231
8.2	Universalism, particularism, and ethical beliefs	232
8.3	Ethical beliefs, institutional requirements, and social control	234
8.4	GLOBE attributes of ethical leaders	237
8.5	OECD guidelines for ethical managerial behavior	240
8.6	Global Corruption Index	241
8.7	Pressures for and against OECD guideline compliance on bribery and corruption	243
8.8	Strategies for managing ethical conflicts	254
9.1	Culture, work values, and behavior	265
9.2	Vacation policies in selected countries	267
9.3	Culture and the psychological contract	270
9.4	Gender wage gaps across nations	281
9.5	Strategies for managing work and motivation	285
10.1	Advantages and drawbacks of global teams	296
10.2	Influences on global team synergy	298

10.3	Characteristics of co-located and dispersed global teams	301
10.4	Strategies for managing dispersed global teams	307
10.5	Managing tasks and team processes	309
10.6	Leadership and global team building strategies	313
10.7	Can people be trusted?	315
10.8	Developing mutual trust	316
10.9	Strategies for managing global teams	319
10.10	IBM's dispersed global development team for South Korean bank	322
11.1	Key relationships in living and working globally	328
11.2	Implications of employer-initiated and self-initiated global assignments	330
11.3	Long- and short-term global assignments	331
11.4	Long-term global assignments	332
11.5	Short-term global assignments	335
11.6	Challenges of living and working globally	336
11.7	Family considerations in global assignments	340
11.8	Career considerations in global assignments	341
11.9	Stages in psychological adaptation to a new culture	345
11.10	Strategies for coping with culture shock	348
11.11	Acculturation strategies in local cultures	351
11.12	Influences on acculturation success	353
11.13	Coping strategies of returning expatriates	354
11.14	Strategies for living and working globally	358
12.1	Stages in developing multicultural competence	367
12.2	Cultural, organizational, and situational contexts	368
12.3	Global management skills	369
12.4	Model for global managers	371
12.5	Learning from the past, looking to the future	375
A.1	Kluckhohn and Strodtbeck's cultural dimensions	379
A.2	Hofstede's cultural dimensions	380
A.3	Hall's cultural dimensions	381
A.4	Trompenaars' cultural dimensions	382
A.5	Schwartz's cultural dimensions	383
A.6	GLOBE project's cultural dimensions	384
A.7	Core cultural dimensions	386

Guided tour

Learning strategy for book

The learning strategy for this book is organized around a 3-stage developmental process:

Global challenges

Stage I begins our analysis by discussing both the challenges facing managers and how various managerial roles and responsibilities can often differ across cultural and organizational boundaries.

Global understanding

Stage II focuses on developing a deeper awareness and critical analysis of the complex cultural, organizational, and situational contexts in which global managers increasingly find themselves.

Global management

Stage III then builds on this foundation to focus on developing specific multicultural skills managers can use to survive and succeed in today's competitive global environment.

Recognize global challenges:

1. Management across cultures: an introduction
2. Global managers: challenges and responsibilities (with global management model)

Develop global understanding:

3. Cultural environments (including map of cultural environment and Appendix summarizing various models of national cultures)
4. Organizational environments (including map of organizational environment)

Develop global management skills:

5. Communicating across cultures
6. Leading global organizations
7. Negotiating global partnerships
8. Managing ethical conflicts
9. Managing work and motivation
10. Managing global teams
11. Managing global assignments
12. Lessons learned

A **global management model** is introduced early in the text to guide in the development of critical analysis skills as the book progresses.

Learning strategy for chapters

Each chapter also follows a learning strategy aimed at building bridges between theory and practice using a range of real-world examples, applications, discussion questions, and cases.

Chapter introduction
- Management challenge
- Chapter outline

Chapter content
- Concepts, research, and examples
- Applications and questions
- Manager's notebook: - summary points and action strategies

Chapter review
- Key terms
- Discussion questions
- Case study

Chapter introduction

Each chapter begins by highlighting the **management challenges** that serve as the basis for the chapter. **Chapter outlines** organize the text.

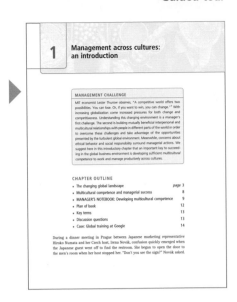

Chapter content

The **text** brings together what we currently know—and, in some cases, what we don't know—about the problems global managers may face in the field and the global skills they require to survive and succeed. These materials are based on current theory and research.

Applications are interspersed throughout each chapter to illustrate how concepts under study apply in practice. Application questions encourage students to develop an understanding of what managers did in particular situations and how they might have done it better.

Manager's notebooks summarize chapter lessons and their implications for managerial action.

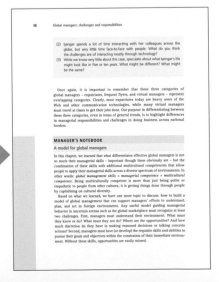

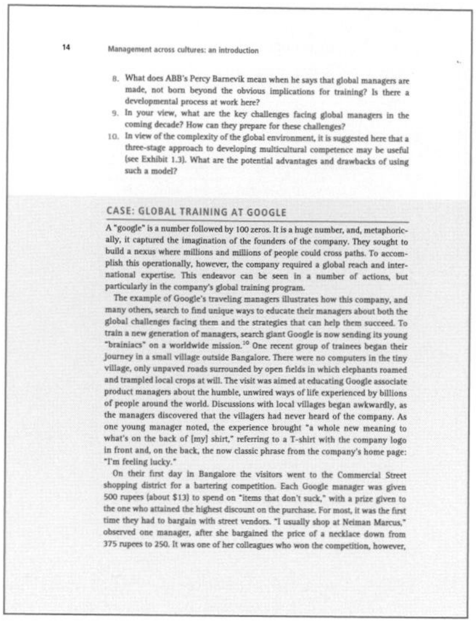

14 Management across cultures: an introduction

8. What does ABB's Percy Barnevik mean when he says that global managers are made, not born beyond the obvious implications for training? Is there a developmental process at work here?
9. In your view, what are the key challenges facing global managers in the coming decade? How can they prepare for these challenges?
10. In view of the complexity of the global environment, it is suggested here that a three-stage approach to developing multicultural competence may be useful (see Exhibit 1.3). What are the potential advantages and drawbacks of using such a model?

CASE: GLOBAL TRAINING AT GOOGLE

A "google" is a number followed by 100 zeros. It is a huge number, and, metaphorically, it captured the imagination of the founders of the company. They sought to build a nexus where millions and millions of people could cross paths. To accomplish this operationally, however, the company required a global reach and international expertise. This endeavor can be seen in a number of actions, but particularly in the company's global training program.

The example of Google's traveling managers illustrates how this company, and many others, search to find unique ways to educate their managers about both the global challenges facing them and the strategies that can help them succeed. To train a new generation of managers, search giant Google is now sending its young "brainiacs" on a worldwide mission.[10] One recent group of trainees began their journey in a small village outside Bangalore. There were no computers in the tiny village, only unpaved roads surrounded by open fields in which elephants roamed and trampled local crops at will. The visit was aimed at educating Google associate product managers about the humble, unwired ways of life experienced by billions of people around the world. Discussions with local villages began awkwardly, as the managers discovered that the villagers had never heard of the company. As one young manager noted, the experience brought "a whole new meaning to what's on the back of [my] shirt," referring to a T-shirt with the company logo in front and, on the back, the now classic phrase from the company's home page: "I'm feeling lucky."

On their first day in Bangalore the visitors went to the Commercial Street shopping district for a bartering competition. Each Google manager was given 500 rupees (about $13) to spend on "items that don't suck," with a prize given to the one who attained the highest discount on the purchase. For most, it was the first time they had to bargain with street vendors. "I usually shop at Neiman Marcus," observed one manager, after she bargained the price of a necklace down from 375 rupees to 250. It was one of her colleagues who won the competition, however,

Chapter review

Key terms highlight chapter concepts for purposes of review, while **discussion questions** probe both the conceptual and managerial implications of the materials under study.

Each chapter concludes with a **case study** for applying the problem-solving skills learned.

Learning strategy online

Instructors can access a comprehensive set of 600 downloadable **PowerPoint slides** online at www.cambridge.org/steers. These slides are designed to review the materials covered in each chapter, including key concepts, chapter applications, manager's notebooks, end-of-chapter discussion questions, and cases.

An online **instructional resources package** is also available to instructors that includes suggestions for use of in-text materials and PowerPoint slides; web links to author-recommended videos, cases, exercises, and simulations; team problem-solving activities; and supplemental downloadable global management cases and exercises by the authors.

Preface

This is a fantastic time to be entering the business world, because business is going to change more in the next 10 years than it has in the last 50.

Bill Gates, Founder, Microsoft[1]

Success in the global economy requires a number of ingredients, including innovative ideas and products, access to raw materials and competitive labor, savvy marketing strategies, solid financing, sustainable supply chains, and predictable logistical support. The central driver in this endeavor, however, is the manager – who is perpetually caught in the middle. Indeed, no one ever said being a manager was easy, but it seems to get more difficult with each passing year. As competitive pressures increase across most industries and services, so too do the pressures on managers to deliver results. Succeeding against the odds often catapults a manager into the higher echelons of the organization, with a concomitant increase in personal rewards. Failure to deliver often slows one's career advancement, though, if it doesn't stop it altogether. The stakes are very high for managers and organizations alike.

With this in mind, what do managers need to know to survive and succeed in this complex and turbulent environment? Certainly, they need to understand both micro- and macroeconomics. They need to understand the fundamentals of business practices, including strategy, marketing, operations and logistics, finance, and accounting. They also need to understand issues such as outsourcing, political risk, legal institutions, and the application of emerging technologies to organizational operations. In addition to this knowledge, however, managers must understand how to work with other people and organizations around the world to get their jobs done. We refer to this as *multicultural competence*, and it is the focus of this book.

This book is aimed at managers from round the world. It is not intended to be a North American book, a European book, a Latin American book, and so forth. Rather, it aims to explore managerial processes and practices from the standpoint of managers from all regions of the globe – China and Brazil, India and Germany, Australia and Singapore – as they pursue their goals and objectives in the field. This is done in the belief that the fundamental managerial role around the world is a relative constant, even though the details and specifics of managerial cognitions and actions may often vary – sometimes significantly – across cultures. Taken together, our goal in this book is to help managers develop an enhanced behavioral repertoire of cross-cultural management skills that can be used in a timely fashion when they are confronted with challenging and at times confusing situations. It is our hope that future managers, by better understanding cultural realities on the ground, and then using this understanding to develop improved coping strategies, will succeed when many of their predecessors did not.

As a result, this book focuses on developing a deeper understanding of how management practices and processes can often differ around the world, and why. It draws heavily on recent research in cultural anthropology, psychology, economics, and management as it relates to how managers structure their enterprises and pursue the day-to-day work necessary to make a venture succeed. It emphasizes both differences and similarities across cultures, since we believe that this approach mirrors reality. It attempts to explore the psychological underpinnings that help shape the attitudes and behaviors of managers, as well as their approaches to people from other regions of the world. Most of all, though, this book is about learning. It introduces a *global management model* early in the text to serve as a guide in the intellectual and practical development of managers seeking global experience. Further, it assumes a lifelong learning approach to global encounters, managerial performance, and career success.

Throughout this book, our emphasis is on critical analysis, not drawing arbitrary conclusions or selecting favorites. This is done in the belief that successful global managers will focus more on understanding and flexibility than evaluation and dogmatism. This understanding can facilitate a manager's ability both to prepare and to act in ways that are more in tune with local environments. As a result, managers who are better prepared for future events are more likely to succeed – full stop. By integrating these two perspectives – explorations into the cultural drivers underlying managerial action and the common management strategies used in the field – it is our intention to present a more process-oriented look at global managers at work.

The title of this book reflects the twin goals in writing it. First, we wanted to examine how management practices and processes can frequently differ – often significantly – across national and regional boundaries. Managers in different cultures often see their roles and responsibilities in different ways. They often organize themselves and make decisions differently. They often communicate, negotiate, and motivate employees in different ways. Understanding these differences is the first step in developing global management capabilities. Second, we wanted to identify and discuss realistic strategies and tactics that can be used by global managers as they work to succeed across cultures. In other words, we wanted to explore how people can work and manage across cultures – and how they can overcome many of the hurdles along the way. We see these two goals as not just mutually compatible but indispensable for meeting the business challenges ahead.

Like most authors who seek an interested audience, we wrote this book primarily to express our own views, ideas, and frustrations. As both teachers and researchers in the field, we have grown increasingly impatient with books in this area that seem to aim somewhat below the readers' intelligence in the presentation of materials. In our view, managers and would-be managers alike are intelligent consumers of behavioral information. To do their jobs better, they seek useful information and dialogue about the uncertain environments in which they work; they are not seeking unwarranted or simplistic conclusions or narrow rulebooks. Moreover, in our view, managers are looking for learning strategies, not prescriptions, and understand that becoming a global manager is a long-term pursuit – a marathon, not a sprint.

We have likewise been dismayed seeing books that assume one worldview, whether it is British, Chinese, American, French, or whatever, in interpreting both global business challenges and managerial behavior. Instead, we have tried diligently to cast our net a bit wider and incorporate divergent viewpoints when exploring various topics, such as communication, negotiation, and leadership. For example, asking how Chinese or Indian management practices differ from Australian or Canadian practices assumes a largely Western bias as a starting point: "How are *they* different from us?" Instead, why not ask a simpler and more useful question, to find out how Chinese, Indian, Australian, and Canadian management styles in general differ: "How are we *all* different from one another?" Moreover, we might add a further, also useful, question concerning managerial similarities across cultures: "How are we *all* similar to each other?" To achieve this end, we have resisted a one-size-fits-all approach to management, locally or globally, in the belief that such an approach limits both understanding and success in the field. Rather, our goal here is to develop multicultural competence through the development of learning strategies in which managers can draw on their own personal experiences, combined with outside information such as that provided in this book and elsewhere, to develop cross-cultural understanding and theories-in-use that can guide them in the pursuit of their managerial activities.

In writing this book, we were also able to draw on our research and teaching experiences in various countries and regions of the world, including Argentina, Belgium, Brazil, Canada, Chile, China, Colombia, Denmark, Germany, Japan, Mexico, Netherlands, Norway, Peru, Singapore, South Africa, South Korea, Spain, United Kingdom, United States, and Uruguay. In doing so, we learned from our colleagues and students in various parts of the world, and we believe that these experiences have made this a better book than it might otherwise have been. Our aim here is not to write a bias-free book, as we believe this would have been an impossible task. Indeed, the decision to write this book in English, largely for reasons of audience, market, and personal competence, does itself introduce some bias into the end result. Rather, our intent was to write a book that simultaneously reflects differing national, cultural, and personal viewpoints, in which biases are identified and discussed openly instead of being hidden or rationalized. As a result, this book contains few certainties and many contradictions, reflecting our views on the life of global managers.

Few projects of this magnitude can be successful without the support of families. This is especially true in our case, with all three of our families joining together to help make this project a reality. In particular, Richard would like to thank the three generations of women who surround and support him: Sheila, Kathleen, and Allison; Luciara would like to thank her mother, Jussara, for her unconditional support, and her son, Caio, for his inspiration; and Carlos would like to thank his wife, Carol, and daughters, Clara and Isabel, for their continued support and encouragement. Throughout, our families have been there for us in every way possible, and for this we are grateful.

Any successful book is a joint venture between authors, instructors, students, and publishers. In this regard, we were fortunate to have received useful comments from instructors and outside reviewers alike aimed at making this edition superior to the last. Student comments, both in our own classes and those of others, have also helped us improve on the first edition. Finally, we are indebted to the people at Cambridge University Press for their help and support throughout the revision and production process. They lived up to their reputation as a first-class group of people to work with. In particular, we wish to thank Paula Parish, Raihanah Begum, and Jo Lane for their advice, patience, and support through the project. We are indebted to them all.

Richard M. Steers, USA
Luciara Nardon, Canada
Carlos Sanchez-Runde, Spain

NOTE

1. J. D. Meier, "Lessons learned from Bill Gates," sourcesofinsight.com, 2013.

1 Management across cultures: an introduction

MANAGEMENT CHALLENGE

MIT economist Lester Thurow observes, "A competitive world offers two possibilities. You can lose. Or, if you want to win, you can change."[1] With increasing globalization come increased pressures for both change and competitiveness. Understanding this changing environment is a manager's first challenge. The second is building mutually beneficial interpersonal and multicultural relationships with people in different parts of the world in order to overcome these challenges and take advantage of the opportunities presented by the turbulent global environment. Meanwhile, concerns about ethical behavior and social responsibility surround managerial actions. We suggest here in this introductory chapter that an important key to succeeding in the global business environment is developing sufficient *multicultural competence* to work and manage productively across cultures.

CHAPTER OUTLINE

- The changing global landscape — *page* 3
- Multicultural competence and managerial success — 8
- MANAGER'S NOTEBOOK: Developing multicultural competence — 9
- Plan of book — 12
- Key terms — 13
- Discussion questions — 13
- Case: Global training at Google — 14

During a dinner meeting in Prague between Japanese marketing representative Hiroko Numata and her Czech host, Irena Novák, confusion quickly emerged when the Japanese guest went off to find the restroom. She began to open the door to the men's room when her host stopped her. "Don't you see the sign?" Novák asked.

"Of course I do," Numata responded, "but it is red. In our country, a red-colored sign means it's the ladies' room. For men, it should be blue or black." Novák returned to her table, remembering that she too had looked at the sign but had focused on what was written, not its color. She wondered how many other things she and her Japanese colleague had seen or discussed but interpreted very differently.[2]

We live in a contradictory and turbulent world, in which there are few certainties and change is constant. Over time, we increasingly come to realize that much of what we think we see around us can, in reality, be something entirely different. We require greater perceptual insight just as the horizons become more and more cloudy. Business cycles are becoming more dynamic and unpredictable, and companies, institutions, and employees come and go with increasing regularity. Much of this uncertainty is the result of economic forces that are beyond the control of individuals and major corporations. Much results from recent waves of technological change that resist pressures for stability or predictability. Much also results from the failures of individuals and corporations to understand the realities on the ground when they pit themselves against local institutions, competitors, and cultures. Knowledge is definitely power when it comes to global business, and, as our knowledge base becomes more uncertain, companies and their managers seek help wherever they can find it.

Considering the amount of knowledge required to succeed in today's global business environment and the speed with which this knowledge becomes obsolete, it is the thesis of this book that mastering learning skills and developing an ability to work successfully with partners in different parts of the world may well be the best strategy available to managers who want to succeed. Business and institutional knowledge is transmitted through interpersonal interactions. If managers are able to build mutually beneficial interpersonal and multicultural relationships with partners around the world, they may be able to overcome their knowledge gaps. *Our aim in this book, then, is to develop information and learning models that managers can build upon to pursue their job responsibilities, corporate missions, and careers.*

As managers increasingly find themselves working across borders, their list of cultural contradictions continues to grow. Consider just a few examples. Most French and Germans refer to the European Union as "we," while many British refer to it as "they"; all are members. To some Europeans, Japan is part of the "Far East," while, to some Japanese, Europe is part of the "Far East"; it all depends on where you are standing. Criticizing heads of state is a favorite pastime in many countries around the world, but criticizing the king in Thailand is a felony punishable by fifteen years in jail. Every time Nigerian-born oncologist Nkechi Mba fills in her name on a form somewhere, she is politely told to write her name, not her degree. In South Korea, a world leader in IT networks, supervisors often assume employees are not working unless they are physically sitting at their desks in the office. And in a recent marketing survey among US college students, only 7 percent could identify the national origins of many of their favorite brands, including Adidas, Samsung, Nokia, Lego, and Ericsson. In particular, quality ratings of Nokia cellphones soared after students concluded, incorrectly, that they were made in Japan.

There is more. Germany's Bavarian Radio Symphony Orchestra recently deleted part of its classical repertoire from a concert tour because it violated the European Union's new noise at work limitations. US telecommunications giant AT&T has been successfully sued in class action suits for gender discrimination against both its female and male employees. When you sink a hole in one while playing golf with friends in North America and Europe, it is often customary for your partners to pay you a cash prize; in Japan, you pay them. The head of Nigeria's Niger Delta Development Corporation was fired from his job after it was discovered that he had paid millions of dollars of public money to a local witch doctor to vanquish a rival. The penalty for a first offense of smuggling a small quantity of recreational drugs into Western Europe is usually a stern lecture or a warning; in Singapore, it is death. Finally, dressing for global business meetings can be challenging: wearing anything made of leather can be offensive to many Hindus in India; wearing yellow is reserved for the royal family in Malaysia; and white is the color of mourning in many parts of Asia.

When confronted by such examples, many observers are dismissive, suggesting that the world is getting smaller and that many of these troublesome habits and customs will likely disappear over time as globalization pressures work to homogenize how business is done – properly, they believe – across national boundaries. This may be incorrect, however. *The world is not getting smaller; it is getting faster.* Many globalization pressures are currently bypassing – and, indeed, in some cases actually accentuating – divergent local customs, conventions, and business practices, if for no other reason than to protect local societies from the ravages of economic warfare. What this means for managers is that many of these and other local customs will likely be around for a long time, and wise managers will prepare themselves to capitalize on these differences, not ignore them.

The changing global landscape

Much of what is being written today about the changing global landscape is characterized by a sense of energy, urgency, and opportunity. We hear about developing transformational leaders, building strategic alliances, launching global product platforms, leveraging technological breakthroughs, first-mover advantages, global venturing, outsourcing, sustainable supply chains, and, most of all, making money. Action – and winning – seem to be the operational words. Discussions about

Exhibit 1.1 The changing global landscape

global business assume a sense of perpetual dynamic equilibrium. We are told that nothing is certain except change, and that winners are always prepared for change; we are also told that global business is like white water rafting – always on the edge; and so forth. Everything is in motion, and opportunities abound.

At the same time, however, there is another, somewhat more troublesome side to this story of globalization that is discussed far less often, yet it is equally important. This side is characterized by seemingly endless conflicts with partners, continual misunderstandings with suppliers and distributors, mutual distrust, perpetual delays, ongoing cost overruns, political and economic risks and setbacks, personal stress, and, in some cases, lost careers. Indeed, *over 50 percent of international joint ventures fail within the first five years of operation.* The principal reasons cited for these failures are cultural differences and conflicts between partners.[3]

Problems such as these have several potentially severe consequences for organizational success, especially in the area of building workable global partnerships. Although it is not easy to get a handle on all the changes occurring in the global environment, three prominent changes stand out: the evolution from intermittent to continual change, from isolation to increasing interconnectedness, and from biculturalism to multiculturalism (see Exhibit 1.1).

From intermittent to continuous change

Change is everywhere. Companies, products, and managers come and go. This turbulence increasingly requires almost everyone, from investors to consumers, to pay greater heed to the nature, scope, and speed of world events, both economically and politically. Details have become more important. Personal relationships, even though they are under increasing strain, remain one of the last safe havens in an otherwise largely unpredictable world.

Across this changing environment – indeed, as one of the principal causes of these changes – we can see the relentless development and application of new technologies, especially with regard to the digital revolution. Technology is largely held to be a principal driver of globalization and the key to national economic development and competitiveness. Indeed, global business as we know it today would not be possible without technology. It was only with the emergence of affordable and reliable computer and communication technologies that coordination and collaboration across borders became reliable. A few years ago subsidiaries were managed as independent organizations, and managers traveled around the globe for coordination purposes. Today electronic technologies facilitate the transfer of information and make communication through text, voice, and video simple and affordable.

At the same time, globalization has resulted in an increase in the transfer and diffusion of technological innovation across borders, as well as competition among nations to develop and adopt advanced technologies. As business becomes more and more global, the need for better and cheaper technology increases, pushing technological development to new heights. Computers are obsolete as soon as they are out of the box, smartphones integrate new functionalities for managers on the move, and we have cellphone coverage and Internet access in almost every corner of the world. Managers cannot understand globalization or manage globally without understanding the influence of technology on business.

Take the example of the growth of the mobile Web in Vietnam.[4] Internet penetration in Vietnam has grown to 44 percent of the state's 90 million people from 12 percent a decade ago. Much of that is driven by smartphones, which are used by more than a third of the population. This expansion is powering a range of online services, many of which are showing their first signs of serious growth, such as mobile e-commerce. A Vietnamese government agency forecasts the market for e-commerce will generate revenue of $4 billion this year, compared with $700 million in 2012. Data prices are among the lowest in the world. This presents an opportunity for local businesses and at the same time expands the footprint of global technology companies. Active mobile social-media accounts, meanwhile, rose 41 percent in the past year. That is more than China, India, or Brazil, and indicates what might happen in other mobile-first countries such as Myanmar or Nigeria as they race to catch up with Internet usage in more developed countries. And Facebook now has 30 million active users in Vietnam, up from 8.5 million just three years ago, making the country one of Facebook's fastest-growing markets.

From isolation to interconnectedness

In today's increasingly turbulent and uncertain business environment, major changes occur with increasing regularity. The recent collapse of the global financial markets, accompanied by worldwide recession, continues to cause hardships around the world and has led to changes, both political and economic, in rich and poor countries alike. The economic and political power of India and China continues to grow exponentially, and both are struggling to manage the positive and negative consequences of growth and development. Russia is trying to reassert itself politically and economically in the world, overcome rampant corruption in its business sector, and reform its economic system in order to build local companies that can compete effectively in the global economy. Arab nations are struggling for greater democracy and human rights. Japan is trying to rebuild its economy after its recent catastrophic environmental disaster. France is trying to reinvigorate its economy by changing its historically uncompetitive labor policies. Turkey is trying to join the European Union so that its companies can gain greater access to world markets. South Africa continues to struggle to shed the vestiges of its old apartheid system and build a new, stronger economy based on more egalitarian principles. Throughout, there is a swelling consumer demand for higher quality but lower-cost goods and services that challenge most governments and corporations. In a nutshell, welcome to today's increasingly global economy. In this new economy, globalization is not a debate; it is a reality.

This is not to say that the challenges and potential perils of globalization are a recent phenomenon. Indeed, quite the contrary is true; globalization has always been a major part of commerce. What is new, however, is the magnitude of globalization today and its impact on standards of living, international trade, social welfare, and environmental sustainability. In 1975 global foreign direct investment (FDI) totaled just $23 billion; by 1998, a little over twenty years later, it totaled $644 billion; and by 2008, just ten years after that, it totaled $1.5 trillion. It is estimated that, by 2020, global FDI will surpass $3 trillion. Despite regional and worldwide recessions and economic setbacks, global FDI continues to grow at a seemingly uncontrollable rate. What are the ramifications of this increase for organizations and their managers? What are the implications for developed and less developed countries? Is there a role for governments and public policy in this revolution?

Take just one example of this interconnectedness. When the use of ethanol as an additive to gasoline production increased significantly in American and European markets, corn prices around the world skyrocketed, and the price of tortillas in Mexico, a staple food among Mexico's poor, nearly doubled. A short time later, however, the bottom fell out of the ethanol market as oil prices dropped and the price of corn fell.[5] Then, a year later, oil prices skyrocketed again, as did the price of corn. Caught in the middle of all of this is the Mexican peasant, just trying to survive: unintended, yet nonetheless very real, consequences.

From biculturalism to multiculturalism

The increasing intensity and diversity that characterize today's global business environment require managers to succeed simultaneously in multiple cultures, not just one. Gone are the days when a manager prepared for a long-term assignment in

France or Germany – or even Europe. Today this same manager must deal simultaneously with partners from perhaps a dozen or more different cultures around the globe. As a result, learning one language and culture may no longer be enough, as it was in the past. In addition, the timeline for developing business relationships has declined from years to months – and sometimes to weeks. This requires a new approach to developing global managers. This evolution from a principally bicultural business environment to a more multicultural or global environment presents managers with at least three new challenges in attempting to adapt quickly to the new realities on the ground.

- It is sometimes unclear to which culture we should adapt. Suppose that your company has asked you to join a global team to work on a six-month R&D project. The team includes one Brazilian, one Indian, one Portuguese, and one Russian. Every member of the team has a permanent appointment in his or her home country but is temporarily assigned to work at company headquarters in Sweden for this project. Which culture should team members adapt to? In this case, there is no dominant cultural group to dictate the rules. Considering the multiple cultures involved, and the little exposure each manager has likely had with the other cultures, the traditional approach of adaptation is unlikely to be successful. Nevertheless, the group's members have to be able to work together quickly and effectively to produce results (and protect their careers), despite their differences. What would you do?
- Many multicultural encounters occur at short notice, leaving little time to learn about the other culture. Imagine that you have just returned from a week's stay in India, where you were negotiating an outsourcing agreement. As you arrive in your home office, you learn that an incredible acquisition opportunity has just turned up in South Africa and that you are supposed to leave in a week to explore the matter further. You have never been to South Africa, nor do you know anybody from there. What would you do?
- Multicultural meetings increasingly occur virtually, by way of Skype or video conferencing, instead of through more traditional face-to-face interactions. Suppose that you were asked to build a partnership with a partner from Singapore whom you have never met, and that you know little about the multiple cultures of Singapore. Suppose further that this task is to be completed online, without any face-to-face communication or interactions. Your boss is in a hurry for results. What would you do?

Taken together, these three challenges illustrate just how difficult it can be to work or manage across cultures in today's rapidly changing business environment. The old ways of communicating, negotiating, leading, and doing business are simply less effective than they were in the past. As such, as noted earlier, the principal focus of this book will be on how to facilitate management success in global environments – how to become a global manager.

Multicultural competence and managerial success

Globalization pressures represent a serious challenge facing businesses and the way in which they conduct themselves in the global economy, and they have a direct influence on the quality and effectiveness of management. Even so, globalization presents companies with opportunities as well as challenges. The manner in which they respond – or fail to respond – to such challenges will in large measure determine who wins and who loses. Those that succeed will need to have sufficient managers with economic grounding, political and legal skills, and cultural awareness to decipher the complexities that characterize their surrounding environment. Tying this all together will be the management know-how to outsmart, outperform, or outlast the competition on a continuing basis. Although globalization seems to be inevitable, however, not all cultures and countries will react in the same way, and therein lies one of the principal challenges for managers working across cultures.

In view of the myriad challenges such as this, managers viewing global assignments – or even global travel – would do well to learn as much as they can about the world in which they will work. The same holds true for local managers working in their home countries, where the global business world is increasingly challenging them on their own turf. Like it or not, with globalization and competition both increasing almost everywhere, the challenge for managers is to outperform their competitors, individually or collectively. This can be attempted either by focusing exclusively on one's own self-interests or by building mutually beneficial strategic alliances with global partners. Either way, the challenges and pitfalls can be significant.

Another important factor to take into consideration here is a fundamental shift in the nature of geopolitics. The days of hegemony – East or West – are over. No longer do global business leaders focus on one or two stock markets, currencies, economies, or political leaders. Today's business environment is far too complex and interrelated for that. Contrary to some predictions, however, nation states and multinational corporations will remain both powerful and important; we are not, in fact, moving towards a "borderless society." Global networks, comprising technological, entrepreneurial, social welfare, and environmental interest groups, will also remain powerful. Indeed, global networks will increasingly represent power, not traditional or historic institutions. Future economic and business endeavors, like future political, social, and environmental endeavors, will be increasingly characterized by a search for common ground, productive partnerships, and mutual benefits.

The plight of many of today's failed or mediocre managers is evident from the legion of stories about failures in cross-border enterprise. Managers are responsible for utilizing human, financial, informational, and physical resources in ways that facilitate their organization's overall objectives in turbulent and sometimes hostile environments about which they often understand very little. These challenges can be particularly problematic when operations cross national boundaries.

As globalization pressures increase and managers spend more time crossing borders to conduct business, the training and development community has increasingly advocated more intensive analyses of the criteria for managerial success in the global economy. As more attention is focused on this challenge, a growing cadre of management experts is zeroing in on the need for managers to develop perspectives that stretch beyond domestic borders. This concept is identified in many ways, including "cultural intelligence" and "global leadership," but we refer to it simply as multicultural competence.[6] (This topic is discussed in greater detail in Chapter 2.) Whatever it is called, its characteristics and skills are in increasing demand as firms large and small, established and entrepreneurial, strive for global competitiveness.

The concept of multicultural competence and how it can be developed is at the heart of this book. The skills and abilities discussed throughout this volume represent an effort to develop such competence. The fundamental challenge of multicultural competence is not whether or not managers possess it; rather, it is a question of how much they possess. It is a question of degree. Simply put, better trained managers – especially those with higher levels of multicultural competence – tend to succeed in challenging foreign environments more often than those with lower levels of competence. It is as simple as that.

Endeavoring to meet the challenges discussed throughout this chapter is far more the result of hard work, clear thinking, serious reflection, and attentive behavior than any of the quick fixes that are so readily available. To accomplish this, managers will need to develop some degree of multicultural competence as an important tool to guide their social interactions and business decisions and prevent themselves from repeating the intercultural and strategic mistakes made by so many of their predecessors. Clearly, working and managing in the global economy require more than cross-cultural understanding and skills, but we argue that, without such skills, the manager's job is all the more difficult to accomplish. If the world is truly moving towards greater complexity, interconnections, and corporate interrelationships, the new global manager will obviously need to play a role in order for organizations and their stakeholders to succeed.

MANAGER'S NOTEBOOK

Developing multicultural competence

Former Swiss-based ABB chairman Percy Barnevik observed, "Global managers are made, not born. This is not a natural process."[7] Becoming a global manager is the result of a process, a career path streaming through different assignments and cultures. It is a journey, not an end state. Throughout, we suggest that what

Exhibit 1.2 Building global management skills

differentiates effective global managers is not so much their managerial skills – although this is obviously important – but the combination of these skills with additional multicultural competencies that allow people to apply their managerial skills across a diverse spectrum of environments (see Exhibit 1.2). It is this synergistic integration of basic management skills working in tandem with a deep understanding of how organizations and management practices differ across cultures that differentiates the successful from the less successful global managers.

Whether relocating to a foreign country for a long stay, traveling around the world for short stints, or dealing with foreigners in one's home country, managers often face important cultural challenges. Different cultures have different assumptions, behaviors, communication styles, and expectations about management practice. The ability to deal with these differences in ways that are both appropriate and effective goes by many names, but we refer to it simply as *multicultural competence*. It represents the capacity to work successfully across cultures. Being multiculturally competent is more than just being polite or empathetic to people from other cultures; *it is getting things done through people by capitalizing on cultural diversity.*

Multicultural competence can be seen as a way of viewing the world with a particular emphasis on broadening one's cultural perspective as it relates to cross-cultural behavior.[8] In other words, it asks the question: what can we learn from people around us from different cultures that can improve our ability to function effectively in a multicultural world? Multicultural competencies include elements of curiosity, awareness of diversity, and acceptance of complexity. People with multicultural competence tend to open up themselves by rethinking boundaries and changing their behaviors. They are curious and concerned with context, possessing an ability to place current events and tasks into historical and probable future contexts alike. They accept inherent contradictions in everyday life, and have the ability to maintain their comfort level with continual change.

In addition, managers who possess multicultural competence have a commitment to diversity, consciousness and sensitivity, as well as valuing diversity itself. They exhibit a willingness to seek opportunities in surprises and uncertainties, including an ability to take moderate risks and make intuitive decisions. They focus on continuous improvement, with a capacity for self-improvement and helping others develop. They typically take a long-term perspective on activities and plans, focusing on long-term results and not obsessing on short-term problems or results. Finally, they frequently take a systems perspective, including an ability to seek out interdependencies and cause–effect relationships.

It seems clear that, as the world of business draws closer together, companies in all countries will require managers who can work in a truly global environment. In this environment, successful managers bring a depth and breadth of understanding of how to capitalize on cultural differences in ways that enhance corporate goals and employee welfare as well. In large measure, this is what distinguishes between managers who can succeed in their local surroundings and managers who can succeed in the global economy.

Much has been written on the topic of developing global management skills, and much of what has been written is contradictory, simplistic, and sometimes simply incorrect. Successful global managers tend to rely on themselves, including their own perceptions and assessments of what is going on in the world. They often require personal insight more than outside advice. Indeed, what often differentiates successful global managers from unsuccessful ones is the fact that they have developed a way of thinking about the world that is flexible and inclusive and guides their behavior across cultures and national boundaries.

One way to view this is to think about professional development as consisting of *three stages* (see Exhibit 1.3). In the first stage, emphasis is placed on better

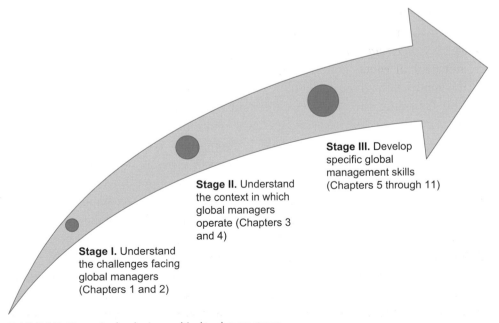

Stage III. Develop specific global management skills (Chapters 5 through 11)

Stage II. Understand the context in which global managers operate (Chapters 3 and 4)

Stage I. Understand the challenges facing global managers (Chapters 1 and 2)

Exhibit 1.3 Stages in developing multicultural competence

understanding the various challenges facing managers. In the second stage, emphasis shifts to better understanding the cultural, organizational, and situational environments in which management occurs. Finally, in the third stage, emphasis is placed on learning specific global management skills, as well as understanding where and how to use these skills. Taken together, we view these three stages as a roadmap to developing multicultural competence.

The case below on global training programs at Google illustrates how these three strategies can be combined to facilitate multicultural competence that benefits managers, employees, customers, and the long-term goals of the company.

Plan of book

As just noted, we view management success in the global arena as consisting of three interrelated components: understanding global challenges; understanding global environments; and developing global management skills. As such, this book has been organized around this assumption as a three-step developmental process. As Arie de Geus of Royal Dutch Shell says, "In the future, the ability to learn faster than your competitors may be the only sustainable competitive advantage."[9] The aim of this book is to support this mission.

1. Understanding global challenges (Chapters 1 and 2). Managers must first understand the challenges and obstacles they face, as well as the opportunities. They must understand their jobs and how their efforts fit into the larger organizational objectives. And they must have a mental model of what is needed to succeed in the field and how the various parts fit together. Such a global management model is presented in the following chapter, and we will build on this model throughout the book.

2. Understanding the global environment (Chapters 3 and 4). Managers must next understand how to assess the local environments in which they work and make suitable choices among available alternatives. While there are many ways to break up this environment for the purposes of analysis and understanding, we suggest that a productive approach is to visualize three interrelated environments: cultural, organizational, and situational. That is, to accomplish their tasks and responsibilities, managers must succeed in all three environments simultaneously. Taken together, this environment creates both demands and constraints on managerial action. These limitations raise two pertinent questions for global managers: what must I do as a manager – that is, what is expected of me to succeed – and, second, what must I avoid doing as a manager? What actions should I avoid in order not to offend others or lose opportunities? Within these two limitations, managers are free to make informed choices among their

available options concerning their present and future actions. The question here is: what are my options, and how can I best use my managerial skills on behalf of the organization? Again, the global management model introduced in Chapter 2 is designed to be helpful.

3. Developing global management skills (Chapters 5 through 11). Once the local environment is better understood and choices have been made, managers must have (or develop) suitable global managerial skills to carry out their actions. As discussed in this book, we view these skills as including cross-cultural communication, leadership, negotiation and global partnerships, ethics, work and motivation, team management, and living and working successfully abroad. This section of the book is oriented very specifically to skills development and action planning. We conclude with Chapter 12 that aims to summarize and integrate the materials presented throughout the book.

KEY TERMS

changing global landscape (characteristics) • multicultural competence

DISCUSSION QUESTIONS

1. MIT economist Lester Thurow suggests that companies must, in essence, change or die. Do you agree with this assertion? Why or why not? In which ways might this statement be correct and in which ways might it be misleading?

2. It was also suggested in the chapter that the world is not getting smaller; it is getting faster. Do you agree or disagree with this statement? If so, what does this mean for global managers?

3. Experts seem to agree that for most businesses, globalization is the pathway to survival. But most does not mean all. What are some characteristics of businesses that can thrive – or even prosper – without globalization? Explain.

4. Over 50 percent of international joint ventures fail within the first five years of operation. What, if anything, can future managers, not past managers, do to reduce this failure rate?

5. Three characteristics of the changing global landscape were discussed in this chapter (Exhibit 1.1). Do you believe each of these characteristics is inevitable or might future events serve to nullify or change the directions of one or more of these trends? Why?

6. Like societies, corporations are moving towards increasingly multicultural organizations. What are the positive and potentially negative consequences of this trend for corporations, employees, and societies at large?

7. Why is multicultural competence so important for managerial and corporate success? Explain.

8. What does ABB's Percy Barnevik mean when he says that global managers are made, not born beyond the obvious implications for training? Is there a developmental process at work here?

9. In your view, what are the key challenges facing global managers in the coming decade? How can they prepare for these challenges?

10. In view of the complexity of the global environment, it is suggested here that a three-stage approach to developing multicultural competence may be useful (see Exhibit 1.3). What are the potential advantages and drawbacks of using such a model?

CASE: GLOBAL TRAINING AT GOOGLE

A "google" is a number followed by 100 zeros. It is a huge number, and, metaphorically, it captured the imagination of the founders of the company. They sought to build a nexus where millions and millions of people could cross paths. To accomplish this operationally, however, the company required a global reach and international expertise. This endeavor can be seen in a number of actions, but particularly in the company's global training program.

The example of Google's traveling managers illustrates how this company, and many others, search to find unique ways to educate their managers about both the global challenges facing them and the strategies that can help them succeed. To train a new generation of managers, search giant Google is now sending its young "brainiacs" on a worldwide mission.[10] One recent group of trainees began their journey in a small village outside Bangalore. There were no computers in the tiny village, only unpaved roads surrounded by open fields in which elephants roamed and trampled local crops at will. The visit was aimed at educating Google associate product managers about the humble, unwired ways of life experienced by billions of people around the world. Discussions with local villages began awkwardly, as the managers discovered that the villagers had never heard of the company. As one young manager noted, the experience brought "a whole new meaning to what's on the back of [my] shirt," referring to a T-shirt with the company logo in front and, on the back, the now classic phrase from the company's home page: "I'm feeling lucky."

On their first day in Bangalore the visitors went to the Commercial Street shopping district for a bartering competition. Each Google manager was given 500 rupees (about $13) to spend on "items that don't suck," with a prize given to the one who attained the highest discount on the purchase. For most, it was the first time they had to bargain with street vendors. "I usually shop at Neiman Marcus," observed one manager, after she bargained the price of a necklace down from 375 rupees to 250. It was one of her colleagues who won the competition, however, by purchasing a deep burgundy *sherwani* – a traditional Indian outfit – for one-third of the original asking price.

From India, the group traveled to Japan, to visit the company's Shibuya headquarters and network with fellow employees, learn about regional markets, and study the local culture. The visitors shared the product "roadmap" for the next year with their Japanese colleagues, answered questions, and then heard what the engineers and managers in each location were focusing on. They also got a sense of the local marketplace by talking to local Googlers, customers, and partners. In Tokyo, they learned that Yahoo! Japan was clobbering the competition – it's like Google and AOL and eBay rolled into one – but that Google had captured the imagination of the Japanese people. It was the no. 2 brand in the country, behind Toyota.

Tokyo's legendary electronics district, Akihabara, was chosen for another group competition, ostensibly to sharpen the product knowledge, business skills, and street smarts of the global travelers. They were divided into small teams and given $100 to buy the strangest gadgets they could find. Diving into stalls full of electronic gizmos, they found items such as a USB-powered smoke-removing ashtray and a stubby wand that, when waved back and forth, spells out words in LED lights.

Next the group traveled to China, and came face-to-face with the realities of doing business there. They immediately recognized the conflict of balancing the company's freewheeling management style with China's rigid government rules – and censorship. At Google headquarters in Beijing, the visiting managers interviewed local English-speaking consumers. Here they learned the stark realities of how effective the Chinese government can be at tilting the playing field to benefit the home team, Baidu.com, by occasionally blocking access to Google's site and by insinuating a nationalistic element into the choice. The lesson was clear to the visiting managers: Baidu knows more about China than Google. The journey continued, as did the learning.

In the case of Google, two principal learning strategies were used. First, Google managers were intentionally placed into unfamiliar circumstances in which they quickly had to seek understanding and be aware of their first-hand experiences. They needed to reflect and make sense of these experiences and identify important lessons for the future. Second, at the same time these managers had to organize what they saw and develop theories-in-use for future actions that could be tried when they returned to the field.

CASE QUESTIONS

1. From what you can learn, what is your assessment of Google's global training program? What are its positive – and negative – points?
2. Are all three stages of the global management developmental process as illustrated in Exhibit 1.3 included in Google's training program? Explain.

3. If you were a participant in this program, what do you think you would learn to make you a better global manager?

4. Would Google's approach to global training work better in some types of organizations than others? Explain.

5. If you were in charge of Google's training program, what might you do to improve its effectiveness? Why?

6. (*Optional research question*) Identify some examples of global management training programs sponsored by other companies or organizations. Do these programs share certain characteristics? What are some of the differences? Which approach to global training do you think would generally prove to be most effective, and why?

NOTES

1. "60 Minutes," CBS television, 1998.
2. Personal communication.
3. See www.hewitt.com.
4. James Hookway, "Vietnam's mobile revolution catapults millions into the digital age," *Wall Street Journal*, June 12, 2015.
5. Timothy Wise, "The cost to Mexico of US corn ethanol expansion," *Global Development and Environment Institute*, Tufts University, May 2012.
6. Richard M. Steers, Carlos J. Sanchez-Runde, and Luciara Nardon, *Management across Cultures: Challenges and Strategies*. Cambridge University Press, 2010.
7. Percy Barnevik, cited in Philip Harris, Robert Moran, and Sarah Moran, *Managing Cultural Differences*. Amsterdam: Elsevier, 2004, p. 25.
8. Mansour Javidan and Richard M. Steers, *The Global Mindset*. Amsterdam: Elsevier, 2007.
9. Arie de Geus, "Planning as learning," *Harvard Business Review*, March 1988.
10. Steven Levy, "Google goes globe-trotting," *Newsweek*, November 12, 2007, pp. 62–4.

2 Global managers: challenges and responsibilities

MANAGEMENT CHALLENGE

IBM strategic planner Michael Cannon-Brooks observes, "You get very different thinking if you sit in Shanghai or São Paulo or Dubai than if you sit in New York."[1] If managers in different regions of the world think differently, what does this mean for negotiating and building successful partnerships, building global teams, or motivating employees from different cultures? As companies face an increasingly complex global business environment, a logical question arises: can organizations today be managed in the same way they were in the past? In other words, does a changed environment – one characterized by multiple economic and political systems, divergent social norms and values, and highly diverse educational and skill levels – require us to reassess both the managerial role in general and management practices in particular? Indeed, is the very definition of management changing? Moreover, how should today's managers best prepare themselves for greater involvement in global assignments in this new world? Key to success here will be their ability to understand changes in the managerial role as played out across cultures.

CHAPTER OUTLINE

- Traditional management models — *page* 19
- Context of global management — 21
- Rethinking management models — 25
- Diversity in global assignments — 30
- MANAGER'S NOTEBOOK: A model for global managers — 38
- Key terms — 41
- Discussion questions — 41
- Case: Two expatriates — 42

APPLICATIONS

2.1 What is a supervisor?   *page* 24

2.2 Dermot Boden, expatriate   33

2.3 Jan Chipchase, frequent flyer   36

2.4 Adhira Iyengar, virtual manager   37

Despite widespread recognition that we live and work in an increasingly interconnected global economy, it is curious how little many people understand about other countries and cultures. When we travel on holiday, we often seek out collective experiences where we can travel with people from our own cultures, eat food that is familiar, and then get back on our tour bus. When we go abroad on business, we often sequester ourselves in meeting rooms in five-star hotels with air conditioning and *BBC World News*. Then we return home saying that we have been to Thailand or Costa Rica or France. Unfortunately, there is a big difference between having *been* somewhere and having *learned* something about where we have been.

And even when we seek deeper understanding, it is often difficult to come by. Indeed, a pivotal question facing both training directors and managers themselves is exactly how to expand global awareness, understanding, and skills. In this pursuit, managers often turn for advice to those who specialize in cross-cultural training and development for help in preparing for foreign assignments. This over-reliance on others – instead of on oneself – can carry risks, however. How do we know if what we hear is correct or biased? And do we wish to stake our careers and the company's success on what we are being told? And once in the field, how can we trust or do business with prospective foreign business partners when we know so little about them, their backgrounds, their approaches to business, and their future intents?

The obvious question here is: what to do? Unfortunately, the answer to this question is not as simple as perhaps it once was. Gone are the days when prospective managers could learn French, or German, or Spanish in college and feel prepared for an international career. Learning foreign languages and foreign cultures is obviously very helpful, but it is often impractical in view of the rapidity with which business opportunities appear and disappear around the world. Besides, today's managers need much more than this.

This challenge of understanding people from other cultures is made more difficult by the increasing speed with which business often occurs. A key factor here is the way in which recent technological advancements have pushed both the pace and complexity of globalization to new heights. Communication and information technology make it possible to collaborate – or compete – globally from anywhere in the world, regardless of one's country of origin or cultural background. As a growing number of organizations have established increased operations around the world, managers' exposure to both partners and competitors from significantly different cultural backgrounds has increased at a rate that has surprised economists and social scientists alike. The implication of this for managers of all types is clear: managers with a capability to think and understand business relationships from a *global* perspective in *real time* will more often than not succeed over those with more limited, nation-based mindsets. Such is the topic of this chapter.

Traditional management models

While definitions of management abound, it is significant that most of these definitions, coming from all parts of the world, lack any notable variance. Management is management – or so we are told. Dating from the early writings of Frederick Taylor, Henri Fayol, Max Weber, Mary Parker Follett, and others in the late nineteenth and early twentieth centuries and continuing through today, most writers have agreed that management involves the coordination and control of people, materiel, and processes in order to achieve specific organizational objectives as efficiently and effectively as possible. Indeed, business historian Claude George has discovered the roots of such a definition dating back to the ancient Samarians, Egyptians, Hebrews, and Chinese well over 6,000 years ago.[2] Neither the concept nor the profession of management is new; indeed, they are widely thought to form a central pillar of organized society: getting things done through coordinated efforts.

While the underlying definition remains the same, variations around this theme can easily be found. Industrial engineers, dating from the time of scientific management proponent Frederick Taylor, have long emphasized production or operations management and the necessity to structure jobs, people, and incentive systems in ways that maximize performance.[3] Similarly, French industrial engineer Henri Fayol, also writing at the beginning of the twentieth century, emphasized the importance of standardized "principles" of management, including the division of work, unity of command, unity of direction, and the subordination of individual interests to the general (i.e., the organization's) interest.[4] Although Taylor focused on workers and Fayol focused on administrative structures, their mantra was the same: organizations must be managed through strength, discipline, hierarchy, and logic (see Exhibit 2.1).

Around this same time, social scientists and other academicians were taking a different perspective on this same phenomenon. German-born psychologist Hugo Munsterberg launched investigations into the application of psychological principles to management and workers. In the process, he created the field of industrial psychology. In his 1913 book *Psychology and Industrial Efficiency*,

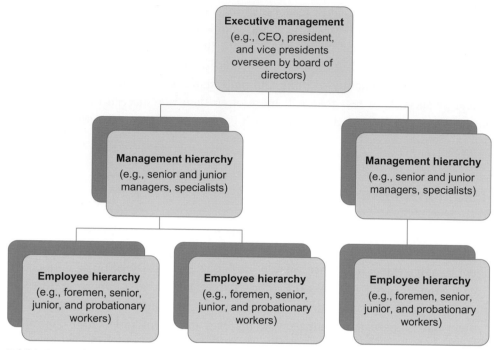

Exhibit 2.1 Traditional "logic" of organization and management

he asserted that the aim of this new discipline was "to sketch the outlines of a new science, which is to intermediate between the modern laboratory psychology and the problem of economics."[5] Meanwhile, German sociologist Max Weber wrote extensively about how organizations organize and operate – or, more accurately, should organize and operate.[6] Weber introduced the concept of bureaucracy as the most perfect form of organization. (Obviously, this term has taken on very different and negative connotations in recent years, but this was its original meaning.) Rules governed everything and little was left to chance. People were hired and promoted on the basis of qualifications – not unlike the ancient Chinese civil service system at the time of Confucius. Power and authority were vested in offices, not individuals. Even here, however, the conclusion was the same: rules and standard operating procedures uniformly enforced by competent managers would lead to efficient operations. The goal remained unchanged.

Now fast-forward 100 years and consider the advice of contemporary writers on management, both Eastern and Western. While contemporary writers have added some depth to the ongoing dialog about the nature and role of management, they have not added much breadth. Consider two contemporary definitions of management: "Management involves coordinating and overseeing the work activities of others so that their activities are completed efficiently and effectively";[7]

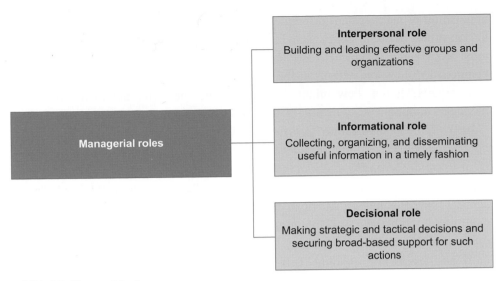

Exhibit 2.2 Managerial roles

and: "Management is the process of assembling and using sets of resources in a goal-directed manner to accomplish tasks in an organizational setting."[8] Once again, the desired end state remains unchanged.

This stability in our conception of management – unchanged over the centuries – implies that all managers do essentially the same work. Indeed, in one of the most frequently cited studies of management, McGill professor Henry Mintzberg concludes that "managers' jobs are remarkably alike," whether we are looking at foremen, company presidents, or government administrators.[9] In the end, "the primary purpose of the manager is to ensure that his or her organization serves its basic purpose – the efficient production of specific goods and services." Mintzberg goes a step further and suggests that all managers serve ten basic managerial roles in varying degrees. These are: figurehead, leader, liaison, monitor, disseminator, spokesperson, entrepreneur, disturbance handler, resource allocator, and negotiator.[10] These traits, in turn, can be organized into three clusters – interpersonal, informational, and decisional – as illustrated in Exhibit 2.2.

Context of global management

While all this may be correct as far as it goes, this line of reasoning seems to ignore, or at least downplay, the challenges facing global managers in performing these roles across cultures. As we discuss throughout this book, cultural differences can play an important role in both the conceptualization and practice of management around the world. People's conceptions of business management, as well as their application of management principles, often result from a combination of cultural backgrounds, personal experiences, and the situations confronting them. Thus, we must ask: would a typical Australian, Polish, or Indonesian manager approach business decisions and actions in the same way as their Indian, Bolivian, or French counterparts? If not, how might their approaches be different? How can global managers simultaneously deal with such diverse worldviews?

Intensifying globalization pressures only add to the problem. *Like it or not, in today's increasingly turbulent and complex business environment, everyone is, or is rapidly becoming, a global manager regardless of where they work.* Ten years ago people focused considerable attention on the differences between British managers, Chinese managers, Mexican managers, and so forth. They were relatively comfortable with their well-intentioned cultural stereotypes. Today these stereotypes have become somewhat blurred, as the global economy becomes a reality and most business is international. This is not to say that substantial differences no longer exist between managers from various countries or the ways in which they do business. Of course they do. Rather, it is to say that the very definition of effective management has changed in ways that have little to do with national origin. Most managers today have to engage with customers, business partners, and employees from various regions of the world. Success or failure depends on these managers' ability to communicate, negotiate, contract, lead, organize, coordinate, and control activities across borders.

Indeed, succeeding in today's demanding global economy requires a greater degree of international and cross-cultural communication, collaboration, and cooperation than ever before. Increasingly, companies must think in global terms, as national and even regional companies are progressively becoming a thing of the past. The future has shifted unequivocally and irreversibly, as have the opportunities, and smart companies and their managers respond accordingly.

The responsibility of managers in all this is to make things happen – to maximize consumer benefit and the company's bottom line. At the same time, society asks – and often demands – that managers pay fair wages, provide safe and equitable working conditions for their employees, follow the laws and regulations in the countries where they do business, protect the environment, act in socially responsible ways, and abide by ethical norms and professional standards. It is an understatement to point out that accomplishing these often conflicting goals is no easy task. In view of this, the question for today's managers is how they can best prepare themselves for this brave new world of international business.

As we have seen, traditional models of management pay only scant attention to cultural – and for that matter, organizational – differences. The assumption is that management is a largely universal pursuit and that the key to good management is to follow prescribed rules and policies. What is missing here is a serious

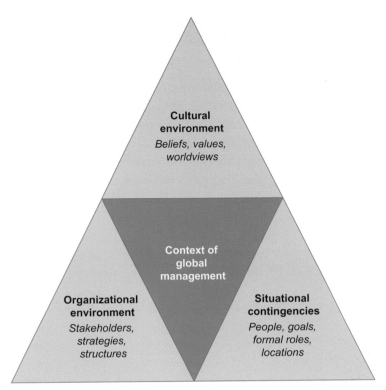

Exhibit 2.3 Context of global management

consideration of how differences in the work environment can – and often do – affect both how management is defined and how it is implemented.

To understand these differences, we must look more closely at the context of global management; that is, the characteristics of the global environment that can limit what managers must do (demands) and what they must not do (constraints), resulting in a more limited set of options for decision-making and action. To operationalize this, we identify three elements of the complex environment surrounding a manager's job (see Exhibit 2.3):

- Cultural environment. What are the predominant cultural trends in a particular encounter that help shape normative behavior? What do we know about the people we are dealing with, or planning to deal with? What are their beliefs, values, and worldviews?
- Organizational environment. What do we know about the organizational environment? Who are the principal stakeholders? What are their leading strategies? How are organizations structured to do business in the global arena?
- Situational contingencies. What are the situational contingencies, the unique factors that go beyond culture and organization that help characterize the environment? This may include people's or company's targeted objectives, the nature

of the work being performed (e.g., marketing, production), the location of the interaction (e.g., office, restaurant, country), the relative positions or roles of the people involved (e.g., superior, subordinate), and so forth.

This is the complex and often contradictory environment in which global managers find themselves and must work to succeed. Each element of this contextual environment is important and each can exhibit considerable variability. The question now is how to put these three contexts of the work environment together to better understand both the managerial challenge, as well as what managers can actually do in the field. Although global managers obviously face a number of demands and constraints in the workplace, they also have a number of opportunities. The challenge is to understand how these can be realized.

APPLICATION 2.1 What is a supervisor?

To see just one example of differences in the contexts that managers face, consider how people in different cultures view the role of supervisors. What does this term mean? What does it conjure up in people's minds? In English, the word "supervisor" carries with it connotations of authority, control, and power; a supervisor is a boss (see Exhibit 2.4). In Japanese, by contrast, the word often assumes a more familial connotation; a supervisor is a senior role model and protector of subordinates, much like parents. Indeed, **kachou** in Japanese means "supervisor" (or, more accurately, "section chief"), but it also means "patriarch" or "family head." In German, the word "supervisor" carries strong connotations of technical competence and expertise. Indeed, a supervisor is sometimes referred to as **meister** (or master technician). German supervisors are generally chosen for their knowledge, technical competence (**technik** in German) and training abilities, and not necessarily for their ability to control others. In Mexico, a supervisor is considered to be a patron, looking after the interests of his or her employees in exchange for allegiance and obedience (**capataz** or **jefe**). Same word, basically, but very different meanings – and sometimes very different behavioral consequences.

Think about it . . .

(1) What are the implications of these different meanings for the supervisory role in the workplace and for those who report to supervisors? Explain.
(2) What is your personal definition of a "supervisor"? Where did your definition come from? How did it develop?
(3) If you were assigned to meet with several supervisors from, say, Turkey or Malaysia, how would you learn about the supervisory role in those locations prior to your meeting?

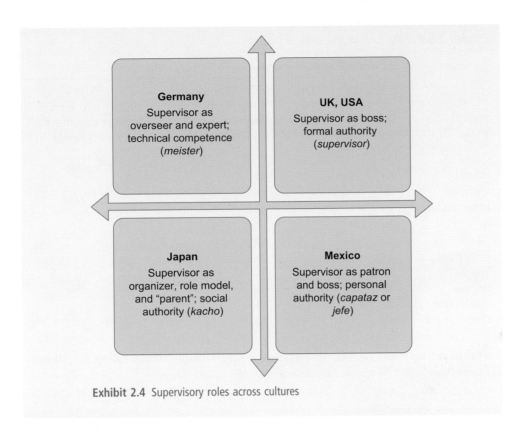

Exhibit 2.4 Supervisory roles across cultures

Rethinking management models

With this discussion in mind, a central thesis of this book is that understanding managerial roles and responsibilities by themselves and in the absence of an adequate understanding of the surrounding cultural, organizational, and situational environment is a highly suboptimal strategy for global managers. Successful managers must understand the context in which their managerial behavior transpires, and, in order to understand this, it is important to know the local environment. This challenge can be seen in two ways. First, how can cultural variations change managerial role expectations? Second, once this is understood, what can managers do to accommodate such differences – if at all?

Managerial roles and practices across cultures

If people often vary across cultures in their thoughts and habits, so too can they vary in their expectations concerning appropriate managerial roles. Two related

Exhibit 2.5 Perceptions of managerial roles

Country	Percentage of managers who agree with each statement		
	"Managers must have the answers to most questions asked by subordinates"	"The main reason for a chain of command is so people know who has authority"	"It is OK to bypass chain of command to get something done efficiently"
China	74	70	59
France	53	43	43
Germany	46	26	45
Indonesia	73	83	51
Italy	66	–	56
Japan	78	50	–
Netherlands	17	31	44
Spain	–	34	74
Sweden	10	30	26
United Kingdom	27	34	35
United States	18	17	32

Source: Data from Andre Laurent, reported in John Saee, *Managing Organizations in a Global Economy* (Mason, OH: Thompson/Southwestern, 2005), pp. 39–42.

issues are relevant here: first, what is the ideal managerial role – the role people say they prefer to see in good managers – and, second, what is the "real" managerial role – the everyday roles that managers play out in real life, warts and all? Theoretically, these two roles should be highly correlated, but in reality significant differences are often found. Not surprisingly, taking these comparisons across borders only adds to the ambiguity.

First, consider how people in various cultures describe their ideal manager. INSEAD professor Andre Laurent conducted one of the more interesting studies on this topic.[11] He focused his attention on understanding the normative managerial role (that is, what is expected of managers) and discovered significant differences across cultures. He asked managers from different cultures a series of questions dealing with effective management. Laurent's results demonstrate wide variations in responses across cultures, as shown in Exhibit 2.5. For each set of responses, note how far apart typical managers are in responding to rather simple statements about appropriate managerial behavior. For each of the three questions, the percentage of managers in agreement ranges from 10 to 78 percent, 17 to 83 percent, and 26 to 74 percent, respectively. These percentages aren't even close. If managers from different countries differ so much in their descriptions of the correct managerial role, it is no wonder that significant differences can be found in actual management style across national boundaries.

Exhibit 2.6 Perceptions of managerial practices

Country	Manager's sense of drive and initiative (percentage of agreement by managers)	Country	Manager's willingness to delegate authority (percentage of agreement by managers)
United States	74	Sweden	76
Sweden	72	Japan	69
Japan	72	Norway	69
Finland	70	USA	66
South Korea	68	Singapore	65
Netherlands	67	Denmark	65
Singapore	66	Canada	64
Switzerland	66	Finland	63
Belgium	65	Switzerland	62
Ireland	65	Netherlands	61
France	65	Australia	61
Austria	63	Germany	61
Denmark	63	New Zealand	61
Italy	62	Ireland	60
Australia	62	UK	59
Canada	62	Belgium	55
Spain	62	Austria	54
New Zealand	59	France	54
Greece	59	Italy	47
UK	58	Spain	44
Norway	55	Portugal	43
Portugal	49	Greece	38

Source: Charles Hampden-Turner and Fons Trompenaars, *The Seven Cultures of Capitalism* (New York: Doubleday, 1993), ch. 1.

A second study, conducted by Cambridge University professor Charles Hampden-Turner and Dutch management consultant Fons Trompenaars, also found significant differences across managers based on culture, as shown in Exhibit 2.6. For example, managers in the United States, Sweden, Japan, Finland, and South Korea showed more overall drive and initiative than leaders in Portugal, Norway, Greece, and the United Kingdom. Note also that Canadian managers placed less emphasis on managerial drive and initiative than their US counterparts. At the same time, managers in Sweden, Japan, Norway, Canada, and the United States tended to be more willing to delegate authority than leaders in Greece, Portugal, Spain, and Italy. These findings, along with those of Andre Laurent, suggest clearly that effective managerial behavior can easily vary across cultures.

Other studies confirm this conclusion. For example, one study found that British managers were more participative than their French and German counterparts.[12] Two possible reasons were suggested for this. First, the United Kingdom may be more egalitarian than France or Germany, and the political environment supports this approach. Second, top British managers tend not to be involved in the day-to-day affairs of the business, and delegate many key decisions to middle and lower-level managers. The French and Germans, by contrast, tend to prefer a more work-centered, authoritarian approach. Although it is true that German co-determination leads to power sharing with employees throughout the organization, some have argued that this has resulted not from German culture but, rather, from German laws. By contrast, Scandinavian countries make wide use of participative leadership approaches, again following from their somewhat more egalitarian culture.

On the other side of the world, Japanese managers tend to be somewhat authoritarian, but at the same time listen to the opinions of their subordinates. One study found that Japanese managers place greater confidence in the skills and capabilities of their subordinates than their counterparts in other cultures.[13] Another feature of Japanese leadership is an inclination to give subordinates ambiguous goals instead of highly specific ones. In other words, many Japanese managers tell their workers what they want in a general way, but leave it to the workers to determine the details and the work plan. This practice is also commonplace in South Korea, and contrasts sharply with typical US managers, who often take a hands-on, management-by-objectives approach to project management.

To illustrate this point, let us return to Mintzberg's ten managerial roles. Although this model was designed around North American managers, it can also be useful in exploring on a conceptual level how culture and managerial roles can intersect. For the sake of example, Exhibit 2.7 illustrates how each of the ten managerial roles can be influenced by cultural differences. For instance, considerable research has indicated that most people in individualistic cultures prefer managers who take charge, while most people in collectivistic cultures prefer managers who are more consultative. Similarly, managers in high-context cultures frequently make extensive use of the context surrounding a message to get their point across, while managers in low-context cultures tend to rely almost exclusively on specific and detailed messages and ignore much of the message context. In short, managerial roles often change – not necessarily in major ways, but certainly in important ways – as we move across borders.

Matching managerial roles to local situations

Finally, it is important for managers to understand their own management style. The fundamental question here is: can you be the manager you are expected to be in

Exhibit 2.7 Cultural influences on managerial roles

Managerial roles	Differences across cultures
Interpersonal roles	
Figurehead	Figureheads have considerable symbolic value in some cultures; in others, being described as a figurehead is not seen as a compliment.
Leader	Individualistic cultures prefer highly visible "take charge" leaders; collectivistic cultures prefer more consultative leaders.
Liaison	Some cultures prefer informal contacts based on long-standing personal relationships; others prefer to use official representatives.
Informational roles	
Monitor	Culture often influences both the extent of information monitoring and which specific information sources receive greatest attention.
Disseminator	In some cultures, the context surrounding a message is more important than the message itself; in others, the reverse is true.
Spokesperson	Culture often influences who is respected and seen as a legitimate spokesperson for an organization.
Decisional roles	
Entrepreneur	Some cultures are highly supportive of innovation and change; others prefer the status quo and resist change.
Disturbance handler	Some cultures resolve conflict quietly; others accept and at times encourage a more public approach.
Resource allocator	Hierarchical cultures support differential resource allocations; egalitarian cultures prefer greater equality or equity in distributions.
Negotiator	Some cultures negotiate all items in a proposed contract simultaneously; others negotiate each item sequentially.

your foreign assignment? How much do you understand this new environment and can you adapt your style to maximize your potential as a manager there? For example, if your management style is highly participative, can you become an autocrat overnight if you need to? And should you? We suggest here that self-awareness is one of the most important skills managers should have. As a result, knowing what others expect of you is of little value if you don't know what you can comfortably be. Hence, before addressing other issues, managers need to know what type of managers they are, what types of behaviors they are comfortable with or willing to learn, and how far they are willing and able to change and still be authentic to themselves and their values.

Considering the important influence of culture in determining what is expected of supervisors and managers, how can a manager be successful across cultures? In many cases, successful managers are found to develop an awareness of cultural differences and adapt their management styles to the extent possible to match local conditions. This strategy is not always the best, however. In several cases, a manager is sent abroad to promote change, and not fitting the local culture may be the manager's most important competitive advantage. In these circumstances, "going native" may not be the best approach.

Rob Coffee and Gareth Jones suggest that the key to a manager's success lies in the ability to conform just enough to the local environment as not to be rejected by the local culture.[14] Conforming too much can undermine the manager's potential to make important changes in the organization, however. Frequently a manager is sent abroad or charged with global operations because of some personal characteristic and particular way of doing things that is linked to his or her cultural background. Losing these abilities may not be in the organization's or followers' best interests. Clearly, alienating the local culture is bound to bring some challenges, but going native may not be the best solution either. The success of global management lies in the fine balance of conforming enough to the key aspects of the cultural context, allowing managers to engage and gain leverage, which can then be used to promote change. The idea here is that managers must conform enough to the new cultural milieu, gaining acceptance as a member, in order to make the necessary connections to make changes. Effective managers understand what it is about the culture that can be changed – and what cannot – and operate within those constraints.

Diversity in global assignments

Thomas A. Stewart, former editor of the *Harvard Business Review*, has observed, "A global manager is set apart by more than a worn suitcase and a dog-eared passport."[15] To the extent that this observation is correct, the onus is clearly on managers to prepare themselves for success in the future. Engaging with managers and entrepreneurs from different cultures opens up considerable opportunities to learn more about ourselves, discover new ways of doing things, and find creative solutions to problems both old and new. It is clearly part of the developmental process for most managers; and, in this pursuit, continual cognitive, analytical, and experiential learning play a significant – and often underappreciated – role.

Global managers come in all shapes and sizes, as well as skills and abilities. Indeed, in today's global economy, almost all managers are involved in some form or another with global management. As such, it is difficult – if not impossible – to develop a precise definition that accurately encompasses all their activities and responsibilities. As a starting point, however, we define a global manager as someone who works with or through people across national and cultural boundaries to accomplish global corporate objectives. Inherent in this definition is the assumption that many – if not all – of these managers work with people from differing cultural backgrounds and, as such, must somehow accommodate or respond to these differences. Also inherent in this definition is the recognition that some of these cross-cultural interactions may be across countries with fewer cultural differences than others (e.g., Canada and the United States or Canada and Saudi Arabia). Indeed, some of these cultural differences can often be found within a single country.

Paramount to this definition is the assumption that global managers are – and must be – different from more traditional managers. They must have a worldview, not a national one; they must understand not just cultural differences but also the ways in which to navigate such differences to achieve corporate objectives; they must seek partnerships, not domination; and, above all, they must have both the competence and the confidence to work with colleagues and partners from around the world. Included within this definition are managers who have very different corporate lifestyles. Some live abroad, some live in airplanes, and some live in virtual space. Some do all three.

For the sake of parsimony, and acknowledging that there are obvious risks in categorizations, we suggest that these global managers can be roughly divided into three somewhat overlapping categories: expatriates, frequent flyers, and virtual managers. We suggest, further, that the characteristics and cultural challenges of each of these types of managers can be quite different (see Exhibit 2.8). While expatriates typically require deep knowledge of a particular country or region, frequent flyers more often require broad knowledge of cultural differences and cultural processes in general. One leads a somewhat stable life, albeit in a foreign country; the other leads a highly mobile existence. This is not to say that one approach is superior to the other, only that they are different and that each plays an important role in global commerce. Added to this is a category of other managers who work largely through computer and information technology and who essentially wander the globe in cyberspace to achieve their results. We refer to these individuals as virtual managers, in recognition of their basic patterns of collegial and business interaction.[16] (Some have suggested that we need to add a fourth category of global managers, namely everyone else, since in fact most managerial positions require some degree of multicultural expertise even when sitting at corporate headquarters simply working with global clients.)

Expatriates

Traditionally, the most common foreign assignments have involved the long-term relocation of parent company managers to various countries in which the parent firm does, or wants to do, business. Firms have often preferred to use expatriate managers for a number of reasons, especially when they needed parent-company representation and control in a distant location, wanted to provide developmental

Exhibit 2.8 Challenges of global assignments

Characteristics and management challenges	Expatriates	Frequent flyers	Virtual managers
Principal management focus	Long-term face-to-face management, where managers are either assigned to reside in a foreign country to oversee company operations or hired to bring special expertise to a foreign firm.	Short-term face-to-face management, where managers with particular expertise (e.g., project management, financial controls) are flown in to plan, implement, or control specific operations.	Virtual (or remote) technical management, often in specialized areas (e.g., logistics, IT), where managers perform most of their tasks and responsibilities via information networks and digital technologies.
Degree of cultural embeddedness and technological dependence	High cultural embeddedness; low technological dependence.	Moderate to low cultural embeddedness and technological dependence.	Low to no cultural embeddedness; high technological dependence.
Primary mode of communication and interaction	Largely face-to-face.	Balance of face-to-face and virtual.	Largely virtual.
Key success factors for working across cultures	Typically requires deep knowledge of the culture(s) and culture–business relationships where they live and work; bilingual or multilingual skills important; understanding global issues – not just local ones – is also critical.	Typically requires moderate understanding of cultural differences and dynamics in general and culture business relationships around the globe; multilingual skills important; deep understanding of global issues critical.	Typically requires at least a modest understanding of cultural differences and variations in business practices around the globe, although a deeper understanding is preferred; multilingual skills often useful.
Typical cultural challenge	*Regional myopia:* overemphasis on local or regional issues and business practices at the expense of global issues and overall corporate objectives.	*Global myopia:* overemphasis on global issues and overall corporate objectives at the expense of local customs and business practices.	*Technological myopia:* ignorance of the impact of cultural differences on the local uses, misuses, and applications of communication and information technology.

opportunities for parent–country managers, or needed to fill skill gaps when locals did not have the skills to do the job themselves.[17] Today, however, the term "expatriate" has come to describe any person working in residence in a foreign country. This could include a Swiss manager working for a Swiss company in South Korea, or a Swiss manager working for a South Korean company in South Korea. Both face similar challenges of living abroad for lengthy periods.

APPLICATION 2.2 Dermot Boden, expatriate

LG's Nam Yong did not set out to hire a group of aggressive Western-style expatriate managers, but he knew LG needed change. The company's South Korean management team had built an engineering powerhouse that excelled at manufacturing high-quality goods, but the company realized that more than four-fifths of its revenue came from overseas and nearly 60 percent of its manufacturing was done outside South Korea. When Nam took over LG Electronics' top job, the company was coasting. It had become a top-five consumer electronics player globally, but had few major hits. Nam believed the company needed to be a trendsetter if it wanted to prosper in the digital age. To shake things up, he asked headhunters to find top talent from multinationals worldwide, regardless of nationality.

Irish-born Dermot Boden, chief marketing officer for LG, was the first non-Korean to be hired by LG as an internal change agent. Nam hired the veteran of Pfizer and Johnson & Johnson to help turn LG into a premium brand. The problem was that LG's marketing was uninspiring. So Boden determined to give the brand a more sophisticated image, with high-end products such as a cellphone co-branded with fashion house Prada and washing machines costing $1,500 or more. He also took a more organized approach to marketing, by hiring a single international advertising agency in London to handle advertising worldwide.

Other foreign expatriates were asked to standardize the hodgepodge of processes and systems that LG had developed around the world. Purchasing, for example, was done by four different business units and was split between factories and subsidiaries in 110 countries. "I'm like a conductor, getting 2,000 purchasing officers to work in concert to make good music," says Tom Linton, a twenty-year veteran of IBM who joined LG as its first chief procurement officer in 2008. Nam said in 2010 that Linton's efforts to reshape the purchasing system had already saved the company hundreds of millions of dollars. Meanwhile, LG's supply chain was equally chaotic. Didier Chenneveau, a Swiss who left Hewlett-Packard (HP), also in 2008, to become LG's chief supply-chain officer, inherited more than ten warehouse management systems, five transportation operations, and four computer systems to monitor the movement of parts and finished products. His goal: to merge everything into a single global system.

Not unexpectedly, Boden and the other foreign managers were not entirely welcomed by local South Korean managers. "The biggest worry was the prospect of Western executives imposing a way of thinking that might not work in our Confucian culture," said marketing manager Choi Seung Hun. "The prospect of communicating with my boss in English gave me a headache," added Lee Kyo Weon, a purchasing manager. Over time, however, both Choi and Lee agreed that the newcomers had made an effort to bridge the cultural gap. The results of this experiment in internationalization are interesting. When an anticipated surge in global sales failed to materialize, LG decided not to renew the contracts of Boden and the other expats. The company announced that it had decided to pursue a different executive strategy, using mostly South Korean executives, not foreign ones. Meanwhile, across town, rival electronics giant Samsung continued to hire more expats.

Think about it . . .

(1) How do you explain the rapid buildup, and equally rapid termination, of the expatriate managers at LG?

(2) What did LG gain – and possibly lose – from its three-year experiment with expatriate managers?

(3) Overall, what lessons emerge from the LG experience for other managers entering into an expatriate experience?

While some of the advantages of expatriate assignments may be fairly obvious, finding people who can actually succeed in expatriate assignments can be problematic. Although traveling abroad (perhaps on a vacation or business trip) is often seen by people as an enjoyable experience, actually living abroad can be frustrating, stressful, and sometimes very unpleasant. For many, staying in a four-star hotel, eating in fine restaurants, seeing new sights, and knowing that soon they will be back in their own bed is far more preferable to setting up a household in a strange neighborhood where few people speak their language, finding new schools for the kids, shopping in local markets stocked with foods they can't identify, and using public transportation. For others, these same experiences provide a sense of adventure and learning. Clearly, the location of the assignment plays an important role as well. Some people will thrive in some locations and fail in others. The challenge for managers – and their companies – is to discover which type of person is fit to which type of assignment before getting on the airplane.

Many people see an international assignment as a great opportunity. It may be an opportunity to advance one's career, to make more money, or to learn new things. It may represent a personal challenge or a way to a more interesting life. Managers who take international assignments report learning new managerial skills, increasing their tolerance for ambiguity, learning new ways of seeing things, and improving their ability to work with others.[18] As noted above, however, living and working abroad is not easy. Long-term international assignments are particularly challenging for managers with family, when a partner may need to give up a career in the home country and may not find suitable employment in the host country, and when children require special attention such as international schooling. A recent survey found that 81 percent of workers declining an expatriate assignment cited family reasons.[19]

Frequent flyers

While extended expatriate assignments are often useful, some have suggested that the days when managers prepared for a long-term assignment in Italy, Thailand, or Costa Rica are rapidly being eclipsed by a new reality in which managers sometimes seem to spend more time in the air than on the ground. Global assignments of shorter duration – often accompanied by increased intensity – are usually focused on specific tasks or projects, and, as such, can often provide easier ways to assess results (see Exhibit 2.8).[20] In addition, there are many managers who would not consider uprooting the family for long-term expatriate assignments but would be interested in shorter international opportunities. This increases the pool of talent available for such postings – a big plus, since the demand for highly qualified international assignees is often higher than the supply.[21] Furthermore, employees often see short-term assignments as being easier on their friends and family, as well as their home-country career opportunities.

The main challenge facing managers on short-term assignments is that they often find themselves in a foreign country without family and friends, and with a very short time to develop relationships and become adjusted.[22] Since assignees are usually sent abroad for a short period in order to solve a specific problem or perform a specific task, they are not given the time to learn the ropes and adjust to the new locale, as would be the case in traditional long-term expatriate assignments. Instead, frequent flyers are often expected to perform as soon as they hit the ground, which increases the challenges – and stresses – of such assignment. Strong pressures to perform – quickly – coupled with a limited social and family life, frequently lead assignees to work long hours, enduring high levels of stress, and, at times, a poor work–life balance.

APPLICATION 2.3 Jan Chipchase, frequent flyer

Jan Chipchase is the founder of Studio D Radiodurans, a research, design, and strategy consultancy that specializes in understanding consumer behavior in emerging markets.[23] Born in London, he was previously Executive Creative Director of Global Insights at Frog Design in California, where he led the firm's global research practice in both mainstream and emerging markets. Before joining Frog Design in 2010, Chipchase was Principal Scientist at Nokia, based out of Tokyo but frequently traveling. The goal of his research has been to understand the ways technology works in different cultures, with a focus on understanding technology three to fifteen years out. He is widely considered a thought leader in the space of consumer and user behavior, and how insights can be applied to the innovation process.

Most of his research is commissioned by commercial clients. He has lived in London, Berlin, San Francisco, Shanghai, Los Angeles, and almost a decade in Tokyo. In one interview, he observed, "I just came back from six weeks on the road: Tokyo, London, Beirut, rural Uganda, Kenya, Spain, and New York. I stayed in the Trump Tower, a $10 shack near the Sudanese border, and traveled with a Hezbollah fixer on a motorcycle." He gained his reputation as an extreme method researcher after spending almost a decade in Nokia's research center and design studio. His former employer, Frog Designs of California, hired him to apply sociology, ethnography, and psychology to product design for clients that include GE and Lenovo.

Chipchase recently ventured to Afghanistan to understand mobile banking for his numerous telecom clients. "I could take my team anywhere in the world to research this," said Chipchase, who typically takes some 10,000 photos when he goes into the field. "But I know, when you go to the more extreme places, you're more likely to see things that exist elsewhere, but aren't quite as visible."

Think about it . . .

(1) Based on this example, it could be argued that the grueling work pace and travel demands could easily burn out many frequent flyers. In your view, what characteristics should a successful frequent flyer have in order to survive in this fast-paced environment?

(2) What are the pluses and minuses of Jan Chipchase's type of job? Would you enjoy having such a job? Why or why not?

(3) What do you think Chipchase will be doing in five years? Why do you think so?

Virtual managers

The same communication technologies that are making globalization a reality and changing the nature of work are also influencing the lives and work habits of global managers. Many of these technologies are not new (e.g., cellphones, Internet). What has been different in recent years, however, has been the ways in which these communication technologies have increased both their operating powers and their interactive capabilities. Many of these technologies have merged into more powerful tools for busy managers. As it became possible to access e-mail and the Web through smartphones and tablets, it has also become possible to travel light and still be constantly connected. It is no longer necessary to carry a laptop and a bag full of cables; it is not even necessary to be in a specific location to connect. Wireless technology makes it possible to perform work anywhere and anytime with minimal equipment, making it possible to be a global manager without leaving one's home base. The key issue here is not having access to the technology, however; rather, it is a manager's ability to use such technology to build workable networks and relationships that collectively serve corporate interests.

APPLICATION 2.4 Adhira Iyengar, virtual manager

Adhira Iyengar, an entrepreneur from Delhi, is a good example of a virtual manager.[24] One recent morning Iyengar got up, prepared a cup of tea, and logged on to her PC. As expected, Debra Brown, her business partner in California, was already logged on and asking questions about Iyengar's latest report to her. As they finished their online Skype meeting, Iyengar looked at her calendar and realized that, again, it was going to be a long day. At 10:00 that morning she had a conference call with Xiang Bingwei (Mr. Xiang, or "Andrew," to use his Westernized name), a client from Shanghai, about some changes in their service contract. At 1:30 in the afternoon she had a video conference meeting with a group of prospective Australian clients. Before the end of the day she had to complete a report and e-mail it to Gabriela Bedoya Cárdenas, a prospective partner in Monterrey, Mexico, and she still needed to prepare for her upcoming trip to Oslo the following week for her yearly face-to-face meeting with her co-workers.

Think about it . . .

(1) Adhira Iyengar clearly lives a busy life. What special qualities or skills does she possess – and what qualities or skills should other virtual workers possess – to survive and succeed in such a harried virtual existence?

(2) Iyengar spends a lot of time interacting with her colleagues across the globe, but very little time face-to-face with people. What do you think the challenges are of interacting mostly through technology?

(3) While we know very little about this case, speculate about what Iyengar's life might look like in five or ten years. What might be different? What might be the same?

Once again, it is important to remember that these three categories of global managers – expatriates, frequent flyers, and virtual managers – represent overlapping categories. Clearly, most expatriates today are heavy users of the Web and other communication technologies, while many virtual managers must travel at times to get their jobs done. Our purpose in differentiating between these three categories, even in terms of general trends, is to highlight differences in managerial responsibilities and challenges in doing business across national borders.

MANAGER'S NOTEBOOK

A model for global managers

In this chapter, we learned that what differentiates effective global managers is not so much their managerial skills – important though these obviously are – but the combination of these skills with additional multicultural competencies that allow people to apply their managerial skills across a diverse spectrum of environments. In other words: *global management skills = managerial competence + multicultural competence.* Being multiculturally competent is more than just being polite or empathetic to people from other cultures; it is getting things done through people by capitalizing on cultural diversity.

Based on what we learned, we have one more topic to discuss: how to build a model of global management that can support managers' efforts to understand, plan, and act in foreign environments. Any useful model guiding managerial behavior in uncertain arenas such as the global marketplace must recognize at least two challenges. First, managers must understand their environment. What must they know or do? What must they not do? Where are the opportunities? And how much discretion do they have in making reasoned decisions or talking concrete actions? Second, managers must have (or develop) the requisite skills and abilities to pursue their goals and objectives within the constraints of their immediate environment. Without these skills, opportunities are easily missed.

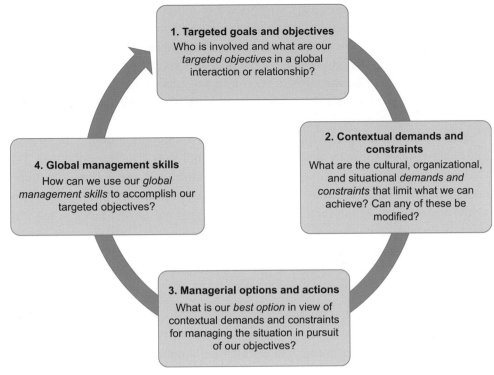

Exhibit 2.9 A model for global managers

The question, then, is how best to accomplish this. For this, we suggest a model – really an organizing framework for understanding a manager's options – based on the classic research of Oxford University professor Rosemary Stewart.[25] Stewart made a cogent argument for rethinking our approach to management, global or otherwise. The goal of her research was both simple and startling:

trying to change how the reader thinks about managerial work. I believe this is necessary because the language commonly used for talking about managerial work takes too little account of what managers actually do. It is often too general, treating managing as primarily a common activity, and also too formal and idealistic, hence divorced from reality.[26]

What is needed, according to Stewart, is "a new way of thinking about the nature and the diversity of managerial jobs and about how individuals actually do them."[27]

Following from this logic, we suggest here a global management model that will form the basis for our explorations throughout this book. As suggested in this model, a manager's first task is to develop a coherent set of targeted goals and objectives (see Exhibit 2.9, box 1). What is he or she trying to accomplish in upcoming global encounters, including contract negotiations, relationship-building, partnership management, managing global workers, and so forth?

Beyond establishing clear goals, strategies, and objectives, the model asks managers to understand various contextual demands and constraints that can enhance or limit managerial actions (box 2). All managerial work is constrained in varying degrees by existing demands (what people must do) and constraints (what people must not do). Demands and constraints are in no small way influenced by local cultures, organizations, and situations, what we refer to as the "context of global management" (discussed above).

Within these limitations, managers typically have multiple managerial options and actions open to them about what is done and how it is done (box 3). The challenge for managers is to understand the demands and constraints – cultural, organizational, and situational – facing each unique problem within their environments and then act within these limitations. This may not always be easy, but it is essential to long-term success.

Finally, none of this can happen unless managers have sufficient global management skills to accomplish their targeted objectives working in a global environment (box 4). Global management skills include:

- Communicating across cultures
- Taking leadership roles in global organizations
- Negotiating global agreements and working with global partners
- Managing in an ethical and socially responsible manner
- Working with and managing global employees
- Working with and managing global teams
- Managing global assignments

The model provides a framework for thinking about the nature of managerial work and how managers do it. We can build upon this model to explore managerial work in a global context. In other words, this basic framework can be adapted such that global managers can visualize the environment in which they work, including constraints on what they can do and demands about what they must do. Within these two sets of parameters, global managers are free – or relatively free – to use their skills, or develop new ones, to achieve their goals and objectives. This is the arena in which they can make decisions (choices) concerning their actions. Within this arena, several logical questions for managers to ask here include the following:

- What am I trying to accomplish?
- What am I able to do?
- What are my options?
- What demands or constraints are negotiable or changeable?
- How can I best use my managerial skills?
- What new skills do I need to learn in order to be successful?

Both as a developmental tool and a managerial guide, this model will hopefully prove useful in understanding how global managers work, and we will return to it throughout the book. This model is not meant to be overly simplistic or overly complex. Instead, it is meant to highlight three key factors that managers must understand and accommodate as they attempt to make good decisions and take appropriate actions.

KEY TERMS

capataz (Spanish) • constraints (model) • context of global management • contextual demands and constraints (model) • cultural environment • demands (model) • expatriates • frequent flyers • global management model • global management skills • global manager • *jefe* (Spanish) • *kachou* (Japanese) • management • managerial options and actions (model) • managerial roles (Mintzberg) • *meister* (German) • organizational environment • situational contingencies • targeted goals and objectives (model) • *technic* (German) • virtual managers

DISCUSSION QUESTIONS

1. In the beginning of the chapter, IBM's Michael Cannon-Brooks points out that managers in different parts of the world can exhibit systematic differences in patterns of thinking. Do you believe this observation to be true? If so, what are the implications both for developing management talent and for a manager's survival and success in the field?

2. Do you believe that there is one common definition for "management" or multiple definitions? Explain.

3. As the world continues to globalize and more and more managers become global managers, what are the downside or negative consequences? What, if anything, can be done about this?

4. How might managers going into the field for the first time make use of the model outlining the context of global management (Exhibit 2.3)? Are there things managers can do in the field to actually increase their knowledge base using this model?

5. Perceptions of managerial practices differ, as illustrated in Exhibit 2.6. How can managers use this information to better prepare for global assignments?

6. In dealing with others in different cultural settings, how can managers determine the right balance between retaining their own authenticity and adapting to local situations? Explain.

7. We identified three types of global managers (expatriates, frequent flyers, and virtual managers). What are the most serious challenges to the success facing

each type of these types of managers? What can each type of manager do to enhance the odds of success working across cultures?

8. From a managerial standpoint, what are the advantages and potential drawbacks of using global management models such as the one illustrated in Exhibit 2.9? Explain.

9. When you consider the various global management skills that can help develop multicultural competence, which skills do you believe you have in abundance and which skills could use more work?

CASE: TWO EXPATRIATES

Mr. Smith and Mr. Zhang (real people, fictitious names) are two expatriates ostensibly doing much the same kind of job: a British expat working in Shanghai and a Chinese expat working in London). What follows is the story of each as seen from their perspective.

"The rules in China are not always transparent," observes Smith, an executive at a Western firm that sells beauty products in China. His firm operates through a network of local individuals who knock on doors and attempt to convince their acquaintances to buy lipstick and shampoo. These salespeople also recruit other salespeople. This direct selling is controversial in many countries, including China. Some officials think it poses a threat to the harmonious society. Direct marketing companies are allowed to operate only under tight conditions designed to keep out scammers. For example, they must maintain a physical presence in the neighborhoods where they do business, so that disgruntled staff and customers have somewhere to go to make complaints.

Smith says his firm is happy to abide by the rules, but this is not as simple as it would be in the West. China's commercial law is sometimes an unreliable guide to what is allowed. For example, is it legal to recruit students to work as part-time salespeople? As far as Smith knows, it is. When some of his employees started recruiting on a university campus, however, the students' parents complained and the government took their side, making it plain that Smith's firm had crossed an invisible line. "I think it's a Confucian thing," he muses. "Chinese people place an immense value on education, and abhor anything that might distract students from their books." His firm now steers clear of students.

Despite his challenges, Smith says that he enjoys working in China. He admires his Chinese sales force. In the United Kingdom, direct selling is typically someone's second job; in China, it is a full-time occupation. Chinese people tend to have large networks of family, friends, and classmates, and they do not hesitate to use them. "It's embedded in the culture," he says. They are not embarrassed to ask for favors or tout business propositions at family dinners. "That really helps us."

The context in which Mr. Zhang works is quite different. English meat pies "are dry and have no flavor," he observes. Moreover, British food is very expensive. Chinese expatriates who are posted abroad do not enjoy the same lavish pay and perks that Western expatriates in China do, especially if they work for state-owned firms. Back home, Chinese managers have housemaids. "They are not used to cooking for themselves," says Zhang, a telecoms executive. When sent to work in rich countries, "they even have to clean their own toilets," he chuckles. All the same, Zhang finds life in London easier than many other Chinese expatriates, because he speaks English well. His pay is low, however, and he was posted to England without his spouse or family. "We don't have the kind of expat package that pays for family expenses, housing, or the kids' education." This can make for a lonely, gloomy time.

Western expatriates in China are typically there because they want to be. Some find the culture fascinating. Most expect to make good money and burnish their résumé. Western multinationals feel obliged to have a presence in China, and since the country is so potentially lucrative they often send their most capable staff there. Wal-Mart's global head of procurement is based in Shenzhen. HSBC's boss moved from London to Hong Kong last year. A spell in China helps a Western executive rise to the top. The converse is not true, though. Chinese executives, especially at state-owned firms, win promotion by cultivating the right people, and those people live in China. Even a few years away from your connections can mean they go cold, threatening your chances of promotion. If you are a senior Chinese manager and you get posted abroad, it may mean you are not doing very well at home, says Zhang; and if you work for a state-owned firm, you cannot refuse to go, he adds.

According to Zhang, an advantage of working in Europe is that the rules governing business are relatively straightforward. "Everything is transparent," he says. Relationships between companies are simpler, too. In China, he says, firms assume that customers will buy only from someone they know or have a relationship with. They therefore spend vast amounts of time catering to clients. Western firms do this too, but not to the same degree. Finally, differences in corporate etiquette can also be significant. If a Chinese vendor gives a presentation and the customer asks him lots of questions he can't answer or raises lots of potential problems, the vendor will be distraught, says Zhang. He will assume that the customer does not like him. If the customer is Western, however, it probably just means that he wants to be given more information. "People here look at the facts, not the person."

Ostensibly, Mr. Smith and Mr. Zhang have identical jobs; they are both expatriates in each other's country and are both are working in marketing and sales. Obviously, though, the jobs are not the same.

CASE QUESTIONS

1. From what you can learn from this case, how would you describe the "context of global management" (cultural, organizational, and situational) for each of these two expatriates (see Exhibit 2.3)? Where are the key differences, if any? What is similar?

2. How might these contextual differences influence the behaviors of Smith and Zhang? Explain.

3. While both Smith and Zhang are expatriates, based on your assessment of this case do both individuals actually have the same jobs? Explain.

4. How might the differences in perceptions of managerial roles (Exhibit 2.5) influence how each approaches his work?

5. Recognizing that you have only limited information here, how can you use the global management model (Exhibit 2.9) to better understand each manager's goals and objectives, contextual constraints, and managerial options? Can you offer any conclusions concerning the specific global management skills each manager may need to improve his performance?

6. (*Optional research question*) Explore how different companies work to prepare expatriates for their global assignments. Are there similarities or differences across these corporate efforts? What suggestions do you have to improve such programs?

NOTES

1. Cited in Luciara Nardon, Richard M. Steers, and Carlos J. Sanchez-Runde, "Developing multicultural competence," *The European Business Review*, May 9, 2013.

2. Claude S. George, *The History of Management Thought*. Englewood Cliffs, NJ: Prentice-Hall, 1972.

3. Frederick Taylor, *Scientific Management*. New York: Harper & Row, 1911.

4. Henri Fayol, *Administration Industrielle et générale*. Paris: Dunod, 1916.

5. Hugo Munsterberg, *Psychology and Industrial Efficiency*. Cambridge, MA: Riverside Press, 1913.

6. Max Weber, *The Theory of Social and Economic Organization*. New York: Free Press, 1927.

7. Stephen Robbins and Mary Coulter, *Management*, 9th edn. Upper Saddle River, NJ: Pearson/Prentice-Hall, 2006, p. 7.

8. Michael Hitt, Stewart Black, and Lyman Porter, *Management*, 2nd edn. Upper Saddle River, NJ: Pearson/Prentice-Hall, 2004, p. 8.

9. Henry Mintzberg, *The Nature of Managerial Work*. New York: Harper & Row, 1973, p. 55.

10. Henry Mintzberg, *Structure in Fives: Designing Effective Organizations*. Englewood Cliffs, NJ: Prentice-Hall, 1993.

11. Andre Laurent, "The cultural diversity of Western conceptions of management," *International Studies of Management and Organization*, 13(1/2) (1983), pp. 75–96.

12. Richard Hodgetts and Fred Luthans, *International Management: Culture, Strategy, and Behavior*, 5th edn. New York: McGraw-Hill-Irwin, 2003.

13. James Abbeglen and George Stalk, *Kaisha: The Japanese Corporation*. New York: Harper & Row, 1985.

14. Rob Coffee and Gareth Jones, *Why Should Anyone Be Led By You? What It Takes to Be an Authentic Leader*. Cambridge, MA: Harvard Business School Press, 2006, pp. 109–33.

15. Thomas Stewart, cited in Philip Harris, Robert Moran, and Sarah Moran, *Managing Cultural Differences*. Amsterdam: Elsevier, 2004, p. 1.

16. We include *inpatriates* (foreign managers assigned to positions in the parent company's home country) in the same category as expatriates, since they share the same kinds of problems and challenges; the only difference is the reverse nature of their assignment. We also lump *telecommuters* (who work largely from home via networks) and digital nomads (who work via networks from anywhere in the world, depending upon where they happen to be) into the category of virtual managers, since both manage or do business largely using computer-mediated technologies.

17. Marja Tahvanainen, Denice Welch, and Verner Worm, "Implications of short-term international assignments," *European Management Journal*, 23(6) (2005), pp. 663–73.

18. Nancy Adler, *International Dimensions of Organizational Behavior*. Mason, OH: Thompson, 2008.

19. Martha J. Frase, "International commuters: are your overseas assignments creating risky stealth-pats?," *HR Magazine*, March, 2007, pp. 91–5.

20. Carla Joinson, "Cutting down the days: HR can make expat assignments short and sweet," *HR Magazine*, April, 2000, pp. 93–7.

21. *The Economist*, "Traveling more lightly: staffing globalization," June 24, 2006, pp. 23–4.

22. Helene Mayerhofer, Linley Hartmann, Gabriela Michelitsch-Riedl, and Iris Kollinger, "Flexpatriate assignments: a neglected issue in global staffing," *International Journal of Human Resource Management*, 15(8) (2004), pp. 1371–89.

23. "Most creative people in business," *Fast Company*, August 21, 2015; "Jan Chipchase," *Fast Company*, June 2011, p. 128.

24. Luciara Nardon and Richard M. Steers, "The new global manager: learning cultures on the fly," *Organizational Dynamics*, 37(1) (2008), pp. 47–59.

25. Rosemary Stewart, *Choices for the Manager*. Englewood Cliffs, NJ: Prentice-Hall, 1982.

26. Stewart, *Choices for the Manager*, p. vii.

27. Stewart, *Choices for the Manager*, p. vii.

3 Cultural environments

MANAGEMENT CHALLENGE

With this chapter, we begin Stage II in developing *multicultural competence* by focusing on understanding the context in which global managers operate (see Exhibit 1.3 in Chapter 1). This chapter examines cultural environments, while Chapter 4 focuses on organizational environments. According to the *Talmud*, an ancient book of wisdom, "We do not see things as they are; we see them as we are."[1] We are a product of our cultures, and these cultures lead us to adopt different conceptions of reality. Without understanding how to navigate diverse cultural beliefs, values, and traditions, managers are left to take their chances in today's high-stakes and ever-changing environment. From a managerial standpoint, turning in one direction can lead to success; turning in the other can lead to failure. As a first step, managers can ask two questions: What is meant by the rather amorphous term "culture"? And what is the relationship between culture, contexts, attitudes, and behaviors? Managers who understand these issues are typically better prepared to compete and build successful partnerships.

CHAPTER OUTLINE

- Culture, socialization, and normative behavior   *page* 48
- Descriptive models of culture   52
- Culture and institutional environments   59
- Cultural complexities and contradictions   63
- Cultural diversity and multiculturalism   70
- MANAGER'S NOTEBOOK: Working across cultures   72
- Key terms   77
- Discussion questions   77
- Case: Anna Håkansson – from Sweden to Bahrain   78

APPLICATIONS

3.1 Customer service at Mitsukoshi   *page* 51

3.2 Traffic fines in Finland   59

3.3 Islamic legal systems and global business   62

3.4 Women executives in the Middle East   63

3.5 Seat assignments to Tel Aviv   69

3.6 Multiculturalism in Singapore   71

Grasshoppers are considered pests in North America, pets in China, and appetizers in Thailand. What does this suggest about the influence of local differences on perceptions of even the lowly insect? Indeed, what does this suggest about how and why tastes in general can differ so starkly across nations and regions? If different cultures can have such differing views about grasshoppers, imagine what they can do with people.

Philosophers and social scientists have long noted that if you want to understand why people – including managers – behave as they do, a good place to begin is with a serious look at the cultural environment in which they work. Think about the following three observations:

- Talmudic wisdom (cited above) dates from well over 2,000 years ago, yet is as true today as it was when it was initially written. Culture influences our perceptions of world events and thereby influences our values, attitudes, and behaviors. It tells us what is acceptable and what is not. If cultures differ, though, so do our perceptions, values, and judgments. What may be pleasant, attractive, agreeable, or acceptable in one culture may not be in another.
- More than 700 years ago Chinese scholar Wang Yinglin compiled a volume of ancient wisdom thought to be from Confucius and called the *Trimetric Classic*, in which he observed that "all people are basically the same; it is only their habits and environments that differ."[2]
- Much more recently, Wharton professor Robert J. House observed, "Ample evidence shows that the cultures of the world are getting more and more interconnected and that the business world is becoming increasingly global. As economic borders come down, cultural barriers will most likely go up and present new challenges and opportunities for business. When cultures come in contact, they may converge in some aspects, but their idiosyncrasies will likely amplify."[3]

The Talmud, a Confucian scholar, and a modern-day business professor, each coming from a very different time and place in history, all understood what has too frequently eluded many contemporary managers: culture can make a difference in determining how we think and how we behave. This is equally true in our personal lives as it is in our work lives. Unfortunately, too many managers have ignored even the most rudimentary cross-national differences while working overseas, and, as a result, have missed significant opportunities both for themselves and their companies.

Culture, socialization, and normative behavior

Along with economic and political considerations, the cultural environment of global management incorporates much of the *macro environment* in which organizations operate (see Exhibit 3.1). Included here are not just the social norms and beliefs that prevail in a society, but also social organization and cultural diversity. Moreover, the nature of social institutions should also be considered to the extent that they are influenced by fundamental cultural characteristics.

To understand how the cultural context works, we need to step back and learn more about cultures and how they can differ – sometimes significantly – both across and within countries and regions. To do so, in this chapter we examine five aspects of the cultural context that has relevance for managers: (1) the basic concept of culture as it relates to socialization and the creation and reinforcement of normative beliefs; (2) different models for describing cultures; (3) culture and institutional environments; (4) cultural complexities and contradictions; and (5) cultural diversity and multiculturalism. We begin with a simple question: What is culture? Unfortunately, this question is not as simple as it may appear.

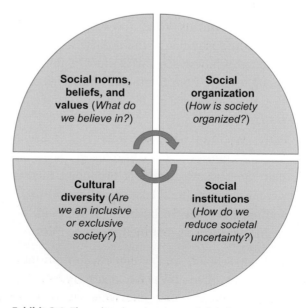

Exhibit 3.1 The cultural environment of global management

What is culture?

Culture is both simple and difficult to understand. It is simple because definitions abound that are easily understood by any reader. At the same time, however, culture can be difficult to comprehend, because of its subtleties and complexities. The ancient Chinese Taoist philosopher Lao Tzu once observed that "water is the last thing a fish notices," using water as a metaphor for culture.[4] In other words, most people are so deeply immersed in their own culture that they often fail to see how it affects their patterns of thinking or their behavior; they are too close to it. It is only when we are "out of the water" that we become aware of our own cultural biases and assumptions.

A key issue in dealing with different cultures relates to how we recognize culture when we see it. What do we mean by the term culture? One of the main challenges managers face when working across cultures is teasing out cultural influences from other phenomena in the world surrounding us. For example, where does culture end and personality begin? What is universal behavior and what is not? In this regard, finding a suitable working definition of culture can be challenging.

Hofstede defines culture as the collective programming of the mind that distinguishes the members of one human group from another.[5] Meanwhile, cultural anthropologist Clyde Kluckhohn defines culture as the collection of beliefs, values, behaviors, customs, and attitudes that distinguish the people of one society from another.[6] Researchers in the Global Leadership and Organizational Behavior Effectiveness (GLOBE) project define culture as shared motives, values, beliefs, identities, and interpretations or meanings of significant events that result from common experiences of members of collectives that are transmitted across generations.[7] Fons Trompenaars defines culture as the way in which a group of people solves problems and reconciles dilemmas.[8] Ann Swidler also took a problem-solving approach, viewing culture as a "toolkit" of symbols, stories, rituals, and worldviews that help the people of a culture survive and succeed.[9] Finally, cultural anthropologist Clifford Geertz defines culture as the means by which people communicate, perpetuate, and develop their knowledge about attitudes towards life.[10] Culture is the fabric of meaning in terms of which people interpret their experience and guide their actions.

While all these definitions are useful and share a great deal in common, they all have nuanced differences that may have more to say to academicians than managers. Taken together, these definitions suggest that, from the standpoint of global management, *culture is perhaps best thought of as addressing three questions: who are we, how do we live, and how do we approach work?* These three questions focus attention on individuals, environments, and work norms and values, and the answers to these questions allow us to draw some inferential conclusions about work and society and how managers in general should behave as they work across cultures.

Characteristics of cultures

Three characteristics of culture common to these definitions are particularly salient for our discussion here:

- Culture is shared by members of a group, and, indeed, sometimes defines the membership of the group itself. Cultural preferences are neither universal around the world nor entirely personal; they are preferences that are commonly shared by a group of people, even if not by all members of the group. The fact that most Koreans and Mexicans like spicy food does not require that all of them prefer such cuisine, nor does it require that all Dutch and Canadians avoid it.
- Culture is learned through membership in a group or community. Cultures, in the form of normative social behavior, are learned from elders, teachers, officials, experiences, and society at large. We acquire values, assumptions, and behaviors by seeing how others behave, growing up in a community, going to school, and observing our family.
- Culture influences the attitudes and behaviors of group members. Many of our innate beliefs, values, and patterns of social behavior can be traced back to our particular cultural training and socialization. After we grow up, culture still tells us what is acceptable and unacceptable behavior, attractive and unattractive, and so forth. As a result, culture heavily influences socialization processes in terms of how we see ourselves and what we believe and hold dear. This, in turn, influences our normative behavior, or how we think those around us expect us to behave.

Exhibit 3.2 illustrates the relationship between human, cultural, and personal preferences. Research by a number of social psychologies suggests that personality is influenced by a combination of learned and inherited attitudes and behaviors. A key part of this development is the culture in which people are nurtured. To some extent, we are a product of where we were brought up and how we were socialized. Culture, in turn, is influenced by human nature or biological programming. Culture resides between these two and the line that separates them is at best blurred. There are many situations where it is impossible to know for sure why someone is behaving in a certain way. And the reality is, in most instances it does not really matter. Managers need to be effective working across diverse populations, which includes an understanding of cultural differences but is not restricted to it. More important is identifying what is universal and what is not. The erroneous belief that a value, belief, or assumption is universal is likely to bring misunderstandings. For this reason, in this book we will highlight cultural differences in an attempt to bring awareness to non-universal assumptions.

Culture often sets the limits on what is considered acceptable and unacceptable behavior; it pressures individuals and groups into accepting and following *normative behavior*. In other words, culture determines the rules of the road that guide

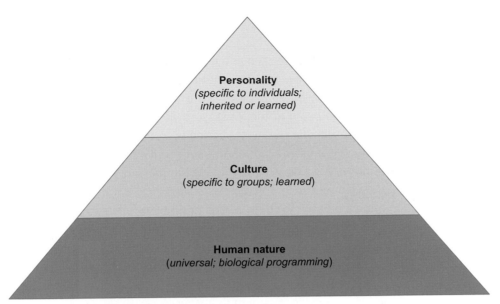

Exhibit 3.2 Culture, personality, and human nature
Source: Adapted from Geert Hofstede, *Culture's Consequence: International Differences in Work Related Values* (Thousand Oaks, CA: Sage, 1980); and D. Thomas and K. Inkson, *Cultural Intelligence for Global Business: People Skills for Global Business* (San Francisco, CA: Berret-Hoehler, 2003).

what people can do. Indeed, newspapers and periodicals are filled with examples of people who set out to break a "culture barrier." Rightly or wrongly, these barriers are typically established to ensure uniform practice, stability, and security among members of a society, and, as a result, societies often take a dim view of people who buck the system.

APPLICATION 3.1 Customer service at Mitsukoshi

Is customer service the same all over the world? Yes, in the sense that customers are served (some better than others, of course), but also no, in the sense of the mindsets and information processing of the customer service representatives. For example, foreign observers have long noted how naïve Western customers in their home countries can sometimes be in responding favorably to widespread promises of customer satisfaction. By contrast, many Japanese sales clerks such as those at the high-end Mitsukoshi Department Store do not guarantee customer satisfaction; instead, they aim to do their best and believe that satisfaction will follow.[11] But no guarantees. For many Japanese salespeople, a guarantee of satisfaction sounds too pretentious, almost like an invasion of privacy. "Who are we to judge whether customers will really be satisfied?" the logic goes.

This behavior is related to differing images concerning the relationship between buyer and seller. In the West, this is seen as a horizontal exchange among equals. Japanese, however, tend to view the relationship with customers in more hierarchical terms, in which the buyer is more like a master and the seller like a servant. Expressions often heard in the West, such as "The customer is always right," make little sense within a hierarchical framework, because the very assessment of right and wrong implies a position of superiority by those making the assessment. If customers are always right in the West, they are beyond right and wrong in Japan. As a consequence, commercial relationships in the West focus on the transaction and its balance for both buyers and sellers, while caring for the relationship and a mixture of loyalty and interdependence is generally stressed in Japan.

Finally, sales clerks in Japan typically take buyers' complaints, remarks, and requests at face value, while trying to understand exactly what they want. This is done with a lack of personal involvement that Westerners often see as too cold or lacking in emotion. The Japanese salesperson presents product information without drawing conclusions for the customer, unlike Western tactics, whereby, in what often resembles a contest of wills, sellers try to persuade customers of the need to purchase the product – preferably immediately, because it is "on sale." In Japan, sales clerks who interject themselves into the sale too much lead to customer doubts about the quality of the product or service. Instead, they will frequently take themselves out of the buyer's equation and let the product speak for itself.

Think about it . . .

(1) What is your definition of good customer service? Explain.
(2) How can the viewpoints of both customers and sales clerks influence this definition in practice? What happens when these two viewpoints are far apart?
(3) How might cognitive processes or thought processes among customer service clerks differ across cultures? Why?

Descriptive models of culture

To understand the changes and challenges around the world, many researchers suggest we need some kind of tool or mechanism with which to compare cultural and subcultural differences and similarities. Such a mechanism can provide a heuristic to gain conceptual entry into why some people think and act differently from others. Many researchers – and many global managers – begin by comparing cultures on various cultural dimensions, such as hierarchical or egalitarian, individualistic or collectivistic, and so forth. Although comparing cultural dimensions may provide only a thumbnail sketch of some general trends between two or more cultures, it can be useful as a starting point for cross-cultural understanding.

Even this simple strategy is not without its problems, however. As noted cultural anthropologist Edward Hall once observed, "I have come to the conclusion that the analysis of culture could be likened to the task of identifying mushrooms. Because of the nature of the mushrooms, no two experts describe them in precisely the same way, which creates a problem for the rest of us when we are trying to decide whether the specimen in our hands is edible."[12] Hall makes an important point here. While the success of global managers frequently rests on their understanding of cultures and cultural differences, the experts who advise them are not always in agreement. To apply Hall's metaphor, however, managers have to decide which mushrooms are edible and which are not. They need to know which practices or behaviors will create barriers to conducting business and which will open a path to partnership.

Models of national cultures

For many managers, the study of culture often begins with a comparison of different countries using several cultural dimensions (e.g., individualism/collectivism). For example, if a manager from Paris is traveling to Budapest, it can be helpful to understand differences in cultural trends between the two locales prior to arrival. While such models clearly do not explain everything managers need to know to succeed, they can be a useful starting point.

A number of such models are available and have been widely adopted (see Exhibit 3.3). These include the works of Edward T. Hall, Geert Hofstede, Fons Trompenaars, and Robert House and his GLOBE project associates. Each attempts to capture the essence of cultural differences through the use of multiple dimensions or measures. In doing so, each model highlights different aspects of societal beliefs, norms, and/or values. In Exhibit 3.3, we briefly summarize each of the four models. (Models of national cultures are examined in more depth in the Appendix.) This is followed by a brief comparison between the models in search of commonalities.[13]

A useful cultural model has been suggested by Edward T. Hall, a noted cultural anthropologist. Hall proposed a framework based on his ethnographic research in several societies, notably Germany, France, the United States, and Japan.[14] His research focused primarily on how cultures vary in interpersonal communication, but also included work on personal space and time. These three cultural dimensions are summarized in Exhibit 3.3. Many of the terms used today in the field of

Exhibit 3.3 Popular models of national cultures

Hall	Hofstede	Trompenaars	GLOBE project
Context: Extent to which the context of a message is as important as the message itself. *Space:* Extent to which people are comfortable sharing physical space with others. *Time:* Extent to which people approach one task at a time or multiple tasks simultaneously.	*Power distance:* Beliefs about the appropriate distribution of power in society. *Uncertainty avoidance:* Extent to which people feel threatened by uncertain or unknown situations. *Individualism–collectivism:* Relative importance of individual vs. group interests in society. *Masculinity–femininity:* Assertiveness vs. passivity; material possessions vs. quality of life. *Time orientation:* Long-term vs. short-term outlook on work, life, and relationships. *Indulgence-restraint:* Societal emphasis on enjoyment and need gratification vs. strict social control to suppress or regulate gratification.	*Universalism–particularism:* The degree to which rules are uniformly or situationally applied. *Individualism–collectivism:* Do people derive their identity from within themselves or from their group? *Specific vs. diffuse:* Are an individual's various roles compartmentalized or integrated? *Neutral vs. affective:* Are people free to express their emotions or are they restrained. *Achievement vs. ascription:* How are people accorded respect and social status? *Time perspective:* Do people focus on the past or the future? *Relationship with the environment:* Do people control the environment or does it control them?	*Power distance:* Degree to which people expect power to be distributed equally. *Uncertainty avoidance:* Extent to which people rely on norms, rules, and procedures to reduce the unpredictability of future events. *Humane orientation:* Extent to which people reward fairness, altruism, and generosity. *Institutional collectivism:* Extent to which society encourages collective distribution of resources and collective action. *In-group collectivism:* Extent to which individuals express pride, loyalty, and cohesiveness in their organizations and families. *Assertiveness:* Degree to which people are assertive, confrontational, and aggressive in relationships with others.

Hall	Hofstede	Trompenaars	GLOBE project
			Gender egalitarianism: Degree to which gender differences are minimized.
			Future orientation: Extent to which people engage in future-oriented behaviors such as planning, investing, and delayed gratification.
			Performance orientation: Degree to which high performance is encouraged and rewarded.

Exhibit 3.3 (*cont.*)

Source: Based on Edward T. Hall, *The Silent Language* (New York: Anchor Books, 1981); Edward T. Hall and Mildred R. Hall, *Understanding Cultural Differences* (Yarmouth, ME: Intercultural Press, 1990); Geert Hofstede, *Culture's Consequences: International Differences in Work Related Values* (Thousand Oaks, CA: Sage, 1980, rev. 2001); Fons Trompenaars, *Riding the Waves of Culture: Understanding Cultural Diversity in Global Business* (London: McGraw-Hill, 1993); Robert House, Paul Hanges, Mansour Javidan, Peter Dorfman, and Vipin Gupta, *Culture, Leadership, and Organizations* (Thousand Oaks, CA: Sage, 2004).

cross-cultural management (e.g., monochronic and polychronic) are derived from his work. Hall's model, especially as it related to intercultural communication will be discussed further in Chapter 5.

A second important model has been proposed by Dutch management researcher Geert Hofstede.[15] In his classic book, *Culture's Consequences*, Hofstede compares culture to the "software of the mind" that differentiates one group or society from another. In other words, while people all have the same hardware, their brains and patterns of thinking and behaving can be very different. Hofstede's model was derived from a study of employees from various countries working for major multinational corporations and was based on the assumption that different cultures can be distinguished on the basis of differences in what they value. In other words, some cultures place a high value on equality among individuals, while others place a high value on hierarchies or power distances between people. Likewise, some cultures value certainty in everyday life and have difficulty coping with unanticipated events, while others have a greater tolerance for ambiguity and seem to relish change. Taken together, Hofstede argues that it is possible to gain considerable insight into organized behavior across cultures on the basis of these value dimensions. Initially, Hofstede asserted that cultures could be distinguished along four dimensions, but later he added a fifth dimension focusing on long- and short-term orientation based on his research with Michael Bond. More recently, a sixth dimension was added: indulgence vs. restraint (see Exhibit 3.3).

Building on the work of Hofstede, Dutch management researcher Fons Trompenaars has presented a somewhat different model of culture based on his study of Shell and other managers over a ten-year period.[16] His model focuses on variations in both values and personal relationships across cultures. It consists of seven dimensions, as shown in Exhibit 3.3. The first five dimensions focus on relationships among people, while the last two focus on time management and society's relationship with nature.

Finally, in one of the most ambitious efforts to study cultural dimensions, Robert House led an international team of researchers that focused primarily on understanding the influence of cultural differences on leadership processes.[17] Their investigation was called the GLOBE study. In their research, the GLOBE researchers identified nine cultural dimensions (see Exhibit 3.3). While several of these dimensions have been identified previously (e.g., individualism/collectivism, power distance, and uncertainty avoidance), others are unique (e.g., gender egalitarianism and performance orientation).

Based on this assessment, the GLOBE researchers collected data in sixty-two countries and compared the results. Systematic differences were found in leader behavior across the cultures. For example, participatory leadership styles that are often accepted in the individualistic West are of questionable effectiveness in the more collectivistic East. Asian managers place a heavy emphasis on paternalistic leadership and group maintenance activities. Charismatic leaders can be found in most cultures, although they may be highly assertive in some cultures and passive in others. A leader who listens carefully to his or her subordinates is more valued in the United States than in China. Malaysian leaders are expected to behave in a manner that is humble, dignified, and modest, while American leaders seldom behave in this manner. Indians prefer leaders who are assertive, morally principled, ideological, bold, and proactive. Family and tribal norms support highly autocratic leaders in many Arab countries. Clearly, one of the principal contributions of the GLOBE project has been to systematically study not just cultural dimensions but also how variations in such dimensions affect leadership behavior and effectiveness.

Taken together, these models attempt to accomplish two things. First, each model offers a well-reasoned set of dimensions along which various cultures can be compared. It offers us a form of shorthand for cultural analysis. We can break down assessments of various cultures into power distance, uncertainty avoidance, and so forth, allowing us to organize our thoughts and focus our attention on what other-wise would be a monumental task. Second, some of the models offer numeric scores for rating various cultures. For example, we can use Hofstede's measures to say that Germany is more egalitarian than France. Regardless of whether these ratings are highly precise or only generally indicative of these countries, they nonetheless force managers to confront cultural differences and consider the managerial implications.

Critics of this research point out – with some justification – that all four theories and the research underlying their creation and use focus too much on comparing central tendencies between cultures and not enough on comparing the differences within each culture. In other words, are all Indonesians or Kenyans or Bulgarians alike? Obviously not. Moreover, is it inaccurate to suggest that there are only a few differences between the peoples of either East Asia (Chinese, Korean, Japanese) or Western Europe (Dutch, French, Germans, Italians). Again, the answer is "No." Do these criticisms hold up? Do they change the basic argument about cultural differences influencing the way people see the world and respond to it? Probably not. As already noted, however, although the use of cultural dimensions is certainly helpful, it should be considered as only the beginning of a more detailed study.

Common themes across models: core cultural dimensions

Even so, while each of these models focuses on different aspects of culture, we believe that, taken together, they serve to amplify one another and reinforce their utility as critical evaluative components in better understanding global manage-ment and the world of international business. Each model has added something of value to this endeavor.

With this in mind, if we compare the various models of cultural dimensions, five dimensions emerge as being the most commonly used by researchers and managers alike in trying to differentiate between cultures (see Exhibit 3.4).[18] While not a perfect fit, we can nevertheless find fairly common agreement. We refer to these as core cultural dimensions. Each dimension focuses on one of five fundamental questions about cultures as they relate to social interaction and management practices in the global economy.

(1) Power distribution *(hierarchical vs. egalitarian)*. How are power and authority distributed in a society? Is this distribution based on concepts of hierarchy or egalitarianism? What are societal beliefs concerning equality or privilege?
(2) Social relationships *(individualistic vs. collectivistic)*. What is the fundamental building block of a society: individuals or groups? How does a society organize for collective action?
(3) Environmental relationships *(mastery-oriented vs. harmony-oriented)*. On a societal level, how do people view their relationship with their surrounding

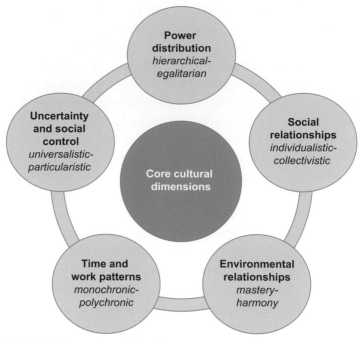

Exhibit 3.4 Core cultural dimensions
Source: Based on Luciara Nardon and Richard M. Steers, "The culture theory jungle: divergence and convergence in models of national culture," in Rabi S. Bhagat and Richard M. Steers (eds.), *Cambridge Handbook of Culture, Organizations, and Work* (Cambridge University Press, 2009), pp. 3–22.

environment? Is their goal to control or master their environment or to live in harmony with it?

(4) Time and work patterns (*monochronic vs. polychronic*). How do people in a society organize their time to carry out their work and non-work activities? Do people approach work in a linear (i.e., one thing at a time) or a nonlinear (i.e., everything at once) fashion?

(5) Uncertainty and social control (*universalism vs. particularism; also called rule-based vs. relationship-based*). How do societies try to reduce uncertainties and control the behavior of their members? Do they focus primarily on rules or relationships? In other words, do they work to control people through rules, policies, laws, and social norms that are uniformly applied across society (universalism) or do they attempt to control people through rules or laws that are often tempered by personal relationships, in-group values, or unique circumstances (particularism)?

Taken together, these five core cultural dimensions highlight key aspects of cultural differences that can have a bearing on how business and management is conducted – or not conducted – around the world. Like the models on which it is based, these core cultural dimensions provide a quick cultural snapshot of the central tendencies in one country. They are a good starting point to investigate cultural differences between countries, but their utility will vary depending on the countries involved and the particular situation.

APPLICATION 3.2 Traffic fines in Finland

A good example of how cultures can differ can be found in Finland, a country that stresses egalitarianism with a passion. Many Finnish laws are universalistic and based on the principle of equity if not equality. For example, traffic fines vary based on personal income; the more you make, the more you can afford to pay. Police departments maintain direct computer access to internal revenue files to calculate the fines on the spot. Hence, when Jaako Rytsola, a young Finnish entrepreneur, was stopped driving his BMW at 43 miles per hour in a 25-mile-per-hour zone, his speeding ticket cost him $72,000. Similarly, when 27-year-old millionaire Jussi Salonoja, also in a BMW, was caught doing 40 miles per hour in a 25-mile-per-hour zone, he was fined $225,000. A government minister noted that this was a "Nordic tradition." They have both progressive taxation and progressive punishment. However, another driver fined $60,000 for going 10 miles over the speed limit had a different opinion. "Finland is impossible to live in for certain kinds of people," he noted.[19]

Think about it . . .

(1) What is your opinion of the fairness of tying traffic fines to personal income? Why might this be fair or unfair?
(2) Do you think the kind of car you drive influences whether or not you get stopped by the police? Is this true in all cultures?
(3) Would you enjoy being a manager in a country that genuinely stresses equality – including equality with your subordinates?

Culture and institutional environments

At the height of the recent global economic crisis, Bank of America announced it would cut 30,000 jobs over three years in a bid to save $5 billion per year. The cost-cutting drive was part of a broader effort to reshape and shrink the bank as it coped with fallout from years of poor investments and what many considered to be poor management decisions. Shortly after the announcement, Bank of America's stock price *increased* significantly.

In difficult economic times, when demand declines for services or production, companies around the world face the same challenge: what to do with excess employees. While the challenge may be the same, however, corporate responses are not. In much of North America, like the situation at Bank of America, reduced demand for services often leads logically – and culturally consistently – to employee lay-offs. Although widely recognized as causing hardship to people, lay-offs are often deemed to be a prudent business and management response to a financial crisis. In Germany or the Netherlands, however, long-standing social legislation makes it much more difficult – and more costly – to downsize employees. As a result, Dutch and German companies will often seek other remedies, such as seeking early retirements or job sharing. Finally, in Japan, lay-offs are rare (although they still occur), since organizations risk losing their public reputation, which can affect their business and future hiring opportunities. Lay-offs violate fundamental Japanese social norms regarding paternalism in the workplace. As a result, Japanese companies will frequently decide to transfer redundant employees to other parts of the organization or its subsidiaries, even if they too are overstaffed. Same problem, but very different responses – and it is all part of the institutional environment facing managers.

Culture and institutional environments go hand in hand. Indeed, they are frequently mutually reinforcing. The institutional environment generally consists of the legal-political environment, which either encourages or discourages individuals and companies from pursuing certain strategies that governments or society at large either support or oppose (see Exhibit 3.5). Governments obviously have considerable power to control organizations through the passage of laws and policies, technology transfers to favored companies, financial support, legal strictures on investment policies, import–export policies and constraints, and so forth. This arena is sometimes referred to as business–government relations, and a major debate in international business is the extent to which business and government should have an adversarial relationship or a cooperative one.

Nowhere is this difference more notable than when comparing the institutional environments and business–government relationships between Japan and the United States. If there is a principal difference in the business strategies of Japanese and US firms, it is Japan's preoccupation with gaining market share, as opposed to the US preoccupation with achieving short-term net profits or higher stock prices. This fundamental difference results from several differences in the two business environments, which allow many Japanese firms to take a longer-term perspective than their US competitors.

First, consider the institutional environment in which most US firms operate. This environment is characterized by the following: distant and often adversarial

Normative beliefs and values	Institutional requirements	Goal: Social control, stability, and continuity
Societal beliefs, norms, and values encourage and reinforce what society deems to be correct and proper	Laws, regulations, and public policies aimed at reinforcing societal norms and values	Encourage "correct" actions that are consistent with societal needs and goals through social (e.g., ostracism) or legal (fines) sanctions

Exhibit 3.5 Normative beliefs, institutional requirements, and social control

business–government relations are common, including having the government as the principal regulator. The principal purpose of the company is to maximize stockholder wealth. Investors stress short-term transactions and returns on investment. A clear link exists between earnings per share and stock price. Managers are frequently offered stock options and large bonuses for superior performance. Finally, undervalued companies are frequently subject to hostile takeovers.

Now consider the very different institutional environment found in Japan. In contrast to much of the West, Japan's institutional environment is characterized by a strong and ongoing cooperative business–government relationship that permeates the core business environment, including government targeting of strategic industries and support for local industries. The principal purpose of a company is to build value over the long term to benefit investors, employees, and the nation. Investors stress long-term stock appreciation instead of earnings per share. Dividends are paid at a constant rate as a percentage of the par value of the stock, not as a percentage of profits. Managers are seldom offered stock options or large bonuses for superior performance. Few outside board members are present to defend stockholder interests. Finally, undervalued companies are typically protected by sister companies from outside takeovers.

As a result of these differences, Japanese firms are better positioned to focus their attention on attaining strategic objectives (such as gaining market share) instead of financial objectives (such as keeping stockholders happy). This competitive advantage occurs for three principal reasons. First, low profits and high retained earnings support growth. Second, close relationships with banks allow the use of high levels of debt to support growth. Finally, Japanese stockholders routinely accept low dividends and management's absolute control of the firm.

APPLICATION 3.3 Islamic legal systems and global business

Leaving Japan and the United States, we turn now to the Middle East for another example of institutional environments. Columbia University anthropologist Lawrence Rosen has written extensively on the differences between Western and Islamic countries with respect to the functioning of the legal system.[20] According to Rosen, property in the West is viewed, for legal purposes, in terms of ownership ("Who owns this land?"); this is an objectivist approach. By contrast, under Islam, property is viewed in terms of its relationships to others ("Who is associated with this land?"); this is a subjectivist approach. Because the idea of a divisible self is unimaginable in Islam, power is both institutional and personal, with the implication that judges (and managers, we may add) are expected to rule without consciously trying to exclude their personal feelings and attitudes.

Judges, then, will open widely the bounds of relevance to ascertain the ties of indebtedness of the various parties to a dispute, often getting people back to negotiate their own agreements with their kin rather than enunciating particular rights. Judges will assess witness reliability according to the nature and intensity of the witnesses' social ties rather than primarily relying on their objective expertise, and they will ascertain facts according more to their evaluation of the person and his or her past history than by observable circumstances. Rosen also stresses that, because of their greater effect on their networks of relationships, educated and wealthier people are also held to higher legal standards in Islamic cultures.

For managers, the ethical landscape looks very much the same. Business contracts make heavy use of both personal contacts and networks and are largely transitory when conditions change in more particularistic cultures than in universalistic ones.

Think about it . . .

(1) How is the Islamic legal system different from the prevailing legal codes in the West?
(2) What is the impact of these differences on individual and group behavior?
(3) How can these differences impact non-Islamic businesspeople doing business in the Middle East?
(4) What might "foreigners" do to deal with these legal differences in ways that no one is offended?

Cultural complexities and contradictions

The related concepts of culture and cultural differences were introduced above as a means of seeing beyond overt behaviors and better understanding why and how some people act differently from others. What is often missed in these generalizations, however, is that individuals within the same society may use different strategies to deal with identical challenges. As a result, it is unwise to stereotype an entire culture. Instead, we need to look for nuances and counter-trends, not just the principal trends themselves. We also need to look for differences in *context* – the events and environments surrounding people as they form their attitudes and behavioral patterns. Failure to recognize this often leads to failed personal and business opportunities.

Think about the issue of equal opportunity in the workplace. The fight for equal opportunity has been a long and difficult struggle in many nations of the world, north, south, east, and west. For many, this struggle has been quite vociferous, because the underlying beliefs are so strong. What people often fail to recognize here, however, is that to a large extent societal and corporate practices regarding equal rights are embedded in our core beliefs and values. As a result, it is important to be able to compare such beliefs and practices across cultures, as well as within them. For example, some cultures stress sex role differentiation. In other words, men and women are expected to play different roles in society, and, as such, should be treated differently. Other cultures have increasingly stressed minimizing sex role differentiation, believing that men and women should share responsibilities both at home and at work. Still other cultures strive for flexibility and tolerance. As a result of these cultural differences, many people are quick to criticize the beliefs of others as being either overly paternalistic or overly indulgent. For the keen observer, though, differences can often be found just under the surface.

To see how this works, consider the fact that an increasing number of highly educated women are expanding their career opportunities throughout the Middle East. Nahed Taher is just one of these women.

APPLICATION 3.4 **Women executives in the Middle East**

Nahed Taher is the first woman CEO of the Gulf One Investment Bank, based in Bahrain.[21] As a former senior economist at the National Commercial Bank, Taher has been immersed in plans for financing public sector projects, including expansion of the terminal that handles Mecca pilgrims at Jeddah's King Abdulaziz International Airport. She also oversees financing for a water desalination plant for Saudi Arabian Airlines, as well as Saudi copper, zinc, and gold mines. Taher may be an unusual example of an Arab executive, but she is increasingly becoming a common one. In fact, business leaders such as Taher are gaining power despite the odds. Ten women executives from the Middle East made the *Forbes* "World's 100 most powerful women" list.

How are women such as Taher managing to break through the global glass ceiling in the Middle Eastern region? In many cases, the increasing globalization of the world's economy has played an important role. The economic liberalization of several Muslim countries in recent years, along with the privatization of large parts of government-run companies, has helped Muslim businesswomen get a greater foothold. "Now opportunities are open to everyone," says Laura Osman, the first female president of the Arab Bankers Association of North America. "The private sector runs on meritocracy." In fact, banking in the Muslim world is populated by a growing number of women, even in the historically all-male executive suite. Sahar El-Sallab is second in command at Commercial International Bank, one of Egypt's largest private banks. Indeed, four out of ten Commercial International Bank employees and 70 percent of its management staff are women. Similarly, Maha Al-Ghunaim, chairman of Kuwait's Global Investment House, has steadily grown the investment bank she founded into more than $7 billion in assets. Recently it won permission to operate in Qatar, and next wants to establish a presence in Saudi Arabia.

Muslim businesswomen also sit in the top ranks of large conglomerates. Imre Barmanbek runs one of Turkey's largest multinationals, Dogan Holding. Lubna Olayan helps oversee the Olayan Group of Saudi Arabia, one of the biggest multinationals in the Middle East, with investments in more than forty companies. The top ranks of the conglomerate run by the Khamis family of Egypt also include several women. Originally from India, Vidya Chabria is chairman of the United Arab Emirates' Jumbo Group, a $2 billion multinational that operates in fifty countries, with interests in durables, chemicals, and machinery products. It also owns Jumbo Electronics, one of the Middle East's largest Sony distributors of consumer electronics, as well as worldwide brands in information technology and telecom products. Thus, while Muslim women may still have a way to go to reach "equality" in the business world, progress can be seen. "Just being a woman in our part of the world is quite difficult," says El-Sallab of Egypt's Commercial International Bank; "but if you have the proper education, credibility, and integrity in the way you handle your job, intelligent men will always give you your due."

At the same time, an increasing number of young educated Arab women are finding their way into the lower and middle managerial ranks as well, albeit slowly. In Saudi Arabia, for example, new government policies are working to recruit more women for vital private and public sector jobs by offering child care, transportation and, in some cases, segregated factories. The state-run Saudi Industrial Property Authority, for example, is building 13 special zones designed to encourage business owners to hire more Saudi women. The zones are located near urban areas to make commutes short and offer training centers to teach manufacturing skills. Still, much of the recent hiring of women is by foreign companies. An example is Zahra al Khalifa, a young engineering graduate recently hired by GE for their Saudi operations. Multiple hurdles for women still exist, however, and the toughest part of the job is often outside the shop. "Most of our customers are men," al Khalifa observed. "They are not comfortable dealing with females yet."[22]

Think about it . . .

(1) How can we reconcile stereotypes about Arab and Muslim women with examples of successful businesswomen working in the Middle Eastern region such as those mentioned here?

(2) Do the women discussed here exhibit any common personal characteristics that may have helped them succeed?

(3) What other examples of cultural stereotypes from other parts of the world can you identify that are either overly simplistic or simply incorrect? Why do we have such stereotypes?

(4) Considering the example of Zahara al Khalfi, what else might the Saudi and other Arab governments do to overcome traditional impediments to women working in industry?

The examples of Nahed Taher and her colleagues raise an old dilemma. Even though cultural differences have been acknowledged across nation states and regions for centuries, there is no consensus regarding the role of cultural differences in global business. Do cultural constraints really matter if people operating in a global arena are able to overcome them? When dealing with this question, most people fall into one of two groups: believers and non-believers. Believers argue that, on the basis of available research evidence and practical experience, culture does matter, because what works in London will likely not work in Guangzhou, Bangalore, or Moscow. They point out that people who have worked abroad are well aware how different things can be in places around the world, and that much of this difference can be explained only by cultural characteristics. Non-believers, in turn, argue that people are different in general, and that no two Indians (or Chinese, or Russians, or Saudis) behave in exactly the same way. They argue further that organizations in one country can – and often must – operate very differently from those in another country.

Finally, they argue that, from the standpoint of research, the variance explained by culture is often small, and numerous other factors may be equally (or perhaps more) important in explaining behavioral differences across borders, including legal, political, and economic differences and available technologies.

Which of these positions is a more accurate reflection of reality, and what are the implications for global managers? While both research and practical experience suggest that culture does matter, research and practical experience also suggest that culture alone is insufficient to explain the behavior of our foreign counterparts. Otherwise, how can we explain the success of these women in a male-dominated culture?

For this reason, we must be cautious in our interpretation of cultural phenomena. Strong preconceptions about the role (or lack thereof) of culture may blind us to the ways in which culture often does matter. Understanding the role of culture in management practice requires a way of thinking about culture that will help to identify cultural influences, and inform the best course of action to deal with them. In other words, we need to understand what culture is and what it does, how our own culture has influenced our way of thinking in terms of working assumptions and personal and group biases, and how to acquire a sufficient understanding of how culture works to be able to tease out cultural influences on various situations in which we find ourselves. This is no easy task, clearly, but it may nonetheless be an important one for global managers.

These examples of successful women also highlight some important limitations of applying simplistic models to complex phenomena. On the one hand, such models provide a good starting point for understanding the influence of culture and the challenges posed by cultural differences. On the other hand, they focus our attention onto a limited set of parameters and may mislead our interpretation of reality. Instead, understanding cultural influences on behavior requires us to seek out underlying complexities and contradictions, which, ultimately, aid us in our ability to act successfully in or across very different environments.

We suggest five limitations on what some people see as homogeneous cultures. All point to the fact that cultures are indeed not homogeneous (see Exhibit 3.6).

(1) Cultures are stable, but change over time. One of the dangers in any attempt to categorize cultures into a set of fixed dimensions is that this implies that cultures are stable and remain unchanged. Although some aspects of culture are indeed stable and persistent, others evolve and change over time, however. In other words, at the same time that groups of people strive to remain faithful to what and who they are, they simultaneously accommodate change and evolve when necessary or desirable. The implication for managers is that the cultures they must work with – including their own – are in a constant state of flux even if some things are unseen.

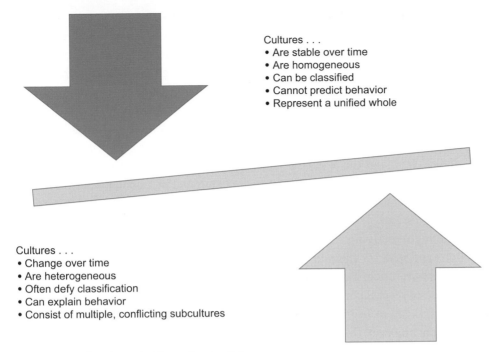

Cultures . . .
• Are stable over time
• Are homogeneous
• Can be classified
• Cannot predict behavior
• Represent a unified whole

Cultures . . .
• Change over time
• Are heterogeneous
• Often defy classification
• Can explain behavior
• Consist of multiple, conflicting subcultures

Exhibit 3.6 Cultural complexities and contradictions

(2) **Cultures are homogeneous, but allow for individuality.** A second problem in
trying to categorize cultures is that such actions imply a degree of homogeneity.
When describing individual cultures (whether through simplified dimensions or
deep descriptive analysis), we focus on shared aspects that are frequently found
across the cultural group. Since cultures are shared, culture, by definition,
includes what is common among members of a group. Members of a cultural
group invest considerable time and effort in tying together the various strands
that collectively represent and define social behavior. Cultures are also
fragmented, however, in the sense that they often allow for internal variations –
individuality – and even significant discrepancies in their midst. Despite
people's tendency to stereotype, logic and personal experience suggest that
variations – sometimes significant – can be found in all cultures. For example,
while people often describe Australia as a highly individualistic culture and
China as a highly collectivistic culture, there are, in fact, many collectivistic
Australians and many individualistic Chinese. Moreover, people may act in
individualistic fashion in some circumstances (e.g., on the job) but collectivistic
in others (e.g., attending religious services). Only by understanding the cultural
context in which behaviors occur can outsiders understand the behaviors that
will be considered proper or acceptable across nation states and those that are
likely to be very different in Cairo, London, and New York.

(3) Cultures are often classified into general categories that overlook subtle but important differences. Descriptions of culture using a limited set of dimensions may lead to the impression that this limited set of adjectives can capture the essence of culture. Experience and observation tell us that culture is more complex and paradoxical, however, with many exceptions and qualifications to any general classification. All cultures contain defining elements that defy universal qualifications. Examples include the Latino notion of *orgullo*, or pride for the accomplishments of their people; the Brazilian *jeitinho*, or flexible adaptability; and the Japanese concept of *kao*, or face (*kao o tateru* for saving face). These unique aspects of culture are enmeshed in, and derived from, unique historical experiences and responses and are not fully captured by general categories and descriptions, which fail to acknowledge the intricacies of the meaning underlying the concepts. Intelligent managers will avoid simple solutions and look for the nuances underlying categorizations, not just the rhetoric.

(4) Cultures can help explain, but not predict, behavior. We have noted above that the use of several core cultural dimensions to describe a particular culture can be a useful way to begin the study of that culture. If this is not done with care or caution, however, this over-reliance on the use of cultural dimensions can lead to an exaggerated assumption of causality or determinism. It is easy to make connections between general cultural characteristics and actions, such as "People from collectivistic cultures prefer working in teams," or "Hierarchical cultures prefer authoritarian leaders." These types of conclusions are problematic, however. Culture both constrains and enables behavior. It provides frameworks for making sense of the world around us, for learning and expanding our horizons. These frameworks are important for interpreting phenomena around us, communicating with others, and organizing social and psychological processes.

(5) Cultures represent a unified whole, but also consist of multiple and often conflicting subcultures. Finally, as noted earlier, a key characteristic of culture is that it is learned. People acquire values, assumptions, and behaviors by seeing how others around them behave and by observing their families. Herein lies a major source for overgeneralizations and stereotypes about national cultures, however. This is because most people within one culture belong to multiple, and often conflicting, subcultures. Subcultures can include levels of education (intellectual culture), professions or specializations (professional culture), normative beliefs about right and wrong and organized religion (religious culture), places of work (organizational culture), geographic locations within a country (regional culture), and so forth. What this means is that people can also acquire additional cultural tools from the various subcultures to which they belong. Culture is a collective, socially constructed phenomenon that exists or emerges whenever a set of basic assumptions or beliefs is commonly held by a group of people. Thus, multiple subcultures coexist within organizations, industries, and

nations. Cultural makeup is layered and influenced by varied group memberships. These multiple layers of culture shape individuals' attention, interpretations, and actions, and the cultural layer that is salient can vary over time. As
such, at a single point in time, people simultaneously belong to one culture and
many cultures, making the study of cultural differences even more problematic.

So what does all this mean for managers? It means that managers are more likely to
succeed to the extent that they are able to focus on the specifics of each situation
surrounding a cross-cultural encounter. They cannot simply look for macro level
cultural variables (e.g., power distance, gender role orientation, etc.) because the
impact of culture on behavior does not happen in a vacuum. It occurs within a
context made up of an organizational reality with specific actors involved. As noted
sociologist Ann Swidler observes, "The debate over whether or how much culture
influences action obscures a crucial insight: that culture's influences vary by
context ... yet there is remarkably little analysis of the contexts in which culture
is brought to bear on action."[23] For many managers, context, not culture, represents
their biggest challenge in succeeding in global transactions.

To see how conflicts can be not just cross-cultural but also multicultural within
one "culture," consider a recent flight by US carrier Delta Airlines from New York to
Tel Aviv.

APPLICATION 3.5 Seat assignments to Tel Aviv

As airplanes get more crowded and passengers experience less room and poorer
service, increased conflicts are both predictable and frustrating for both passengers and flight crews. One recent example reported in the *New York Times*
illustrates this point as it related to cultural differences.[24] During the boarding
process of a fully booked Delta Airlines flight from New York to Tel Aviv, Israel, a
group of Haredi men refused to sit in their assigned seats. Haredi Judaism is a
stream of Orthodox Judaism characterized by a rejection of modern secular
culture. *Haredim* regard themselves as the most religiously authentic group of
Jews, and their religious beliefs forbid them from touching members of the
opposite sex unless they are close relatives or a spouse.

When the men announced that they could not sit next to the women seated
next to them, the flight attendant asked the two women – also from Israel – to
change seats with other male passengers. They refused, saying that they had
reserved and paid for their particular seats and were not moving. They also
claimed sex discrimination. There were no open seats on the entire aircraft so at
least four passengers would have to be moved to resolve the problem. The flight

attendant reported to the captain, but neither knew what to do, and the surrounding passengers became impatient.

Think about it . . .

(1) How would you describe the nature of this conflict? What is its root cause?
(2) If you were the flight attendant or captain, and realizing that you must take concrete action, what exactly would you do and why? What are the potential ramifications of your chosen action?
(3) Should Delta Airlines or the International Air Transport Association work to create policies to manage similar potential conflicts in the future? If so, what might these policies look like?
(4) What are the broader lessons that go beyond this example that might be applied to other situations of cross-cultural and multicultural conflict?

Cultural diversity and multiculturalism

A Canadian sociologist once observed that the principal difference between American and Canadian cultural images is that American culture creates the image of a "melting pot," where everyone strives to be an "American"; while Canadian culture creates the image of a "mosaic," where cultural differences are constantly on display. Maybe true; maybe not. In any case, understanding cultural differences only takes us so far in navigating cross-cultural interactions because each situation is unique. While culture itself obviously matters, it can matter in different ways across different situations. Thus, while understanding how business is conducted in Saudi Arabia, for example, may be interesting, it provides us with little guidance when trying to negotiate a contract with a Saudi manager working for a French company in Brazil. And learning about French and Brazilian cultures, again while useful, still leaves us short in understanding what to do in the current situation.

This example may seem a bit extreme, but it illustrates at least three challenges in cross-cultural encounters that are commonplace:

(1) There is often more than one culture involved in an interaction, and it is not always clear how each one plays out or is dominant in a particular situation. In our illustration, is it the Saudi cultural background of the individual, the company culture perhaps influenced by the French business culture, or the local Brazilian culture where the interaction takes place that determines appropriate – and inappropriate – behaviors?

(2) People often behave differently in cross-cultural situations than they do in intra-cultural situations. Think about it: While you are trying to figure out how to deal with your Saudi counterpart and adjusting your behavior as best as you can, what do you think your counterpart is doing? The same thing.

(3) Cultures are fragmented, and even within a particular cultural environment different behaviors are observed in different subgroups. In order for cultural information to be useful, it is often important to be specific as to which subgroup we are dealing with.

APPLICATION 3.6 Multiculturalism in Singapore

Singapore is widely recognized as a successful multicultural society. Its population of about 5 million consists of roughly 74 percent Chinese, 13 percent Malays, 9 percent Indians, and the rest Eurasians and others. Together they represent numerous diverse religious faiths – Buddhist, Christian, Muslim, Taoist, Hindu, Sikh, and Jewish – all crammed into an area of a little over 700 km^2, making it one of the most densely populated countries in the world. This diversity of peoples living in close proximity to one another is potentially explosive but, remarkably, Singapore is distinguished by a high level of social and cultural harmony.[25]

Why? From independence in 1965, the fledgling democracy sought to integrate the various racial and cultural groups into a peaceful, workable society, with a unifying identity. Without this, many understood that this tiny state, with few natural resources, would likely not have survived. How did the new government accomplish this? Mainly through a high degree of state centralization and intervention; separation of state and religion; maintaining a secular neutralism vis-à-vis religion; recognition of the languages of the major communities, Malay, Chinese [Mandarin], and Tamil, as official tongues, with English as the first language; a system of meritocracy as opposed to one of nepotism and cronyism; and what some opponents call a de facto one-party government, which has ensured continuity of government policy.

A principal tool the government used to forge cultural and religious harmony was the education system. Instruction in the public schools is in English, although pupils also study their mother tongues. A sense of national pride and identity, as well as racial, religious, and cultural consensus, is instilled through a broad-based social studies program. Another means to bring the various groups together was an ethnic integration policy in which each of the major cultures were given a representative quota of homes in various housing blocks. Once that limit has been reached, no further sales of flats to that ethnic group were allowed.

According to one survey, Singaporeans rate citizenship higher than the demands of their religion because of the high degree of religious tolerance, both between government and religions, and between the religions themselves. Second, the main state language, English, does not conflict with the "languages of religion." Third is the lack of a clear ethno-linguistic-religious majority, which prevents the political dominance of a particular group.

Lastly, Singapore's phenomenal economic success and prosperity have served both to minimize tensions and to motivate the various groups to work together to maintain the state's position as one of Asia's more dynamic economies. While not all the citizens of the country are rich, the standard of living is comparable to that in North America and Western Europe. A recent survey found that 11.4 percent of Singaporean households are considered millionaires, the largest proportion in the world.

Think about it . . .

(1) Why do outside observers describe Singapore as a successful multicultural society?
(2) Are these characteristics easily transferrable to other multi-ethnic societies? Why or why not?
(3) What are the challenges facing Singaporeans in living in a multicultural society? Explain.
(4) What are the implications for foreign firms doing business in Singapore?
(5) What can other countries learn from the example of Singapore in seeking to develop more successful multicultural societies?

MANAGER'S NOTEBOOK

Working across cultures

We have now come full circle, from looking for general dimensions with which to compare cultures to understanding that cultures are indeed complex and at times contradictory. Cultures are not easily pigeonholed into groups and categories. As Edward Hall notes, "Culture hides much more than it reveals, and strangely enough what it hides, it hides most effectively from its own participants."[26] Caution is certainly in order.

Added to this is an understanding of the important role that culture and context play in influencing managerial action. These complexities and contradictions raise the intriguing question of how managers should act or react when they find

1. Avoid cultural stereotyping	2. View cultural differences in neutral terms	3. Prepare for unexpected by enhancing your cognitive skills
• Cultural descriptions contain only limited information. • Be as objective as possible in describing cultures; avoid evaluations. • Focus on accurate descriptions of beliefs, values, and norms. • Cultural descriptions should be considered a first guess and a trigger to further exploration. • Cultural descriptions can change over time.	• Cultures are neither good nor bad; they are just different—and can have different behavioral implications. • Remember that most cultures are complex and contradictions can often be found in attitudes and behaviors. • Use your expanded cultural knowledge to view situations through the eyes of others. • Look for subtleties and nuances in interpersonal interactions that explain what others are thinking.	• Self-awareness • Empathy • Information gathering and analysis • Information integration and transformation • Behavioral flexibility • Mindfulness

Exhibit 3.7 Strategies for working across cultures

themselves in the middle of cultural tension or change. A major challenge here is that different cultures often require very different behaviors from their managers, and what is acceptable in one country may be offensive in another. This is not surprising, but it nevertheless presents real challenges for managers when interacting with – and sometimes managing – a global workforce. How should managers behave, and will they be accepted when they are charged with accomplishing corporate objectives in a foreign culture? Should managers be themselves or try to adapt their management style to fit local customs and expectations? Fundamentally, how can they survive and succeed when they don't understand the rules of the game, and the rules that they do understand are often changing or do not apply to the specific individuals or contexts they are dealing with?

To aid in this understanding, we can summarize several coping strategies that may help managers as they try and make sense out of the "strange" behaviors of others (see Exhibit 3.7). More specifically, we discuss three management strategies: avoiding cultural stereotyping, seeing cultures in neutral terms, and preparing for the unexpected.

1.   Avoid cultural stereotyping

Understanding the influence of culture on management practices is an important first step. Managers who are able to understand the ways that culture can influence behavior and have knowledge of how cultures differ are better able to identify cultural phenomena and identify solutions to deal with them. In this regard, the role of cultural stereotypes is clearly relevant.

McGill professor Nancy Adler offers some sound advice on how to avoid making cultural stereotypes or overgeneralizations about the people from any culture.[27]

- Cultural descriptions, by their very nature, contain limited information. Keep in mind that such generalizations often mask other useful information about cultural diversity.
- Cultural descriptions should be limited to describing members of various groups as objectively as possible and should not include an evaluative component (e.g., "This is good," "That is bad").
- Cultural descriptions should provide an accurate description of the beliefs, values, and social norms of a group.
- Cultural descriptions should be considered a first best guess about the behaviors of a cultural group prior to developing more specific information about individual members of the group.
- Cultural descriptions should be modified over time, on the basis of new information gained through observation or experience.

When describing cultures and identifying cultural differences between two or more groups, some caution may be in order, for at least two reasons. First, while common sense would suggest that bigger cultural differences are harder to deal with than smaller ones, experience suggests that this is not always the case. In some situations, managers moving between countries perceived as culturally similar (e.g., the Netherlands and Belgium) find that "small" differences are just as hard to deal with as big ones. Worse, these small differences are frequently overlooked and not dealt with until some damage is done. Second, what may initially seem like a large cultural difference may be overcome by some smaller similarities. For instance, in a recent joint venture between a Brazilian company and a Chinese one (companies from two very different cultures), members found sources of similarity that facilitated the relationship, such as the similar levels of development and the importance of context and relationships in partnerships. In the words of one Brazilian managing director, "The Chinese are the Brazilians of Asia."[28]

2.   View cultural differences in neutral terms

In addition, cultural differences are not a bad thing in the managerial world; they just require a bit more work at times. In many cases, depending on the task at hand, a degree of cultural difference is often seen as leading to improved managerial decision-making and action. For example, a recent study found that Portuguese managers perceived business activities with Brazilians and Spaniards (with whom they are culturally more similar) to be riskier and more difficult than business activities with Scandinavians (culturally very different). It is worth noting, however, that the same managers also felt more "at home" and preferred to socialize and make friends with Brazilians and Spaniards.[29]

What this suggests is that cultural differences are not inherently good or bad, but they can be perceived positively or negatively depending on the situation. Additionally, sometimes differences are not perceived the same way by the two parties. A manager from Portugal may appreciate Danish punctuality, while the Danish manager may find Portuguese tardiness annoying. On the other hand, the Danish manager may appreciate Portuguese flexibility (particularistic or low rule orientation), while the Portuguese manager may find the Danish obsession with rules frustrating.

Most importantly, it is difficult to predict how these identifiable differences will play out when two cultures meet. As a starting point, cultural frameworks create limitations on our ability to think and perceive the environment, suggesting that individuals from different cultures will have different understandings of the situation, and will probably act differently. As individuals interact with each other and the new environment around them, however, new understandings may emerge and new behaviors may be called for. It would be naïve to think that, in a cross-cultural situation, individuals will continue behaving in the same way they would at home for a long period of time. Over time, either they will negotiate a new way to relate or the relationship will not continue. Unfortunately, it is impossible to predict what will work for a particular context and relationship, since several other factors besides culture come into play. For example, who has power? Who are the majority? Who has the money? What is the personality of the ones in power? What is the goal of the relationship? Are there historical issues as well between both cultural groups that may lead to predispositions, or perceptions of superiority, inferiority, or sameness? Referring to the Chinese–Brazilian partnership above, a Chinese manager noted, "My opinion is that working with Brazilians is easier than working with North Americans, with French, or even with people from Singapore. It's amazing, because people from Singapore have the same cultural roots that we have. But, with Brazilians, it's easier because we treat each other as being on the same level. This may be more important than having the same cultural roots or speaking the same language."[30]

Simply put, when two or more cultures come into contact, the starting point for interaction is usually what these cultures bring to the table. The end result, though, will more likely depend on their interactions, the actors and organizations involved, the power differential, and the exchanges that take place. Management researchers Oded Shenkar, Yadong Luo, and Orly Yeheskel, coming from three very different cultures themselves, call this process cultural friction, in reference to the resistance and conflicts that need to be dealt with as two cultures come into contact, including issues of organizational identities, national identities, differences in resources and interests, and asymmetry in power and hierarchy.[31] These issues are dealt with and negotiated in a process of response and counter-response that will shape the relationship between the parties.

3. Prepare for the unexpected

Finally, when facing the complexities of cultural influences and the unpredictability of cultural encounters, an obvious question arises: what can global managers do? An often-overlooked response to this difficult question rests on the speed with which managers can learn and adjust their behavior to fit each unique situation. Here, we do not mean adjusting the behavior to fit the other culture; we mean adjusting the behavior to fit the situation. Sometimes, what is in order is adjusting to the other culture as closely as possible. At other times, though, this behavior would be counterproductive (e.g., perhaps we really should avoid considering Nahed Taher as a traditional Arab woman). Knowing the difference is what separates successful global managers from the rest.

To this end, several important learning skills can be suggested for global managers:

- Self-awareness. Global managers need to understand that they are complex cultural beings and that their values, beliefs, assumptions, and communication preferences are a product of their cultural heritage.
- Empathy. Global managers must understand that others are also complex cultural beings, whose actions are a product of deep-seated cultural values and beliefs. When misunderstandings occur, competent global managers will search for cultural explanations of confusing or offensive behavior, before judging it.
- Information gathering and analysis. Managers have to uncover hidden cultural assumptions to become aware of how culture is shaping the perceptions, expectations, and behaviors of all involved parties.
- Information integration and transformation. Managers must assimilate the information gathered into a coherent theory of action.
- Behavioral flexibility. Managers need the ability to engage in different behaviors, to switch styles, and to accomplish tasks in more than one way.
- Mindfulness. Global managers must be mindful of themselves, the other, and the interaction. They must pay close attention to their feelings and actions, and others' actions and reactions.

In summary, managers must be keenly aware of their biases (and the biases of others) in their ways of looking at the world. This is not easy, because it requires a continual effort to move from our own perspective to the perspectives of others – or, at least, to try to do so. Understanding others requires – and allows – us to de-center our own self-centered points of view, thereby expanding our personal worldviews. French philosopher Gilles Deleuze has referred to this concept as "being another thought in my thoughts, another possession in my possessions."[32] Throughout the remainder of the book, we discuss in detail several ways in which culture matters, highlighting how culture leads to different perspectives and understandings, and drawing out their implications for management practice.

It is our hope that these discussions will help managers identify their own biases in management understanding and facilitate the recognition of potential cultural problems on the ground.

KEY TERMS

collectivistic culture • core cultural dimensions • cultural environment • cultural friction • cultural stereotypes • culture • egalitarian culture • GLOBE's culture model • Hall's culture model • *haredim* (Hebrew) • harmony-oriented culture • hierarchical culture • Hofstede's culture model • individualistic culture • institutional environment • *jeitinho* (Brazilian) • *kao* (Japanese) • mastery-oriented culture • mindfulness • monochronic culture • normative behavior • *orgullo* (Spanish) • particularistic (relationship-based) culture • polychronic culture • *sharia* (Arabic) • Trompenaars' culture model • universalistic (rule-based) culture

DISCUSSION QUESTIONS

1. In what ways can a better understanding of cultural environments, as illustrated in Exhibit 3.1, prepare managers for foreign assignments? Provide two specific examples to illustrate your point.

2. What is your definition of culture as it relates to global management? How might this definition help us understand how managers succeed or fail in the global economy?

3. Some countries or regions have what is called strong or tight cultures, meaning that their core beliefs are deeply and widely held across community members, while other countries have what is called soft or weak cultures, where belief systems allow for more variability. What accounts for such differences, and what are the implications for managers working in these cultures?

4. What are the relative strengths of each of the four culture models reviewed here (see Exhibit 3.3 for a summary)? Which model would be most useful for global managers, and why?

5. Some people claim that national culture models like those reviewed here are overly simplistic and misleading. Do you agree or disagree with this assertion? What are the benefits and drawbacks of using such models?

6. As illustrated by the core cultural dimensions discussed here (Exhibit 3.4), a number of similarities can be found across various culture models. In your view, what is missing from these models that could be of use to managers seeking to better understand their business partners or competitors?

7. Normative beliefs and institutional requirements both aim to solidify social control, stability, and continuity (Exhibit 3.5). In doing so, they oftentimes create forces against change. In view of this, how would you proceed if you

were trying to modify the laws in a particular country to provide more equitable employment opportunities for women or minorities? What would be your strategy?

8. We tend to paint cultural differences across countries with a broad brush and talk, for example, of the Russian culture or the Indian culture. Obviously there are individual, regional, and other differences within each country. There are also a number of cultural complexities and contractions within all cultures that reduce clarity of understanding. What might managers do to seek out these differences and improve their understanding prior to a foreign assignment?

9. Singapore is a good example of a thriving multicultural society with strong representation of Chinese, Malays, Indian, and Anglo cultures working together. How might a manager prepare for an assignment to this country compared to an assignment to a country with less cultural diversity, such as Korea or Japan?

10. Three general strategies for working across cultures were identified here based on the materials presented in this chapter (Exhibit 3.7). Each strategy calls on managers to change the ways in which they approach cross-cultural inter-actions. How difficult would it be to actually follow these strategies and what can managers do to facilitate a change in their mindset here?

11. If you were asked to create and lead a one-week seminar to educate junior managers about the role of cultural differences in their work environment, how would you organize it? What might be the contents of your program? And who would teach it?

CASE: ANNA HÅKANSSON – FROM SWEDEN TO BAHRAIN

Anna Håkansson, an investment banker at the Swedish Investment Bank in Stockholm, was recently informed that she was being sent to Bahrain to negotiate a contract with senior managers of Bahrain Investment Bank. Having never been to the Middle East, she was unsure how to prepare herself.

She first talked to colleagues who had some experience there to get general descriptions and first-hand experiences from people who had visited there. Next, she ran a Google search and discovered that there were over 21 million hits on Arab culture alone. During this search she uncovered a number of recent articles in various respected sources that helped her to understand what to expect.

She learned that the extended family was the single most important entity of Arab society; playing a pivotal role not only in social life but in economic and political life as well. Even an individual's self-identity is based on a collective self. Each family member shares a collective ancestry, a collective respect for elders, and a collective obligation and responsibility for the welfare of the other family members. It is to the extended family, not to the government, that a person first turns for help. She further learned that a major reason for the resilience of the traditional extended family structure is the extraordinary strength of traditional Islamic social, economic, and political values, as reinforced by traditional beliefs contained in religious teachings and *sharia* law. *Sharia* means the "way" or "path," and provides the legal framework within which the public and some private aspects of life are regulated for those living in a legal system based on Islam.

As Håkansson continued to learn, three characteristics of Arab extended families stood out. First, Arab societies are typically patriarchal societies, maintaining a respect for age and seniority that has largely disappeared in Western societies. The wisdom and authority of elders is seldom challenged. Second, traditional gender roles in Arab societies share a number of common characteristics with other traditional societies, the most notable of which is that men's roles are outside the home as family providers, protectors, and managers, and women's roles are in the home. Men are predominant outside the home – in business and public affairs – and women are to a large degree predominant within the home, particularly in parental decisions. And third, the traditional method for reaching and legitimizing decisions in Arab society is through consultation among those within the group whose opinions are considered important. From consultation emerges consensus, which is binding on all members of the group. Within the extended family, the principal consensus makers are senior male members or elders. This ancient process of consultation and consensus was given religious sanction in Islam.

Based on what she had learned earlier, Håkansson next attempted to find a way to organize everything into a user-friendly format. She looked for a cultural model she could use to make some comparisons between Swedish and Arab societies to solidify what she had learned. She chose a model developed by Dutch management researcher Geert Hofstede. He views culture as the "software of the mind" that differentiates one group or society from another. In other words, while people all have the same hardware, their brains and patterns of thinking and behaving can be very different.

Using this model, she compared the cultures of her native Sweden and Bahrain (see Exhibit 3.8). For Bahrain, she had found that people tend to be low on long-term orientation, high on uncertainty avoidance, moderately high on masculinity, moderately high on collectivism, and high in power distance – that is, a belief in rigid hierarchies. For Sweden, by contrast, she found very different scores. Specifically, Hofstede's scale indicates that Swedes tend to be high on long-term orientation, moderately low on uncertainty avoidance, very low on masculinity, moderately low on collectivism (that is, relatively high on individualism), and low on power distance. In other words, in Sweden we see a society in which egalitarianism is emphasized, including equality of gender and race. Power is widely shared and uncertainty is tolerated, in the belief that it helps facilitate creativity and

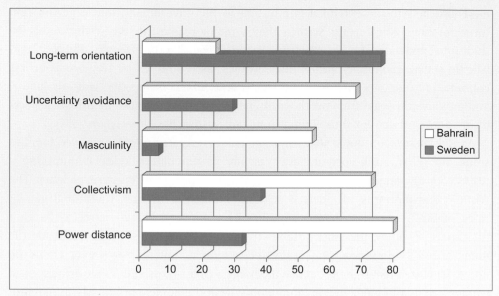

Exhibit 3.8 Hofstede's cultural dimensions for Bahrain and Sweden

innovation. Groups – and, indeed, society itself – are considered to be important by all, but so too is individualism.

Now Håkansson believed she had a concrete comparative framework on which to compare some of the basic differences between the two countries. Based on what she had learned, she further believed she was now prepared for her business trip to Bahrain. But was she?

CASE QUESTIONS

1. What is your opinion of the manner in which Anna Håkansson prepared for her business trip? Could she have done a better job here? If so, how?
2. In what ways do cultural models such as the Hofstede model used here help managers understand how to behave appropriately in foreign countries?
3. Would Anna's conclusions concerning mainstream Swedish and Bahraini cultures differ if she used the Hall or the GLOBE model instead of Hofstede's framework (see Exhibit 3.3)?
4. Are there any lessons from Applications 3.3 and 3.4 that could help Anna better understand the work environment in Bahrain? Explain.
5. Based on what you have learned, identify some of the cultural complexities and contradictions facing Håkansson as she tries to understand the culture of her counterparts in Bahrain (see Exhibit 3.6).
6. What can Håkansson do to minimize the creation of stereotypes about the managers she will meet in Bahrain?

7. Based on what Anna Håkansson has already done to prepare for her upcoming visit, what are the next steps, if any, that you would recommend she take to continue developing her knowledge of business culture in the Middle East?

8. (*Optional research question*) Identify a country you are interested in but have never visited, and follow Anna Håkansson's strategy for learning as much as you can about the country's cultural environment. After your study, what questions remain that would be helpful to know prior to a visit there? How might you gain useful information about these unanswered questions?

NOTES

1. The Talmud is a record of rabbinical discussions pertaining to Jewish law, ethics, customs, and history.

2. Wang Yinglin, *Trimetric Classic* (trans. Herbert Giles). Shanghai: Kelly & Walsh, 1910. The *Three Character Classic*, *Trimetric Classic*, or *San Zi Ji* is one of the classic Chinese texts. It was probably written in the thirteenth century and attributed to Wang Yinglin (1223–96) during the Song Dynasty, but has also been attributed to Ou Shizi (1234–1324). Some writers have attributed the original wisdom collected in this volume to Confucius, although there is no conclusive evidence on this.

3. Robert J. House, "Introduction," in Robert J. House, Paul J. Hanges, Mansour Javidan, Peter W. Dorfman, and Vipin Gupta, *Culture, Leadership, and Organizations: The GLOBE Study of 62 Societies*. Thousand Oaks, CA: Sage, 2004, pp. 1–2 (p. 1).

4. Lao-Tzu, or Laozi, was a philosopher of ancient China and is a central figure in Taoism. Laozi literally means "Old Master" and is generally considered an honorific. Laozi is revered as a god in religious forms of Taoism. Taishang Laojun is a title for Laozi in the Taoist religion, which refers to him as "One of the Three Pure Ones."

5. Geert Hofstede, *Culture's Consequences: International Differences in Work-Related Values*. Thousand Oaks, CA: Sage, 2001.

6. Clyde Kluckhohn, "Culture and behavior," in Gardner Lindzey (ed.), *Handbook of Social Psychology*. New York: McGraw-Hill, 1951, pp. 921–76.

7. House *et al.*, *Culture, Leadership, and Organizations*.

8. Fons Trompenaars, *Riding the Waves of Culture: Understanding Cultural Diversity in Global Business*. London: McGraw-Hill, 1993.

9. Ann Swidler, "Culture in action: symbols and strategies," *American Sociological Review*, 51(2) (1986), pp. 273–86.

10. Clifford Geertz, *The Interpretation of Cultures*. New York: Basic Books, 1973.

11. Jonny Johanson and Ikujiro Nonaka, *Relentless: The Japanese Way of Marketing*. New York: Basic Books, 1996.

12. Edward T. Hall, *An Anthropology of Everyday Life: An Autobiography*. New York: Anchor Books, 1992, p. 210.

13. See Luciara Nardon and Richard M. Steers, "The culture theory jungle: divergence and convergence in models of national culture," in Rabi S. Bhagat and Richard M. Steers (eds.), *Cambridge Handbook of Culture, Organizations, and Work*. Cambridge University Press, 2009, pp. 3–22.

14. Edward T. Hall and Mildred R. Hall, *Understanding Cultural Differences*. Yarmouth, ME: Intercultural Press, 1990.

15. Hofstede, *Culture's Consequences*.

16. Trompenaars, *Riding the Waves of Culture*.

17. House *et al.*, *Culture, Leadership, and Organizations*.

18. See Nardon and Steers, "The culture theory jungle."

19. "Speeding while rich," *The Week*, March 4, 2015, p. 4.

20. Lawrence Rosen, *Law as Culture: An Invitation*. Princeton University Press, 2006, pp. 98–100.

21. Elizabeth MacDonald and Megha Bahree, "Muslim women in charge," *Forbes*, July 30, 2008; Faiza Saleh Ambah, "Saudi women rise in defense of the veil," *Washington Post*, June 1, 2006, p. A12.

22. Ahmed al Omran, "Saudi women move into workforce but face limits," *Wall Street Journal*, January 2, 2016, p. A6.

23. Swidler, "Culture in action."

24. Sarah Gordon, "Delta Airlines flight from New York's JFK Airport was delayed after ultra-Orthodox Jewish passengers refuse to sit next to women," *Daily Mail*, April 15, 2015.

25. "Singapore: model of a pluralistic, multicultural society," Beryl-pieces-asia.blogspot .com, 2012.

26. Edward T. Hall, *The Silent Language*. New York: Anchor Books, 1990, p. 29.

27. Nancy J. Adler, *International Dimensions of Organizational Behavior*, 5th edn. Mason, OH: Thompson, 2008.

28. Guilherme Azevedo, "Brazilian management in China and a theory of the formation of hybrid organizational cultures," paper presented at the European Group of Organizations Studies (EGOS) conference, Amsterdam, July 12, 2008.

29. Susana Costa e Silva and Luciara Nardon, "An exploratory study of cultural differences and perceptions of relational risk," paper presented at the European International Business Academy conference, Catania, Italy, December 15, 2007.

30. Azevedo, "Brazilian management in China."

31. Oded Shenkar, Yadong Luo, and Orly Yeheskel, "From distance to friction: substituting metaphors and redirecting intercultural research," *Academy of Management Review*, 33(4) (2008), pp. 905–22.

32. Martín Hopenhayn, "La aldea global entre la utopía transcultural y el ratio mercantil: paradojas de la globalización cultural," in Ramón Pajuelo and Pablo Sandoval (eds.), *Globalización y Diversidad Cultural: Una Mirada desde America Latina*. Lima: Instituto de Estudios Peruanos, pp. 423–4.

4 Organizational environments

MANAGEMENT CHALLENGE

In this chapter, we examine this second major context in which global awareness and understanding are critical for managers: organizational environments. Organizations come in many shapes, sizes, and forms. Managers need to understand the type of organizations they are working with, the types of solutions they have found to deal with their environments, and the implications of these solutions for managers. In other words, organizations themselves put pressures on managers by defining what is expected or required. Some of the more common challenges managers face with regard to organizations concern the character and goals of their stakeholders, the strategies they pursue, and the fundamental ways in which they organize, make decisions, and create and support corporate cultures that work in support of the organization's overall objectives. These topics are discussed in this chapter, along with the implications for the managers.

CHAPTER OUTLINE

- Organizations and environments — *page* 84
- Stakeholders and global strategies — 86
- Organizing for global business — 88
- Regional organizing models — 92
- Control, participation, and decision-making — 105
- Corporate culture — 109
- MANAGER'S NOTEBOOK: Working with global organizations — 114
- Key terms — 119
- Discussion questions — 119
- Case: Co-determination at Volkswagen — 121

APPLICATIONS

4.1 Germany's *Mittelstand* firms   *page* 87

4.2 Uber technologies   91

4.3 Corporate culture at Dentsu   111

4.4 Corporate culture at Alibaba   112

Facebook executive Sheryl Sandberg speaks from experience when she says, "We try to be a strengths-based organization, which means we try to make jobs fit around people rather than make people fit around jobs. We focus on what people's natural strengths are and spend our management time trying to find ways for them to use those strengths every day."[1] Sandberg emphasizes that business success at Facebook and elsewhere relies not just on people but also on getting the best from people. Organizations are the vehicles through which this is accomplished. Globalization requires a diversity of options, not a one-size-fits-all approach to organization and management. This includes having a global vision and strategy, but it also means tailoring corporate strategies to fit both local conditions and available resources. In this endeavor, the principal stakeholders of an organization (e.g., investors, employees, customers, governments, etc.) play a major role.

The message here is simple: different stakeholders, different strategies; different strategies, different structures. But this is only the beginning. Given an organization's unique business strategy, the key question for managers is how to organize their critical resources – including human resources – to effectively pursue their strategy. This is the principal focus of this chapter.

Organizations and environments

What is an organization and why is it important to understand organizational processes? Simply put, an organization is a system of consciously coordinated activities of two or more persons aiming to achieve common objectives. Organizations prosper or fail in line with the extent to which they – and their managers – are successful in achieving both effectiveness and efficiency in the common pursuit of these goals. Organizations are not just about how to put people into boxes – or cubicles. Instead, they serve as a principal command and control system for focusing human, financial, and physical resources on the accomplishment of valued tasks. And organization designs live or die on the basis of their ability to assist managers with their responsibilities.

But organizations are also so much more. Geert Hofstede argues that "there are no universal solutions to organizational and management problems. Organizations are symbolic entities; they function according to implicit models in the minds of their members, and these are culturally determined."[2] Organizations provide managers with a set of rules, policies, procedures, and norms of behavior to guide action in the form of standard operating procedures and organizational cultural norms. This can be thought of as the *micro environment* in which managers work and is heavily influenced by prevailing cultures and institutions. Organizational culture may either replicate or reject national cultural values and norms, creating a micro environment in which national norms are reinforced or do not apply. For example, even though punctuality may not be the norm in a particular cultural environment (e.g., Greece), an organization in that country may reject this cultural norm and enforce punctuality in its activities for very sound reasons (e.g., maintaining global flight schedules at Olympic Air). Indeed, many global organizations deal with the challenges posed by multiple national cultures by creating clear behavioral guidelines across the organization.

To succeed in any of these jobs, it is imperative that managers understand as much as possible about the organizational environment in which they work. In this chapter, we examine four aspects of organizations as they relate to managerial performance in the field: global strategy, organizational structure, organizational decision-making, and corporate culture. Throughout, the role of stakeholders, market pressures, and economic constraints in helping shape the organizational environment will become evident (see Exhibit 4.1).

Exhibit 4.1 The organizational environment of global management

Stakeholders and global strategies

Simple logic – not always a good guideline for global interactions – suggests that strategy-making follows a relatively predictable format, often referred to as the strategic management cycle. The relationships involved in this cycle have been seen largely in terms of a one-way causal relationship. That is, mission determines strategy, which in turn determines structure, which governs management practice, which ultimately determines the extent to which the organization succeeds in achieving its mission.

However, recent evidence suggests a far more complex and interactive relationship. Specifically, while mission and values may help determine an organization's initial strategy and goals – at least in the early years of the venture – organization design and even management practices can also influence strategy in significant ways, especially as the organization matures and is confronted by new challenges and economic realities. Likewise, strategy can influence structure, but so too can management practices. Finally, these interactive relationships are played out in a business environment that is itself multifaceted and interactive. This includes such external factors as geographic location; the cultural milieu(s) in which organizations work; legal conventions and local customs; variations in political and institutional support; a country or region's factor endowments; the specific sector of the economy where the organization does business (e.g., industry vs. services); available investments, technologies, and markets; and environmental challenges and goals. In other words, the simple strategy–structure–management paradigm is found to be sorely lacking in explanatory power as organization theory crosses borders. In particular, what is lacking here is recognition that the key issue in organizational success may not be its strategy; it may be its stakeholders.

Not surprisingly, a company's stakeholders (e.g., investors, customers, employees, etc.) can have a major influence on both the determination of the company's mission and its strategy. Various stakeholders place demands, expectations, and constraints on enterprise activity and, obviously, these demands frequently differ across the various stakeholders, some wanting better return on their investment and others that want a more socially or environmentally responsible organization. Most strategists understand this. However, what many global managers fail to understand is that the nature and power of a stakeholder group can be influenced by the predominant culture in which the enterprise does business. While in theory all stakeholders are created equal, in fact some have far more power than others.

For example, some companies routinely face a stakeholders group where power and influence is fairly centralized. In Korea, Argentina, the United Kingdom, and the United States, for example, investors, customers, and governments often have considerable influence over enterprise mission and strategy, while employees and the public-at-large do not. At the same time, in Germany, Japan, and Norway, a different situation exists. That is, investors, customers, and governments still have a major influence over missions and strategies but so, too, do employees and the public-at-large. Moreover, foreign firms that do business in Sweden or Germany, for example, face this broader or more distributed stakeholder group and must accommodate these different constituencies. To see how strategy-making is done in an environment characterized by broad-based constituents and stakeholders, consider the example of Germany's *Mittelstand* firms. Here, investors are important, but so too are the employees, the state, and local communities.

APPLICATION 4.1 Germany's *Mittelstand* firms

Most people are familiar with the names of a number of large and successful German companies, including Siemens, BMW, Volkswagen, Daimler, Beyer, and BASF. What many people fail to realize, however, is that the real strength of the German economy actually relies less on these large companies and more on its 2.5 million small and medium-sized firms. These so-called *Mittelstand* (or small to medium-sized) *firms* account for over two-thirds of the nation's economy and over 80 percent of its private-sector employment. Examples of *Mittelstand* firms include Rational (high-end restaurant ovens), Trumpf (computer-based machine tools), and Playmobil (educational toys).[3]

Germany's *Mittelstand* firms compete in the global marketplace through a global strategy that has served them well for several decades. This strategy can be summarized as follows: First, because of their high cost structure, most *Mittelstand* firms ignore markets characterized by low prices and prefer instead to focus on markets where quality or other product uniqueness can command a high price. Within these markets, they focus on making superior products using advanced technologies and/or superior craftsmanship. They then compete based on customer satisfaction, not short-term profit maximization. To supplement this effort, German firms hire and train the best workers they can find, not the cheapest. They make extensive use of apprenticeship programs as a competitive weapon. All employees, regardless of level in the organization, are empowered to an extent seldom seen elsewhere to help achieve the firm's mission. This is largely done through co-determination and employee involvement. Finally, German firms prefer to take a long-term perspective to market development and can be patient when necessary. This is largely possible because most companies have close ties with major German banks and other financial institutions are patient about getting a return on their investment, unlike North America where investors often require a shorter payback period.

Unfortunately, recent increases in the cost of labor and production in Germany have increasingly threatened the competitiveness of many of these *Mittelstand* firms. As a result, some firms are beginning to curtail many of their German-based operations in favor of manufacturing facilities in other lower-cost countries (notably in Asia and Eastern Europe). Increasing emphasis is being placed on using technology to increase productivity. Even so, the future remains highly uncertain. Despite their current success, many worry that *Mittelstand* firms might eventually price themselves out of global markets in the future because of their high cost structure. In the final analysis, how much will customers pay for German craftsmanship? On the other hand, if quality has been the long-term basis of a firm's competitiveness, what are the risks of changing (or devaluing) this strategy?

Think about it . . .

(1) From what you have learned about these middle-sized firms, who are the principal stakeholders and what do they want?
(2) How might the nature of Germany's *Mittelstand* firms influence their strategy-making processes?
(3) As the world continues to globalize, what do you think is the future of Germany's *Mittelstand* firms. Why?

Organizing for global business

For many firms, the choice of an appropriate organization design for conducting global business typically evolves over time as firms increase their involvement in global activities. This evolutionary process often begins with some form of domestic organization design, in which international activities are largely an appendage to the more central domestic activities, and evolves over time into a more integrated global organization design that places international business at the center of the organization's strategy. Domestic organization designs are most commonly found when a national firm initially begins to export a product that it has long made for the home market. This endeavor requires some structure to oversee successful implementation, but, because the venture is new and may not be successful, most organizations approach it with caution, using trusted local managers.

When a firm decides to sell its products abroad, or when its overseas sales volume increases, it frequently establishes an export department. This is a separate department within the home company's headquarters that is assigned specific responsibility for overseas transactions. Again, this is simple to establish and run. As companies become more sophisticated in differentiating among their global markets, they soon realize that localized expertise represents a strategic asset for satisfying local customer demands. In such cases, firms frequently establish international divisions. While export departments are usually located in corporate headquarters in the home country, international divisions are most often located overseas near the firm's principal global markets. Local managers are hired, again to get close to principal customers and markets, and to provide a worldview for headquarters on future business opportunities abroad.

When international activities become a more prominent aspect of the total business, most companies reorganize in order to capitalize on this growing business sector. They then often select one of the typical global organization designs (see Exhibit 4.2). Companies go to great lengths to identify a design that will provide the best combination of such knowledge and support the firm's strategic objectives. An appropriate organization design should help the firm integrate four types of strategic information in order to facilitate successful competition: (1) area knowledge, involving an understanding of the local area's culture, economics, and social conditions; (2) product knowledge, involving an understanding of local customer needs and possible markets for company products; (3) functional knowledge, involving local access to expertise in the various functional areas of business, such as finance, production, etc.; and (4) customer knowledge, involving an understanding of each customer's particular needs for sales and service.

Most of these organization designs are straightforward. Two may need further explanation, however: global matrix and global network designs. Global matrix organizations represent a blend of two of the other global designs working in tandem (e.g., integrating a global functional design with a global product design). As with any matrix organization, each manager would have two supervisors, leading to improved communications and flexibility but reduced accountability and job clarity. In addition, driven by an increasingly dynamic environment, some organizations use Web-based global network designs to break the organization into groups with loose links, relying on regional groupings and regional headquarters and the creation of teams and projects that link different units around the world. Web-based networks are also popular in coordinating the efforts of multiple companies coordinating their technologies and patents to create single products (e.g., high-tech products). These teams are often highly dynamic, thus changing the relationship between the units over time. This design is flexible and allows for strategy diversity and fast learning, but may be difficult to control and may generate high levels of ambiguity.

Exhibit 4.2 Global organization designs

Global organization design	Basis of organization	Principal applications
Global product	Worldwide responsibility for specific product groups (e.g., laundry products, baby products) assigned to different global operating units.	Establish separate worldwide divisions (possibly at corporate HQ) for each principal product group. Popular design for companies that emphasize relatively standardized product development and marketing of global products (e.g., baby products in one division, laundry products in another).
Global area design	Geographic regions of the world (e.g., Asia-Pacific, Latin America, Europe).	Establish several regional HQs around world that are each responsible for development and marketing of tailored products in various regions (e.g., selling different candies in the United Kingdom and the United States). Popular design when products require localization to suit different tastes.
Global function	Functional areas (e.g., finance, operations, marketing).	Establish global units for various functional responsibilities (e.g., divisions for global marketing, global finance, etc.). Popular design when company has relatively narrow product line that is easily transferred around the world (e.g., global airline).
Global customer	Unique needs of customers (e.g., business-to-business transactions, franchise business).	Establish separate worldwide divisions for similar products but different consumer groups (e.g., selling tires in bulk to automobile manufacturers and to local tire replacement companies). Popular design when building customer relations in competitive markets is critical.
Global matrix	Combination of two global designs (e.g., integrating global area with global product design).	Establish dual reporting lines for managers in various product or services groups (e.g., reporting to a manufacturing manager on production and quality specifications and to a marketing manager on number of units sold). Popular design in mass assembly or mass services companies (e.g., automobiles, chemicals).
Web-based global networks	Loosely coupled Web-based organizations (e.g., Uber Technologies).	Establish a cluster of business units from around the world (sometimes from different companies) to design, build, or deliver a globalized product or service. Popular design in high-technology industry for new product development requiring multiple and interrelated technologies.

APPLICATION 1.2 Uber Technologies

One of the clearest examples of a Web-based global network design is Uber Technologies, the highly successful ride-sharing service that uses private drivers and private cars around the world to compete head on in the heavily regulated taxi industry. Uber drivers typically are not licensed as public drivers, their cars are not taxed or regulated, and fees are established online – away from the snooping eyes of government regulations. As a result, costs – and consequently prices – are typically much lower than traditional taxis.

Needless to say, some governments and most unionized taxi drivers oppose this budding industry. Recently, France went so far as to arrest the executives of the local Uber service there, charging them with running an illegal taxi service.[4] Similar charges have been brought in Korea, the Netherlands, and Indonesia. After the arrests in France, the company announced "We are keen to continue talking with the French government about the regulatory framework for services like Uber. There is a way forward – with regulation that is focused on the needs and safety of the public, while also allowing more people to take advantage of these new economic possibilities."

Think about it . . .

(1) Uber Technologies represents an example of technological innovation combined with an entrepreneurial organization design for doing business and forcing changes on a very traditional industry in many countries around the world. Do you support having Uber as an unregulated (or lightly regulated) competitor in a heavily regulated industry? Why or why not?

(2) What happens to the jobs of traditional taxi drivers if Uber succeeds? Is this fair or necessary?

(3) What would you recommend as a way out of this conflict? Or is there a way out? Explain.

(4) Is there a technological imperative in international business; that is, do new proven technologies always win out over older technologies in the long run? Are there times when technological or economic changes should be forcibly slowed down by governments to protect local cultures, jobs, and residents? Explain.

Understanding the relationship between global strategy and organizational design is critical for managers, as it provides information as to what the priorities of the organization are (product standardization versus country adaptation) and, as such, influences the degree of managerial discretion. For example, an organization following a particular global strategy and structure may wish to replicate its home organizational culture and processes in the foreign location and allow little room for adaptations. Headquarters may monitor the foreign manager's actions and attend to behavior that indicates a deviation from the home country's way of doing things. On the other hand, an organization following a strategy that aims to adapt to local conditions may grant local managers considerable discretion with regard to how to manage the organization so long as the financial goals of the subsidiary are met. Likewise, understanding where one fits into the organization structure provides managers with key information regarding the perceived importance of their role and the types of pressures they are likely to face, whether locally or from headquarters.

Regional organizing models

Managers can learn a great deal about both strategy and structure by studying local or regional trends in organization design. These designs can tell us who the primary beneficiaries of an organization are, who holds power and influence, the rights and privileges of rank-and-file employees, managerial role obligations, and how decisions are made. In many ways, *a company's unique organization design is like its own personal fingerprint*. It can provide insights into a company's character, values, ambitions, management systems, and operating procedures. Comparing these designs can help us understand how cultural differences can influence how businesses operate and how management is conducted. This can also help managers who have to work with highly diverse organizations from multiple countries.

While a country-by-country discussion is beyond the scope of this book, it is possible to identify four of the more common models based on the central question of who derives the greatest benefit from an organization's operations. We refer to these as regional organizing models.[5] Obviously, all regional organizations have multiple stakeholders, and many major or minor groups benefit in various ways (e.g., investor returns, employment, local community development). The question here, however, is: who stands to gain the most as a general trend? What we find when we begin exploring the role of cultural differences in organization design is that there are systematic differences across regions not only in management style but also in principal beneficiaries. This is not to say that all organizations within a single culture share common objectives and principal beneficiaries – they don't – but trends can nevertheless be discovered that can help us understand why companies look different and operate in different ways across various regions of the world.

We examine four regional models of organization here as examples: investor, family, network, and mutual benefit (see Exhibit 4.3).

Exhibit 4.3 Regional models of organization

Characteristics	Investor model	Family model	Network model	Mutual benefit model
Country examples	American, Australian, British, and Canadian companies	Chinese *gong-si*, South Korean *chaebol*, Mexican *grupo*	Japanese *kaisha* and *keiretsu*	German *konzern*, Danish *selskabet*, Dutch *bedrijf*, and Swedish *företag*
Primary beneficiaries	Principal emphasis on stockholders and investors as principal beneficiaries	Principal emphasis on extended family members as both investors and principal beneficiaries	Sequential emphasis on corporate network, individual company shareholders, and permanent employees	Relative balance between stockholders and investors, most employees, local community, and public-at-large
Center of power and influence	Centralized power largely held by investors and stockholders and delegated to top executives	Centralized power held by family with government backing and tightly controlled through family management	Moderately distributed power held by investors, sister companies, key banks, unions, and government	Widely distributed power held by investors, partners, managers, works councils, unions, and government
Trends in management selection	Professional education	Family membership	Seniority	Technical mastery
Trends in decision-making	Top-down centralized management common, but not universal	Top-down centralized management, often with government involvement and support	Consultation with employees up, down, and across hierarchy, but final decisions typically made at top	Collaboration between managers, works councils, and unions on key decisions
Employee rights and job security	Weak legal protection of employee rights and job security for all employees	Weak legal protection of employee rights and job security for all employees	Weak legal, but strong social, protection of employee rights and job security for all "permanent" employees	Strong legal protection of employee rights and job security for almost all employees

Exhibit 4.3 (*cont.*)

Characteristics	Investor model	Family model	Network model	Mutual benefit model
Variability in basic model	Wide variations within basic model	Few variations in basic model	Moderate variations in basic model	Few variations in basic model

Source: Based on Richard M. Steers, Luciara Nardon, and Carlos Sanchez-Runde, "Culture and organization design: strategy, structure, and decision-making," in Rabi S. Bhagat and Richard M. Steers (eds.), *Cambridge Handbook of Culture, Organizations, and Work* (Cambridge University Press, 2009), pp. 71–106.

Investor model of organization (e.g., US, UK, Canada)

Many books on the topic of organization design and management structure assume that managers organize their resources in fairly similar ways. Typically, what they are talking about here is what may be described as an investor model of organization. A good example of this approach to organization and control can be found in what are often described as predominantly "Anglo" cultures, including Australia, Canada, New Zealand, the United Kingdom, and the United States. Most companies in this cluster make use of some type of investor structure as their chief organizing framework. In other words, the investors typically exert significant power and influence over the organization, management, and ultimate destiny of the firm, and recoup most of the profits or return on investment for themselves as owners. Indeed, in the United States, for example, commercial law requires that executives manage the firm for the exclusive benefit of investors (within legal and regulatory limits). They are not therefore allowed, for example, to provide greater benefits to employees or customers unless they can demonstrate that such actions clearly benefit investors. It is simply against the law.

Identifying a "typical" company in any culture is a challenge, but perhaps nowhere is this challenge greater than with respect to US firms. As elsewhere, US companies reflect the culture(s) in which they do business, and since the United States is strongly multicultural it is not surprising to find major differences across companies – even in similar industries. All the same, it is possible to develop a general portrait of what such a company looks like in terms of its basic organization structure and management processes (see Exhibit 4.4). Based on what we know about prevailing American cultural patterns, consider how we might describe a typical US firm.

- **Mastery-oriented.** Many investor organizations stress individual or group achievement and responsibility, control over the environment, a linear approach

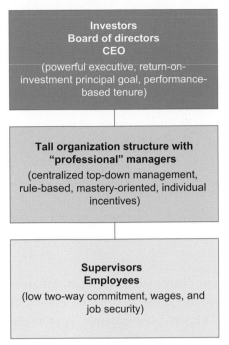

Exhibit 4.4 Example of US investor model of organization
Source: Based on Richard M. Steers, Luciara Nardon, and Carlos Sanchez-Runde, "Culture and organization design: strategy, structure, and decision-making," in Rabi S. Bhagat and Richard M. Steers (eds.), *Cambridge Handbook of Culture, Organizations, and Work* (Cambridge University Press, 2009), pp. 82–5.

to decision-making, respect for rules and policies and a sense of order, and a belief that, at least in theory, anyone can rise to the top.

- **Powerful CEOs.** CEOs and company presidents often get most of the credit for company successes and much of the blame for failure; they also get much of the money, regardless. US CEOs tend to have considerable power as decision-makers and leaders so long as they succeed. Indeed, we often hear about the "imperial CEO." If they do not succeed, however, they tend to disappear rather quickly.

- **Professional management.** At the same time, these companies typically make use of so-called "professional managers." This is not to imply that other forms of management are not professional; rather, it is to emphasize that such companies rely heavily on outside, professionally trained, and presumably impartial managers (e.g., free from nepotism) to run their companies.

- **Fluid organization design.** Organization design in typical US firms tends to be rather fluid. They tend to have many alliances and partners and frequently reinvent themselves when the need arises (e.g., under conditions of financial exigency). When they need capital to expand the business, market research for a new product, or in-depth legal advice, most US firms typically go outside the company. Likewise, manufacturing and service companies alike often rely on outside suppliers and distributors that have only a tenuous relationship with the company.

- Low employee job security. Employees on *all* levels are often viewed as factors of production, rather than valued members of the organization. Indeed, in some US companies, so-called "permanent" employees are routinely hired and fired on the basis of variations in workloads. From an accounting perspective, they are considered as part of a firm's variable costs, not fixed costs. Moreover, the use of contingent workers is on the rise, partly to save money and partly to increase operating efficiency. Not surprisingly, employee commitment to organizations is on the wane.

It is important to note here that it would be a mistake to assume that organization and management practices are identical – or even similar, in some cases – across the broad so-called "Anglo" cluster.[6] For example, London Business School professor Nigel Nicholson has noted that typical governance rules in the United Kingdom are quite different from those in the United States. As a rule, British companies are far less tolerant of power aggregation than are their American counterparts. For example, they tend to oppose unitary boards of directors and strongly prefer the separation of the roles of chairman and CEO between two people, unlike the tendency in the United States to integrate these two roles into one person. They also dislike dual-share voting systems, and have rules that prevent banks from owning major shares in companies. British firms are also far less encumbered with layers of lawyers, spend far less money on government lobbying, and have generally weak trade associations. In general, then, Nicholson notes that British firms tend to be more liberal than their US counterparts and maintain more liquidity and fluidity in ownership. If British firms are more liberal in ownership and governance, however, they tend to be more conservative in management policies and practices. The ethos of British management is highly pragmatic, achievement-oriented, and entrepreneurial, but is often opposed to "out-of-the-box" thinking, weak on leadership, strong on financial management, and frequently poor on vision, community, and integration.

At the same time, systematic differences between the United States and Canada can also be noted. Adler offers the following observations. Compared to Americans, Canadians tend to understate their strengths and perhaps overstate their weaknesses.[7] They do not usually claim to be the best at something. Canadians strongly believe in collegiality. For example, Canada is one of the leaders in creating middle-country initiatives, whereby a group of countries in the world tries to get something done (instead of trying to go it alone). Canadians tend to be more formal than

Americans – titles and family names are important. Canadians are generally more polite and less confrontational than their American counterparts. Canadians are also less explicitly and publicly religious. Finally, Canadians believe in more collective responsibility across society in such areas as education and healthcare. All this is not to say that overlaps do not occur; obviously, they do. Assuming that Americans and Canadians live identical lifestyles or share identical values can only lead to lost opportunities for global managers, however.

In summary, some might argue that, in making comparisons between American and British firms, and, indeed, firms in Australia, Canada, and New Zealand, the key issue is whether within-group variance is larger or smaller than between-group variance. In other words, commonalities can be found among all the countries that comprise the so-called "Anglo" cluster. Part of the reason for these similarities can be found in the historic British influences in all these cultures. Even so, in recognition of the strong individualism found in this cluster, it is not surprising to find that it is difficult to make generalizations about organization design and management practice. At the same time, part of the difference here can be found in the increasing cultural heterogeneity of people inhabiting all these countries. Diversity is increasing throughout. Indeed, as these countries become increasingly multicultural, perhaps the term "Anglo" will lose much of its meaning as a descriptor of this cluster of countries. In fact, these countries and cultures may begin evolving in very different directions in the future.

Family model of organization (e.g., China)

A distinguishing characteristic of the family model of organization is the centrality of family members in the routine operations of the firm. Frequently, multiple family members hold different positions in the corporate hierarchy. Such firms are typically run by the head of the family – often, although not exclusively, male. Moreover, family members are the principal beneficiaries of corporate operations and success. The family model can be seen in numerous variations. We focus here on the example of China, although this model can be found in many places throughout the world (e.g., South America, Southeast Asia, the Middle East).[8]

When Westerners attempt to describe Chinese culture, they invariably begin – correctly or incorrectly – with Confucianism.[9] Confucius promulgated a code of ethical behavior that was meant to guide interpersonal relationships in everyday life. This code is summed up in the so-called five cardinal virtues. These consist of filial piety, absolute loyalty to one's superiors, strict observance of seniority, subservience to superiors, and mutual trust between friends and colleagues. Although these principles suggest a way of living in the broader society, they also have implications for business practices today. Confucius and his followers saw the universe – and hence society – as a hierarchical system ruled by an educated aristocratic elite. Concepts such as democracy and equality were disdained, while learning and education were highly prized. Confucian society stressed the virtues of self-discipline, hard work, diligence, and frugality.[10] Hence the fundamental nature of human relationships is not interactions among equals but, rather, interactions among unequals. In other words, correct interpersonal behavior is determined by one's age, gender, and position in society, and a breach in this social etiquette carries with it severe penalties.

These five cardinal virtues are reinforced by several social patterns that characterize traditional Chinese society, as well as business practices.

- *Guānxi*. This represents a strong personal relationship between two people with implications of a continual exchange of favors.[11] Two people have *guānxi* when they can assume that each is conscientiously committed to the other regardless of what happens. This bond is based on the exchange of favors (i.e., social capital), not necessarily friendship or sympathy, and it does not have to involve friends. It is more utilitarian than emotional. Failure to meet one's obligations under this arrangement causes a severe loss of face, however, and creates the appearance of being untrustworthy.
- Face. Face is largely interpreted to mean dignity, self-respect, and prestige.[12] This is based both on the upholding of correct relationships between individuals and on the protection of one's face. All social interactions must be conducted in a manner in which no party loses face. Hence, if an individual cannot keep a commitment, however small, he or she loses face. Similarly, a person loses face when he or she is not treated in accordance with his or her station or position in society. Thus, a senior manager will lose face if it becomes known that a junior colleague is earning a higher salary or was promoted ahead of him or her.
- Rank. Confucian principles were designed to recognize hierarchy and differences between class members. As a result, the behavioral requirements of individuals differed according to who was involved in the relationship. Among equals, certain patterns of prescribed behavior existed. You can see this today when two strangers discover upon meeting for the first time that they both attended the same high school or college. An instant bond emerges and there is a sense of immediate camaraderie. On the other hand, for people from outside this common background or clan, frequently there is hostility or distrust. Foreign observers note that some people can be very blunt and impolite when talking with total strangers, yet very hospitable and generous when dealing with friends or acquaintances. It is a question of belonging.
- Harmony. Within one's broad circle of acquaintances, there is a clear responsibility for maintaining group harmony. Again, this principle stresses harmony between unequals – that is, it links persons of unequal rank in power, prestige, or position. Since strong personal relationships outside the family tend to occur only

between persons of equal rank, age, or prestige, harmony is the means of defining all other necessarily more formal relationships. It is everyone's responsibility to maintain this harmony continually among one's acquaintances and family members, and considerable effort is invested in doing so, including gift giving.

In view of China's strong cultural traditions, it is not surprising that its companies, both large and small, reflect this heritage. Chinese companies are generally called *gong-si* (pronounced "gong-suh"). Although the term originally referred to private family-owned enterprises, recent Chinese corporate law now uses this term to refer to all companies, regardless of whether they are large or small, family-owned or state-owned. To clarify this difference, smaller and medium-sized family-run enterprises are now often called *jia zu gong-si*. An illustration of a typical family-run company is shown in Exhibit 4.5. In brief, its characteristics are as follows.

- Flat and informal structure. *Gong-si* companies have little formal structure, few standard operating procedures, and little specialization.[13] While they lack formal structure and procedures, personal relationships are likely to take precedence over more objectively defined concerns, such as organizational efficiency. Who one knows is often more important than what one knows, and employee loyalty is sometimes preferred over actual performance.

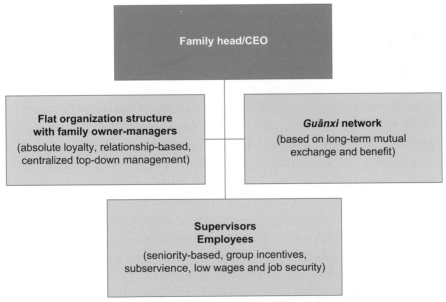

Exhibit 4.5 Example of Chinese family model of organization (*gong-si*)
Source: Based on Richard M. Steers, Luciara Nardon, and Carlos Sanchez-Runde, "Culture and organization design: strategy, structure, and decision-making," in Rabi S. Bhagat and Richard M. Steers (eds.), *Cambridge Handbook of Culture, Organizations, and Work* (Cambridge University Press, 2009), pp. 91–4.

- Relationship-based. Decisions are frequently based either on intuition or on long-standing business exchange relationships. According to Darden business professor Ming-Jer Chen, if these family firms have a competitive advantage, it lies in their small size, flexibility, network of connections, and negotiation skills.[14]
- Family management. Top management positions are often filled with family members, sometimes despite a lack of managerial competence.[15]
- Business as private property. Business owners tend to regard the business as the private property of the core family (not an individual), and are therefore reluctant to share ownership with outsiders or to borrow from individuals or organizations unrelated to the family in some way.
- Family revenue. Following from Confucian thought, the family is the most fundamental revenue and expenditure unit. Within a family, each member contributes his or her income to a common family fund. Each member then has a right to a portion of this money, while the remainder belongs to the family as a whole. The interests of the entire family take precedence over individual members and others outside the family.

Network model of organization (e.g., Japan)

Next, we turn to a look at the network model of organization, frequently found in Japan. An overview of Japanese culture includes a strong belief in hierarchy, strong collectivism, a strong harmony orientation, moderate monochronism, and strong particularism. Hierarchy beliefs in Japan can be seen in the deep respect shown to elders and people in positions of authority. In many circumstances, their directives are to be obeyed immediately and without question. This belief follows from early Confucian teachings (see above). Indeed, the concept of authority in Japan differs from that typically found in the West. Western views of authority see power generally flowing in one direction: down. The supervisor or manager gives directions; those below him or her follow them. Authority is a one-way concept. In Japan and many other Asian countries, by contrast, power still flows downwards, but those exercising power must also look after the welfare and well-being of those they manage. In other words, a supervisor expects his or her directives to be followed without question, but will also spend considerable time guiding, coaching, and teaching subordinates so that they can progress in their careers. Subordinates – and in many cases their families too – will be looked after. Thus, authority here is seen as a two-way street; both sides (superiors and subordinates) have a role to play. By deferring to those above you, you are in essence asking them to look after you.

Japan is also a highly collectivistic nation. Groups generally take precedence over individuals, and people gain their personal identity through their group membership. An old saying, "The nail that sticks out will be hammered down," best exemplifies the importance of this belief. (Contrast this to the old American and British saying, "The squeaky wheel gets the grease.") As a result, employees naturally gravitate towards groups at work, and group achievement surpasses individual achievement on the job. Seniority-based or group-based rewards are frequently preferred over performance-based individual rewards.

Harmony – both with other people and with nature – is also a strong characteristic. Japan's respect for its surrounding environment is legendary. This is not to say they refrain from changing or challenging nature; rather, they typically attempt this in ways that do as little harm as possible to the environment. Likewise, most Japanese will go to great lengths not to offend anyone or create open conflict or argumentation. As a result, communications in Japan tends to emphasize context at least as much as content. Nonverbal signs and signals are frequently used to convey thoughts in cases when words may be inappropriate. Finally, many observers have noted that Japanese society tends to be highly particularistic: while clear rules of law pervade society, exceptions are routinely made for friends and family or for powerful and influential people.

Japan's large and highly diversified companies represent a unique approach to organization that has served their members and their country well over the years.[16] These organizations are referred to as *keiretsu*. A *keiretsu* refers to a uniquely Japanese form of corporate organization, consisting of a network of affiliated companies (*kaisha*) that form a tight-knit alliance to work towards each other's mutual success (see Exhibit 4.6). The example shown here is for the Kirin Holdings *kaisha*, part of the Mitsubishi *keiretsu*. The design of these types of organizations is rooted in Japanese history and is successful largely because it is congruent with the national culture.[17] Japanese *keiretsu* typically consist of a group of interlocking companies clustered around one or more banks, a lead manufacturer, and a trading company, overseen by a president's council consisting of the presidents of the major group companies.

Common features of *keiretsu* include the following:

- Internal financing. Financing is most likely to come from inside the Japanese conglomerate's own financial institutions (e.g., company-owned banks or insurance companies), while marketing research and even legal advice is frequently carried out within the group. Within each horizontal *keiretsu*, a company-owned bank or banks perform several functions, including internal financing for company operations and new ventures.
- Trading companies. Japanese companies tend to have large and highly competent trading companies (*sogo shosha*). These organizations provide member companies with ready access to global markets and distribution networks, and maintain offices throughout the world to continually look out for new or expanded markets. At the same time, their field offices collect and analyze market

Exhibit 4.6 Example of Japanese network model of organization (Kirin Holdings *kaisha*, Mitsubishi *keiretsu*)
Source: Based on Richard M. Steers, Luciara Nardon, and Carlos Sanchez-Runde, "Culture and organization design: strategy, structure, and decision-making," in Rabi S. Bhagat and Richard M. Steers (eds.), *Cambridge Handbook of Culture, Organizations, and Work* (Cambridge University Press, 2009), pp. 85–91.

and economic intelligence that can be used by member companies to develop new products or otherwise get a jump on the competition. They frequently assist member companies with various marketing activities as well, and facilitate imports into Japan for their business customers.

- **Weak executives.** Compared to many other companies around the world, executives have less power, and decision-making is distributed throughout the firm. Executives are prized for being consensus builders more than autocratic decision-makers.
- **Long-term employees.** In contrast to many of their Western counterparts, Japanese firms tend to treat their employees as a fixed cost, not a variable cost, and relationships with suppliers tend to be closer and more stable over time.
- **Enterprise unions.** Japanese unions, called enterprise unions, tend to be company unions and are more closely associated with company interests than is the case in the West.

Mutual benefit model of organization (e.g., Germany, Netherlands, Scandinavian countries)

A fourth approach to organization and management can be seen in the mutual benefit model of organization. This model is common in Germany, the Netherlands, and the Scandinavian countries and, once again, it is derived from the long-standing cultural traditions found in this region of the world. This model is based on societal assumptions about collective participation and the common good. We focus here on Germany as one variation on this model.

A number of social scientists have attempted to describe German culture in general terms. Hofstede, for example, has described the typical German as relatively individualistic (although not so extreme as Americans), high on uncertainty avoidance and masculinity, and relatively low on power distance.[18] Hall and Hall add that Germans tend to be very punctual about time, follow schedules closely, demand order, value their personal space, respect power and position, and seek detailed information prior to decision-making. Indeed, Hall and Hall quote a French executive as saying that "Germans are too busy managing to think creatively."[19] As discussed in Chapter 3, cultural anthropologists suggest that the dominant German culture includes a mastery orientation, moderate individualism and egalitarianism, a strong rule-based orientation, and a monochronic approach to time.

To foreign observers, Germans tend to be conservative, formal, and polite.[20] Formal titles are important in conversations, and privacy and protocol are valued. In business, Germans tend to be assertive, but not aggressive. Although firms are often characterized by strict departmentalization, decisions tend to be made on the basis of broad-based discussion and consensus-building among key stakeholders. Negotiations are based on extensive assessments of data and plans, and, since Germany is a low-context culture (where message clarity counts – see Chapter 5), communication is explicit and easily understood by foreigners.

As with companies in any country, it is difficult to generalize about the nature or structure of the typical large German company (*Konzern* in German). A representative model is nevertheless presented in Exhibit 4.7.

- Supervisory and management boards. German firms are typically led from the top by two boards. At the very top is the supervisory board (*Aufsichtsrat*), which, much like a board of directors in US firms, is responsible for ensuring that the principal corporate objectives are met over the long term. Its members are typically elected for five years and can only be changed by a vote of 75 percent of the voting shares. The supervisory board, in turn, oversees the activities of the management board (*Vorstand*), which consists of the top management team of the firm and is responsible for its actual strategic and operational management.

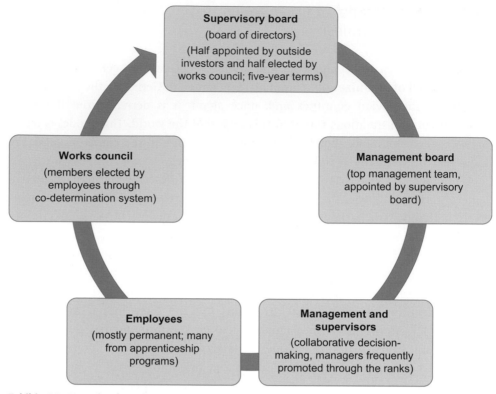

Exhibit 4.7 Example of German mutual benefit organization (*Konzern*)
Source: Based on Richard M. Steers, Luciara Nardon, and Carlos Sanchez-Runde, "Culture and organization design: strategy, structure, and decision-making," in Rabi S. Bhagat and Richard M. Steers (eds.), *Cambridge Handbook of Culture, Organizations, and Work* (Cambridge University Press, 2009), pp. 94–7.

- Co-determination and works councils. A major feature of mutual benefit structures is the enhanced power that employees at various levels of the organization have in decisions affecting the future of the organization. In Germany, this is called co-determination (*Mitbestimmung*). As part of this, works councils, elected from rank-and-file employees, are represented on company supervisory boards and participate significantly in both strategy formulation and management practice.
- *Meister*. From the first-line supervisor (usually held by a *Meister*, or master technician) on up, managers are respected for what they know rather than who they are. They tend to be less controlling than many of their US counterparts. Instead, it is assumed that workers and supervisors will meet deadlines, guarantee quality and service, and do not require close supervision. Independence within agreed-upon parameters characterizes the working relationship between managers and the managed.

- *Technik.* Behind the organizational facade of German firms is a particular notion of technical competence commonly referred to as *Technik.* This describes the knowledge and skills required for work.[21] It is the science and art of manufacturing high-quality and technologically advanced products. The success of *Technik* in German manufacturing is evidenced by the fact that over 40 percent of Germany's gross domestic product (GDP) is derived from manufacturing. Indeed, Germany is responsible for over a half of all EU manufactured exports. It is for this reason that knowledge of *Technik* represents a principal determinant in the selection of supervisors and managers.

Control, participation, and decision-making

Making timely, relevant, and – hopefully – wise decisions concerning the future directions of a firm is clearly a principal function of management. Critical to this process is where, when, and how information is sourced for optimum results. In other words, who has useful and important information or viewpoints that can lead to better decisions and who can be ignored, for reasons either of confidentiality or efficiency? Clearly, there are considerable and often heated disagreements on this issue. At the heart of this disagreement are the twin issues of management control and employee involvement or participation in decision-making.

While many heuristics are available to examine the extent of organizational control and employee involvement in managerial decision-making, we make use of a long-standing and simple framework.[22] This approach has seen widespread use among scholars and managers, due in part to its strong empirical base and in part to its down-to-earth approach to understanding how problems are actually addressed and resolved up and down the organizational hierarchy. This model offers a three-level classification scheme based on the amount of employee participation that is generally allowed by managers and organizations, allowing for variations around each (see Exhibit 4.8): centralized, consultative, and collaborative.[23]

Centralized decision-making (e.g., USA, UK, Canada)

If we look at a typical decision-making process in many of the so-called "Anglo" countries (e.g., Australia, Canada, New Zealand, United Kingdom, United States), we often find a process that centralizes power squarely in the hands of line managers. Here, the initial problem identification is largely a managerial or supervisory responsibility; workers' opinions are often ignored or not offered in the first place. Once a problem or issue has been identified, it is management's responsibility to analyze and resolve it, often with the help of senior managers or outside specialists

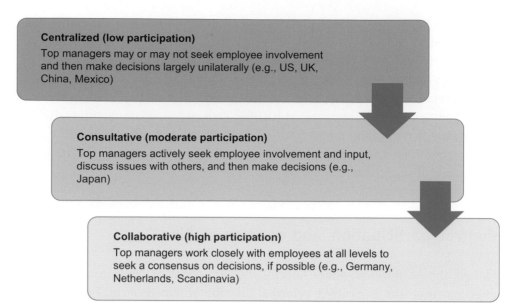

Centralized (low participation)
Top managers may or may not seek employee involvement and then make decisions largely unilaterally (e.g., US, UK, China, Mexico)

Consultative (moderate participation)
Top managers actively seek employee involvement and input, discuss issues with others, and then make decisions (e.g., Japan)

Collaborative (high participation)
Top managers work closely with employees at all levels to seek a consensus on decisions, if possible (e.g., Germany, Netherlands, Scandinavia)

Exhibit 4.8 Employee participation in organizational decision-making
Source: Based on Richard M. Steers, Luciara Nardon, and Carlos Sanchez-Runde, "Culture and organization design: strategy, structure, and decision-making," in Rabi S. Bhagat and Richard M. Steers (eds.), *Cambridge Handbook of Culture, Organizations, and Work* (Cambridge University Press, 2009), pp. 107–15.

and consultants. Decisions are then passed down to lower-level employees in the form of changed work procedures. Not surprisingly, since the people at the bottom of the hierarchy often have little understanding of management's conclusions or intents, decision implementation tends to be slow, as management now has to persuade workers to go along with the decision. Frequently, extrinsic rewards (i.e., externally administered rewards, such as pay or bonuses) need to be used instead of intrinsic rewards (i.e., internally administered rewards, such as pride in accomplishment or job satisfaction) as a result of this process.

Meanwhile, the decision process described above is not dissimilar from that commonly found in Chinese *gong-si*, or family-based companies. Despite being a collectivistic country, China is still hierarchical, leading to centralized power in decision-making. Problem identification is typically carried out either by supervisors or owner-managers using fairly rigid management and production control systems. The owner-managers then discuss and analyze the problem, often in consultation with extended family members or *guānxi* relationships. Because of the autocratic decision style, the rapid announcement of a decision to rank-and-file employees by management is possible (see Exhibit 4.9). Rapid acceptance and implementation of an owner-manager's decision by largely contingent employees is also possible, because of a combination of loyalty to the owner-manager and fear of the consequences of non-compliance. Employees' intrinsic motivation to implement decisions

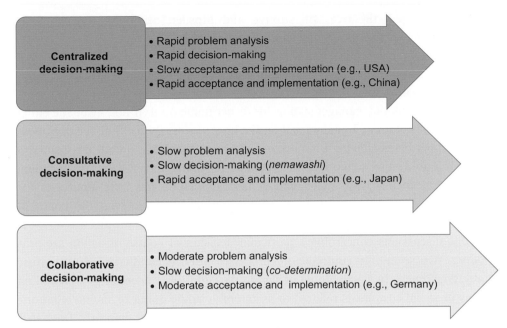

Exhibit 4.9 Decision analysis and implementation speed
Source: Based on Richard M. Steers, Luciara Nardon, and Carlos Sanchez-Runde, "Culture and organization design: strategy, structure, and decision-making," in Rabi S. Bhagat and Richard M. Steers (eds.), *Cambridge Handbook of Culture, Organizations, and Work* (Cambridge University Press, 2009), pp. 107–15.

may be high, due to custom and loyalty to the firm, but extrinsic motivation may also be high, due to the importance of job security and income.

Consultative decision-making (e.g., Japan)

Managerial decision-making in a typical Japanese *kaisha* (company) reflects Japanese culture and is seen by many observers as being quite distinct from that in the West. Not surprisingly, Japanese firms endorse the concept of problem-solving on the basis of consensus up and down the hierarchy.[24] The system by which this is done is usually called *ringi-seido* (often shortened to simply *ringi-sei*), or circle of discussion.

When a particular problem or opportunity is identified, a group of workers or supervisors will discuss various parameters of the problem and try to identify possible solutions. At times, technical experts will be brought in for assistance. If the initial results are positive, employees will approach their supervisor for more advice and possible support. The whole process is generally referred to in Japan as *nemawashi*. The word *nemawashi* is derived from a description of the process of preparing the roots of a tree for planting.[25] The concept here is that, if the roots are properly prepared, the tree will survive and prosper. Similarly, if a proposal is properly prepared, it too should survive and prosper.

When a group has achieved informal consensus, a formal proposal is then drafted for submission up the chain of command. This formal document, known as a *ringi-sho*, is reviewed by successively higher levels of management. If a manager agrees with the proposal, the manager stamps his or her name on it; if not, he or she either refrains from stamping it or stamps it on the reverse side. By the time the document reaches upper management, it has become clear whether it has broad-based support or not. If it does enjoy support, in all likelihood top management will formally adopt the proposal. In this way, upper management frequently has little input into the decision-making process. If a proposal has universal support up the chain of command, top managers will be hard-pressed to oppose it.

While discussions concerning a particular decision or course of action are proceeding, two seemingly contradictory processes often occur that tend to confuse many Westerners. In Japan, doing or saying the right thing according to prevailing norms or social customs is referred to as *tatemae*, while doing or saying what one actually prefers to do (which may be difficult) is referred to as *honne*.[26] Thus, in a conversation or meeting, to some Westerners a Japanese manager may speak in contradictions, or, worse, speak insincerely. In reality, the manager may simply be saying what he or she believes he or she is obliged to say, while hoping that through subtle signals the recipient of the message will discover his or her true desire or intent. This can be confusing to many Westerners, and requires them to listen carefully and observe body language as well as formal speech (e.g., reading someone's face). After all, Japan is a high-context culture (see Chapter 5), while most Western nations are not.

A key point to remember here is that the *ringi-sei* process tends to result in slow decisions, which is often a disadvantage in a fast-paced and competitive global business environment. This process yields considerable support for and commitment to the emergent solution when it is achieved, however. By contrast, many Western decisions are typically made unilaterally much higher up in the management hierarchy, but, once they have been made, they frequently face considerable opposition or apathy as managers and workers attempt to implement them. As a result, strategic planning is frequently accomplished more quickly in the West, while strategic implementation is frequently accomplished more quickly in Japan.

Collaborative decision-making (e.g., Germany, Netherlands, Scandinavian countries)

Finally, the decision-making process found in many German, Dutch, and Scandinavian firms tends to be more participative than any country in either the Anglo or the Asian clusters. This is due in large measure to the presence of co-determination laws and works councils.

Collaborative decision-making can be highly complex, on account of the knowledge and power of the various stakeholders. In this process, problems are most frequently identified either by supervisors or workers through a combination of job experience and sophisticated production control processes. Lower-level employees in a section or department begin by working with supervisors to help identify the underlying causes of the problem, as well as possible solutions. Next, department heads, section chiefs, and supervisors meet to discuss and develop a proposal to remedy the situation. Technical experts and works council members are frequently consulted as needed to achieve the best possible solution. The problem and possible solutions are then passed up the management hierarchy. Management discusses the problem and possible solutions widely and then makes a formal decision, often in consultation and negotiation with works council members and the local industrial union leadership.

The resulting decisions are likely to be widely accepted by rank-and-file employees, because of the representative process through which they were made; workers at all levels have had a voice throughout the process. As a result, decision implementation typically proceeds at a moderate pace, although union resistance may still occur because of structural or contract issues. Employees' intrinsic motivation to implement the decision is typically reasonably high, since their representatives had a voice in determining it and the decision typically does not threaten job security.

In summary, as we have seen throughout this discussion on organizational decision-making, a lot is heard about the role of employee participation and involvement. In some countries, employee participation is a preciously guarded right; it is assumed. In other countries, workers have no expectations of employee participation; indeed, they often see managers who seek their opinions as being weak. In still other countries (some include Canada and the United States in this category), participation is often honored more in rhetoric than in actual practice. In other words, although many companies may proclaim their interest in the opinions of subordinates, they are often more interested in results than in process. Consider: how do managers determine how much participation to encourage or allow among their subordinates, and what should they do if the advice offered by colleagues or subordinates is self-serving, excessively expensive, or simply unrealistic?

Corporate culture

The behavioral manifestations of organization design are typically brought to life through a firm's corporate culture. (This is also called organizational culture, but we prefer the word "corporate" here to avoid confusion.) *If management structures are the fingerprints of organizations, then corporate cultures are their personalities.* Organizations provide managers with a set of rules, procedures, and norms of behavior to guide action in the form of standard operational procedures and organizational cultural norms. The corporate culture reflects the norms, values, and approved (and proscribed) behaviors of particular companies, divisions, or departments within organizations. It represents the *perceived* organizational realities as they affect individuals and groups of employees.

Corporate culture may either replicate or reject national culture values and norms, creating a micro environment in which national norms are reinforced or do not apply. For example, even though a country may embrace a polychronic time orientation, an organization in that country may reject this cultural norm and enforce punctuality in its activities. Indeed, many global organizations deal with the challenges posed by multiple national cultures by creating clear behavioral guidelines across the organization. In intra-organizational interactions, organizational norms and rules may serve to decrease the impact of multiple institutional environments. In inter-organizational relationships, the organizational environment may exacerbate differences. Through the development and reinforcement of norms of behavior, organizations define what is expected of managers.

The fundamental challenge facing managers is how to identify – quickly – the type of culture they are dealing with. Corporate culture expert Edgar Schein suggests three possible ways (see Exhibit 4.10).[27]

1. Symbols and behaviors. Observe the manifestations of culture through the presence of artifacts and patterns of behavior. Organizations look and feel different from one another. Upon arriving at a new organization, we can observe symbols or physical characteristics that can provide important information. For example: are there offices or is it one open floor? Are doors open or closed? Is the environment formal or informal? How are people dressed? We can also observe patterns of behavior. Are there particular ways in which a number of people behave and others seem to treat this behavior as normal (e.g., interrupting in meetings, arriving late, answering the phone)?

2. Power distribution. Study the power structure of the organization and seek to understand how a person can obtain, maintain, or lose power. This will point to what is really valued in this organization. Another cue here is an organization's reward and punishment system. In other words, who or what gets rewarded or punished, and why?

3. Problem-solving processes. Analyze how an organization confronts problems. How do they respond? Are they primarily proactive or reactive? Do they panic quickly or are they ready for almost any change or challenge?

To see how this works, take a look at how many companies around the globe attempt to build an aggressive, and hopefully creative, corporate culture through

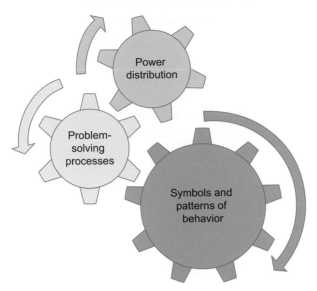

Exhibit 4.10 Influences on corporate culture

moderate risk-taking and physical hardship. Creating physical challenges for junior managers is nothing new, but the verve with which companies pursue it seems to be on the rise. Let's travel to Japan and China to see two different examples of global corporate cultures.

APPLICATION 4.3 **Corporate culture at Dentsu**

As employee inductions go, advertising agency holding group Dentsu probably has one of the most creative.[28] And definitely the most exhausting. Every July since 1925, the Japanese headquartered company – which owns huge global agencies including Carat, Isobar, and McGarry Bowen – has sent all its new hires and recently promoted executives to climb the country's 12,388-foot-high mountain, Mount Fuji. The message to new hires: "Welcome to the company. Now climb this mountain."

Mount Fuji is not considered a particularly dangerous peak, but a few climbers do die each year from high winds, exposure, and falls. The summit has only two-thirds the oxygen of sea level, and ropes and crampons are required: it's a daunting task. Hundreds of Dentsu employees begin the trek up the volcanic mountain in the afternoon, finally reaching the summit for sunrise at around 4:30 a.m. Everyone that is physically able to is required to take part – from senior execs to junior staff straight out of college.

When they finally reach the top of their ascent, Dentsu's weary team members write postcards to their clients, sending them from a conveniently located post office at the summit. Climbers also pray in front of the Shinto shrine for the company's future growth.

Christopher Demetrakos, who worked at Dentsu in Japan for thirteen years, explained the thinking behind the climb: "The message is: 'We are going to conquer the one symbol that represents Japan more than anything else. And, once we do that, it will signify that we can do anything.'"

Dentsu's headquarters in downtown Tokyo is also emblematic of its ambition: The agency's 6,200 employees are spread across forty-five of the building's forty-eight floors in an effort to isolate teams working on various creative accounts and stop them from interacting with other teams. Elevator use is not encouraged.

Think about it . . .

(1) In a few words, how would you describe the corporate culture of Dentsu?
(2) Do you believe that this culture serves Dentsu's long-term corporate object-ives? Explain.
(3) How is it possible for a company like Dentsu to retain its corporate culture for such a long time?
(4) Would you wish to work for this company? Why or why not?

While Dentsu illustrates the use of physical challenges to help build an achievement-oriented corporate culture, another mechanism that is often found in organizations is enthusiasm; that is, get employees involved in work life almost to the point of making work a game. China's Alibaba is a good example of this approach.

APPLICATION 4.4 Corporate culture at Alibaba

As discussed earlier in this chapter, hierarchy, collectivism, and other Confucian principles tend to characterize traditional Chinese companies. What many people do not realize, however, is that an ever-increasing number of new high-tech start-ups in China are beginning to create a very different corporate culture. It is not Western, it is not traditional Chinese; it is a third way.

On the fourth floor of the headquarters of e-commerce titan Alibaba is a massive workspace filled with hundreds of salespeople. This is Alibaba's army of cold callers. They telephone clients who have storefronts on the Web, urging them to buy keyword advertising or to pay to boost their online rankings. Each salesperson inhabits a cubicle furnished with a desk, a plastic sunflower, and a mirror – the last a reminder to smile, because it's an article of faith at Alibaba that a customer can hear a smile over the phone. "*Liuqian!*" yells one woman, popping up from her cubicle: "Six thousand!" She has just persuaded a client to buy 6,000 yuan of keyword advertising. On cue, all her colleagues raise their assigned celebratory device: a long plastic stick with three plastic hands at the end of it. The sound of three hands clapping is *click-click-click-click* nonstop on a good day. This is also the odd noise of China's changing organizational cultures.

Since corporations began popping up in China during the economic liberalization of the 1980s, workplace culture has been defined by what one might call the "Great Wall" model – a divide between the haves (the executives) and the have-nots (the workers). Today the old ways are under attack. With the Communist authorities increasingly aware of the nation's social divisions and potential restiveness, China has opened up to influences from other cultures, and practices from abroad have crept into corporate life quickly, particularly in the Internet sector.

Leaders such as Ma Yún (Jack Ma in the West), founder and CEO of Alibaba, have been inspired by the examples of Silicon Valley's tech titans.[29] Like Ma, a new cohort of Chinese executives – educated and professionally seasoned in other countries – is returning home with new thinking about management and work, including a more "in the trenches" ethos, a heightened appetite for risk, and a different understanding of innovation. These execs have earned a well-known nickname: *haigui*, or "sea turtle," which in Mandarin is harmonious with the word for a person who goes overseas and then returns home to China.

Ma studied at Hangzhou Teacher's College. Although he is not a sea turtle himself, his ranks at Alibaba include numerous alumni from major universities outside China. He got the idea for Alibaba after a visit to the United States. After starting the company, he and other executives went on a world tour, meeting the chiefs of long-lasting, successful corporations including General Electric and HSBC. He concluded that they all had not just strong corporate values but also a unified sense of purpose, that what made the difference between short-term and long-term success was a distinct organizational culture. So he organized Alibaba around six core values: customers come first; the embrace of change; integrity; passion; commitment to your job; and teamwork and cooperation. What resulted was a "Silicon Valley company" refracted through his unique Chinese lens – much like the Chinese versions of Western goods that you might find for sale on Alibaba.

Signs of Ma's whimsical management style are all over Alibaba's Hangzhou campus: from the three-handed celebration devices to an enormous statue of a naked man in the central courtyard to the receptionists' daily costume changes during festivals and holiday seasons. Employees even get cake on their birthday.

There are also interest-free loans for qualified employees to buy their first homes – and build more loyalty to Alibaba. The cafeteria even features a special menu for pregnant women. In hiring and in promotions, cultural fit is as much a priority as technological expertise. In quarterly evaluations, staff members are judged on Alibaba's six-point value system. The goal is to cultivate a team spirit that will drive profits and, according to Ma, "keep the state-owned enterprises up at night." None of this, however, can explain why some applicants have been asked to do headstands in job interviews!

Think about it . . .

(1) What is your assessment of Alibaba's six core values? Is there anything particularly Chinese about these values?
(2) In your opinion are corporate cultures more closely associated with their industry (e.g., high-tech start-ups, automobiles, pharmaceuticals) or with their national cultures (e.g., Chinese, French)? Why?
(3) In many ways, Alibaba uses a traditional Chinese family structure for organizing, yet this approach seems to be in harmony with high-tech firms in its industry. How do you think this is possible?
(4) The corporate culture at Alibaba is a combination of team spirit (e.g., *liuqian*), paternalistic employee benefits (e.g., housing assistance), and whimsy (e.g., three-handed celebration). If you returned to this company in five or so years, do you think it would have the same corporate culture or might it be different? Why or why not?
(5) Does the example of Alibaba provide a model for other high-tech start-ups from other cultures? Why or why not? What cultural limitations might serve to limit the adoption of this model?

MANAGER'S NOTEBOOK

Working with global organizations

What are the lessons here? For starters, organizations are complex entities, and frequently not easily understood. They are not just about how to put people into boxes or cubicles. Instead, they serve as a principal command and control system for focusing human, financial, and physical resources on the accomplishment of valued tasks. Organization designs live or die on the basis of their ability to assist managers with their responsibilities. Globalization requires a diversity of answers, not a one-size-fits-all approach to organization and management. This includes having a global vision and strategy, but it also means tailoring organizational designs to fit both local conditions and the available resources.

The choice of an appropriate organization design typically evolves over time as companies increase their involvement in global activities. This evolutionary process often begins with some form of domestic organization design, in which international activities are largely an appendage to the more central domestic activities, and evolves over time into a more integrated global organization design that places international business at the center of the organization's strategy.

In addition, making timely, relevant, and wise decisions about the future directions of a firm is, clearly, a principal function of management. Critical to this process is where, when, and how information is sourced for optimum results. In other words, who has useful and important information or viewpoints that can lead to better decisions and who can be ignored, for reasons either of confidentiality or of efficiency? At the heart of this disagreement is the issue of employee involvement and participation in decision-making.

Corporate culture (also called organizational culture) reflects the norms, values, and approved behaviors of particular companies, divisions, or departments within organizations. It may either replicate or reject national culture values and norms, creating a micro environment in which national norms are either reinforced or do not apply. In intra-organizational interactions, organizational norms and rules may serve to decrease the impact of multiple institutional environments. In inter-organizational relationships, the organizational environment may exacerbate differences through the development and reinforcement of norms of behavior; organizations define what is expected of managers.

The challenge for managers, then, is how to learn enough about how particular organizations operate to be able to work with them. In this endeavor, we can suggest three general management strategies (summarized in Exhibit 4.11).

1.   Understand the relationships between stakeholders, strategies, and structures

It has been suggested throughout this book that looking for relationships represents an excellent learning tool. With regard to stakeholders, strategies, and structures, several lessons seem important.

We have seen in this chapter how culture can influence the ways in which firms approach strategic decisions. In Germany, for example, social pressures and the legal environment both require corporations to look beyond the exclusive interests of investors and stockholders in determining policy. The principle of co-determination requires this. Employees and the local communities must also be considered, as well as environmental issues and high ethical standards. In Japan, we

1. Understand the relationships between stakeholders, strategies, and structures	2. Understand the characteristics of local work environments	3. Learn about other organizations by better understanding your own
• Understand stakeholder power and influence in the strategy-making process. • Understand how your organization differs from others in terms of their strategic objectives and organizing frameworks. • Look for interactions between strategic decisions and structures. • Remember that strategies and structures can evolve over time. • Consider the role of cultural differences in strategy–structure relationships.	• Understand how decisions are made across organizations, including the role of employee involvement. • Understand constraints on organizational decision-making. • Understand your own organizational culture. • Understand differences in organizational cultures across companies, including artifacts and behaviors, power distributions, and problem-solving mechanisms. • Learn how you as an outsider can work with people from a different organizational culture.	• Learn more about the relationships between your own culture and local organizing frameworks. • Based on this, learn more about other cultures as they play out in organizational settings. • Continue to develop your multicultural skills to be prepared for differing environments. • Finally, learn the rules of the game regardless of where you are working.

Exhibit 4.11 Strategies for working with global organizations

saw how close business–government relations also dictate how firms make strategic choices, and how government policies can support corporate strategies, especially in the area of exporting. At the same time, other countries (e.g., the United Kingdom, the United States) have more of an adversarial relationship between business and government, and – sometimes by law – companies are required to favor investors and stockholders over all other stakeholders as the principal beneficiaries of corporate actions. The point here is simple: it would be naïve for managers from any country to assume that organizations around the world approach basic strategic decision-making in the same manner. Each company experiences unique, but nevertheless very real, constraints on how it approaches its strategy, both short- and long-term, and these constraints can vary widely from country to country.

Strategy and structure frequently interact with one another; each influences the other. Clearly, part of the reason behind this is that cultural differences influence organization design and management practice alike. It goes beyond this, however. Regardless of local cultural variations, organizations and their managers comprise learning systems, which build on past experiences and future expectations in ways that can change both the structure of the organization and its management strategies and practices.

Remember that both strategies and structures continually evolve to varying degrees in response to global and local changes. Another influence can be found in the rapid evolution of information and computer-mediated technologies, which have the power to change the ways in which fundamental communications occur through the firm and with its partners.

When dealing with business partners or prospective partners in other organizations, it is critical to understand what their strategy is, how they are organized, and how decisions are made. For example, recognizing the location of your counterpart in his or her organization structure will provide important information as to how much power the person has and how much discretion he or she has in making a decision. Understanding his or her decision-making style is equally critical, because, although you may be pressed to reach a quick agreement, your counterpart may not be able to do that given the organizational constraints he or she faces. Be patient when you can.

The four organizing frameworks discussed here are highly correlated with the cultural traits of their home countries. Japan is a collectivistic society that fosters inclusion and group membership. Not surprisingly, major Japanese *keiretsu* (as well as smaller firms) make use of a group mentality and paternalism in structuring their firms and managing their people. Everyone "belongs" to the company – and the company belongs to them. By contrast, Germany is a more individualistic country, but is still largely egalitarian in nature. As such, German firms may be somewhat more bureaucratic, but they still provide a strong basis for employee participation and involvement at all levels. Thus, while both Japanese and German firms foster employee participation, the basis for such inclusion is very different: participation in Japanese firms is based on societal norms, while in Germany it is based on the prevailing legal system. Meanwhile, non-family employees in a Chinese *gong-si* seldom have expectations of participation. Finally, terms such as "employee participation" or "involvement" are frequently heard throughout the corridors and factories of American and Canadian enterprises, but such words often carry little real meaning beyond the rhetoric. The lesson here is simple: cultures do matter when attempting to understand or manage organizations around the world.

2. Understand the characteristics of local work environments

A second management strategy that follows from the above discussion relates to understanding the unique characteristics of local work environments. In this chapter, we have focused on two aspec · of the work environment in which wide differences can often be found across borders: decision-making processes and organizational cultures.

One of the most important things managers do is make decisions concerning the use and applications of their company's limited resources. As a result, understanding how decisions are made in different organizations and different countries is an important part of doing one's job. In particular, managers need to understand both the principal constraints on decision-making processes and the role of employee involvement. Who (e.g., particular people or units) is involved in making key decisions and how much discretion do they actually have? What level of information do people want from others to make a decision? Some people want to know everything, while others simply want to know if they trust the other party. What criteria do people use to judge whether a decision is good or bad?

Whether managers are assigned to a new location within their own organization or are working with people from other companies, one key question stands out as a critical factor in success: understanding the local organizational culture. Organizational cultures often specify – sometimes overtly, but sometimes covertly – the rules of the road. They both limit and encourage behaviors, and in this sense influence success in no small way. As a result, regardless of the assignment, managers are advised to learn to recognize and understand local artifacts and behaviors, power distributions, and problem-solving mechanisms. Finally, managers would do well to learn how they as outsiders might fit in or whether this would be an impossible task. Throughout, the best advice is to know one's surrounding environment in ways that can work to your advantage.

3. Learn about other organizations by better understanding your own

Finally, although managers may have a familiarity with the operations of their own firm, understanding the general trends – and idiosyncrasies – of various local firms can be far more difficult than it may appear. To the extent that this is correct, what frames of reference can managers use when trying to understand the organizational models in other countries? From a managerial standpoint, three action recommendations emerge from this analysis that have to be resolved for managers to work successfully with organizations across cultures (see Exhibit 4.12):

- Managers must develop an understanding of cultural trends, organizational patterns, and management styles in their own country. This is often easier said than done. We often assume, incorrectly, that we already know this, but looking deeper might reveal that we have something to learn here.
- Based on this local understanding, and as discussed earlier in the book, managers must develop sufficient insight into and understanding of the other countries and cultures with which they or their companies do (or wish to do) business.
- Managers must continue to develop their management and multicultural skills so that they can successfully bridge these two cultures and help meet corporate objectives.

Exhibit 4.12 Learning from different organizational models

Throughout this endeavor, managers should strive to understand the subtle – and not so subtle – rules of behavior within organizations. Understanding the general behavioral patterns of a national culture is not enough; managers need also to understand the rules of behavior within the particular organization with which they are doing business. Developing the skills to quickly observe patterns of behaviors and gather information about expectations is critical for survival in such a multicultural business environment. This is particularly true with regard to understanding different organizational cultures. As illustrated above, organizations that can outwardly appear to be similar may conceal significant differences in what is acceptable and what is expected. To the extent that managers can gain insight into this by doing their homework prior to arrival, their ease in making the rules play to their advantage is enhanced.

In summary, it should again be noted that, although the organizing models discussed here represent central tendencies in various countries, wide variations can obviously be found everywhere. As a result, while these frameworks may be instructive for the purposes of general comparisons across cultures, they are not intended to represent universal patterns of organization.

KEY TERMS

co-determination (German) • Confucianism (Chinese) • corporate (organizational) culture • domestic organization design • enterprise unions (Japanese) • face (Chinese) • family model of organization • five cardinal virtues (Chinese) • global matrix organizations • global network designs • global organization designs • *gong-si* (Chinese) • *guānxi* (Chinese) • *honne* (Japanese) • investor model of organization • *kaisha* (Japanese) • *keiretsu* (Japanese) • *Konzern* (German) • management board (German) • *meister* (German) • *mittelstand* firms (German) • mutual benefit model of organization • *nemawashi* (Japanese) • network model of organization • organization • organizational environment • regional organizational models • *ringi-sei* (Japanese) • *ringi-sho* (Japanese) • *sogo shosha* (Japanese) • stakeholders • strategic management cycle • supervisory board (German) • *tatemae* (Japanese) • *technik* (German) • trading companies • Web-based global network design • works councils (German)

DISCUSSION QUESTIONS

1. Geert Hofstede argues that organizations are symbolic entities and function according to implicit models in the minds of their members, and these are culturally determined. Do you agree or disagree with this statement? Why? Provide an example of how this assertion may be correct.

2. In what ways can a better understanding of organizational environments (as illustrated in Exhibit 4.1) prepare managers for foreign assignments? Provide two specific examples to illustrate your point.

3. What factors influence the relationship between strategy and structure in global organizations? Why might knowledge of this be important for global managers working in the field? Explain.

4. We saw an example of Web-based global network organization design at work in Uber Technologies. In what circumstances are such designs most useful to long-term organizational success across borders? In what circumstances are they potentially harmful?

5. Why might we say that a company's unique management structure is like its own personal fingerprint? To the extent that this statement is correct, how might it influence managerial development and managerial behavior? Explain.

6. What are the strategic and managerial advantages and potential drawbacks of each of the four regional organizing models discussed here (investor, family, network, and mutual benefit)? In which type of organization would you personally prefer to work, and why?

7. The organization design and managerial practices of many traditional Chinese (and other Asian) companies are heavily influenced by Confucian principles. As the world continues to globalize and competitiveness increases in importance, are these principles helpful or detrimental to long-term organizational prosperity? Why?

8. Outside observers have argued that Japanese *keiretsu* structures are so closely knit that they represent unfair competition for foreign companies. That is, it is difficult – some would say impossible – to penetrate the network and get a piece of the business. Is this a fair criticism? What might foreign companies do to penetrate these closely held networks?

9. What is your opinion of the role of employee participation or some form of co-determination in organizations around the world? Is employee participation an inalienable (or human) right or is it simply a management technique used in some countries to improve performance? Explain.

10. Corporate cultures vary considerably both within and across national borders. Why should global managers care about such variations so long as they know the specific individuals within a company that they need to work with?

11. Three strategies were suggested here concerning ways to improve managers' capabilities to work with organizations across cultures (Exhibit 4.11). How might you set up a workshop to inform managers about these strategies and demonstrate how they can be applied? What topics would you include, and why?

CASE: CO-DETERMINATION AT VOLKSWAGEN

From its headquarters in Wolfsburg, Germany, Volkswagen has consistently tried to accomplish two seemingly contradictory goals: remain a sales leader in the global auto industry while at the same time building and maintaining a worker's paradise for its employees. The success – or failure – of Volkswagen's efforts over time is emblematic of the challenges of Germany's co-determination system.

On several occasions over the past, however, the company's prospects looked grim as global car sales dropped. During one such crisis, sales dropped 20 percent in one year, requiring a massive reduction in working hours by company employees. Indeed, the company determined that it had 30,000 more workers than it needed in Germany alone. Its supervisory board concluded that poor economic conditions would likely remain for several years and that in order to survive it had to find a way to quickly reduce its operating costs by 20 percent to match the decline in sales.

As Volkswagen faced this challenge, the business and social environment in which key decisions would be made differed sharply from those the company would have faced in the United States. For starters, 20 percent of Volkswagen's stock is owned by the state of Lower Saxony, where the company's principal manufacturing facilities are located. In addition, 90 percent of all employees at Volkswagen are unionized. Since the company's union contract required approval of over 80 percent of the shareholders on all important decisions, any cost-cutting plan that involved large lay-offs was highly problematic. Lower Saxony and the IG-Metall union also had strong representation on the company's supervisory board, where cost reduction strategies would be openly discussed. As a result, major lay-offs were not a viable option.

In addition to its governance structure, Volkswagen had spent decades developing a culture of cooperation and inclusion among all of its employees. Key features of this culture include: (1) widespread dissemination of detailed information on the state of the company to employees, the IG-Metall union, and works councils; (2) a receptive climate for unions; (3) informal co-determination in advance of formal decisions; (4) an emphasis on consensus in decision-making; and (5) a norm of implementing decisions once they are made.

In creating and supporting this culture, Volkswagen was by no means abandoning its objectives of profitability and shareholder value. Instead, it believed (like many German companies) that all of the principal stakeholders of the company – including employees – should be protected in making major corporate decisions. In other words, capital and labor were seen as joint responsibilities of the company. From the standpoint of top management, VW had to find a solution that was acceptable to both sides. On the one hand, a reduction in labor costs was required to enhance operating efficiency and competitiveness, particularly in the face of reduced demand for its product. On the other hand, the method of achieving this cost reduction had to be acceptable to rank-and-file employees.

CASE QUESTIONS

1. What are the benefits and limitations of the co-determination system as practiced at Volkswagen?
2. What are the implications of the co-determination system for managerial practices and processes?
3. What are the implications for employee selection, training, and rewards?
4. Is the *Meister* concept of supervision significantly different from other supervisory models? If so, how? Where and when might this model be advantageous for organizations?
5. German firms have been criticized for often making strategic decisions more slowly than many of their global competitors. At the same time, most of Germany's large and *Mittelstand* firms remain highly competitive over time. How do you explain this?
6. In view of the success of the co-determination system in Germany (and other Northern European countries), why doesn't Volkswagen apply this or similar systems throughout its global operations?
7. (*Optional research question*) How many countries around the world use some version of co-determination as a core management system? What, if anything, do these countries have in common? Is co-determination the wave of the future in global management or not?

NOTES

1. Anne-Marie Slaughter, "Yes, you can," *New York Times*, March 7, 2013.
2. Geert Hofstede, *Culture's Consequences: International Differences in Work-Related Values*. Thousand Oaks, CA: Sage, 2001, p. 373.
3. The term *Mittelstand* normally refers to German, Austrian, or Swiss small and medium-sized enterprises (SMEs). However, precisely defining what constitutes a *Mittelstand* firm is difficult, since the word actually directly translates as "middle class." *Mittelstand* firms are typically owned and managed by a family, owned by family but run by an outside management team, or partially owned by family but with outside shareholders. German *Mittelstand* firms employ over 70 percent of all employees in private business, according to the Institut für Mittelstandsforschung.
4. Sam Schneider, "Two Uber executives indicted in France," *Wall Street Journal*, July 1, 2015, p. B-1.
5. Richard M. Steers, Luciara Nardon, and Carlos Sanchez-Runde, "Culture and organization design: strategy, structure, and decision-making," in Rabi S. Bhagat and Richard M. Steers (eds.), *Cambridge Handbook of Culture, Organizations, and Work*. Cambridge University Press, 2009, pp. 71–106.

6. It should be remembered that the term "Anglo" came into widespread use by cultural anthropologies and social psychologists in the 1970s and 1980s to describe this cluster, and much has changed in the intervening years.

7. Nancy Adler, *International Dimensions of Organizational Behavior*, 3rd edn. Cincinatti, OH: Southwestern Publishing, 1997.

8. Ming-Jer Chen, *Inside Chinese Business: A Guide For Managers Worldwide*. Boston, MA: Harvard Business School Press, 2001.

9. Confucius (551 BCE–479 CE) (*Kŏng Fūzĭ*), literally "Master Kong," was a Chinese thinker and social philosopher whose teachings and philosophy have deeply influenced Chinese, Korean, Japanese, Taiwanese, and Vietnamese thought and life. His philosophy emphasized personal and governmental morality, correctness in social relationships, justice, and sincerity. These values gained prominence in China over other doctrines, such as Legalism or Taoism, during the Han Dynasty (206 BCE–220 CE). Confucius' thoughts have been developed into a system of philosophy known as *Confucianism*. It was first introduced into Europe by the Jesuit Matteo Ricci, who was the first to Latinize the name as "Confucius." His teachings may be found in the *Analects of Confucius*, a collection of "brief aphoristic fragments," which was compiled many years after his death. Modern historians do not believe that any specific documents can be said to have been written by Confucius, but for nearly 2,000 years he was thought to be the editor or author.

10. Wenzhong Hu and Cornelius Grove, *Encountering the Chinese: A Guide for Americans*, 2nd edn. Yarmouth, ME: Intercultural Press, 1999.

11. *Guānxi* describes the basic dynamic in the complex nature of personalized networks of influence and social relationships, and it is a central concept in Chinese society. In Western media, the pinyin romanization of this Chinese word has tended to oversimplify the meaning of this term into "connections" or "relationships." Neither of these terms sufficiently reflects the wide cultural implications that *guānxi* describes. At its most basic, *guānxi* describes a personal connection between two people in which one is able to prevail upon another to perform a favor or service, or be prevailed upon. The two people need not be of equal social status. *Guānxi* can also be used to describe a network of contacts, which an individual can call upon when something needs to be done, and through which he or she can exert influence on behalf of another. In addition, *guānxi* can describe a state of general understanding between two people, in which both parties are aware of the other's needs and wants, and take these into account when making decisions or taking action. The term is not generally used to describe relationships within a family, although *guānxi* obligations can sometimes be described in terms of an extended family. The term is also not generally used to describe relationships that fall within other well-defined societal norms (e.g., boss–worker or teacher–student friendship). The relationships formed by *guānxi* are personal and not transferable. When a *guānxi* network violates bureaucratic norms, it can lead to corruption, and *guānxi* can also form the basis of patron–client relations.

12. Christopher Earley, *Face, Harmony, and Social Structure: An Analysis of Organizational Behavior across Cultures*. New York: Oxford University Press, 1997.

13. Sameena Ahmad, "Behind the mask: a survey of business in China," *The Economist*, March 20, 2004, pp. 3–19.

14. Chen, *Inside Chinese Business*.

15. S. Gordon Redding, *The Spirit of Chinese Capitalism.* Berlin: Walter de Gruyter, 1995.

16. Toyohiro Kono and Stewart Clegg, *Trends in Japanese Management: Continuing Strengths, Current Problems, and Changing Priorities.* London: Palgrave Macmillan, 2001; Masahiko Aoki and Ronald Dore (eds.), *The Japanese Firm: Sources of Competitive Strength.* Oxford University Press, 1994.

17. James Abbeglen and George Stalk, *Kaisha: The Japanese Corporation.* New York: Harper & Row, 1985.

18. Hofstede, *Culture's Consequences.*

19. Edward T. Hall and Mildred Reed Hall, *Understanding Cultural Differences: Germans, French and Americans.* Yarmouth, ME: Intercultural Press, 2000.

20. Richard Hill, *We Europeans.* Brussels: Europublications, 1997.

21. Ingrid Brunstein (ed.), *Human Resource Management in Western Europe.* Berlin: Walter de Gruyter, 1995.

22. Victor Vroom and Philip Yetton, *Leadership and Decision-Making.* New York: Wiley, 1973.

23. We use the terms "centralized" and "collaborative" here instead of Vroom and Yetton's original "autocratic" and "group" in view of the nebulous meanings and normative ascriptions associated with the original terms.

24. Hiroki Kato and Joan Kato, *Understanding and Working with the Japanese Business World.* Englewood Cliffs, NJ: Prentice-Hall, 1992.

25. *Nemawashi* is an informal process of quietly laying the foundation for some proposed change or project, by talking to the people concerned, gathering support and feedback, and so forth. It is considered an important element in any major change, before any formal steps are taken, and successful *nemawashi* enables changes to be carried out with the consent of all sides. *Nemawashi* literally translates as "going around the roots," from *ne* (root) and *mawasu* (to go around something). Its original meaning is literal: digging around the roots of a tree, to prepare it for transplant.

26. *Honne* and *tatemae* are Japanese words used to describe recognized social phenomena. *Honne* refers to a person's true feelings and desires. These may be contrary to what is expected by society or what is required according to one's position and circumstances, and they are often kept hidden, except from one's closest friends. *Tatemae*, literally meaning "facade," is the behavior and opinions one displays in public. *Tatemae* is what is expected by society and required according to one's position and circumstances, and this may or may not match one's *honne*. This *honne/tatemae* divide is considered to be of paramount importance in Japanese culture. The very fact that the Japanese have single words for these concepts leads some Japanese experts to see this conceptualization as evidence of greater Japanese complexity and rigidity in etiquette and culture. *Honne* and *tatemae* are arguably a cultural necessity, resulting from a large number of people living in a relatively small island nation. Even with modern farming techniques, Japan today domestically produces only 39 percent of the food needed to feed its people, so close-knit cooperation and the avoidance of conflict remain of vital importance today, as they did in ancient times. For this reason, the Japanese tend to go to great lengths to avoid conflict, especially within the context of large groups. The conflict between *honne* and *giri* (social obligations) is one of the main topics of Japanese drama throughout the ages. In such dramas, the protagonist would typically have to choose between carrying out his obligations to his family or feudal lord and

pursuing a forbidden love affair or other personal interest. In the end, death would often be the only way out of the dilemma.

27. Edgar H. Schein, *Organizational Culture and Leadership*. San Francisco: Jossey-Bass, 1988.
28. "This company makes all its new employees climb Mount Fuji," *Business Insider*, Laura O'Reilly, May 5, 2015.
29. April Rabkin, "What is the sound of three hands clapping?," *Fast Company*, February 2012, pp. 79–98.

5 Communicating across cultures

MANAGEMENT CHALLENGE

The previous two chapters focused on understanding the cultural and organizational environments in which global managers work. The present chapter and the ones that follow build on this knowledge and introduce Stage III of developing *multicultural competence*, as suggested in Exhibit 1.3 in Chapter 1: building global management skills. We begin with cross-cultural communication. Language, communication, and shared meaning are the essence of good management. They are at the heart of effective organizations. In view of this, it is surprising how difficult it can be communicating with others, especially across cultures. Whatever our intent, we sometimes come across to others as impatient, condescending, and sometimes just rude. From a managerial standpoint, such behavior serves only to erect barriers to organizational success. To communicate effectively across cultures, managers need to understand the fundamental influences on both effective and ineffective communication, as well as strategies for reaching a higher level of mutual understanding between people.

CHAPTER OUTLINE

- Interpersonal communication — *page* 128
- Cultural screens on interpersonal communication — 130
- Culture, cognition, and communication — 132
- Culture and communication protocols — 141
- MANAGER'S NOTEBOOK: Communicating across cultures — 149
- Key terms — 155
- Discussion questions — 155
- Case: Roos Dekker, Global Healthcare — 156

APPLICATIONS

5.1 The fourth floor   *page* 134

5.2 Native and non-native speakers   135

5.3 Cultural logic in Brazil and Canada   139

5.4 Summer internship in Ecuador   142

5.5 Making apologies: Toyota and BP   147

5.6 Emotional displays: Germany and Spain   148

Namasté is a common greeting used on the Indian subcontinent. It literally means "I bow to you," and it is used as an expression of deep respect in India and Nepal by Hindus, Jains, and Buddhists. In these cultures, the word (from the ancient Sanskrit) is spoken at the beginning of a conversation, accompanied by a slight bow made with the hands pressed together, palms touching and fingers pointed upwards, in front of the chest. This silent gesture can also be performed wordlessly and carry the same meaning, as is often done at the close of a conversation. As such, *namasté* is a form of both verbal and nonverbal communication. When used appropriately, it signals to the parties to a conversation that the people involved likely understand something about prevailing social norms and values. They are one of "us," and a bond is easily formed. It may be only one word, but it carries significant symbolism.

Communication is all about conveying meaning to others. It is the principal way we reach out to others to exchange ideas and commodities, develop and dissolve relationships, and conduct business. Within one culture or language group, communication can often be problematic – particularly across age groups, geographic regions, and gender. These problems pale into insignificance, however, in comparison to the challenges of communicating across cultures. Not only do the principal communicators have different cultural backgrounds, they come from different organizations and must also work with other team members of employers who also have different backgrounds and expectations. Third parties to conversations (e.g., interpreters) can also add confusion as they attempt to provide clarity.

Simple and often unintended words, behaviors, signs, and symbols can lead to misunderstandings, embarrassment, conflict, and even lost business opportunities. Global managers understand this. *When managers are asked to identify their most serious challenge in the field, the response is almost universal: communicating effectively across cultures.*

We often hear what we want to hear, however. Our frames of reference and personal experiences – and even our worldviews – can all work to filter message transmission and reception by screening in or out what we will likely attend to and by attaching meanings to how messages are interpreted and dealt with. Financial analysts tend to pick up threads of conversation involving money, while sales managers pick up on market opportunities. In any cross-cultural exchange between managers from different regions, the principal purpose of communication is to seek understanding – to seek out ideas, information, customers, and sometimes even partnerships between the parties. Business in general and management in particular both rely on people's willingness and ability to convey meaning between managers, employees, partners, suppliers, investors, and customers. Indeed, it can be argued that most efforts to build or to understand organizations begin with an understanding of basic communication and exchange processes.

Interpersonal communication

Recognizing the importance and difficulty of cross-cultural communication, academics, consultants, and fellow managers have long sought to provide advice to those setting off for global assignments and foreign locations. Much of this advice focuses on learning the rules of the road when dealing with people from other cultures. Managers are told that communication is an interactive process between senders and receivers in which senders encode their messages into a medium and then transmit them through often noise-infested airways to receivers, who, in turn, decode the messages, interpret them, and respond appropriately. Throughout this process, cultural differences and potential cross-cultural misunderstandings are typically subsumed under a broad category of noise. The more a manager can reduce this noise, the greater the message clarity.

Although this advice is useful as far as it goes, it neglects what we consider to be two major impediments to effective communication: attention and interpretation. In other words, messages are effective only to the extent that recipients are both paying attention to them and capable of processing the information in ways that facilitate common meaning. While some may lump these challenges into the general category of "noise," we suggest that in the realm of multicultural communication such a catch-all category can easily lead managers to overlook two of the more critical influences on effective message construction, transmission, understanding, and response.

We suggest here that, in order to significantly enhance communication effectiveness across borders, simple encode–noise–decode models must be augmented with a deeper understanding of the processes underlying them. We further argue that many of these processes do not occur within culturally complex black boxes; in fact, they are often relatively easy for managers to identify and understand if they know what they are looking for.

To this end, we begin with a look at how culture and cultural differences often screen the ways in which people create, send, receive, and interpret messages. As a starting point, we make use of the attention–interpretation–action model, or AIA

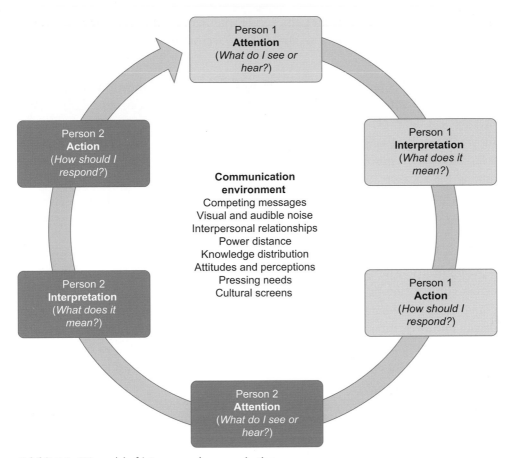

Exhibit 5.1 AIA model of interpersonal communication
Source: Adapted from Luciara Nardon, Richard M. Steers, and Carlos Sanchez-Runde, "Seeking common ground: strategies for enhancing multicultural communication," *Organizational Dynamics*, 40(2) (2011), pp. 85–95.

model, to illustrate the fundamental processes used by managers to communicate (see Exhibit 5.1).[1] As discussed in greater detail below, this model highlights three key ingredients in effective interpersonal communication.

1. Attention. First, when messages are sent, recipients must notice them – that is, they must select out the intended messages from a barrage of other often simultaneous messages for particular attention. The basic question here is: "What do I see or hear?" Hence the challenge for the global manager is how first to capture the attention of the other party.

2. Interpretation. Second, once a message is selected out for attention, the recipients must interpret or decode it. Here the questions are: "What does this message mean to me? How do I make sense out of it?" Again, cultural differences can play a crucial role.

3. Action. Finally, the recipient must decide whether or not to reply and, if so, how to construct and transmit a response. The question in this stage is: "What is an appropriate response?"

Throughout this process, numerous factors in the communication environment can serve to reinforce, attract, or distract attention towards or away from some messages at the expense of others. These factors include other competing messages, the particular languages in use, visual and audible noise, the nature of interpersonal relationships, the power distance between speakers, the degree of shared knowledge among the speakers, attitudes and perceptions, and pressing needs as experienced by both parties. In addition to attracting or deflecting attention, these factors can often serve to influence message interpretation and analysis, as well as message construction and delivery mechanisms.

Thus, while the traditional encode–noise–decode model can be helpful, we prefer an AIA approach as a means of better identifying the challenges facing managers working across cultures. In our view, this approach gives weight not just to what people are doing but also to what they are thinking. It also lays the groundwork for looking more deeply into why, from a manager's viewpoint, it is easier to communicate with some "foreign" counterparts than others. Much of this difference resides in the ways that cultural differences influence the communication process from start to finish.

Cultural screens on interpersonal communication

At its core, communication is all about conveying meaning to others – not just words. Business in general and management in particular both rely on people's willingness and ability to convey meaning between managers, employees, partners, suppliers, investors, and customers. Language and culture not only provide a guide as to what is acceptable behavior and what is unacceptable; they focus attention on different parts of the exchange and provide parameters for interpreting information. Understanding the ways in which culture guides attention and meaning creation is a key component in creating understanding across cultures. Clearly, moreover, the greater this understanding, the greater is the opportunity for the effective exchange of ideas and subsequent business success.

We focus here on the two critical influences mentioned above: two interrelated cultural screens, or lenses, that can affect both interpersonal interactions in general and multicultural communications in particular:[2]

- Culturally mediated cognitions. The first screen involves cultural influences on individual cognitions surrounding communication episodes – that is, how people and messages are often evaluated and processed in the minds of senders and receivers alike.

- **Culturally mandated protocols.** The second screen involves cultural influences on communication protocols, or required behaviors, such as how we construct or shape our messages in ways that may be culturally consistent for us but, we hope, not problematic for our intended receivers.

These two screens often emerge as a result of cultural differences between senders and receivers, and they can have important implications for how various parties to a conversation receive, interpret, and respond to messages (Exhibit 5.2). Cultural screens can perhaps be best understood as part of the communication environment; they represent potential impediments or barriers in the basic AIA model discussed above. In other words, culture routinely influences both how we think and how we behave, and nowhere is this influence more evident than with respect to communication processes. As a result, we suggest that managers committed to improving multicultural communication need to dig deeper and work harder to understand the underlying cultural forces at play in interpersonal communication.

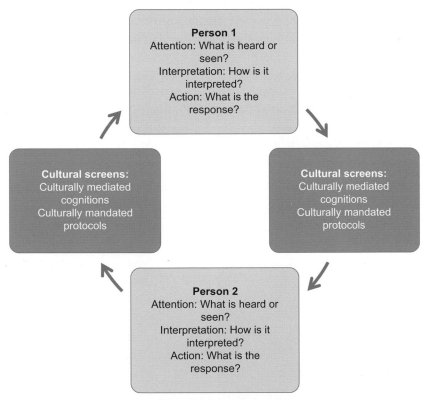

Exhibit 5.2 Cultural screens on interpersonal communication
Source: Adapted from Luciara Nardon, Richard M. Steers, and Carlos Sanchez-Runde, "Seeking common ground: strategies for enhancing multicultural communication," *Organizational Dynamics*, 40(2) (2011), pp. 85–95.

Culture, cognition, and communication

As noted earlier, when people receive messages from others they routinely screen and interpret what they hear and see to determine how to respond. Sometimes they will categorize messages based on their sources ("Is the source believable?"). At other times they will prioritize messages based on the degree to which they think the messages are important ("Do I need to respond immediately or can this wait?"). Such processes require both senders and receivers to pay attention to intended messages; they require cognition. At least four commonly used culturally mediated cognitions can be identified: language and linguistic structures, selective perception, cognitive evaluation, and cultural logic (see Exhibit 5.3).

Language and linguistic structures: choose your words carefully

Consider the challenges posed by language differences, or, more specifically, language competencies. When two American tourists were traveling on a bus in Stuttgart recently and one of them sneezed, a German passenger turned around and

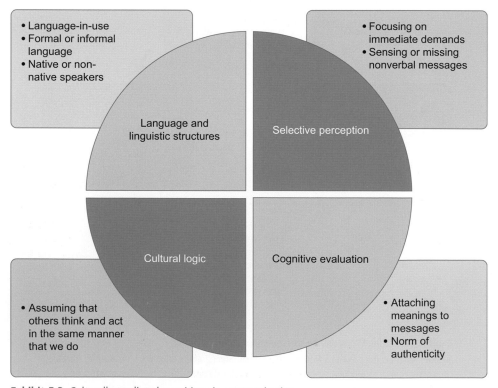

Exhibit 5.3 Culturally mediated cognitions in communication

said, "*Gesundheit.*" One visitor looked at the other and noted, "How nice that they speak English here."[3]

Whether it is correctly or poorly used, language is central to human communication. It plays an important role in initiating conversations and conducting most aspects of human affairs. It facilitates socialization, organization, and management. It also allows us to express our feelings and facilitate problem-solving by thinking, both silently and vocally. Moreover, it is due to language that we are able to retain our histories, passing knowledge from one generation to the next. In this regard, language and linguistic structures (i.e., the manner in which words, grammar, syntax, and the meaning of words are organized and used) are closely linked to cultures, because, while culture provides the meanings and meaning-making mechanisms underlying existence, language provides the symbols to facilitate the expression of such meanings.

Language is always a potential impediment to effective cross-cultural communication. In this regard, there are two issues that are worthy of note. First, which language should be used in a conversation? Some argue that English is increasingly becoming the *lingua franca* of global business; as such, everyone should speak English.[4] Not everyone agrees with this, obviously. Indeed, both Mandarin Chinese and Spanish have more native speakers around the world than English. Why shouldn't everyone speak Chinese or Spanish? Others have suggested that the language to be spoken should be determined by who has the money – consistent with the oft-cited phrase "Serve the customer." If the French are buying, it is logical for both parties to speak French. This debate may never be resolved, since, among other things, mass conversions to a foreign language can threaten the cultural integrity of a country or region.

For managers living largely in the English-speaking parts of the world, there is a second challenge. Which English are we speaking? For example, Norman Schur has compiled a British-English/American-English dictionary that contains nearly 5,000 entries that are translated from one version of English to the other.[5] We are told that to "table" an item means to submit it for discussion in British-English, but to remove it from discussion in American-English. "Lifts" are "elevators," "companies" are "corporations," "corporations" are "municipalities," "sheltered trades" are "domestic monopolies," and "to hire" means "to lease." We are further told that, in the United Kingdom, "shares" are "stocks" and "stocks" are "government bonds." We are told that a clerk in the United States is pronounced "clark", and that schedule is pronounced "shed-ule." Spellings can also differ ("behavior" or "behaviour"). Furthermore, this is all before we recognize that many sectors of both cultures often speak differently and use very different words to communicate. If this were not enough, we must remember that people in Canada, New Zealand, Singapore, and other locales are different still in their choice and use of "English" words.

Languages and their associated linguistic structures are also intricately intertwined with the cognitive processes that affect managerial and employee behaviors, however. Italian film director Federico Fellini observed, "A different language is not just a dictionary of words, sounds, and syntax. It is a different way of interpreting reality."[6] Languages can also vary considerably in their precision. Take English and Chinese, for example. Like other European languages, English consists of over 1 million words, each of which has a relatively constant and precise (though certainly not universal) meaning. By contrast, Chinese is an ideographic language that consists of only about a quarter as many words – or, more accurately, characters. As a result, each character must "work harder"– that is, Chinese characters create meaning through the images and concepts they stimulate, not through dictionary-type definitions. Everything that is written is open to multiple interpretations. Often one Chinese symbol will contain eight or ten different meanings. As a result, using nonverbal signals to support verbal messages takes on added significance in creating shared meanings compared to the West.

APPLICATION 5.1 The fourth floor

Consider how even direct and clear translations of words can still carry different meanings and hence lead to confusion. When a group of Americans attend a meeting scheduled on the "fourth" floor of a New York office complex, they in fact go to the fourth floor (or level in the building), since Americans typically use the terms "ground" and "first" floors interchangeably. Not so the British and most Europeans, who distinguish between the ground and first floors and would thus likely go to the fifth level of the building in London, Paris, or Berlin. When foreign travelers attend a meeting on the "fourth" floor of a Seoul office building, even the more experienced travelers can become puzzled. While the number four (pronounced *sa* in Korean using traditional Chinese characters) is not in itself unlucky, as "many" believe, its oral pronunciation sounds very similar to the word for "death" – something that is seldom, if ever, discussed in local society. As a result, many South Korean buildings either use the English letter "F" ("fourth") for this floor or they simply don't have one. (Note that many older high-rise buildings in the United States don't have a thirteenth floor for similar reasons.)

Think about it . . .

(1) What does something as simple as the location of the fourth floor in a building tell us about cross-cultural communication processes?
(2) Can you identify a similar example from your own culture in which a particular word carries an entirely different meaning elsewhere?
(3) What can managers do to avoid similar, but potentially more serious, misunderstandings in interpersonal communication?

Languages also provide subtle yet powerful cues about what to account for in our dealings with other people (respect, social distance, and so forth). For example, languages vary in the number and type of forms of address available to people when meeting others. In English, for example, there is typically only one word for "you." Native speakers use this same word when speaking to almost any person, regardless of age, gender, seniority, or position. On the other hand, Romance languages, such as Spanish and French, distinguish between a formal and an informal mode of address (*usted/tú* in Spanish, *vous/tu* in French). In Japanese, there are many equivalent words for "you," depending on someone's age, seniority, gender, family affiliation, and position. The implication of these linguistic differences is that, depending on the language being spoken, managers must attend to different cues and focus on different aspects of their context and message.

Those who are not conscious of these differences risk missing key information about situations facing them, leading to further communication errors. Needless to say, knowledge of the other party's language helps develop understanding that goes beyond the content of the messages exchanged. Indeed, learning the language of the host country is one of the most common recommendations offered by expatriates to young managers for understanding a different culture.

Finally, the choice of language in cross-cultural conversations can serve as a major impediment to successful job completion, as, for example, when everyone in a team or organization is required to speak in the dominant language.

APPLICATION 5.2 Native and non-native speakers

Consider what happens when a native English-speaking supervisor meets with a global team or work group consisting largely of non-native English speakers. More specifically, consider what happens when an Anglo-American supervisor from California meets with her Eastern European product development team, consisting of members from Romania, Slovakia, and Croatia. (We use English as an example here, but any other language would yield similar results.) As illustrated in Exhibit 5.4, our native English-speaking supervisor will likely have an easier time in the exchange than her Eastern European counterparts. This, in turn, might lead the supervisor to conclude that the non-native speakers are less educated, less intelligent, less committed, more obstinate, and so forth. At the same time, the European non-English speakers may face numerous frustrations trying to make themselves heard and understood, with potentially serious, if unintended, consequences. Their lack of a broad vocabulary can often lead to the use of simple sentences to discuss complex issues, with predictable results. Moreover, when two non-native speakers talk together in a third language (e.g., English), the possibilities for confusion multiply even further.

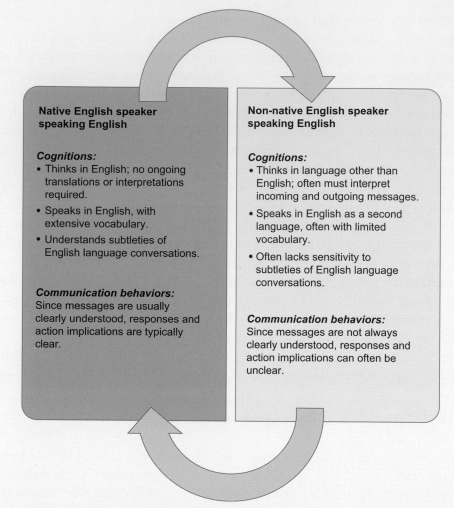

Exhibit 5.4 Native and non-native speakers

Think about it . . .

(1) When a native speaker meets with a non-native speaker to negotiate a contract, what can each side do to ensure an open and accurate exchange of ideas? Explain.

(2) If English is increasingly becoming the international language of business, why bother to learn a second language, such as German, Chinese, or Spanish?

Selective perception: eye of the beholder

Since people cannot simultaneously focus on all the events surrounding them at a given time, they use selective perception to choose what to focus on and what to ignore. In other words, they make mental choices about what is important, useful, or threatening, and focus their mental powers on these particular issues. As such, the information that becomes important is in the eye of the beholder – the information he or she is expecting or looking for – while other potentially useful information is often left by the wayside.

Throughout this process, cultural differences can play a key role. Consider an example dealing with nonverbal communication. While nonverbal communication is commonly used throughout much of Asia as a way to convey information with subtlety (e.g., rejecting a request without anyone losing face), many in the West simply fail to notice it. They are not looking for it. In fact, many managers in the West much prefer to hear and speak plainly and publicly – "Say what you mean, and mean what you say." As a result, Asians often believe they have communicated a message (nonverbally) when in reality it was not received, while Westerners believe no communication was forthcoming since they did not hear any words. Both sides can experience frustration. To overcome such problems, communications expert Richard Lewis reminds us: "Silence is a form of speech, so don't interrupt it."[7]

Selective perception and nonverbal communication can be seen in many different ways. What may be comfortable to one person may be offensive to another. Consider the plight of a visiting British professor who was reading to his poetry class at the prestigious Ain Shams University in Cairo. Reflecting on what he was reading, the professor became so relaxed that he inadvertently leaned back in his chair and crossed his legs, thereby revealing the sole of one of his shoes to his students. Obviously, in much of the Muslim world, this is a serious insult. The following morning the Cairo newspapers carried banner headlines about the student demonstrations that resulted. They denounced what they saw as British arrogance and demanded that the professor be sent home immediately.

Cognitive evaluation: interpreting words and actions

When people see or hear something, they have a tendency to categorize the information so they can make judgments about its authenticity, accuracy, and utility. They try to relate it to other events and actions so they can make sense out of it and know how to respond. This process is called cognitive evaluation, and culture can play a major role. For example, research has shown that Americans, raised in an individualistic society, often rely on the isolated properties of people or objects they are examining in order to attach meaning or enhance understanding. As a result, when they see an individual they tend to mentally classify him or her as a man or woman, black or white, professional or blue-collar, and so forth. By contrast, Chinese, raised in a more collectivist environment, tend to classify people on the basis of criteria that emphasize relationships and contexts. As a result, they are more likely to see someone first as a member of a particular group, clan, or organization, instead of focusing on his or her individual characteristics.

At the same time, people tend to have better recall of information when it is consistent with their cultural knowledge and values. For example, many managers from mastery-oriented cultures tend to recall the specific successes of their subordinates that involved sales or financial achievements, but not their interpersonal or team-building successes. In more harmony-oriented cultures, managers tend to recall more about their subordinates' interpersonal or team-building successes, regardless of their sales or financial successes.

When inferring the mental states of other people, research indicates that several cultures in North America and Western Europe emphasize a norm of authenticity (i.e., a belief that external actions and emotional displays are, or should be, generally consistent with internal states), while East and Southeast Asian societies often tend to consider such beliefs as immature, impolite, and sometimes bizarre.[8] For example, "speaking one's mind" or "telling it like it is" frequently appears in a positive light to many Westerners, but not to many Asians. Many in Asia give more importance in communication processes to what is left unsaid instead of what is said in open and direct ways, while the opposite tends to apply in many Western societies. In this regard, note that many wedding ceremonies in the West contain the admonition to the audience "Speak now or forever hold your peace." In other words, speak up if you have something to say. No such statement is heard in most Asian ceremonies.

Finally, reasoning processes also play out differently in communication across cultures. In other words, when people face the possibility of alternative interpretations of specific events (e.g., the success of a work team), they will almost invariably choose the interpretation that is most consistent with their own cultural outlook. For example, managers from highly individualistic cultures will typically attribute team success to the team leader's skills and efforts, while managers from more collectivistic cultures will typically attribute it to the skills and efforts of the entire team. Likewise, managers in individualistic cultures will often attribute team failure to the team members, while managers from more collectivistic cultures will accept blame for such failures. These examples illustrate the power of cognitive evaluations in terms of what is said and what remains unsaid, and how both are interpreted.

Cultural logic: assumptions about shared meanings

Interpersonal communication is an interactive process, requiring two or more people to exchange thoughts, ideas, emotions, questions, proposals, and so forth in an effort to find common ground. It is at the heart of how we do business, negotiate contracts, lead groups, work with team members, and motivate employees. In this regard, one of the aspects of communicating with people from different countries is the cultural logic that underlies any message.[9] (Some refer to this as "cultural logics," to emphasize the fact that this process consists of a series of logical assumptions that do not necessarily represent a unified whole – that is, cultures have a variety of logics relating to different aspects of social interaction.) When people converse with one another, they often rely on these culture-based logical assumptions to facilitate the conversation.

Cultural logic is the process of using one's own assumptions about normative behavior to interpret the messages and actions of others, thereby hypothesizing about their motives and intentions. It is the process by which people attribute meaning to the words and actions of others on the basis of the local meanings embedded within their own culture. Cultural logic provides people with a system of assumptions about what is mutually known and understood among individuals (i.e., a common ground). People often rely on this logic to facilitate communication and reduce what needs to be said to a manageable level, since it is often too difficult and time-consuming for people to express all the thoughts and assumptions behind everything they say. A shared cultural logic helps people fill the gaps left by what is unsaid, thereby facilitating the process of creating a shared meaning. It also allows for simplified and rapid communication. When moving across cultures, however, there is often an assumption of a common knowledge that, in fact, is not common.

APPLICATION 5.3 Cultural logic in Brazil and Canada

To illustrate how cultural logic works, consider a recent interchange between a Canadian sales representative and her potential Brazilian customer. In order to schedule an appointment with Sergio, Sarah contacted him to propose a meeting in her office the following Monday at 9:00 in the morning. In doing so, she created a mental image of the message she was trying to convey, using her own cultural logic (in this case, relying on her Canadian emphasis on punctuality). To do so, however, she required some form of verbal shorthand – that is, she needed to make some assumptions about what was in Sergio's mind, or else her message might become excessively long and risk being ignored. To this end, she assumed that Sergio would make the same assumptions about the use of words that she was making. For example, she would have assumed that "9:00" meant 9:00, not later in the morning, when she had other appointments. She also assumed that Sergio would understand her message, and his agreement to the meeting indicated that he would arrive at 9:00 a.m. sharp.

While Sarah was making her assumptions, however, so too was Sergio, and his assumptions about the message differed considerably. Following his own cultural logic (particularly the Brazilian perception of time), Sergio assumed that "9:00" was only a targeted or approximate time, and that slippage in the time schedule was perfectly acceptable, since he had other commitments around the same time. He further assumed that Sarah was also flexible and that she would agree with his loose interpretation of when the meeting would begin. After all, since she had invited him, she must have understood his culture.

The end result of this episode is predictable. Using their own very different cultural logics, both Sarah and Sergio ran the risk of being disappointed or frustrated when they met. Had both parties – or even one party – understood their variability in cultural logic, perhaps the results would have turned out differently. Instead, due to a miscommunication regarding what time the meeting should actually take place, Sarah risked coming away from the meeting thinking that Sergio was unreliable; while Sergio risked concluding that Sarah was too rigid to base a partnership on. The result could easily have been a lost business opportunity.

Think about it . . .

(1) Is either Sarah or Sergio correct in this situation? Why or why not?
(2) How could this misunderstanding with respect to time have been handled differently?
(3) Have you personally experienced a similar event in which differences in cultural logic led to conflict or confusion?

Together, these four cultural screens on cognition – language and linguistic structures, selective perception, cognitive evaluation, and cultural logic – are likely to influence the communication process. Referring back to the AIA model discussed above, languages help determine the structures and meanings underlying intended messages; selective perceptions guide people's attention to particular parts of intended messages; cognitive evaluations guide the process of attaching meaning to received messages; and cultural logic guides senders' choices of what needs to be communicated and receivers' interpretation of the message. Managers who understand how these cultural screens can mediate the process of attention–interpretation–message creation can thus improve their chances of finding the common ground necessary for effective communication and productive exchanges.

Culture and communication protocols

All cultures and subcultures foster socio-normative beliefs and values that guide members' thoughts and actions. These beliefs include what members can and can't do as well as what they should and shouldn't do. This is a world of obligations, responsibilities, and privileges, which together form the interpersonal foundations of a culture. Not surprisingly, these norms and values influence how we choose to converse not just with members of our own culture but with members of others as well. Included here are a variety of expected communication protocols, or behaviors, such as appropriate topics for discussion, message formatting, conversational formalities, and acceptable behaviors (see Exhibit 5.5).[10] Each of these is likely to influence what people attend to in a message, how they interpret it, and how they respond.

Appropriate topics for discussion: hold your tongue

What people can and cannot talk about varies by culture. Consider just one example that happened to one of the authors recently. When asked by a South Korean friend

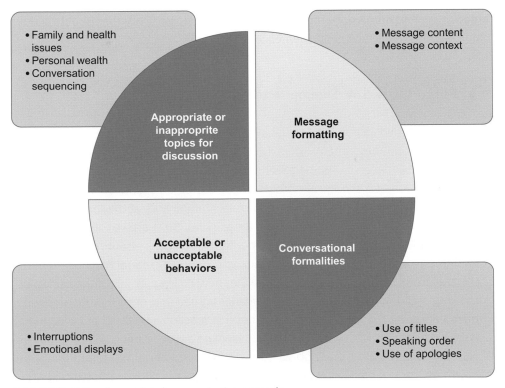

Exhibit 5.5 Culturally mandated communication protocols

how the family was doing, the visitor replied that his younger brother had recently died. The Korean friend looked puzzled, and there was an awkward moment of silence. Then he responded, "Did you see the baseball game last night?" This was obviously not a subject he wished to discuss.

In some cultures, it is perfectly acceptable to ask about one's family; indeed, it is often considered impolite not to ask. In other cultures, however, this topic is off limits. Likewise, some cultures prefer not to talk about illness or bad fortune, perhaps in the belief that not talking about something will make it less likely to happen. Other cultures do talk about healthcare issues, sometimes including the topic of serious illness or even death; others resist doing so, as just noted. People in some cultures may also brag to anyone who will listen about how much money they've made or how they used questionable tactics to make a sale; others prefer not to discuss this, even if true. It is typically inappropriate to discuss money in France or personal matters in England. Moreover, people are expected to talk about themselves in South Asia and Latin America, but not in Germany or the Netherlands.

Equally important here is the ordering or sequencing of conversational topics. While many Western managers believe in avoiding "small talk" and getting right down to business ("Time is money!"), managers in South America and East and Southeast Asia typically believe that conversations must first be warmed up with broad or general discussions on topics other than business. Only then should serious conversations about business commence.

APPLICATION 5.4 Summer internship in Ecuador

IESE MBA student Shipa Patel, originally from India and raised in Europe, spent her summer business internship in Mindo, Ecuador, working for a non-profit ecological foundation.[11] As she tells her story, the very first day of her arrival in Mindo, she realized she knew nothing about the organization, its workings, its people and its context. She felt like a complete stranger and, at the same time, did not feel she had a lot of time to explore these issues. So she asked the managing director of the foundation to introduce her to its members, about forty Ecuadorians. She thought it would be a good idea to convene a general meeting so that she could explain her work plans and ask her new colleagues about the principal challenges of their jobs. The general manager agreed and most members joined the meeting. At the meeting, however, her first reaction was that her colleagues were hiding things from her. They did not seem receptive to her questions; things were not clearly stated; and nobody took a proactive stance. She found that she had to do most of the talking, while the others basically nodded with sympathetic faces. Under the pressure of time, what seemed to Shipa to be an efficient approach to communication was not actually working.

After the meeting, she kept wondering what had gone wrong. Almost by chance, she began talking with members in the street, on her way to and from work, and during evenings at the local coffee shop. It surprised her that people were so forthcoming and vocal in their opinions, after their comparative silence in the meeting. She soon realized that they felt much more comfortable communicating one-to-one, in a non-formal setting. Talking in front of a meeting audience was a communication style alien to most of the members. Then she realized that she had put her colleagues in a very uncomfortable position by asking them to voice their concerns in front of others. She also possibly intimidated them by taking notes; this was just an efficient way of recording impressions and ideas, but they felt threatened by this and were extremely reserved in the little they said.

So Shipa changed her tactics and found that one-on-one conversations outside the office were extremely informative and could eventually develop a basic view of the organization and its problems. Yes, it paid a price in terms of time and work efficiency, but she finally got what she needed. Her only wish was that she could have understood earlier that when people travel to places that work differently, they may need to change their expectations of accomplishments in order to get things going. They may lose some efficiency but they may still be effective overall.

On reflection, other cultural factors were at play in the first meeting, too. People often defaulted to the opinion of those higher up in the ranks, and nobody actually argued against what other members contributed. In fact, the members only attended the meeting in the first place because the manager asked them to do so.

Commenting on her experience, Shipa concluded:

This experience improved my understanding of different communication dynamics and challenged my preconceptions about information gathering and sharing. It is important to adapt to new contexts, changing your own behavior as needed, even eventually at the price of efficiency. Personal exchanges, in pairs or small groups, often take a lot of time and patience on the part of the outsider, but it is an integral part of integrating in a closely-knit community. It is a normal part of the ritual of relationship-building in some cultures, and an important precursor to effective communication that will then eventually happen.

Think about it . . .

(1) In your view, what are the principal reasons why Shipa's Ecuadorian colleagues did not open up to her?

(2) As a foreigner and stranger, how could Shipa have approached the situation better in the first place?

(3) What are the lessons here for foreigners and strangers – and new global managers – traveling to a new location?

Message formatting: content and context

Communication is so pervasive in our everyday lives and so intertwined with culture that some researchers argue that it is impossible to separate communication from culture. For them, culture *is* communication. For instance, noted anthropologist Edward Hall points out that people communicate with each other through behaviors, not just words, suggesting that cultural assumptions in general are often part of a silent language used to convey meaning without words. Silent communication is the use of nonverbal or visual communication (e.g., facial expressions, gestures, the use of personal space, opulent surroundings, etc.) to convey messages to senders or receivers alike. Such messages are typically subtle in nature and can be difficult to notice unless one is looking for them. Senders usually intend such messages to be received or discovered by others, however. In fact, to someone who can "read" these silent messages, they can sometimes scream very loudly. Or as British communication consultant Richard D. Lewis says, "whatever the culture, there's a tongue in our head. Some use it, some hold it, and some bite it. For the French it is a rapier, thrusting in attack; the English, using it defensively, mumble a vague and confusing reply; for Italians and Spaniards it is an instrument of eloquence; Finns and East Asians throw you with their constructive silence."[12]

The importance of silent, or nonverbal, communication can be found in a recent finding that *verbal communication typically carries less than 35 percent of the intended meaning in two-way conversations*. In some cultures, this percentage is even lower. This suggests that nonverbal characteristics become extremely important when communicating across cultures. To make matters worse, research also suggests that, when verbal and nonverbal messages contradict each other, we are more likely to believe the latter.[13] The meaning of the message is not explicit in the content of the message, and has to be sought out.[14]

As was discussed in Chapter 3, Hall's model of cultural differences suggests that this difference lies in how much message context surrounds the message content.[15] Hall distinguishes between high- and low-context cultures, as shown in Exhibit 5.6. In low-context cultures, such as those in Germany, Scandinavia, and the United States, the context surrounding the message is far less important than the message

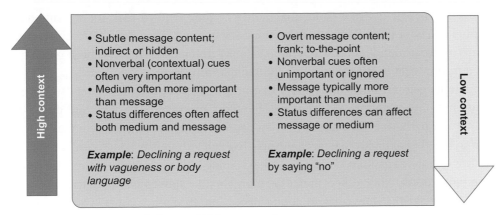

Exhibit 5.6 Communication in low- and high-context cultures

itself. The context provides the listener with little information relating to the intended message. As a result, speakers must rely more heavily on providing greater message clarity, as well as other guarantees such as written documents and information-rich advertising. Language precision is critical, while assumed understandings, innuendos, and body language frequently count for little.

By contrast, in high-context cultures, such as those found in many parts of Asia and the Middle East, the context in which the message is conveyed – that is, the social cues surrounding the message – is often as important as the message itself. Indeed, the way something is said can even be more important in communicating a message than the actual words that are used. Here, communication is based on long-term interpersonal relationships, mutual trust, and personal reputations. People know the people they are talking with, and reading someone's face becomes an important – and necessary – art. As a result, less needs to be said or written down. These subtleties in communication patterns often go unnoticed by many outsiders, who listen very carefully to every word that is spoken – only to miss the real message.

For example, in ethnically diverse Nigeria, communication styles vary considerably across regions. In the southwest, where the people are largely from the Yoruba tribe, people's communication employs proverbs, sayings, and songs to enrich the meaning of what they say. This is especially true when speaking their native language, although many of the same characteristics have been carried into their English-language usage. The Yoruba often use humor to prevent boredom during long meetings or serious discussions. They believe that embedding humor in their message guarantees that what they say is not readily forgotten. By contrast, Nigerians who live in other regions of the country, including the Igbo and Hausa, tend to speak more directly. Nigerians also make extensive use of nonverbal behavior (e.g., facial expressions) to communicate their views. In discussions, Nigerians frequently begin with a general idea and then slowly move to the specific, often using a somewhat circuitous route. Their logic is often contextual – that is, they tend to look for the rationale behind behavior and attempt to understand the context. Thus, behavior is viewed in terms of its surrounding context, and not simply in terms of what has been observed. As a result, what is not said is often more important than what is.

Experienced managers understand that how a message is constructed can have a profound impact on how it is received. Should a message be explicit and direct, or subtle and perhaps even obtuse? To what degree should messages be communicated through verbal or nonverbal mechanisms? To what extent is message content more – or less – important than message context? Some cultures emphasize rigid written communication, while others prefer the more flexible spoken communication. Some cultures prefer that messages from outsiders come through "proper" channels (e.g., up the formal chain of command), while others prefer the use of informal channels (e.g., close associates or friends).

The principal challenge for managers here is sending clear and meaningful messages that are understood by other parties without offending them. An equally important challenge, however, is conveying these messages in culturally appropriate ways that may be unfamiliar to the message senders. For example, a typical Western manager with little experience using nonverbal communication techniques runs the risk of doing more harm than good when trying to be culturally sensitive. Nonverbal communication means much more than being silent or making awkward facial expressions. It is an art form to be studied and practiced, again suggesting the importance of ongoing learning and reflective experience.

Conversational formalities: understand etiquette

Conversational formalities encompass formal or implicit guidelines and rules governing what constitutes acceptable or preferred formal conversational etiquette. Every culture places constraints on how, when, and where we speak to others, and the knowledgeable manager can benefit from such understanding. Such formalities include the use of titles, the manner in which ideas or proposals are presented, and the role of apologies.

It is easy to say that some cultures are more formal than others, but it is necessary to ask what this means. There is typically an underlying purpose in the use of formalities. The use of titles, for example, can represent a sign of respect or a sign of power – not necessarily the same thing. Similarly, an absence of titles can indicate an egalitarian culture that eschews artificial status-based boundaries or a close relationship between parties. Clearly, the informed manager needs to understand these differences.

Conversational formalities also include knowing when and where apologies are required. Formal apologies are used throughout much of East and Southeast Asia to restore harmony after an unpleasant incident or crisis. They demonstrate empathy and acceptance of responsibility. By contrast, apologies in many Western countries are often used to admit guilt, and, as a result, are used only sporadically.

APPLICATION 5.5 Making apologies: Toyota and BP

To understand how this works, consider the public apology by Toyota CEO Akio Toyoda before a US congressional investigation over a series of safety problems involving the company's cars. Toyoda drew widespread attention, because few people could remember when a Western CEO had done such a thing. Toyoda apologized not only to his customers but also to stockholders for the company's declining profits and to employees for recent lay-offs. He observed: "In the past few months, our customers have started to feel uncertain about the safety of Toyota's vehicles, and I take full responsibility for that. Today, I would like to explain to the American people, as well as our customers in the US and around the world, how seriously Toyota takes the quality and safety of its vehicles." Japan's *Asahi Shimbun*, one of Japan's largest newspapers, wrote in an editorial that Toyoda's testimony "not only determines Toyota's fate, but may affect all Japanese companies and consumer confidence in their products. President Toyoda has a heavy load on his shoulders."

In the West, such behavior by a CEO is often interpreted as a sign of weakness or lack of confidence – or, worse still, acceptance of legal responsibility. Witness the recent actions by BP CEO Tony Hayward, also before a US congressional investigation, following an oil spill in the Gulf of Mexico. Hayward offered a tepid apology and downplayed the long-term environmental implications. Some of his statements were: "I think the environmental impact of this disaster is likely to have been very, very modest"; "There is no one who wants this over more than I do. I would like my life back"; and "What the hell did we do to deserve this?" He also stressed that many other companies were also involved in the oil leak, not just BP. Two crises, and two very different public responses.

Think about it . . .

(1) Why is the symbolism underlying the apologies from these two companies so different?

(2) Should either Toyota or BP have handled this situation differently? Why or why not?

(3) In working across cultures, what is your opinion of the proper role of apologies? When are they appropriate and when are they inappropriate? Why?

Acceptable behaviors: behave yourself

Finally, cultures often place constraints and expectations on what are considered to be acceptable behaviors that accompany interpersonal interactions. For example, research has shown that managers in North America are often expected or encouraged to be assertive and take the initiative in conversations; in much of Asia, by contrast, managers are often expected to remain silent and wait for an invitation to speak. Managers in North America are often allowed to leave a conversation once the main topic is finished; managers in Spain are generally expected to linger awhile and talk about other things before departing. Many North American managers tend to communicate linearly, with explicit links between topics and ideas, favoring a planned approach to communication; many Asian managers prefer a more nonlinear approach, following a circular pattern of communication; and many managers from the Mediterranean region tend to favor a zigzag approach, in which tangential ideas may be explored and elaborated before returning to the main point.

Moreover, it is not uncommon for more than one manager to speak at the same time throughout much of Latin Europe, while managers in Northern Europe are more likely to wait until another speaker finishes. Conversations in much of Latin America tend to have very few lapses of silence – indeed, silence or "dead air" often makes such people uncomfortable, forcing them to speak again. By contrast, silent periods are very common in East and Southeast Asia, and few feel uncomfortable.

Finally, disagreements throughout much of Asia are often communicated with silence; disagreements in Spain are often communicated through emotional out-bursts; and disagreements in Northern Europe tend to be clearly, calmly, and directly stated and discussed. Similarly, praise is a common motivational strategy for many supervisors in North America, but is typically reserved only for extraordinary accomplishments in Russia. In France and Indonesia, by contrast, praise is sometimes considered offensive to employees because it suggests that the supervisor was surprised that the employees had done so well.

APPLICATION 5.6 Emotional displays: Germany and Spain

Differences can also be seen in what are considered to be acceptable displays of emotions. Consider a recent example of a Spanish manager assigned to work in Germany. The day after she arrived in Germany, she received news that a close relative had suddenly died. The woman was emotionally upset and burst into tears. She was appalled by the lack of sensitivity of her German colleagues, who did not inquire about what had happened or provide emotional support. On the other hand, her German colleagues were surprised by her reaction and thought she was immature and unprofessional. Thus, while outward displays of emotions are often acceptable and even expected at times in Spain, these same behaviors are often considered inappropriate, and taking interest in a colleague's personal affairs can be deemed rude and unprofessional in Germany.

Think about it . . .

(1) Who is right here? Should the Germans have been more sensitive and understanding of the Spanish woman's misfortune, or should she have been more respectful of the local culture? Why?
(2) Can you identify a particular emotional display that is inappropriate in your own culture? Why is it inappropriate?

Cultural protocols therefore serve as a very useful tool in facilitating communication both within and between cultures. It is through these protocols that people signal what parts of the message are important and how they should be interpreted. They also guide message senders by providing a repertoire of acceptable responses depending upon the situation. Ignorance of these simple mechanisms is often blamed for much of the noise and miscommunication across cultures. In this regard, managers who understand these required behaviors are better able to focus attention on salient comments and events, make more sense out of the messages they receive, and craft more effective replies and responses in their global endeavors.

MANAGER'S NOTEBOOK

Communicating across cultures

What did we learn in this chapter? In any cross-cultural exchange between managers from different regions, the principal purpose of communication is to seek common ground – to seek out ideas, information, customers, and sometimes even partnerships between the parties. But communications are effective only to the extent that recipients are both paying attention to the message and capable of processing the information in ways that facilitate common meaning.

To better understand this, the attention–interpretation–action model was introduced that highlights three key ingredients in effective interpersonal communication: attention, interpretation, and message (or response). Cultural screens are potential impediments or barriers in the basic AIA process. Two cultural screens that affect both interpersonal interactions in general and multicultural communications in particular were discussed. These screens often emerge as a result of cultural differences between senders and receivers, and can have important implications for how various parties to a conversation receive, interpret, and respond to messages. The first screen involves cultural influences on individual cognitions surrounding communication episodes – that is, how people and messages are often evaluated and processed in the minds of senders and receivers alike. The second involves cultural influences on communication protocols, or required behaviors, such as how we construct or shape our messages in ways that may be culturally consistent for us but, hopefully, not problematic for our intended receivers.

Consider the following dilemma: You are a partner in a small, but global, electronics firm that does business primarily in Western Europe and East Asia. You are trying to sell your IT services to two small companies, one in Spain and one in South Korea. When you try to telephone each of the presidents of the two small firms, however, no one answers. Question: should you leave a message informing them that you will call back at a particular time? The correct answer is "Yes and no." Why? In Spain it is perfectly acceptable to leave a message for others (including more senior people) saying that you will call back at a given time. Of course, the person you are calling has no obligation to be there when you call back, but at least you can record your intent. In doing so, you are being polite in saying that you will take the responsibility to link up at a future time. By contrast, leaving such a message on the phone of someone in South Korea (particularly if he or she is older) is often considered rude and inconsiderate, because it obligates the other person to sit by the phone at a specific time waiting for your call. Many Koreans consider constraining the behavior of their superiors an offense against social norms. Instead, etiquette requires that you either leave no message or leave a simple message saying that you called but without reference to a possible callback time.

Routine behaviors such as these can have major ramifications for success or failure in social situations around the globe, and, while a lack of understanding here can be appreciated or even forgiven, it nevertheless seldom leads to positive outcomes. Once again, we return to the inescapable conclusion that global managers must be well prepared for new situations and new contacts if they wish to succeed. Center stage in these preparations is knowing how and when to talk – and what to say.

With increasing globalization and the associated need to communicate on an almost daily basis with people from different cultures, developing the abilities and skills to communicate effectively across cultural boundaries is fundamental to all managers. To a manager (or anyone else, for that matter), the realization that, despite his or her best efforts, the message was met with a blank stare, a grimace, inaction, or actions that demonstrated a lack of understanding can be distressing. When this same manager fails to understand either why the message was unsuccessful or how to improve future communication, however, frustration can turn into despair.

Following the global management model outlined in Chapter 2, perhaps the best place to begin any efforts to improve communication across borders is to identify factors in the external environment that can serve to inhibit or open opportunities for effective interpersonal communication. Each interaction is likely to be unique, based on the situation facing the parties involved, so this seems like a logical starting point. This cautions against a generalized approach to cross-cultural communication. Much energy can be wasted in such efforts.

A number of cultural, organizational, and situational factors can emerge to limit managerial options and choices. For example, communication in high-context cultures will likely focus as much on what is not said (e.g., nonverbal communication) as on what is. Likewise, company formalities or status systems may provide hints about appropriate behaviors during meetings. Finally, the location of a meeting (on-site or off-site) or the language-in-use can also serve to constrain what is said or how it is said. This exhibit illustrates only some of the possible impediments to effective communication. The point here is very simple: the more managers understand about the limitations surrounding their communication endeavors, the greater the possibility that they will select communication channels that will be appropriate – and effective.

As the above discussion suggests, a lot can go wrong when communicating across cultures if environmental factors are ignored. This is not a new conclusion. Over 2,000 years ago Roman poet Horace observed, "A word, once sent abroad, flies irrevocably."[16] Differences in language, cultural logic, expectations and interpretations regarding message content, context and communication protocols may all distort meanings and jeopardize communications. With this in mind, we now come to the issue of what global managers can do to reduce or minimize such impediments to clear communication. As noted above, although cultural processes are multifaceted, complex, and at times secretive, there are nonetheless concrete strategies that managers can initiate to adapt to such differences in their interactions with others. In this regard, managers have at least three choices or options to pursue in order to improve the likelihood of finding common ground with other parties (see Exhibit 5.7). They are all "doable" for managers committed to learning and skills building.

1. Expand your knowledge and understanding of cultural dynamics

If managers are serious about improving their global communication skills, an important step that has been discussed throughout this book is investing the time and energy required to learn more about how the world of work often differs across cultures, as well as the implications of such differences for management. In practice, this is not as difficult as it may at first appear. Exploring other cultures is not unlike learning computer games; at some point it becomes intuitive, allowing the manager to work almost seamlessly in settings that previously seemed alien. Of particular importance here is knowledge of how local beliefs, values, and behavioral

(1) Expand knowledge and understanding of cultural dynamics	(2) Recalibrate perceptual and critical analysis skills	(3) Enhance behavioral repertoire of applied communication
• Develop a greater understanding of your own culture and its common communication patterns. • Develop in-depth knowledge of the beliefs, values, and behavioral expectations of other key cultures. • Expand relevant foreign-language skills for both increased understanding and improved communication. • Seek advice from local cultural experts, when appropriate.	• Examine your own reasoning, as well as the reasoning of others. • Explore the assumptions you make about others. • Use your expanded cultural knowledge to view situations through the eyes of others. • Look for subtleties and nuances in interpersonal interactions that explain what others are thinking. • Seek to understand the "whys?," not just the "whats?," in the comments and behaviors of others.	• Broaden your message-formatting skills, including nonverbal communication skills. • Develop country-specific knowledge of appropriate topics, formalities, and behaviors. • Develop your active listening skills, with particular attention to common communication failures across cultures and possible resolution strategies.

Exhibit 5.7 Strategies for communicating across cultures

expectations can differ across cultures and how managers can prepare themselves for such differences. Much of this learning can be accomplished through independent reading and study, sponsored programs on cross-cultural issues, discussions with foreign nationals, and focused observations of what others are doing. None of this is difficult to accomplish.

Multicultural learning can also be facilitated by language study. Understanding the language of one's counterparts can go a long way towards capturing the essence of cultural differences – an important factor in working successfully across borders. Although it is often noted that "everyone" speaks English, there is ample room for misunderstandings and missed cues when people are forced into an unfamiliar language, as we have seen above.

Finally, in expanding cultural knowledge, it is also important not to forget one's own culture. Frequently managers take their own culture for granted and fail to realize that their own social environment creates its own screens that affect communication. Self-awareness about one's culture can serve as a useful point of departure for better understanding others. It can also serve to enhance one's understanding of how one is viewed by others.

2.   Recalibrate your perceptual and critical analysis skills

Based on this expanded knowledge and understanding of cultural differences, a second communication strategy emerges that involves seeking a better understanding of the cognitive processes underlying the comments and actions of others. This is not as extreme as it may sound. We are not suggesting altering basic cognitive processes; rather, we suggest recalibrating them. In other words, on the basis of their newly acquired multicultural awareness and understanding, managers should be in a position to use somewhat modified cognitive templates or frames of reference when trying to understand why people with different cultural backgrounds do or say what they do. Recent research has shown that experienced global managers often exhibit an ability to look behind external appearances or behaviors and try to understand the "why's?," not just the "what's?" They work to understand interpersonal interactions through the eyes and ears of others. They look for subtleties and nuances in social interactions that may help explain what others are thinking. They observe more than they judge. To a large extent, these are learned behaviors that motivated managers can develop with practice.

It will be remembered from Chapter 1 that Google developed a training program for new managers in which participants are sent abroad in small groups to India, China, and Japan to learn first-hand how business works. Participants live in the local economy and meet with local managers, shopkeepers, and farmers to explore divergent worldviews. The assumption underlying Google's endeavor is that these first-hand experiences will enhance their employees' critical thinking skills in cross-cultural interactions.

At the same time, successful global managers seek to understand their own beliefs and values, assumptions, biases, and perceptions. Stepping outside one's comfort zone allows managers to take a fresh look at situations that confront them. Are their assumptions about certain situations correct, or are there alternative assumptions that are equally valid? Developing shared meanings requires letting go of previous judgments and understandings, and tolerating uncertainty until a new understanding can be created. The point for managers to understand is that they may be "right" with respect to something, but in a cross-cultural environment what is right is relative. Arriving at a common meaning requires an ability to tolerate uncertainty and ambiguity in order to seek a deeper understanding of what one's counterparts are trying to say or do.

3. Enhance your applied communication skills

Finally, on a very practical level, managers can improve their knowledge of various communication protocols, which can vary from culture to culture. In addition to knowing where or when certain languages are preferred or required (discussed above), developing message-formatting skills can be critical to successful communication, especially as it relates to the use of nonverbal communication techniques, such as reading facial expressions and other forms of body language. Numerous cultures use such techniques as a core communication strategy, and misreading these – or ignoring them completely – can lead both to missed signals and missed opportunities.

Related to this is the need for managers to broaden their knowledge of what topics may be required or forbidden in certain conversations or messages (e.g., talking about money, illness, or families), what formalities are required or preferred in various communication arenas (the use of titles, bowing, dress codes, seating arrangements), and what behaviors are acceptable or unacceptable (e.g., raising one's voice, interrupting, verbal rejections, touching someone). In this regard, many companies offer their employees extensive training programs in local business practices and social etiquette prior to sending them on overseas assignments. Some companies sponsor entire corporate "universities" aimed at developing an extensive managerial and cultural skills set for global managers.

Finally, developing active listening skills has long been recommended for managers facing ambiguous situations. This is particularly important in cross-cultural settings, when communication failures can be commonplace. Recognizing such failures – not always an easy task – and finding a remedy can be key to saving a conversation and possible business deal. Again, corporate training programs can be of great assistance here.

In closing, as we have noted before, no one ever said that the manager's job was easy. Because of this, managers look logically for tools and techniques that can help them achieve their goals and objectives. In this pursuit, improved multicultural communication skills rank – or should rank – at the top of any manager's list of desired attributes. None of the three communication strategies discussed here is necessarily easily attained, but all are required if enhanced multicultural communication is to be achieved. Enhancing these skills requires both effort and commitment. It requires a mindset that sees the managerial role as a continual developmental process characterized by experience, reflection, analysis, and, most importantly, learning.

We began this chapter by pointing out that multicultural communication is frequently cited as one of the most serious challenges facing global managers. We close by observing that cross-cultural communication is also one of the most important sources of business opportunity. It is through communication that relationships are formed, conflicts are resolved, and innovative ideas are created and shared. While the perils of poor cross-cultural communication may appear daunting at first glance, we believe that increased awareness of the ways in which cultural differences can affect how meaning is constructed in interpersonal interactions is an important first step towards improved communication. We further believe that, in order to succeed, managers must be willing to make the effort and risk some initial missteps and perhaps embarrassment. In the end, effective multicultural communication is a matter of personal commitment and a willingness to learn. Above all, however, it is a willingness to listen. As the Venetian explorer Marco Polo reportedly observed long ago, "It is not the voice that commands the story; it is the ear."[17]

KEY TERMS

AIA model • cognition • cognitive evaluation • communication environment • cultural logic • cultural screens • culturally mandated protocols • culturally mediated cognitions • high-context cultures • language and linguistic structures • low-context cultures • message content • message context • *namasté* (Sanskrit, Hindi) • noise • nonverbal communication • norm of authenticity • selective perception • silent language

DISCUSSION QUESTIONS

1. How can managers apply the AIA model (Exhibit 5.1) as they prepare for a series of negotiation sessions with a potential global partner?
2. This chapter discussed two types of cultural screens: culturally mediated cognitions and culturally mandated protocols. Other than language barriers, why is it so difficult to communicate clearly across cultures? Why are there so many screens?
3. Considering the various cultural screens (see question #2), which screens may be easier to accommodate than others, and what can managers do to make this happen?
4. In what ways, both positive and negative, have virtual communication techniques such as text messaging or Skype changed the way companies conduct global business communication? What is gained here? What is lost?
5. What can managers do to improve communication processes with non-native speakers who are members of a global team?
6. Do you believe global managers must speak multiple languages to succeed? Why or why not?
7. Application 5.3 provides an example of how cultural logic works. Can you provide two additional examples to illustrate the importance of this problem for global managers?
8. Studies have found that verbal communication typically carries less than 35 percent of the meaning in two-way conversations. Why is this percentage so low? What can be done to increase it?
9. Why do you think some cultures seem to emphasize high-context communication, while others seem to emphasize low-context communication?
10. How would you organize a workshop on the topic of increasing people's nonverbal communication skills? What would you do?
11. Do you believe it is possible for most people to recalibrate their perceptual and critical analysis skills, as discussed in the Manager's Notebook section of this chapter? Provide an example of how this may be accomplished.

CASE: ROOS DEKKER, GLOBAL HEALTHCARE

Roos Dekker works in Rotterdam, Netherlands, for Global Healthcare, a major global leader in home and business healthcare electronics.[18] Her responsibilities include coordinating global logistics for the company's healthcare products, including supplies and product deliveries. In this regard, she must coordinate her efforts with other logistics managers around the world, including Javier Gutiérrez. Gutiérrez works in Buenos Aires for Global Healthcare Argentina (GHA), which represents the manufacturing, import and export, and distribution operations of Global Healthcare throughout South America. Operating through about a dozen plants in the region (mostly Brazil and Argentina), GHA makes components and products specializing in consumer electronics, small appliances, lighting equipment, and electronic medical equipment, which are then distributed and sold under the Global Healthcare brand.

Although Dekker and Gutiérrez are both logistics coordinators, they report to different supervisors in different divisions of the company, Global Healthcare and GHA. Organizationally, they are on the same level in the company hierarchy. Still, they must coordinate their efforts and work together to achieve maximum results for the entire enterprise. Dekker and Gutiérrez both speak fluent English, and have worked together several times, although they have never met in person and each knows very little about the other.

Recently, Roos Dekker was given an assignment involving major product deliveries from South America to the European Union. For reasons she did not know, these deliveries arrived in Europe at a slower pace than was scheduled, and she was under considerable pressure to catch up. Her point of contact for this problem was Javier Gutiérrez. Dekker tried several time to contact Gutiérrez, mostly by e-mail, but failed to get any definitive response regarding the late shipments.

Finally, out of desperation, Dekker sat down at her computer and wrote one more e-mail to Gutiérrez expressing her frustration. When she finished writing the message, she realized that she had to cool off a bit before sending it, and put the message away for one hour. When she returned, she decided that she should edit the message so it was just the facts. Still, she needed to express her sense of urgency. She edited his message as follows and sent it to Gutiérrez:

To: Javier Gutiérrez, GHA, Argentina
From: Roos, Global Healthcare, Netherlands
Re: Recent shipments to Global Healthcare-Europe

Dear Javier

I just had a conversation with Mr. Van den Berg (my boss) about the late shipments from Argentina and Brazil. He is concerned that this delay may have significant impact on our division results as we are losing sales. He blames us for these delays and asked me to provide a report justifying the delays as soon as possible.

I need the following information from you today:

- A full explanation for the cause of the shipment delays,
- A detailed timetable with a realistic forecast of when the shipment will arrive,
- A specific plan of action to get GHA back on track and avoid these delays in the future.

From now on, I would like to receive a copy of all shipment reports coming out of Brazil and Argentina.

Regards,
Roos Dekker

The next day, Gutiérrez sent his response to Dekker:

To: Roos Dekker, Global Healthcare, Netherlands
From: Javier Gutiérrez, Global Healthcare Argentina
c/c: Antonio Rodriguez, Global Healthcare Argentina
Re: Shipments to Global Healthcare-Europe

Dear Ms. Dekker:

I am not surprised that your boss is upset. However, I think you may have misunderstood the situation. I do not wish to be rude here, but you leave me no choice but to be frank. I am the logistics coordinator here, not the boss. The management of GHA schedules both production and deliveries, and several people are involved in these decisions, including the labor unions. If we push the workers too hard, they will shut down entire plants and this helps no one, as you would agree.

In addition, GHA has many recipients within Global Healthcare, not just your division, and to make matters more complicated, our Asian markets are growing faster than those in the EU and they, too, are demanding more product. And you know of all the customs issues we had in the last few weeks due to the new regulations regarding medical equipment and the additional paperwork required to satisfy safety requirements that came at a time in which we are short staffed. And should I remind you that this particular order is a special order that was outside the original forecast and has been accommodated as a special case.

I don't understand how you can blame me for the delays? Can't you see that this just makes things worse? And how can you expect me to provide you with information that I don't have? I can't provide you with the information that you requested until I hear from the production and legal departments. We work for an international firm and should work together to resolve issues, not just blame others for our problems. That is what I most believe.

I am sending a copy of this message to Mr. Antonio Rodriguez (my boss) as it is important that we all become aware of what is happening. I suggest you inform your boss that he needs to be patient and learn to respect his colleagues and partners in other countries.

Sincerely,
Javier Gutiérrez

CASE QUESTIONS

1. What are the key cultural, organizational, and situational context variables in this case?
2. Using the AIA model of interpersonal communication (see text), diagram the communication episode (or cycle) involving Roos Dekker and Javier Gutiérrez.
3. In your view, what was Roos Dekker's principal intention in sending her original message?
4. What cultural assumptions did she make about Gutiérrez or South America in composing her message? Were these accurate?
5. In what ways might the cultural backgrounds of both Dekker and Gutiérrez serve to reduce message clarity this exchange?
6. Is either party in this exchange of memos violating any communication protocols? If so, where?
7. After reading Gutiérrez' response, what are Dekker's options? If you were Dekker, what would you do?
8. (*Optional research question*) Explore some of the various types of cross-cultural communication training programs that are available (online or onsite) for managers. What is the basis of these programs – how do they work? Which, if any, of these programs do you believe might be the best approach to improving one's communication abilities in foreign environments? Why?

NOTES

1. Luciara Nardon, Richard M. Steers, and Carlos Sanchez-Runde, "Seeking common ground: strategies for enhancing multicultural communication," *Organizational Dynamics*, 40(2) (2011), pp. 85–95.
2. Nardon, Steers, and Sanchez-Runde, "Seeking common ground," p. 86.
3. Larry A. Samovar, Richard E. Porter, and Edwin R. McDaniel, *Communication between Cultures*. Belmont, CA: Thomson/Wadsworth, 2007, pp. 165–7.
4. *Lingua franca* (from Italian, literally meaning "the Frankish language") is a language that is systematically used to communicate between persons not sharing a mother tongue, in particular when it is a third language, distinct from both persons' mother tongues. "Lingua franca" is a functionally defined term, independent of the linguistic history or structure of the language. It may also refer to the de facto language within a more or less specialized field. A synonym for "lingua franca" is "vehicular language." Whereas a *vernacular* language is used as a native language in a single speaker community, a *vehicular* language goes beyond the boundaries of its original community, and is used as a second language for communication between communities. For example, English is a vernacular in England, but is used as a vehicular language (that is, a lingua franca) in the Philippines.
5. Norman Schur, *British English: A to Zed*. New York: HarperCollins, 1991.
6. Cited in Nardon, Steers, and Sanchez-Runde, "Seeking common ground."

7. Richard D. Lewis, *When Cultures Collide*. London: Nicholas Brealey, 2006, p. 63.

8. "Authenticity," *Stanford Encyclopedia of Philosophy*. Stanford University Press, 2014.

9. Nick Enfield, "The theory of cultural logic," *Cultural Dynamics* (March 2000), pp. 35–64.

10. Nardon, Steers, and Sanchez-Runde, "Seeking common ground."

11. We thank IESE MBA graduate Shipa Patel for sharing this experience.

12. Lewis, *When Cultures Collide*, p. 94.

13. Samovar et al., *Communication between Cultures*, pp. 165–7.

14. Gary P. Ferraro, *The Cultural Dimension of International Business*, 5th edn. Upper Saddle River, NJ: Pearson/Prentice-Hall, 2005, p. 80.

15. Edward T. Hall, *The Silent Language*. New York: Anchor Books, 1981.

16. Horace, *The Satires, Epistles, and Art of Poetry* (trans. John Conington). Oxford University Press, 2010.

17. Marco Polo, cited in Laurence Bergreen, *Marco Polo: From Venice to Xanadu*. New York: Vintage Books, 2007, p. 1.

18. The names of the company and employees in this case have been changed.

6 Leading global organizations

MANAGEMENT CHALLENGE

Despite the plethora of books on leadership, we still know very little about how or why leadership efforts succeed or fail. And we know even less about how to train leaders, global or otherwise, despite the innumerable training programs available. One thing is clear, however: leadership is not a quality or skill that can be easily replicated around the world. Leadership in Singapore, for example, is based on fundamentally different traditions and assumptions from those in the Netherlands, and these differences cannot be ignored. As a result, the challenge for global managers is to develop a sensitivity and understanding of how leadership efforts play out across countries and cultures, as well as how to behave when placed in or near such responsibilities. We explore this topic in this chapter, looking at the topic from different angles. We also discuss what is probably the most comprehensive study of global leadership (called GLOBE). Throughout, examples are used to illustrate the different faces of leadership across both cultures and organizations.

CHAPTER OUTLINE

- Dimensions of organizational leadership · · · · · · · · · · · · · · · · *page* 162
- Contemporary approaches to cross-cultural leadership · · · · · · · · 164
- Limitations on contemporary approaches · · · · · · · · · · · · · · · · · 171
- GLOBE leadership study · 174
- Women leaders: challenges and opportunities · · · · · · · · · · · · · · 179
- Leadership in China and the West · 182
- MANAGER'S NOTEBOOK: Leading global organizations · · · · · · · · 185
- Key terms · 188

• Discussion questions   188
• Case: Emerson Electric – Suzhou   190

APPLICATIONS

6.1 Carlos Ghosn, Nissan   *page* 166

6.2 Heroines of Reykjavik   168

6.3 Masataka Shimizu, TEPCO   170

6.4 Patronage and *pok chow* in Malaysia   173

6.5 *Jogo de cintura*, Brazil   178

6.6 Women leaders in India   181

A recent World Economic Forum in Davos, Switzerland, brought together over 1,000 corporate executives, 50 heads of state, and 300 cabinet ministers to discuss world challenges ranging from deficits to competitiveness to deadly diseases. At the conclusion of the conference, an observer from *The Economist* characterized the meeting as having one overriding theme: the importance of developing global leaders – in corporations, nation states, and NGOs. "The two most popular words in the business lexicon today are 'global' and 'leadership.' Put them together and people in suits start to salivate."[1] Indeed, global leadership is both an important topic and a topic about which we understand far less than we pretend.

More books have been written about leadership than any other topic in the field of management. Many of these books examine various theories of leadership, comparing the relative advantages and disadvantages of each. Other books represent serious empirical studies of actual leader behavior. Still others are popular books that seem to offer a secret elixir designed to transform ordinary managers into extraordinary leaders. What most of these books fail to do, however, is to recognize that leadership processes can vary significantly across geographic regions. In other words, much of what is written about leadership views is largely in Western terms based on Western beliefs, values, and cultures, and then offers this model to the world as a precursor to managerial and organizational effectiveness. This viewpoint is unhelpful to managers charged with the responsibility to get things done globally.

Consider two observations on leadership, one from China and one from the US, both interesting and each diametrically opposed to the other. Leadership expert Warren Bennis has said, "Leadership is like beauty; it is hard to define, but you know it when you see it."[2] But Chinese philosopher Lao Tzu suggested, "A leader is best when people barely know he exists, who talks little, and when the work is done and the aim fulfilled, people will say, we did this ourselves."[3] What do these two observations tell us? Research has consistently demonstrated that some cultures (e.g., those in France, Russia, and the United States) prefer leaders who take charge and are visible and assertive, while others (e.g., those in China and Japan) prefer leaders who are much less visible and move behind the scenes to accomplish things. Some cultures (e.g., those in Mexico and Spain) prefer leaders who stand above the crowd and command respect, while others (e.g., those in Malaysia and Laos) prefer leaders who are humble and remain part of the crowd. Some cultures aren't sure what they want.

Dimensions of organizational leadership

An age-old debate in the management community involves the difference between management and leadership as concepts that are central to determining organizational effectiveness. To some, there are stark differences between the two constructs of leadership and management; to others, these differences are negligible. Why? Some people see management as focusing on operational issues involved in getting things done through people (e.g., planning, decision-making, controlling, coordinating, etc.), while leadership involves the influence processes through which managers accomplish this (i.e., "lead"). One is mundane; the other is sexy. Others see management and leadership as being so closely intertwined that it becomes almost impossible to separate the two: good managers are good leaders, and vice versa.

There are two ways to view this ongoing debate. The first view (the academic approach) involves attempts to tease out structural and behavioral differences between these two constructs – that is, what do leaders do compared to what managers do? How does each contribute to organizational success or failure? How do we train leaders? The second view (the managerial approach) involves recognizing that, for global managers, the integration of these two issues is probably more important than differentiation. In other words, on the street and in the workplace, managers must, in fact, do both if they are to succeed (one requires the other), and if they fail all this becomes moot. Hence the critical question becomes: how do we train managers, including their leadership capabilities?

Our approach here assumes the latter view – that is, we view leadership as an integral and inseparable part of good management. We define leadership as the ability of a manager to influence, motivate, and enable others within the organization to contribute towards the effectiveness and success of the enterprise. Some managers may be charismatic; others may not. Some situations or locations may suggest participative managers; others may not. Some cultures may value team-oriented managers; others may not. In the end, what matters most is how individual managers can see and understand the on-the-ground situational and cultural realities and then capitalize on their own unique personal skills and abilities

Exhibit 6.1 Dimensions of organizational leadership

(including their approaches to leadership) to get the job done by working through people from different cultural backgrounds.

In this pursuit, we recognize three dimensions of organizational leadership, as shown in Exhibit 6.1: strategic, managerial, and team leadership. The reason this distinction is important, as we shall see later, is that particular leadership efforts are often dependent on the target of leadership; that is, leading a small work team often requires different strategies and approaches (perhaps more interpersonal relationship-building skills) than leading a conglomerate (perhaps more strategic skills), even if the long-term objectives of the firm are the same. Leadership is not a glove that fits all sizes or occasions; it must be tailored and the context in which it is used must be accommodated.

In addition, we also recognize a fourth dimension of leadership that is, or should be, integrated throughout the organizational hierarchy. This is ethical leadership, and it is particularly important when doing business in the global arena where trust, ethics, and social responsibility become so critical. This chapter will focus largely on strategic and managerial leadership. Ethical leadership is discussed in Chapter 8, while team leadership is discussed in Chapter 10. Hence, a major portion of the remainder of this book focuses on leadership processes in the belief that these processes are crucial for global managers to succeed.

Here is the challenge. Whether in Thailand or Morocco, Australia or Costa Rica, global leaders up and down the hierarchy face the same problem: how to adapt their leadership style to fit local circumstances in order to achieve corporate objectives. When managers turn to the myriad materials written on the topic of leadership, however, they are often hard-pressed to find meaningful support. As managers around the globe increasingly face the challenges of leading employees from different cultural backgrounds with divergent expectations about hierarchy, power, and interpersonal relations, it becomes all the more important for them to understand how cultural dynamics can influence effective leadership. With this in mind, in this chapter we explore global leadership processes, as well as what managers can do to prepare for such organizational and managerial realities.

Contemporary approaches to cross-cultural leadership

We begin with a simple question: *beyond simple definitions, what exactly is leadership?* It is universal or situation-specific? Is it visible or invisible? Is it in-born or can it be developed? Does it manifest itself differently in different people or cultures? As we will see, the answer to these questions can be very complex. Much of the confusion limiting our understanding of leadership processes in different countries can be traced to the initial assumptions we make about the topic. These assumptions guide what we choose to focus on. As we know from research on selective perception, people typically discover things on the basis of what they are looking for. Perhaps the best place to begin, therefore, is with the assumptions that typically inform a search for the essence of global leadership. In our experience, managers generally approach this issue in one of three different ways (see Exhibit 6.2).[4]

Universal approach: leader as leader

Some managers – and some organizational researchers – consider leadership to be a generalizable, or universal, behavior regardless of where it is exercised. In other words, leadership is leadership is leadership. We refer to this as the universal approach. Underlying this approach is the belief that leadership traits and processes are relatively constant across cultures. To the extent that this is correct, the goal of managers is to adopt a leadership model, such as charismatic leadership, under the assumption that its applicability is universal regardless of location. Most Western theories of leadership are built on this premise.

A good example of this can be seen in the ongoing debate in the West over the relative merits of transformational and transactional leadership. Advocates of transformational leadership (often called charismatic leadership), whereby managers work to create a universally accepted vision of where the group or organization should go and then use moral persuasion to reinforce this mission,

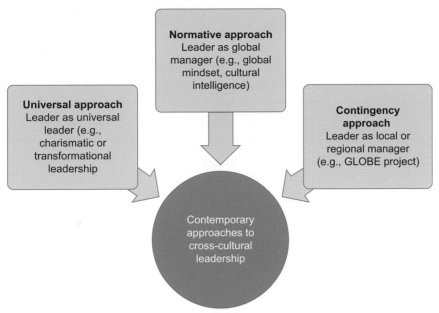

Exhibit 6.2 Contemporary approaches to cross-cultural leadership
Source: Adapted from Richard M. Steers, Carlos Sanchez-Runde, and Luciara Nardon, "Leadership in a global context: new directions in research and theory development," *Journal of World Business*, 47(4) (2012), pp. 479–82.

argue that such an approach is superior to the transactional leadership model, in which it is concrete exchange relationships with employees that largely determine results. The problem here is that recent research in Japan by Rikkyo University professor Jun Ishikawa found that neither of these approaches is very effective in that country.[5] Transformational leaders are often seen as being too abstract, while transactional leaders are sometimes seen as being too mercenary – and both are criticized for being too manipulative. Instead, successful Japanese managers tend to prefer something called gate-keeping leadership, in which they work to reduce the barriers to successful performance among their subordinates. Here is the problem: if these Western theories fail to work in Japan, one wonders where else they might also fail (e.g., Brazil, Russia, Egypt, India etc.).

In this regard, it is unfortunate that, despite decades of research supporting situational approaches to leadership effectiveness, companies still routinely sponsor leadership training programs that stress a few "keys" to successful leadership and ignore critical variations in local environments. One might suggest that many of these programs are doomed to failure from the outset. Having said this, the question still remains whether there are people who are genuinely universal leaders; that is, leaders almost wherever they go. One such example may be Carlos Ghosn.

APPLICATION 6.1 Carlos Ghosn, Nissan

What can happen when an executive from one culture is sent to run a company in another? Ask yourself: what might happen when a Brazilian of Lebanese descent with a French passport and work experience in the United States is sent to Japan to turn around an ailing company? This is precisely what happened to Carlos Ghosn. When Nissan was looking for a strategic partner, it turned to France's Renault. Renault agreed to send out one of its top executives as Nissan's new CEO. Outsiders, and many within Nissan itself, predicted that he would be gone within a year; traditional Japanese business culture would force him out.

After spending several months reviewing Nissan's operations, Ghosn announced a draconian turnaround plan, including closing five Japanese factories and terminating 16,000 employees. The plan shaved operating costs by over $10 billion. Still in control after a year, Ghosn next addressed Nissan's traditional inward-looking corporate culture. He moved swiftly to redirect company managers' attention by refocusing their efforts on improving profits and enhancing customer satisfaction. He established a network of Western-style multinational cross-functional teams to reexamine and reinvigorate each of the firm's core activities. He even began openly discussing a Western-style pay-for-performance compensation system for managerial and non-managerial employees alike to replace the existing seniority system, which was deeply entrenched in Japanese work culture. Moreover, to drive the point home that Nissan would become a truly global firm, not just a Japanese firm operating internationally, Ghosn suggested that henceforth the company's official language should be English, not Japanese.

While all this was going on, and despite an incredibly busy work schedule, Ghosn began studying the Japanese language, never becoming proficient but learning enough to converse in simple ways and show employees his commitment to the firm and its Japanese culture. This also aided in his efforts to better understand local customs and practices. Looking back on his efforts, what Ghosn had done in short order was to challenge the traditional Japanese approach to organization and management and force employees at all levels not to Westernize but to globalize – to build a new management system that focused more on the global than the local. The result was a new way of managing that ultimately led the company to record profits and an enhanced reputation.

Think about it . . .

(1) What is it about Carlos Ghosn that made him a suitable candidate for this position?

(2) What actions did Ghosn initiate at Nissan that may be explained at least in part by his personality, and what actions are simply the results of his approach to management? Is there a relationship here?

(3) What explains Ghosn's success in helping to transform Nissan into a global competitor?

(4) Is it generally easier for outside (i.e., foreign) executives to implement major organizational and managerial changes in global companies such as Nissan than for local executives? If so, why? When might this not be the case?

(5) In the realm of conjecture, when Ghosn leaves Nissan, do you think the company should appoint another foreigner or a Japanese CEO? Why?

Normative approach: leader as global manager

A second approach to thinking about leadership in a global context is to focus on enduring personal skills and abilities that are thought to characterize effective "global" managers. These models are prescriptive in nature, and suggest how managers should approach leadership in global settings. We refer to this as the normative approach. The focus is on the leader as a global manager. It is assumed that a common set of leader traits and abilities apply to all managers regardless of where they are working.

Recent work on the global mindset, cultural intelligence, and global leadership illustrate this approach. There are many definitions for this general phenomenon, but most of them center on a common theme. A global mindset can be defined formally as "a highly complex cognitive structure characterized by an openness to and articulation of multiple cultural and strategic realities on both global and local levels, and the cognitive ability to mediate and integrate across this multiplicity."[6] Simplified, this definition incorporates three skills: (1) an openness and attentiveness to multiple realms of action and meaning; (2) a complex representation and articulation of cultural and strategic dynamics; and (3) a mediation and integration of ideals and actions oriented towards global and local levels alike.

For example, successful global leaders are thought by some to exhibit cosmopolitanism, cognitive complexity, mental inquisitiveness, honesty, humility, and personal resiliency (see Exhibit 6.3 for details). Leaders who possess this cluster of skills and abilities are thought to be prepared to manage effectively throughout much of the world. As a result, the management development question is how to instill these traits and abilities into people who have to work successfully around the world in highly diverse cultural settings. Whether these traits are indeed commonplace among successful managers in different parts of the world has yet to be demonstrated, however.

Exhibit 6.3 Global mindset of effective leaders

Dimensions of a global mindset	Global mindset characteristics
Personal work style	High "cultural quotient"
	Flexibility and open-mindedness
	Effective global communicator and collaborator
	Skills in being a global team player
	Ability to balance global and local goals, behaviors, and management practices
General perspectives	Ability to take broad, long-term systems perspective
	Emotional resilience and personal autonomy
	Ability to embrace and support change
	Ability to work across organizational boundaries
	Ability to operate seamlessly in cross-cultural and cross-functional environments
	Thirst for global learning as a path for career development

Source: Based on Mansour Javidan, Richard M. Steers, and Michael A. Hitt, *The Global Mindset* (Amsterdam: Elsevier, 2007).

APPLICATION 6.2 Heroines of Reykjavik

Leading as global managers – putting a global mindset into practice – is much easier said than done, especially when the world seems to be collapsing around you. And in this pursuit, is the concept of a global mindset in leadership gender-neutral, or might men and women approach this challenge differently? The recent global economic collapse provides a good case in point.

With a total population of just over 300,000, the tiny nation of Iceland was overwhelmed by the recent global economic crisis.[7] Commenting on the crisis, Halla Tómasdóttir observed, "A lot had gone wrong, some things didn't make sense and it couldn't go on that way. We warned it would happen." Tómasdóttir was general director of the chamber of commerce when she issued those warnings, but nobody wanted to listen. She then parted ways and started her own company together with banker Kristin Petursdottir, a former manager at the British subsidiary of the crisis-stricken Icelandic bank Kaupthing. Together, they formed Audur Capital, a financial and investment company that would take a new path. Today, Audur Capital is one of the few firms in the Icelandic finance sector that is actually turning a profit.

At Audur, there is a simple recipe for success: having a global mindset combined with what Tómasdóttir calls **emotional capital**. "We've brought greater female values into the financial world," Tómasdóttir says. The company isn't interested in investments that quickly generate high yields. Instead, they focus on sustainable investments in projects that make as much sense socially and environmentally as they do for the investors themselves. The women call their business maxim "emotional capital," or "profit with principles." She continues:

We have five core feminine values. First, risk awareness: we will not invest in things we don't understand. Second, profit with principles – we like a wider definition so it is not just economic profit, but a positive social and environmental impact. Third, emotional capital. When we invest, we do an emotional due diligence – or check on the company – we look at the people, at whether the corporate culture is an asset or a liability. Fourth, straight talking. We believe the language of finance should be accessible, and not part of the alienating nature of banking culture. Fifth, independence. We would like to see women increasingly financially independent, because with that comes the greatest freedom to be who you want to be, but also unbiased advice.

Men are in a minority at Audur, but Tómasdóttir is keen to hire more. "There are fewer of them, but they are not tokens, we have hired them on merit. Now, if we have two equally competent people, we would positively discriminate in favor of the man because we want balance," she says, without a flicker of irony.

Think about it . . .

(1) Is the concept of "emotional capital" consistent with the idea of a global mindset? Why or why not?

(2) Do you believe men and women generally have different values in business, such as those discussed at Audur Capital? If so, what are the equivalent "male" values that the other banks in Iceland apparently exhibit?

(3) In your opinion, why might the "female" values at Audur have led to greater success in the highly competitive global banking and investments industry than those of their male counterparts?

(4) Could this success story have occurred in countries with less gender equality? Why or why not?

(5) What are the leadership lessons for global managers in other countries?

Contingency approach: leader as local manager

The third approach, which we refer to as the contingency approach, begins with the assumption that there are no universals in describing effective leadership. In other words, successful leaders in New York may fail in Tokyo or Paris if they are unable to modify their behaviors to suit the unique local environments. This approach looks at leadership as a culturally embedded process, not a series of personal traits of the manager or followers. Here the focus is on the leader as a local manager, not a global one, and it is assumed that the characteristics for success will vary with the situation.

A good example of this approach can be found in the recent GLOBE leadership project, a multinational study of culture and leadership in sixty-two countries. The principal finding of the GLOBE study is that, to a large degree, leadership is culturally contingent – that is, the qualities of effective leaders often vary across cultures. For example, successful US managers tend to score higher than their Chinese counterparts on such characteristics as assertiveness, performance orienta- tion, and individualism, while Chinese managers tend to score higher than Americans on power distance and uncertainty avoidance. The important point here is that GLOBE was able to track systematic trends in leadership characteristics across cultures. The GLOBE project is discussed in more detail below.

Another good example of how culture can influence leadership is symbolic leadership. Symbolic leadership occurs when people – usually senior executives or CEOs – accept full responsibility for setbacks or crises on behalf of the entire organization. This is commonplace throughout much of Asia, for example, and sometimes offered even when the executives are not at fault. The belief here is that, through voluntary resignation, harmony is restored and the organization can move forward. Not surprisingly, symbolic leadership is seldom seen in the West when things go wrong. Indeed, it can be seen as a sign of weakness.

APPLICATION 6.3 Masataka Shimizu, TEPCO

When companies succeed, it is commonplace to reward managers – and, hope- fully, other employees. What happens when companies fail, though? What is management's responsibility? In some countries, the decline in stock prices or other setbacks can signal the demise of CEOs by disgruntled stockholders. In others, CEOs are seldom held accountable, even if they were directly responsible for the failure. What happens, however, if a company experiences a natural disaster for which it is not responsible? Should company CEOs be held accountable?

This is what happened at Tokyo Electric Power Company (TEPCO) in 2011 in the wake of Japan's worst natural disaster in memory.[8] Some 20,000 people died and over 1 million were left homeless as a result of an earthquake, followed by a tsunami, followed by a nuclear meltdown in Fukushima. Many people were angry that TEPCO did not do more to prevent or resolve the crisis. Anger mounted as people watched helplessly as their fortunes and futures vanished. In an effort to ameliorate the situation and restore harmony, TEPCO executives publicly accepted responsibility for the problems and announced that their executives would take a 50 percent pay cut and that this money would go to help recent victims of the natural disaster. Company employees also agreed to a 25 percent pay cut. All told, the power company expects to save about $660 million annually, which it will use to compensate victims of the natural disaster.

A short time later, in an act of symbolic leadership, TEPCO's president, Masataka Shimizu, resigned in disgrace following the largest financial loss in the company's history. The key word here is "resignation," not "termination," as might have happened in the West. One wonders how many executives in other countries would have taken a similar course of action.

Think about it . . .

(1) Should Masataka Shimizu have resigned his post as president over this crisis? Why or why not?
(2) Why is symbolic leadership such as that illustrated in this example common in some countries, but not others?
(3) Should more executives and CEOs in Western companies be held more accountable for the failures of their companies, even if they were not directly responsible for the setbacks? Why or why not?

Limitations on contemporary approaches

While all three of the contemporary leadership models discussed here add value to our efforts to understand leadership in a global context, it is our opinion that they all miss the mark in sufficiently explicating the leadership construct as it relates to global diversity. As a result, our ability to help global managers prepare for overseas assignments remains somewhat limited. In particular, we suggest that focusing more squarely on two issues could advance our understanding of leadership processes: (1) the meaning of leadership as a cultural construct; and (2) the variations in local expectations regarding leader behavior. In short, in our view we must move beyond traditional Western models of leadership and take a more cosmopolitan approach to the subject.

Leadership as a cultural phenomenon

First and foremost, it is important to recognize that leadership is a cultural construct. Its meaning is embedded in the diverse cultures in which it is exercised, and changes accordingly. Most important here, it is not a Western construct that is easily expanded to global dimensions.

To understand this, consider our opening question once again: what is leadership? The difficulty in answering this question lies in the differing meaning of the construct itself in different cultures. In other words, leadership means different things to different people. In most Anglo-Saxon countries (e.g., the United Kingdom, the United States, Australia), leadership generally has positive connotations. Leaders tend to be respected, admired, and, indeed, sometimes revered, whether they are in the political or business arena. Clearly, this is not a universal truth. The opposite view of leaders can also be found in many countries (e.g., Mexico, Egypt, Romania), where widespread distrust and fear of power or the dislike of privilege prevail.

Moreover, a direct translation of the word "leader" into different languages can invoke a variety of images, including dictator, parent, expert, and first among equals. Some of these terms have strong connotations of highly directive or authoritarian styles of leadership that many people reject. Leaders are not necessarily to be trusted. We wonder about their motives and true goals, or about other potentially undesirable behaviors and characteristics. At the same time, in many egalitarian societies, terms such as "followers" or "subordinates" are also seen as being inappropriate. For instance, subordinates in the Netherlands are frequently referred to as co-workers (*medewerkers*) instead of subordinates, and leaders are careful to avoid appearing condescending.

With such a diversity of opinions concerning the characteristics of effective leaders, how is it possible to reach agreement on even a simple definition of leadership? Moreover, what does this diversity of views suggest about our ability to apply largely Western-based leadership theories across borders? What does this say about our ability to build or implement leadership development programs that can be used effectively in various regions of the world? What does this say about so-called leadership "gurus" who travel the world with their packaged leadership programs?

To make matters even more complex, not only does the term "leader" translate differently across various cultural groups, but also the meanings that are construed from these translations can also differ, sometimes significantly. For example, in individualistic societies (e.g., Australia, Canada, the United Kingdom) leadership typically refers to a single person who guides and directs the actions of others, often in a very visible way. In more collectivistic societies (e.g., South Korea, Japan, and China), however, leadership is often less associated with individuals and more closely aligned with group endeavors. In hierarchical societies (e.g., Saudi Arabia, Mexico, Indonesia) leaders are often seen as being separate and apart from their followers, while in more egalitarian societies (e.g., Sweden, Denmark) they are often seen as more approachable and less intimidating. Indeed, the rather common

Anglo-American celebration of the accomplishments of various leaders stands in stark contrast to Lao Tzu's ancient observation cited above, that effective leaders work quietly and let workers (or employees) take the credit.

Culture and leader expectations

The second concern with existing approaches to leadership focuses on the expectations surrounding the behavior of successful leaders, including the cultural underpinnings of such expectations. These expectations arise from society at large, local circumstances, subordinates, co-workers, and the leaders themselves. The GLOBE study (discussed further below) clearly contributes to this understanding, but more is required concerning the fundamental normative beliefs and processes underlying a leader's behavior. In other words, we need to have a better understanding of the "why's?" and "how's?" underlying the process, not just the "what's?" or "who's?"

If there is any doubt about the systematic variability in what constitutes effective leader behavior, we need look no further than the observations by various managers and employees from different countries. In the West, the French expect their leaders to be cultivated – highly educated in the arts and mathematics. The Dutch stress egalitarianism and are skeptical about the value and status of leaders. Terms such as "leader" and "manager" can even carry a stigma in some organizations. Americans are often schizophrenic in their choice of leaders; some like leaders who empower and encourage their subordinates, while others prefer leaders who are bold, forceful, confident, and risk-oriented.

By contrast, in the East, Chinese leaders are expected to establish and nurture personal relationships, practice benevolence towards subordinates, be dignified and aloof but sympathetic, and treat the interests of employees like their own. Malaysians expect their leaders to behave in a manner that is humble, modest, and dignified. Japanese leaders are expected to focus on developing a healthy relationship with their employees as employees and managers share the same fate. In short, expectations concerning appropriate leader behaviors can vary considerably across cultures. This is a point not lost on experienced expatriates and frequent flyers.

APPLICATION 6.4 Patronage and *pok chow* in Malaysia

Patronage is very common among all of the ethnic groups that comprise Malaysia. Under this system, individual workers develop mutually beneficial bonds between themselves and a patron who will support their livelihood in exchange for loyalty and service. Among the poorer classes of Malaysia's ethnic

Chinese, this practice can be seen in the tradition of **pok chow**, which translates roughly as gang contracting.

Under this system, individual workers band together under a leader who finds work for the crew, organizes the activities of crew members, and distributes compensation. *Pok chow* crews are especially popular in the construction industry in Malaysia, where employers only have to deal with crew leaders and can dispense with other complicated organizational procedures or requirements.

A strong collectivistic norm keeps crew members together through good times and bad, and changes in crew membership are rare and usually associated in some way with family membership. Patronage systems like this are common in many parts of the world, most notably in Southeast Asia, Latin and South America, and sub-Saharan Africa – all cultures characterized by high levels of collectivism and hierarchical values.

Think about it . . .

1. Have you seen work teams similar to *pok chow* crews in other countries or regions? Do they share the same or different characteristics as a work team?
2. What factors keep these work teams together?
3. What leadership or supervisory skills are required of the leader of a *pok chow* team?

GLOBE leadership study

What can we conclude from all this about the meaning and application of leadership across cultures? To start, we learn to be cautious about a one-size-fits-all portrait of successful leaders. A good leader is not always a leader in the dictionary sense. Recent research seems to back this up. One of the more intriguing modern studies of leadership behavior across borders was conducted by a multicultural team of researchers who led the GLOBE project.[9] This project examined the relationship between culture and successful leadership and management patterns in sixty-two countries around the world. The project members' initial research led them to propose the nine GLOBE cultural dimensions: power distance, uncertainty avoidance, humane orientation, institutional collectivism, in-group collectivism, assertiveness, gender egalitarianism, future orientation, and performance orientation. These dimensions are discussed in greater detail in Chapter 3.

Based on this, the researchers then identified twenty-two leadership attributes that were widely seen as being, in their view, universally applicable across cultures

Exhibit 6.4 GLOBE cultural perspectives on leadership effectiveness

Behaviors and traits universally considered facilitators of leadership effectiveness	Behaviors and traits universally considered impediments to leadership effectiveness	Culturally contingent beliefs about facilitators of leadership effectiveness
Trustworthiness, integrity Visionary, charismatic Inspirational and motivational Communicative, team builder	Antisocial, self-protective, loner Non-cooperative, malevolent Autocratic, dictatorial	Individualistic, autonomous Status-conscious Risk taking

Source: Based on Mansour Javidan, Peter W. Dorfman, Mary Sully de Luque, and Robert J. House, "In the eye of the beholder: cross-cultural lessons in leadership from Project GLOBE," *Academy of Management Perspectives*, 20(1) (2006), pp. 67–90 (pp. 73–6).

(e.g., encouraging, motivational, dynamic, decisive, having foresight) and eight leadership dimensions that were seen to be universally undesirable (e.g., uncooperative, ruthless, dictatorial, irritable). Several other attributes were found to be culturally contingent, however – that is, their desirability or undesirability was tied to cultural differences (see Exhibit 6.4 for details). These included characteristics such as being ambitious and elitist. Here it was found that people in some cultures favored traits in leaders that people in other cultures rejected. For example, some cultures (e.g., those in the United Kingdom, Germany, France, and the United States) often romanticize their leaders and give them exceptional privileges and prestige; they are held in high esteem. At the same time, however, other cultures (e.g., those in the Netherlands and Switzerland) denigrate the very concept of leadership and are often suspicious of people in authority. They worry about abuse of power and rising inequality.

The GLOBE researchers distilled their findings into six relatively distinct leadership dimensions: autonomous, charismatic/value-based, humane, participative, self-protective, and team-oriented (see Exhibit 6.5). Two of these leadership styles (charismatic/value-based leadership and team-oriented leadership) were strongly endorsed in all regional country clusters used in the study. Even so, the magnitude of this endorsement varied across regional country clusters. For example, both charismatic/value-based and team-oriented leadership styles were most widely accepted in the Anglo, Asian, and Latin American clusters. They were still accepted in other regions of the world, but with less intensity.

Meanwhile, the other leadership styles were found to be more culturally contingent. Humane leadership was strongly endorsed in the Asian, Anglo, and sub-Saharan African clusters, and less strongly endorsed in the Latin American and Nordic clusters. Autonomous leadership was generally seen as neither facilitating

Exhibit 6.5 GLOBE leadership dimensions

GLOBE leadership dimensions	Characteristics of dimensions	Regions where leadership dimensions are widely endorsed
Autonomous leadership	Individualistic, independent, unique	Endorsed in eastern European and Germanic clusters; weaker endorsement in Latin American cluster.
Charismatic/value-based leadership	Visionary, inspirational, self-sacrificing, decisive, performance-oriented	Endorsed in all regions, but particularly in Anglo, Asian, and Latin American clusters; weaker endorsement in Arab cluster.
Humane leadership	Modest, tolerant, sensitive, concerned about humanity	Endorsed particularly in Anglo, Asian, and sub-Saharan African clusters; less so elsewhere.
Participative leadership	Active listening, non-autocratic, flexible	Wide variations in endorsements across all regions, but less so in Arab and Latin American clusters.
Self-protective leadership	Self-centered, procedural, status-conscious, face-saving	Wide variations in endorsements across all regional clusters.
Team-oriented leadership	Collaborative, integrating, diplomatic	Endorsed in all regions, but particularly in Anglo, Asian, and Latin American clusters; less so in Arab cluster.

Sources: Adapted from Robert J. House, Paul J. Hanges, Mansour Javidan, Peter W. Dorfman, and Vipin Gupta, *Culture, Leadership, and Organizations: The GLOBE Study of 62 Societies* (Thousand Oaks, CA: Sage, 2004); Peter Dorfman, Mansour Javidan, Paule Hanges, Ali Dashmalchian, and Robert J. House, "GLOBE: a twenty year journey into the intriguing world of culture and leadership," *Journal of World Business*, 47(4) (2012), pp. 504–18.

nor inhibiting a leader from being effective. Within the Eastern European and Germanic clusters, however, this leadership style was considered to be more positively related to outstanding leadership than in other culture clusters. Finally, for self-protective leadership and participative leadership, there was substantial variability in the degree to which these styles were endorsed within the different country clusters. For more details and country breakdowns using the GLOBE methodology, see Exhibit 6.6.

In this exhibit, scales range from 1.0 to 7.0, depending on how important each society on average sees the six dimensions for leadership effectiveness, with 1.0 being very unimportant and 7.0 being very important. Two things should be remembered here. First, these are mean scores, and considerable variations can be found within them. Second, it is probably more useful to look at these numbers as

Exhibit 6.6 Cultural beliefs about leadership styles

Country	Autonomous leadership	Charismatic leadership	Humane leadership	Participative leadership	Self-protective leadership	Team leadership
Australia	3.95	6.09	5.09	5.71	3.05	5.81
Brazil	2.27	6.01	4.84	6.06	3.50	6.17
Canada*	3.65	6.16	5.20	6.09	2.96	5.84
China	4.07	5.57	5.18	5.05	3.80	5.57
Denmark	3.79	6.01	4.23	5.80	2.82	5.70
Egypt	4.49	5.57	5.14	4.69	4.21	5.55
Greece	3.98	6.02	5.16	5.81	3.49	6.12
India	3.85	5.85	5.26	4.99	3.78	5.72
Ireland	3.95	6.08	5.06	5.64	3.01	5.82
Israel	4.26	6.23	4.68	4.96	3.64	5.91
Japan	3.67	5.49	4.68	5.08	3.61	5.56
Mexico	3.86	5.66	4.71	4.64	3.86	5.75
Nigeria	3.62	5.77	5.48	5.19	3.90	5.65
Philippines	3.75	6.33	5.53	5.40	3.33	6.06
Poland	4.34	5.67	4.56	5.05	3.53	5.98
Russia	4.63	5.66	4.08	4.67	3.69	5.63
Singapore	3.87	5.95	5.24	5.30	3.32	5.77
South Korea	4.21	5.53	4.87	4.93	3.68	5.53
Spain	3.54	5.90	4.66	5.11	3.39	5.93
Sweden	3.97	5.84	4.73	5.54	2.82	5.57
Thailand	4.28	5.78	5.09	5.30	3.91	5.76
Turkey	3.83	5.96	4.90	5.09	3.58	6.01
United Kingdom	3.92	6.01	4.90	5.57	3.04	5.71
United States	3.75	6.12	5.21	5.93	3.16	5.80

*English-speaking population.

Sources: Robert J. House, Paul J. Hanges, Mansour Javidan, Peter W. Dorfman, and Vipin Gupta, *Culture, Leadership, and Organizations: The GLOBE Study of 62 Societies* (Thousand Oaks, CA: Sage, 2004); Peter Dorfman, Mansour Javidan, Paule Hanges, Ali Dashmalchian, and Robert J. House, "GLOBE: a twenty year journey into the intriguing world of culture and leadership," *Journal of World Business*, 47(4) (2012), pp. 504–18.

relative differences, not numeric ones. In any case, these results and the GLOBE study in general provide some evidence that acceptable managerial behaviors – including leader behaviors – are to some degree culturally contingent. To see how this works in actual practice, consider an example from Brazil.

APPLICATION 6.5 *Jogo de cintura*, Brazil

According to the findings of the GLOBE study, Brazilian managers tend to be – or try to be – charismatic, participative, and team-oriented. In Brazil, a manager's personal style is considered of great significance and it could almost be said that his or her vision or bearing is viewed as of equal importance to their technical abilities. Relationships are of key importance in this South American culture, and the boss and subordinates work hard to foster a relationship based on trust and respect for personal dignity. First and foremost, however, managers are expected to manage. The boss is expected to give direct instructions and it is expected that these instructions will be carried out without too much discussion or debate. If there is debate it should be done in private to avoid showing public disrespect to the hierarchy.

On an operational level, while managers in many countries (e.g., Japan, Canada, Denmark) value advance planning, Brazilian managers often rely on luck and improvisation. Brazilians rely on a practice called *jeitinho*, which corresponds to a last-minute approach to find solutions to problems, which may include breaking rules, asking for favors, or creative fixes. Brazilian leaders are expected to have *jogo de cintura*, that is, finding creative and improvisatory solutions to deal with problems. It is a general belief that there is no need for worrying about obstacles, as almost everything can be arranged in the end. This "arrangement of things" is mostly related to exemption to certain rules and the use of favors. In this sense, personal contacts play an important role. For example, if a manager missed a deadline to turn in a document to the Human Resources department, but he or she had a friend working in this department, the manager could easily ask her to turn in the document, even though the manager missed the deadline, knowing that she would probably help and things would be fine. Such an approach might drive managers from some other countries crazy, but it works well in Brazil; it gets the job done.

Think about it . . .

(1) For many people, waiting until the last minute to solve problems and then bending the rules to help accomplish this sounds more like chaos or perhaps irresponsibility than leadership. What is your opinion of this seeming contradiction?

(2) What is the unique role of personal relationships in making this approach to management work?

(3) How easily would it be to transfer this leadership style to other cultures or countries? In what other countries might this approach work? Why? And where would this approach definitely not work?

Women leaders: challenges and opportunities

More women than ever before are managers and business owners, according to a recent study by the International Labour Organization, although there is still a dearth of women at the very top of the corporate ladder. In 80 of the 108 countries for which ILO data are available, the proportion of women managers has increased over the last 20 years. But only 5 percent of the CEOs of the world's largest corporations are women.[10] And the larger the company, the less likely the head will be a woman.

Looking globally, a recent study by Thornton International Business Report in forty-five countries found that the percentages of women leaders in both large and small public and private companies ranged from a high of 43 percent in Russia to 9 percent in Japan (see Exhibit 6.7). Commenting on the report, Erica O'Malley, Thornton's managing partner of diversity and inclusion, noted that "It's no longer feasible for global businesses to adopt a sit-and-wait policy when it comes to promoting women to senior management roles, particularly when so many other nations – developed and emerging – are more rapidly realizing the benefits of diverse senior leadership." Still, Thornton also reported that the vast majority of organizations worldwide aren't taking the time to train women for leadership

Exhibit 6.7 Percentage of women in senior leadership positions (rank order)

Country (and rank)	% Women leaders	Country (and rank)	% Women leaders	Country (and rank)	% Women leaders
1. Russia	43	16. Chile	30	31. Ireland	23
2. Indonesia	41	17. Italy	30	32. Singapore	23
3. Latvia	41	18. Finland	29	33. Australia	22
4. Philippines	40	19. Greece	29	34. Brazil	22
5. Lithuania	39	20. Mexico	28	35. Spain	22
6. China	38	21. South Africa	26	36. USA	22
7. Thailand	38	22. Sweden	26	37. UK	20
8. Estonia	37	23. Taiwan	26	38. Denmark	14
9. Armenia	35	24. Vietnam	26	39. Germany	14
10. Georgia	35	25. Argentina	25	40. India	14
11. Peru	35	26. Malaysia	25	41. UAE	14
12. Poland	34	27. Turkey	25	42. Switzerland	13
13. Botswana	32	28. France	24	43. Netherlands	10
14. New Zealand	31	29. Norway	24	44. Japan	9
15. Belgium	30	30. Canada	23		

Source: Chad Brooks, Thornton International Business Report, cited in *Business News Daily* (March 11, 2014), p. 2.

Exhibit 6.8 Percentage of board of director's seats held by women

Board seats held by women

>20%	10–20%	5–10%	<5%
Finland	Australia	Belgium	Bahrain
Norway	Austria	Brazil	Chile
Sweden	Canada	China	India
UK	Denmark	Greece	Japan
	France	Indonesia	Kuwait
	Germany	Ireland	Oman
	Israel	Italy	Portugal
	Netherlands	Malaysia	Qatar
	Poland	Mexico	South Korea
	South Africa	New Zealand	Russia
	Turkey	Singapore	Saudi Arabia
	Switzerland	Spain	Taiwan
	USA	Thailand	UAE

Source: Catalyst, "Quick take: women on boards."

roles. Only 11 percent of businesses globally have a program to support and mentor women, with 70 percent of companies not even considering starting such programs.

At the same time, women represent more than 20 percent of board members in just four countries – Finland, Sweden, Norway, and the United Kingdom – the ILO says, citing a Catalyst report covering board seats in forty-four countries (see Exhibit 6.8).[11] But the study also noted that when it comes to a woman being the chairperson of a company board, the percentages decline sharply. "While data from different sources vary, they generally show the small degree to which women are leading boards – generally in the range of zero to a few per cent," the report said.

Today, women own and manage more than 30 percent of all businesses, ranging from self-employed, micro and small enterprises to medium and large companies. More specifically, they represent around 24 percent of all employers in all regions, except the Middle East and North Africa, where they are around 6 percent. However, women tend to be concentrated more in micro and small enterprises. And while women are gaining access to more and higher levels of leadership and management, there is a tendency for them to be clustered in particular managerial functions. These tend to be in areas that are not on a path to the chief executive role. The study concludes: "Women are often siloed in managerial functions such as human resources, public relations and communications, and finance and administration, and are therefore only able to go up the ladder to a certain point in the organizational hierarchy."

The irony here is that, according to ILO studies, having more women at the top can help the bottom line. It cautions that there may not be a direct causal link and notes the argument that companies that promote women to top jobs are often those that invest in research, innovation, and technology. But the ILO found that several studies have concluded women's participation in decision-making is positive for business outcomes. McKinsey & Company, for example, found that European companies with more women in their top management teams had 17 percent higher stock price growth, and that their average operating profit was almost double their industry average. And a recent Credit Suisse study based on a database of the number of women sitting on the boards of the 2,360 companies constituting the MSCI AC World Index found that over the previous six years, companies with at least one female board member outperformed by 26 percent those with no women on the board in terms of share price performance.

However, these studies leave three key questions unanswered. First, if the numbers are correct, why is it that women leaders can change the bottom line for global firms? Is there a type of distinctiveness in women's leader style that facilitates success? Second, will women be given the opportunity to serve as leaders at or near the top of corporations around the world? And third, if the trend towards more women leaders around the world continues, what are the implications for developing better theories of leadership that account for gender differences?

APPLICATION 6.6 Women leaders in India

India is a land of strong tradition, but also of dynamic change.[12] One of the more notable changes is the increasing number of women who hold leadership positions in local companies or who have begun their own entrepreneurial firms. In past decades a small number of women have risen to the top and quietly broken through the barriers of social conformity, both at home and in the workplace, to become successful entrepreneurs and professionals. In recent years, however, this stream has become a flood. Some, such as Indu Jain of the privately held Bennett Coleman, is CEO of India's biggest media house. She has reached billionaire status, according to *Forbes* magazine.

Kiran Mazumdar-Shaw started one of India's first biotech companies, Biocon, while Lalita Gupte and Kalpana Morparia run India's second largest bank, ICICI Bank. There are more. Simone Tata built one of the first indigenous cosmetic brands, Lakme, now a unit of Hindustan Lever. Anu Aga turned around an ailing company, the engineering firm Thermax Group, to become a highly profitable venture. Priya Paul became the president of Apeejay Surrendra Group at the age of twenty-four when her father was killed. Sulajja Firodia Motwani, managing director of Kinetic Motor, collaborated with firms in South Korea, Italy, and Taiwan to grow her company from a niche moped maker to a manufacturer of a full range of two-wheelers and auto components. Finally, Neelam Dhawan, as managing director for Microsoft India, has led a 35 percent growth spurt in the past five years.

Why are women doing so well in India? One reason is the country's long tradition of valuing education, so women who achieve academically are seen as smart and savvy. Another reason is this: "What really made them successful is their sheer determination to break through," says Indira Parikh, president of the Foundation for Management Education in Pune, outside Mumbai. Their formula for success is identical to those of their male counterparts: skills, drive, and opportunity. Finally, there is little evidence that these women leaders in India behave differently from their male counterparts. Consistent with the GLOBE findings, their behaviors are more Indian than female or male, although this finding may not be true around the world. In working with subordinates, they are described as encouraging, motivating, dynamic, and decisive – which, again, is consistent with GLOBE's overall view of effective leaders.

Think about it . . .

(1) In general, do you believe that gender or national culture represents a more significant influence on leadership style and effectiveness around the world? Why?
(2) Some countries and cultures provide fewer leadership opportunities for women than others. Is this an issue that should be addressed locally or globally? Why?

Leadership in China and the West

When Westerners interact with Chinese managers and leaders, they often come away from the experience confused and frustrated. Common Western responses include perceptions that Chinese leaders refuse to act decisively, fail to respond candidly, are ambiguous about their goals and objectives, and generally don't act like "leaders." To many Western executives, this appears to be ineffectual or even deceitful, making it difficult to build good working relationships. If we examine leadership through a cross-cultural lens, however, the picture can look quite different.

Exhibit 6.9 Leadership patterns in China and the West

Leadership characteristics	Western traditions	Chinese traditions
Beliefs	Seek to achieve ideal end state (*eîdos* and *télos*).	Seek to balance countervailing forces (*yin* and *yang*).
Goals	Establish and pursue aspirational goals; manage the results.	Create conditions conducive to success; manage the process.
Logic	Logic of application; articulate objectives and determine reasonable means to desired ends.	Logic of exploitation; place oneself in a position to exploit opportunities as they emerge.
Preferences	Preference for action; capture the initiative.	Preference for patience; let events come to you.

Source: Adapted from Carlos Sanchez-Runde, Luciara Nardon, and Richard M. Steers, "Looking beyond Western leadership models: implications for global managers," *Organizational Dynamics*, 40(3) (2011), pp. 207–13.

According to the French philosopher François Jullien, the different foundations of leadership in Eastern and Western traditions can be traced to ancient Chinese and Greek thought. These foundations are based on the separate paths these two civilizations followed in their efforts to make sense out of human behavior (see Exhibit 6.9). What is generally referred to as Western civilization traces its origins to the culture, beliefs, and traditions of ancient Greece. The Greeks developed the concept of *eîdos* (ideal) as an ideal form that humans should aspire to and achieve as *télos* (goal). In this scheme, the work of a leader consists of bridging the gap between *télos* as an ideal state and reality (or actual practice) with a goal of achieving perfection.

By contrast, the concept of an ideal or archetype that could serve as a model for action and a desirable final state of affairs never developed in ancient China. Instead, reality in China was seen as a process emanating from the interaction between opposing and complementary forces, or *yin* and *yang*. Order did not result from an ideal to be accomplished but from a natural propensity of processes already in motion. Because the emphasis was on current processes evolving here and now, Chinese thinking focused on very concrete and specific situations of everyday life, rather than abstractions of the essence of an ideal form. Because Chinese thinking did not abstract and generalize in the search for an ultimate *eîdos*, traditional Chinese language did not include words for essence, God, being, ethics, and the like. Indeed, even today's modern Chinese language incorporates these concepts only out of a need to translate such concepts from Western languages.

Understanding this difference helps explain the separate paths of social thought and practice in these two divergent regions of the world. In many cases, Western thinking is difficult to understand or interpret without reference to concepts such as "the ideal." In many ways, current management thought as taught in many parts of the world is based on the original Greek concept of the ideal of purposeful action. Strategy appears as the art of arranging means towards desired end states. Corporate vision and mission make for a concrete definition of organizational ideals. Executives manage by objectives, and leaders strive actively to move the firm closer to achieving business goals and ideals that are carefully and publicly defined and implemented.

Chinese tradition, on the other hand, emphasizes positioning oneself in the flow of reality in a more passive way, so that we can discover its coherence and benefit from its natural evolution. Rather than establishing a set of objectives for action, one has to flow within the potential of each situation and the dynamics that the situation affords. A common metaphor that can be found in traditional Chinese texts tells of a general and his soldiers benefiting from a given evolution of events, rather than behaving with particular heroism or bravery. As such, leaders must locate themselves in such a position that the desired path of events becomes the only viable alternative, the same way that they do not force the enemy (militarily or commercially) into a situation in which their only alternative is to behave bravely against them.

Performance in the Western tradition results from minimizing the gap between the goal and the achievement, the planned and the attained. Action in the West is seen as a separate entity, an external disruption to the natural order of things. In China, by contrast, performance results from a minimization of action itself, leaving the situation to achieve its full potential in terms that benefit the organization. Chinese leaders thus focus on continual processes following their own internal dynamics, uninterrupted. Western action is seen from the Chinese perspective as being extemporaneous, quick, direct, and costly, while the Chinese "effortless action" is slow, indirect, progressive, and natural. Western leaders act, while Chinese leaders transform. Transformation – as opposed to action – extends itself through time, as if without beginning and end, imposing itself albeit in natural ways. Because it comes from the inside of the situation, it imposes itself softly, without resistance. Changes emanate by themselves and do not require heroic efforts and determination, as they are part of a continuous progression that is barely noticed.

This does not mean that the concept of action is not present in traditional Chinese thought. It is a subdued type of action, though: slow, subtle, anticipatory, and naturally inserted in the natural flow of events. Rather than sudden action, occasions are anticipated, providing for the outcome of what will naturally appear. As a result, Chinese leaders pursue objectives in modest ways, silent and almost anonymous, vis-à-vis the grandiloquent apparatus and appearance of the heroic decision-maker often seen or imagined in the West. Action is freed from activism and becomes discreet and subtle, confounded in the course of events, ignorant of particular protagonists.

MANAGER'S NOTEBOOK
Leading global organizations

This chapter looked at the important but complicated topic of leadership. What are the basic findings? Leadership can be viewed as an integral part of good management. Some managers may be charismatic; others may not. Some situations or locations may suggest participative managers; others may not. Some cultures may value team-oriented managers; others may not. In the end, what matters is how individual managers see and understand the situational and cultural realities, and then capitalize on their own unique personal skills and abilities, including their approaches to leadership, to get the job done.

It is important to recognize that leadership is a cultural construct. Its meaning is embedded in the diverse cultures in which it is exercised, and changes accordingly. Most important here, it is not a Western construct that is easily expanded to global dimensions. In this regard, the GLOBE researchers identified twenty-two leadership attributes that were widely seen as being universally applicable across cultures (e.g., encouraging, motivational, dynamic, decisive, having foresight) and eight leadership dimensions that were seen to be universally undesirable (e.g., uncooperative, ruthless, dictatorial, irritable). Several other attributes were found to be culturally contingent, however. In other words, their desirability or undesirability was tied to cultural differences.

The different foundations of leadership in Eastern and Western traditions can be traced to ancient Chinese and Greek thought. These foundations are based on the separate paths these two civilizations followed in their efforts to make sense out of human behavior. What is generally referred to as Western civilization traces its origins to the culture, beliefs, and traditions of ancient Greece. In this scheme, the work of a leader consists of bridging the gap between an ideal state and reality (or actual practice) with a goal of achieving perfection. By contrast, the concept of an ideal or archetype that would serve as a model for action and a desirable final state of affairs never developed in ancient China. Instead, reality in China was seen as a process emanating from the interaction between opposing and complementary forces, or *yin* and *yang*. Order did not result from an ideal to be accomplished but from a natural propensity of processes already in motion. Because the emphasis was on current processes evolving here and now, Chinese thinking focused on very concrete and specific situations of everyday life, rather than abstractions of the essence of an ideal form.

What are the leadership implications of these findings for global managers – and local managers who find themselves working increasingly with global firms? Business success in the global arena is predicated on achieving and maintaining a competitive edge. In this endeavor, managers are charged with the responsibility of outperforming their opponents using the toolkit that is available to them. Simply put, the better the toolkit, the greater the probability of success. In particular, the more that managers can understand the environment in which they work, as well as themselves as potential leaders, the greater their odds of success.

Leadership effectiveness can be influenced in no small way by what local cultures mean by leadership. Do they want leaders who are subtle or overt? Do they base leadership on rules or relationships? How are leaders chosen? Similarly, the owner-ship patterns of an organization can determine who becomes a leader, as well as what is expected of him or her. For example, owner-managers sometimes become leaders by definition, while leaders in investor firms may have to fight their way into leadership positions or use charisma to gain attention and support. Leadership patterns are also often influenced by whether the group or team is on-site (face-to-face) or virtual. Each location here can require very different behaviors. Finally, trust levels between leaders and followers are often important, and are often earned in different ways. The lesson for leaders here is to consider the environment as a source of multiple contingencies that must be met with the leadership style that is used or allowed.

Within these constraints, which can differ from event to event, managers usually have multiple choices in their leadership endeavors. At least three factors come into play here: the personal traits of both leaders and followers; the expectations of both leaders and followers, including the extent to which these expectations are in agreement; and the actual leader behaviors on the ground. These factors suggest that managers placed in leadership roles might profitably begin by making sure that they understand themselves as potential leaders (which is easier said than done), as well as the characteristics of the followers and the situations in which they will find themselves.

1.   Understand yourself as a leader

First, it can be highly instructive for managers facing global assignments to think about how they conceptualize leadership and managing people (see Exhibit 6.10). What does the concept of leadership mean to them as managers? Do they believe in a one-size-fits-all approach to leadership or a more tailored approach that recognizes local differences? Do they take a universal, or normative, or contin-gency approach? What are the limitations of their approach in the field in which it matters? Finally, is there a better – perhaps broader – way to do this? Spending some time considering just what leadership means can go a long way towards preparing managers for success in upcoming global assignments. We see a good example of this when comparing Chinese traditions and leadership patterns with those of the West in the example of Emerson Electric at the end of this chapter, but there are many more examples that come to the same conclusion.

1. Understand yourself as a leader	2. Clarify leadership expectations	3. Manage leader behaviors
• Understand how you get things done working with others. • Understand your own particular leadership style. • Understand what additional skills you should learn to be a more effective leader.	• Clarify the expectations you have about yourself as a leader. • Clarify the expectations you have about others as followers. • Clarify the expectations others have about you as a leader.	• Be authentic, but mindful of local constraints. • Tie available rewards to followership. • Be honest and transparent in your leadership efforts. • Continually listen for feedback about your leader behavior.

Exhibit 6.10 Strategies for leading global organizations

A related part of this consideration is the particular leadership skills that individual managers need to develop as part of their overall approach to management. How complete are their communication or negotiation skills? How much do they understand – or can they learn – about the environment in which they work? It goes without saying that the more managers can understand how they approach leadership, as well as the skills they possess to do the job, the greater the likelihood of success.

2.   Clarify leadership expectations

With this understanding – and with their antennae out – managers on global assignments can and should go the extra mile to understand the uniqueness of the local environment and work to accommodate cultural differences when they exist. Understanding environments – cultural, organizational, and situational – represents a necessary first step in preparing to lead multicultural groups or organizations. In fact, there are many ways to accomplish this, including reading books about particular cultures, talking with people who are familiar with various cultures, and keeping one's eyes open when traveling to new locations. However it is accomplished, the global manager either learns to learn quickly about how leadership processes work or runs the risk of suffering the consequences.

A major part of this challenge deals with expectations. Specifically, what are managers' expectations about their own leadership capabilities? What do they expect from others and, equally important, what do others expect of them? Expectations clarify rules and roles and can support efforts to reduce employee anxieties about how their boss (their leader) will operate. As such, the power of these expectations – as well as efforts to clarify them all round – should not be ignored or downplayed.

3. Manage leader behaviors

Global managers are advised to be authentic – that is, be themselves to the extent that local conditions will allow. "Going native" often risks losing authenticity as a manager, leading to confusion and even distrust among subordinates. Indeed, there are many examples of foreign leaders who were chosen largely because they would approach their jobs in radically different ways, not local ones. The challenge for global managers is not to capriciously try to imitate local behaviors – a task fraught with risk and often doomed to failure. Rather, it is to try to understand local conditions and then act in authentic ways that are compatible, but not necessarily synonymous, with local expectations. Being unique can often prove to be a successful behavioral strategy, so long as such behavior is clearly understood by others to be supportive of local goals and objectives and not contradictory to cultural values and expectations. In this regard, global managers who are well prepared in advance of their assignments may have greater leeway in the exercise of leadership than they might imagine. For this to occur, however, a solid understanding of local conditions must come first.

Finally, it is important to remember the simple fact that working with people from different cultural backgrounds can be very challenging, but it can also potentially be very rewarding. For many managers, though, it doesn't happen easily. To the extent that this is correct, the onus is on managers to prepare themselves for success in the future. Leading people from different cultures – and, in fact, being led by people from different cultures – opens up considerable opportunities to learn more about ourselves, discover new ways of doing things, and find creative solutions to problems both old and new. It is clearly part of the developmental process for managers. In this pursuit, continual learning plays a significant – and often underappreciated – role.

KEY TERMS

charismatic leadership • contingency approach to leadership • emotional capital • ethical leadership • gate-keeping leadership • global mindset • GLOBE leadership project • *jeitinho* (Brazilian) • *jogo de cintura* (Brazilian) • leadership • managerial leadership • *medewerkers* (Dutch) • normative approach to leadership • *pok chow* (Malaysian) • strategic leadership • symbolic leadership • team leadership • transactional leadership • transformational leadership • universal approach to leadership • *yang* (Chinese) • *yin* (Chinese)

DISCUSSION QUESTIONS

1. There is an age-old debate concerning whether leaders lead from the front or the rear. Two quotes early in this chapter illustrate this dichotomy: "Leadership

is like beauty; it is hard to define, but you know it when you see it" and "A leader is best when people barely know he exists, who talks little, and when the work is done and the aim fulfilled, people will say, we did this ourselves." Under what circumstances should leaders be highly visible or largely invisible? Explain.

2. The interrelationship between management and leadership can be confusing, particularly in the global arena. Part of this issue is semantic, but part is very real. In your view, under what circumstances must managers be leaders and when can managers just be managers?

3. This chapter discussed four dimensions of organizational leadership: strategic, managerial, team, and ethical. In what ways are all four of these dimensions important for global leaders? Explain.

4. Three contemporary approaches to cross-cultural leadership were introduced in this chapter: universal, normative, and contingency. How might each of these three approaches help us understand leadership processes across cultures? What are the potential drawbacks of each approach?

5. The concept of a "global mindset" has been suggested to characterize the basic leadership traits and abilities of managers working globally. Do you agree or disagree that such a mindset is universally applicable around the world? Explain.

6. Is it possible to build a theory of leadership that is widely applicable around the world? If so, what factors would need to be part of such a theory?

7. Why has the GLOBE leadership study received so much attention among both researchers and managers? In your view, what are the principal lessons of this study for managers?

8. In your view, do men and women approach leadership in fundamentally different ways? If so, is culture or gender more important in determining a leader's style?

9. It was noted in this chapter that leadership processes in China (and much of East and Southeast Asia) stem from ancient Chinese traditions, while many of the leadership practices in the West (notably Europe and North America) stem from ancient Greek traditions. After hundreds of years of global trade and other interactions between these two regions, as well as recent globalization activities, why have we not seen more movement towards a merger of these two trends in leadership practices?

10. The three strategies for leading global organizations summarized in Exhibit 6.10 suggest that successful leadership requires actions – and trust – on the part of both leaders and followers. How can managers work to better understand themselves and their expectations as leaders when working across borders? How can managers work to better understand and meet the expectations of their subordinates?

CASE: EMERSON ELECTRIC – SUZHOU

When Emerson Electric opened its new manufacturing facility in Suzhou, near Shanghai, the initial aim of the facility was to be the company's showcase operation throughout East and Southeast Asia.[13] When it opened, a US-educated Taiwanese manager, supported by a small group of American expatriates, led the initial management team. Although the operation became an early success in meeting its production quotas, cross-cultural conflicts and leadership issues began to emerge from the very beginning. These issues were centered in three principal areas: the nature of team dynamics, the focus on leadership initiatives, and divergent views of time.

The US view of team dynamics favored team diversity, encouraging multiple viewpoints in team meetings to tease out alternative solutions to complex problems. Along with this diversity of opinions came the predictable interpersonal conflicts. Members were encouraged to confront such conflicts head-on in the hopes of leading to more creative innovative solutions. Better results, rather than the quality of personal interactions, signaled the success of the operation. For the Chinese, however, this created an uncomfortable work environment that they were not used to. To many Chinese, teams should have a single, clear, and unified vision, transmitted through a single voice established by the leader. Conflict indicated poor understanding and leadership of the situation. It was something to be avoided, for it signaled a lack of direction, and might cause someone to lose face.

In addition, these prevailing team dynamics rested on a particular approach to leadership that was more Western than Eastern. The Americans followed a largely functionalist approach to management and interpersonal relations, in which leader competence was viewed in terms of task accomplishment, which was seen as instrumental for success. By contrast, the Chinese approach to leadership was largely "personalist" in nature. In other words, it was the personal integrity of each manager that was deemed instrumental for the success of the new plant. The Chinese valued personal integrity in an effort to win the trust and respect of their followers, while the Americans valued job competence and expected their followers to perform well on the tasks at hand. Chinese management rested on individual commitment, often of a personal nature, whereas the Americans valued professional competence.

These different approaches to team leadership also influenced the way managers dealt with confrontation and misunderstandings. In line with the more personal Chinese approach, interpersonal exchanges among participants provided a basis for developing mutual relationships (*guānxi*). This, in turn, facilitated problem resolution. By contrast, the Americans often preferred the more confrontational "trial-style" alternatives. They emphasized company policies and rules, rather than personal interactions. They saw formal behavior as a sign of professionalism.

The Chinese saw this approach as being childish, since, in their view, norms and regulations seldom allowed for the complexity that was required to actually resolve complex issues and problems.

Finally, time perspectives also affected the quality of the interactions between the Chinese and the Americans. In particular, American managers usually favored relatively short time horizons, since they were expatriates who saw their positions as stepping stones to further career advancement. To advance, they needed short-term recognition of results. By contrast, their Chinese counterparts, who had no goals of leaving either China or Emerson, preferred a longer-term perspective. They largely believed that results would follow from setting the proper course of events in motion. Results would then happen naturally; they did not need to be forced.

As a result of these differences, conflicts and misunderstandings continued until Emerson stepped in and largely replaced the American management team with Chinese leaders who were more attuned to local conditions. Today the Suzhou facility is a star player in the Emerson Electric network of companies. This is in no small part attributable to the wisdom of the firm in developing leadership and management practices that were compatible with, and supportive of, the local operating environment. If there is a lesson to be drawn from this example, it is that leadership style is not universal. Local cultures and conditions can have a profound influence on the success of global ventures.

CASE QUESTIONS

1. This case is an example of managerial leadership at the Suzhou facility. However, such leadership should fit with the overall strategic goals and objectives of the entire company (strategic leadership). How is it possible to solve this managerial leadership problem in a way that is consistent with Emerson's overall strategic goals?

2. Did Emerson employ – or try to employ – any of the three contemporary approaches to leadership (Exhibit 6.2). If so, was it a successful approach for them?

3. Culture plays an important role in this case. Is this case a "battle of cultures" between the two major players or is something else going on here?

4. How would you apply the work of the GLOBE study to understand this case? Explain.

5. What does this case teach us about the limitations of creating global teams across cultures? What are the lessons for managers?

6. How did the Chinese and Americans involved in this case each view leadership and leadership effectiveness? Was it possible to reach a compromise on this issue? Why or why not?

7. Differences in time perspectives were also a problem in this case. To the Chinese, the Americans seemed obsessed with short-term results, which disturbed continuity and long-term performance. To the Americans, the Chinese seemed too laissez-faire about scheduling, which jeopardized their position with senior executives who expected short-term results. Both sets of pressures were to some degree beyond the control of the people at Emerson. Could some kind of compromise have been reached here that might satisfy everyone?

8. Was the resolution of this conflict appropriate or was there a better way for Emerson Electric to move forward? Explain.

9. What are the primary lessons of this case for global managers?

10. (*Optional research question*) Based on this case and the three suggested strategies for leading global organizations (Exhibit 6.10), how would you develop a short-course training program that brings together both Chinese and American partners in learning more about leading global subsidiary factories like the one at Suzhou?

NOTES

1. "Davos man and his defects," *The Economist*, January 26, 2013.
2. Warren G. Bennis, *On Becoming a Leader*. Reading, MA: Addison-Wesley, 1989, p. 1.
3. William G. Boltz, "Lao Tzu Tao Te Ching," in Michael Loewe (ed.), *Early Chinese Texts: A Bibliographical Guide*. Berkeley, CA: Institute of East Asian Studies, 1993, pp. 269–92.
4. Richard M. Steers, Carlos Sanchez-Runde, and Luciara Nardon, "Leadership across cultures: new directions in research and theory development," *Journal of World Business*, 47(4) (2012), pp. 479–82.
5. Jun Ishikawa, "Transformational leadership and gatekeeping leadership: the role of norms for maintaining consensus and shared leadership in team performance," *Asia Pacific Journal of Management*, 29(2) (2012), pp. 265–83; Jun Ishikawa, "Leadership and performance in Japanese R&D teams," *Asia Pacific Business Review*, 18(2) (2012), pp. 241–58.
6. Orly Levy, Sully Taylor, Nakiye Boyacigiller, and Schon Beechler, "Global mindset: a review and proposed extensions," in Mansour Javidan, Richard M. Steers, and Michael A. Hitt (eds.), *The Global Mindset*. Amsterdam: Elsevier, 2007, pp. 11–48 (p. 29).
7. Manfred Ertel, "Cleaning up men's messes: Iceland's women reach for power," *Spiegel*, April 22, 2009, pp. 23–6.
8. "Tokyo Electric Power pay cuts all around," *Bloomberg Business Week*, May 2, 2011, p. 20.
9. Robert J .House, Paul J. Hanges, Mansour Javidan, Peter W. Dorfman, and Vipin Gupta, *Culture, Leadership, and Organizations: The GLOBE Study of 62 Societies*. Thousand Oaks, CA: Sage, 2004; Peter Dorfman, Mansour Javidan, Paule Hanges, Ali Dashmalchian, and Robert J. House, "GLOBE: a twenty year journey into the intriguing world of culture and leadership," *Journal of World Business*, 47(4) (2012), pp. 504–18.

10. Chad Brooks, Thornton International Business Report, cited in *Business News Daily*, March 11, 2014, p. 2.
11. Catalyst, "Quick take: women on boards: 2014" (www.catalyst.org).
12. Megha Bahree, "India's most powerful businesswomen," *Forbes*, September 1, 2006.
13. Juan Antonio Fernandez and Liu Shengjun, *China CEO: A Case Guide for Business Leaders in China*. Hoboken, NJ: Wiley, 2007.

Negotiating global partnerships

CHAPTER OUTLINE

- Negotiations and global partnerships   *page* 196
- Preparing for cross-cultural negotiations   201
- Negotiating strategies and processes   207
- Managing conflicts and compromise   211
- Managing agreements and contracts   214
- MANAGER'S NOTEBOOK: Negotiating global partnerships   218
- Key terms   221
- Discussion questions   221
- Case: Perils of being a junior manager   222

APPLICATIONS

7.1 Airbnb, Cuba   *page* 198

7.2 Apple iPhone   200

7.3 GM–SAIC partnership   204

7.4 Bargaining at Teotihuacán   206

7.5 Changed circumstances at Cosco   217

Negotiating agreements and building global partnerships can be a perilous enter-prise. The stakes are often very high, both for the firms and for the negotiators. Indeed, problems often begin as soon as negotiations are opened, with each side trying to gain an advantage at the other's expense (e.g., lower prices, royalty distributions, proprietary technology, market access, and so forth). If and when a contract is signed, the problems only multiply. How do we manage the partnership? Who is in charge? How do we build trust between the partners? How do we harmonize our long-term interests? Indeed, what is the meaning of the contract on which the partnership itself is based? Throughout the process, moreover, the personalities and private agendas of the principal negotiators and their teams and organizations have different goals, demands, and constraints, which can also play a significant role in determining success or failure. Learning from others may be the best way to avoid similar problems in the future.

Did you ever wonder how Pfizer built such a successful global pharmaceutical firm? In part by absorbing other failed pharmaceutical companies like Pharmacia and Upjohn that had the technologies and patents but not the necessary global management know-how to succeed. Several years back, Sweden's Pharmacia and America's Upjohn Pharmaceutical began working on a merger. The goal was to combine both companies' strengths and become a stronger player in the highly competitive global pharmaceutical industry. When the original merger was pro-posed, however, early disagreements arose among the executives over where to locate their new corporate headquarters.[2] Upjohn had long been headquartered in Kalamazoo, Michigan, and suggested that the new venture be run from there. Not surprisingly, Pharmacia, headquartered in Stockholm, had a different idea and suggested Sweden as its preferred location. After considerable negotiation, neither side would yield so it was decided to move the new headquarters and its 100-person executive staff to London instead. The new venture would be known as Pharmacia Corporation. Principal manufacturing centers for the new 30,000-employee com-pany would remain in Kalamazoo, Stockholm, and Milan (a major pharmaceutical hub), and division managers from these operations would fly back-and-forth to London as needed. It was an inauspicious beginning.

Additional clashes between the parties began almost immediately. The hard-driving, mission-oriented Americans from Upjohn routinely clashed with the more consensus-oriented Swedes from Pharmacia. The Americans wanted more cost cutting and accountability, while the Swedes wanted to keep their employees informed and sought feedback on how to move the company forward. American managers scheduled meetings throughout the month of August, a common holiday time for the Swedes. At the same time, the more internationally experienced Swedes were surprised by the parochial manner and lack of sophistication of their American counterparts. Swedish managers had long worked with people from across Europe and tended to be more adaptable and flexible than their American counterparts. Upjohn's culture had banned smoking and required drug and alcohol testing of its employees, while Pharmacia's culture served liquor in the company cafeteria and provided ashtrays in each conference room. Finally, the Upjohn-based CEO kept his managers on a tight leash and required frequent reports, budgets, and staffing updates. Swedish members of the executive team considered this detail of reporting to be a waste of time, and soon simply stopped complying until the CEO finally resigned. Meanwhile, the Swedes concluded that the Americans were trying to take over the partnership and began resisting calls for cooperation. No one was happy.

To put the conflict into perspective, a Swedish executive observed, "I see in America a more can-do approach to things. They try to overcome problems as they arise. A Swede may be slower on the start-up. He sits down and thinks over all the problems, and once he is reasonably convinced he can tackle them, only then will he start running."[3] Another Swedish executive added, "The Swedish approach is more the engineering approach: 'Tell me why and how this thing works.' The American approach is much more direct. Their attitude is: 'Don't teach me to be an expert, just tell me what I need to know to do my job.'"[4]

The original impetus behind the merger was the compatibility of product lines of the two companies. Together, the new company was well placed in the global marketplace with a broad range of highly competitive pharmaceutical products. However, the ongoing cultural conflicts between members of the executive team led to lost opportunities and less than anticipated sales and profits. In the end, New York-based Pfizer acquired Pharmacia, closed its London headquarters, and fired most of its top executives.

Negotiations and global partnerships

The question here is what went wrong and why? Different goals, self-interests, and perceptions regarding how things should be done helped jeopardize the partnership before it actually began, creating conflicts that were difficult to resolve. Compounding the problem was the "us-versus-them" climate that quickly emerged.

And management and problem-solving styles were dramatically different. Think about it: Did one side – or both sides – commit errors that caused the failure of a potentially mutually beneficial partnership? Would they recognize these errors as errors? Or was this partnership an idea that was just not going to happen and neither side could do much about it?

In fact, problems such as these are actually fairly common. Promising partnerships fail to get off the ground due to conflicts and misunderstandings during the negotiation process. Others flounder shortly after the ink on the contract is dry, again due to conflicts and misunderstandings and promises between partners that are not delivered. The question, then, is how to do it better, and this is the topic of this chapter.

Benefits of global partnerships

In today's turbulent business and technological environment, many contemporary global firms from around the world often have no choice but to seek, secure, and successfully manage various international joint ventures and strategic alliances if they intend to survive and succeed over the long haul. Indeed, there are many reasons for this, most of which are based on corporate responses to opportunities and threats in the global business environment.[5] In particular, the major benefits of global partnerships can be summarized as in Exhibit 7.1.

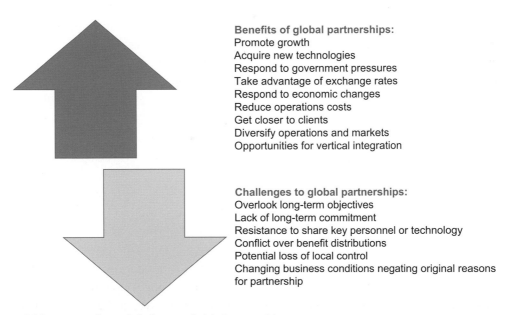

Benefits of global partnerships:
Promote growth
Acquire new technologies
Respond to government pressures
Take advantage of exchange rates
Respond to economic changes
Reduce operations costs
Get closer to clients
Diversify operations and markets
Opportunities for vertical integration

Challenges to global partnerships:
Overlook long-term objectives
Lack of long-term commitment
Resistance to share key personnel or technology
Conflict over benefit distributions
Potential loss of local control
Changing business conditions negating original reasons for partnership

Exhibit 7.1 Benefits and challenges of global partnerships

What does this long list of benefits have in common? Collectively, these actions serve the long-term interests of the partner firms by providing growth opportunities, operating efficiencies, protection from external threats, and, at the end of the day, increased revenues and profits. No wonder that strategic partnerships have become so popular in recent years. As management expert Peter Drucker observed, "alliances, joint ventures, minority stakes, know-how agreements, and contracts will increasingly be the building blocks of successful firms in the future."[6]

APPLICATION 7.1 Airbnb, Cuba

If you don't know much about Cuba, Airbnb's decision to begin booking rooms there sounds pretty unremarkable.[7] After all, Airbnb operates in more than 190 countries, and its offerings are as diverse as they are plentiful. But consider this: Cuba currently has only about a 5 percent open Internet penetration rate, or access to Internet not controlled by the government. And its economy still runs almost entirely on cash. The idea of Airbnb – a company that provides an online marketplace for vacation rentals and processes digital payments – catching on there sounds almost absurd. How did such a digitally driven start-up launch in a country where most people have no daily Internet access and no bank account – and with more than 1,000 potential B&B hosts? By building a partnership in which Airbnb helped its less experienced Cuban partners with technology and Internet access in exchange for rental access to Cuba's beautiful environment.

Since few Cubans had access to the Internet in their homes, many middlemen with Internet access entered the local market to communicate with future guests. But the system was primitive and spotty in coverage. Enter Airbnb, which taught the middlemen how to use the website, and helped them add information. "Maybe they didn't have high-quality photographs in their homes," Airbnb's Molly Turner says. "Maybe their availability was written on paper and not kept online anywhere. Our team did a lot of work behind the scenes talking to hosts and making sure that the information was up to date and current." For the most part, Airbnb was organizing, monetizing, and publicizing the local B&Bs. That was not a small thing.

The middleman-reliant, cash-driven solution is most likely a temporary one. The same policy changes that allowed Airbnb to legally operate in Cuba also allow credit card companies like MasterCard and American Express to operate there. Cuba only recently got its first free public Wi-Fi hotspot. In the long term, Airbnb's initiative allows it to get a foot in the door in what is poised to become a very lucrative tourist destination. The country presents a rare opportunity for the start-up to establish its Cuban market before major hotel chains have the chance.

Airbnb is staking a claim in the business early on by working to create a genuine mutually beneficial partnership.

Think about it . . .

(1) Airbnb is an aggressive and innovative company that takes reasonable risks to grow the company. What particular risks is it taking in expanding into Cuba?

(2) Would you make a financial investment in Airbnb if you had an opportunity? Why or why not?

(3) In general, is there a risk in moving quickly in developing new global partnerships? How might some of these risks be reduced or managed?

Drawbacks to global partnerships

At the same time, while numerous benefits of global partnerships can be identified, it is equally important to recognize some potential drawbacks.[8]

In the haste to create a global partnership, long-term objectives and aspirations can sometimes remain ill defined, leading eventually to an incompatibility of goals as the partnership gets down to managing details. The example of Pfizer illustrates how this can happen.

Partnerships can also fail because of a lack of long-term commitment by one or both partners. The question here is how much a partner is willing to invest in time and resources to insure success. As Wharton Professor Howard Perlmutter observes, "If you [a typical Western company] have a joint venture with a Japanese company, they will send twenty-four people here to learn everything you know, and you will send one person there to tell them everything you know."[9] This hardly sounds likes a strategy for success.

Negotiated partnerships can flounder because one or more partners resist providing key – and often proprietary – information relating to the operations of the venture to their partners. A joint venture between Ford and Mazda stalled for several years when Mazda refused to allow their Ford engineering counterparts access to their research laboratory, despite the fact that Ford then owned 33 percent of Mazda. The conflict was finally resolved by allowing Ford engineers into the Mazda labs, but only for short periods of time.

Conflicts can emerge over how earnings are distributed. Some partners may wish to reinvest earning in research on future products, while other may wish to return all earnings to stockholders or equity partners. This happened when US-based

Rubbermaid broke off an alliance with Dutch DSM Group to manufacture and distribute its products throughout Europe, Africa, and the Middle East because DSM refused to reinvest earnings in future product development, a key to the long-term success of the venture as Rubbermaid saw it.

A major pitfall to successful partnerships is the threatened loss of local control by one partner to another. In point of fact, any partnership involves some loss of autonomy, and in many cases a partner realizes – sometimes too late – that it has lost control over decisions that it values. One partner may wish to continually introduce new products, while the other partner may wish to push older products as long as possible. In other cases, partnerships can lead to one partner buying out the other. One study found that of 150 terminated joint ventures involving Japanese firms, three-quarters ended because the Japanese partner bought out the other partner.[10]

Finally, some partnerships falter because the business conditions change, suggesting more productive strategies for one or both partners. Economic conditions or customer tastes require companies to reassess their business practices and at times previous cooperative arrangements no longer serve the needs or objectives on the firm.

APPLICATION 7.2 Apple iPhone

A good example of some of the drawbacks of global partnerships comes from the increasingly confrontational relationship between Apple, Samsung, and Ericsson. Apple's iPhones are very popular worldwide. Apple does not actually make the phones, however.[8] The components come from a variety of suppliers, while Foxconn, a Taiwanese firm, carries out most of the assembly at a plant in Shenzhen, China. Korean-based rival cellphone manufacturer Samsung Electronics turns out to be a particularly important supplier of Apple. It provides some of the phone's most important components, including the flash memory that holds the phone's apps, music, and operating software and the applications processor that makes the whole thing work. Together, these account for over one-quarter of the component cost of an iPhone. This puts Samsung Electronics in the somewhat unusual position of supplying a significant proportion of one of its principal competitor's chief products in the cellphone market.

Supplying Apple is actually part of Samsung's business model: acting as a supplier of components for others gives it the scale to produce its own products more cheaply. For its part, Apple is happy to let other firms handle component production and assembly, because this leaves it free to concentrate on its strengths: designing elegant, easy-to-use combinations of hardware, software, and services. Stranger still, Apple has sued Samsung on several occasions over the design of Samsung handsets and tablets, claiming that Samsung copied hardware and design features from Apple products. Samsung retaliated by counter-suing.

Now Swedish-based rival – and third partner – Ericsson is suing both Apple and Samsung, claiming its own patent infringements, and claiming tens of millions on unpaid licensing fees from both firms.[11] Still, the three firms' mutually beneficial strategic alliances in both software and hardware continue. Why?

Think about it ...

(1) How is it possible for three companies to work closely together in global strategic alliances when they are not only direct competitors in the market-place, but also suing one another in court?
(2) What does this global partnership tell you about the future of global strategies and competitiveness in dynamic industries such as consumer electronics?
(3) What are the management challenges for Apple, Samsung, and Ericsson in making this long-term relationship work?
(4) Are there lessons from this strategic partnership for other global companies?

Preparing for cross-cultural negotiations

So what have we learned about successful global partnerships? And what have we learned about relationship-building and working with global partners? British management consultant Charles Handy has observed that the most important skills that will be needed in the organizations of the future will be "the ability to win friends and influence people at a personal level, the ability to structure partnerships, and the ability to negotiate and to find compromises. Business will be much more about finding the right people in the right places and negotiating the right deals."[12] If this is correct, what can managers do to prepare themselves?

Successful negotiations, both locally and globally, begin with preparation. In this regard, we can identify three basic initial steps preceding any serious bargaining process (see Exhibit 7.2).

Selecting the right partner

In view of the high "divorce rate" among international joint ventures and strategic alliances, a key question emerges concerning how and where to find the right

Exhibit 7.2 Preparing for cross-cultural negotiations

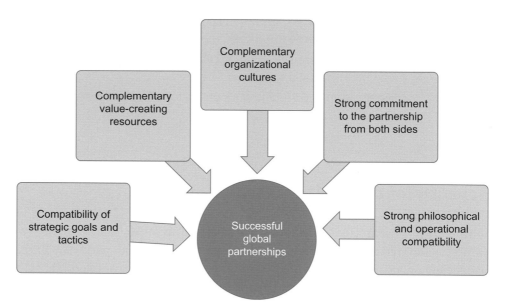

Exhibit 7.3 Key success factors in cross-cultural partnerships

partners and then negotiate a workable partnership. This challenge faces many, if not most, global partnerships today. In this regard, consider what it is that a company most requires in partners in order to expand its business in ways that are both efficient and effective and support its overall mission. Five key success factors can be identified (see Exhibit 7.3):

1. **Solid compatibility of strategic goals and tactics.** First and foremost among these factors is insuring that prospective partners have goals and objectives that mutually reinforce one another's long-term objectives and short-term tactics. Without this congruence, organizational and managerial efforts are likely to dissipate while each partner expends time and resources trying to go

its own separate way. We saw this problem with both the GE–Siemens and the Rubbermaid–DSM alliances above.

2. Complementary value-creating resources. In addition, partners' approaches to methods, systems, inputs, and distribution channels should be similar and therefore understandable and comfortable to each partner. Moreover, ideally each partner would contribute assets to the partnership that the other partner may not have in abundance. The long-standing alliance between Samsung Electronics and Corning Glass is a case in point. When Samsung decided to enter the television market, it had little understanding of critical glass technologies that were critical to manufacturing success. At the same time, Corning was looking to expand its overseas ventures in East Asia based on its previous success in Japan. Both needed partners. As a result of the partnership, Samsung provided a highly educated workforce and capital to match Corning's highly sophisticated glass technology. Both learned from each other and complemented one another through their particular resource contributions to the enterprise.

3. Complementary corporate cultures. Successful partners typically have complementary corporate (or organizational) cultures. Partnering with a firm that has a secretive organizational culture is likely to be unsustainable for a company that thrives on openness. As noted above, Ford and Mazda had this problem in the early years of their alliance. This is not to say that successful partners must have open and cooperative cultures, although this certainly makes partnerships more likely to succeed. Rather, it is to suggest that at the very least that, whatever the cultures are, they should be compatible in their characteristics.

4. Strong commitment to the partnership. A major factor in selecting successful partners is the degree to which both partners have a strong interest and commitment to creating and managing a successful partnership. In the failed venture between General Electric and Siemens, both partners had only a tepid interest in making the venture succeed, with predictable results.

5. Strong philosophical and operational compatibility. Finally, successful partnerships tend to share a common philosophical outlook, as well as strong operational capabilities. They share things in common and, as organizations, often look alike in many ways. At the same time, they frequently share basic philosophies of operational and human resource management. For example, when US-based Davidson-Marley was looking for a British partner, they sought (and found) a viable partner who shared many common characteristics that they felt would be required in order for the venture to succeed.[13] Both used consensus-style management. Both were part of a larger organization that was highly decentralized. Both desired to move to the Continent with a manufacturing presence. Both had similar views on how to grow the business. Both had similar philosophies about both running the business and managing human resources. Both sought an open and fair relationship. As a result, the two partners got off to a good start and began business well along on the learning curve.

APPLICATION 7.3 GM–SAIC partnership

A good example of matchmaking – finding the right partners – is illustrated in the strategic partnership between General Motors (GM) and Shanghai Automotive Industrial Corporation (SAIC) to design and build cars.[14] This venture has been growing in both size and importance since its inception more than a decade ago. The goals of each partner are very clear, as are the required tasks to succeed. When asked to explain GM's Asian expansion, GM executive Steve Girsky observes, "It's simple: do the math." GM's joint ventures sold more than 2 million vehicles in China last year – more than it sold in the United States – and it expects to double that number in five years. SAIC is now the largest automaker in China and is eager to expand its technological capabilities, product lineup, and penetration of foreign markets, and it relies on GM for expertise and know-how. The partners already cooperate in a dozen ventures covering almost every aspect of automotive engineering, manufacturing, and distribution, and any disputes are kept far from public view. The explosion of Chinese auto sales opens up some interesting possibilities. Over the coming ten years, GM believes China will grow by another 12.7 million units – in effect adding another market the size of the United States – and that GM's share will rise along with it. These two companies have worked to understand each other and build a working partnership. SAIC received automotive technology and manufacturing skills; GM received new markets and competitively priced cars.

Think about it . . .

(1) What are GM's long-term strategic objectives in this venture? What are SAIC's long-term strategic objectives?
(2) How much overlap is there between these two sets of goals? In particular, in what areas do these two firms differ in their long-term objectives?
(3) What specific talents or skills must the managers on both sides of this venture have in order to continue with this successful partnership? Explain.

Developing a negotiating strategy

Finding suitable partners may not be as easy as first thought, therefore. Again, the marriage metaphor can be useful in understanding this mating game. Once a potential partner has been identified, however, companies turn their attention to the negotiation process with the aim of building a useful partnership. The negotiation process is the first step in relationship-building, and represents an opportunity for both parties to determine the nature, scope, and ground rules for the partnership. As discussed above, despite the many benefits of a global partnership, there are several drawbacks, and partners must obviously work hard to make it work. During the negotiation process, partners have an opportunity to learn about each party's organizational and national cultures, their interests, commitments, and potential synergistic opportunities to create value.

Unfortunately, when negotiating such a partnership, negotiators frequently commit the mistake of focusing exclusively on signing the deal, assuming that, once the contract has been signed, everything else will follow smoothly. In reality, however, signing a contract is just the beginning of most partnerships. Given the high rate of failure in global partnerships, the real challenge is not signing the contract but putting the deal into practice. Companies that are able to use the negotiation process to get to know their future partners can often foresee and prevent future problems and avoid undue hardships. For these situations, negotiations expert Danny Ertel suggests that negotiators need a new implementation mindset focused on implementation, not just negotiation.[15] He notes that the product of a negotiation isn't a document; it's the value produced once the parties have done what they agreed to do. Negotiators who understand that prepare differently from how dealmakers do. They don't ask, "What might they be willing to accept?" but, rather, "How do we create value together?" They also negotiate differently, recognizing that value comes not from a signature but from real work performed long after the ink has dried. To this end, he suggests five approaches towards an implementation mindset.

1. Start with the end in mind. Think about how the deal will work twelve months after it has been signed. How will you know when it is successful? What can go wrong? These questions focus negotiations on the implementation phase, making the partnership work after the deal has been signed.
2. Help the other side to prepare. Surprising the other party in order to win concessions is likely to backfire, as the other party will not be able to deliver on its promises and both sides will lose.
3. Treat alignment as a shared responsibility. If your interests are not properly aligned, problems will likely emerge at some time in the future. It is worthwhile investing in time to gain acceptance by all those involved in the deal, who will have to make the deal work later on.
4. Send one clear message. Share information with everyone involved in the deal. Withholding information may create early wins, but it will cause problems in the implementation phase if one of the parties feels deceived.
5. Manage negotiations like a business process. Signing a contract is just the first step; the implementation of the deal brings with it important associated costs. To ensure that the implementation is smooth, negotiators use careful preparation and post-negotiation reviews.

Managing the negotiation process

Successful international negotiators are comfortable in multicultural environments and are skilled in building and maintaining interpersonal relationships. A career in this arena is not for the faint-hearted, however; this is a difficult job that requires a number of very specific skills, as well as an ability to handle significant amounts of conflict and stress. Successes come slowly and failures are commonplace. Even so, it is possible to identify a number of personal factors that often differentiate between successful and unsuccessful negotiators: a tolerance of ambiguity; patience, patience, patience; flexibility and creativity; a good sense of humor; solid physical and mental stamina; cultural empathy; curiosity and a willingness to learn new things; and a knowledge of foreign languages.

Among these recommendations, the one suggesting knowledge of a foreign language is perhaps the most controversial. Specifically, how important is it to speak two or more languages? Moreover, when negotiating with a foreign partner, which language should be used? And when should it be used?

APPLICATION 7.4 Bargaining at Teotihuacán

Consider the peril when someone speaks only one language and uses an interpreter for negotiations. A British manager was recently on a business trip to Mexico City and her local host took her to visit the famous Teotihuacán pyramids outside the city.[16] Near the great Pyramid of the Sun, they ran across a Mexican peasant who was selling silver jewelry. The manager found something she liked, and her Mexican host offered to help her negotiate. The peasant made an initial offer, and the visitor's host translated and then suggested a low counter-offer. "If we counter with this, he will then counter with that," said the host.

Not surprisingly, the peasant rejected the counter-offer and offered only a slightly lower price. The host then suggested a higher counter-offer, again explaining that, if she offered x, the peasant would likely come back with y. Bidding and counter-bidding went on like this for several minutes. Finally, the frustrated visitor, who had made little headway in gaining an advantageous price, gave in and agreed to pay almost full price for the item.

At that, the poor Mexican peasant looked at the British manager and asked, in near-perfect English, "Would you like to charge this on your Visa card?" The lesson here is very simple: if you do not understand the local language, at least know who you are bargaining with – and who is doing your translation!

Think about it . . .

(1) What are some of the potential problems of using a translator to conduct business across languages? How might these problems be minimized?
(2) Have you ever been in a similar situation, in which you were talking with someone not realizing others were listening? Why did this happen?

Beyond these personal qualities, experts suggest several general strategies that have been found to facilitate successful negotiations, including the following.[17]

1. Concentrate on building long-term relationships with your partner, not short-term contracts. Long-term partners usually yield greater long-term results for both parties.
2. Focus on understanding the organizational and personal interests and goals behind the stated bargaining positions. What do the various parties to the negotiation hope to gain from an agreement?
3. Avoid over-reliance on cultural generalizations. Although there may be cultural trends within specific countries, no nation is monolithic, and people can vary widely in their personal characteristics. In this regard, Nancy Adler and John Graham investigated negotiation behaviors in both domestic and cross-cultural bargaining, and found that people behave differently when they are negotiating with people from their own culture compared to another culture.[18]
4. Be sensitive to timing. Some cultures – and some negotiators – require considerable patience in working towards an agreement, while others demand prompt resolution of all issues or they will go elsewhere.
5. Remain flexible throughout the negotiations. Circumstances, available information, and opportunities often change, and success sometimes hinges on being both prepared and alert.
6. Plan carefully. Nowhere is the old adage "Knowledge is power" more apt than in understanding international negotiations. Solid preparations can make all the difference.
7. Learn to listen, not just to speak. Develop good listening skills to understand both the content and the context of the message. Use body language and facial expressions to identify informal or subtle cues as to intentions.

Negotiating strategies and processes

In many cultures, business is built on long-standing personal relationships. This is as true in Belgium and Chile as it is in China and India. People do business with partners they know, people they can trust. As such, many international negotiations begin with both sides trying to establish a personal bond. This does not necessarily mean they plan to become lifelong friends; rather, each side needs to determine whether the other party is sufficiently trustworthy to conclude an agreement and stick with it. In many countries, it is insulting (as well as unproductive) to begin a business discussion until after such relationships have been firmly established. In these cultures, it is often said that business relationships must be "warmed up" before getting down to serious negotiations. This is a good principle to remember.

Ironically, the one place where such relationships, while important, are not necessarily critical to a successful negotiation is the United States, where legal contracts are frequently seen as a substitute for personal relationships (see below). As a result, US negotiators are notorious for wanting to get down to business immediately – a practice that frequently leads to frustration and failure. More successful US negotiators understand the critical importance of subtleties and patience, not brashness and drive. Accordingly, most successful international managers – regardless of their home country – invest considerable time and effort in getting to know their prospective partners. This frequently includes a variety of social activities (dinners, golf, etc.), at which it is often inappropriate to discuss any business whatsoever. The stage is being set.

Competitive versus problem-solving strategies

Generally speaking, there are two basic strategies for negotiation: competitive negotiation and problem-solving negotiation. The competitive approach views negotiations as a win–lose game, while the problem-solving approach seeks to discover a win–win solution from which both sides can benefit, if at all possible. Exhibit 7.4 illustrates how these two different strategies are played out during negotiation.

In competitive negotiation, each side tries to give as little as possible. They frequently begin with unrealistically high demands and make concessions only grudgingly. Competitive negotiators will, at times, use dirty tricks or other tactics that allow them to win. Little thought is given to building a long-term relationship between the parties. Since starting from inflexible positions often leads to outcomes that satisfy neither side, each side often develops negative attitudes towards the other. As a result, losers in the agreement often seek revenge, such as reneging on parts of the contract at a later date or substituting inferior-quality materials in production orders.

By contrast, problem-solving negotiation begins with the basic tenet that negotiators must separate positions from interests. Instead of defending a company's position as a major goal in the negotiation process, problem-solving negotiators begin by seeking a mutually satisfactory ground that is beneficial to

Exhibit 7.4 Competitive and problem-solving negotiation strategies

Stages in negotiation	Competitive bargaining	Problem-solving bargaining
(1) Preparation	Identify current economic and other benefits your firm seeks from the deal. Prepare to defend your firm's position.	Define the long-term strategic interests of your firm. Prepare to overcome cross-cultural barriers to defining mutual interests.
(2) Relationship-building	Look for weaknesses in your opponent's position. Learn about your opponent, but reveal as little as possible.	Adapt to the other side's culture. Separate the people involved in negotiation from the problems and goals that need to be solved.
(3) Information exchange and first offer	Provide as little information as possible to your opponent. Make your position explicit. Make a hard offer that is more favorable to your side than you realistically expect to achieve.	Give and demand to receive objective information that clarifies each party's interests. Accept cultural differences in speed of response and type of information needs. Make firm but reasonable first offer.
(4) Persuasion	Use dirty tricks and pressure tactics when appropriate to win.	Search for new creative options that benefit the interests of both parties.
(5) Concessions	Begin with high initial demands. Make concessions slowly and grudgingly.	Search for mutually acceptable criteria for reaching accord. Accept cultural differences in starting position and in how and when concessions are made.
(6) Agreement	Sign only if you win and then ensure that you sign an ironclad contract.	Sign when the interests of your firm are met. Adapt to cultural differences in contracts when necessary.

the interests of both sides (see Exhibit 7.5). Dirty tricks are avoided because they poison the development of long-term mutually advantageous relationships. Objective information is preferred whenever possible as a basis for discussion and problem-solving efforts, instead of unrealistic sales pitches or hyperbole. Often problem-solving negotiation facilitates the identification of creative new ways to provide both parties with what they want to achieve. Furthermore, even when mutually advantageous solutions are not found, both sides leave the table believing that sincere efforts were made on both sides. This leaves open the possibility of returning to the bargaining table in the future when another opportunity presents itself.

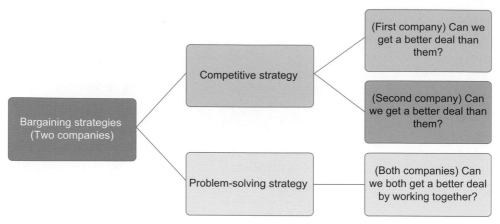

Exhibit 7.5 Examples of competitive and problem-solving negotiation strategies

Three important points emerge from this case regarding the choice between using either competitive or problem-solving bargaining strategies. First, it is very easy in cross-cultural negotiation to misread the intentions of the other party. Hence a detailed understanding of the cultural backgrounds of one's opponent becomes critical in determining whether he or she is stating a highly inflexible position or offering a genuine opportunity to strike a deal. This is why many successful international negotiators always have advisors at their side who are intimately familiar with the culture and traditions of the other party. Second, culture sometimes predisposes negotiators to select one approach over the other. For example, observers note that some US managers believe there has to be a winner and a loser, while many Japanese managers prefer a problem-solving approach. The smart bargainer understands this and adjusts his or her strategy accordingly. Finally, when possible, most experts on international negotiation recommend a problem-solving approach, because it tends to lead to better long-term solutions and relationships. This is particularly true in negotiating global partnerships. Winning now may mean big losses later. It is important to remember that the failure of the partnership may be more expensive than small concessions given during the negotiation process.

Bargaining and concessions

Clearly, the ultimate goal of a negotiation is to arrive at a mutually agreed contract that is legally binding in both countries. To achieve this, concessions must be made. What is interesting here is that culture can, at times, influence how these concessions are determined. In North America, for example, companies frequently use what is called a sequential approach to concession making (see Exhibit 7.6).

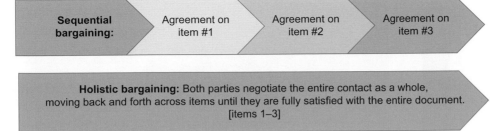

Exhibit 7.6 Sequential and holistic bargaining strategies

In other words, they prefer to go through a proposed contract item by item and get agreement on each item as they proceed sequentially through the proposals.

By contrast, and popular throughout much of Asia, there is the holistic approach to concession-making. In this the two parties work their way through the entire proposed agreement, but do not agree to anything until they have completed their review. They then discuss the contract in its entirety and make final proposals and counter-proposals aimed at reaching a complete agreement. The holistic approach frequently perplexes novice North American negotiators when they learn that a point they thought was already agreed upon resurfaces to be discussed later by their Asian counterparts.

Managing conflicts and compromise

Despite well-intended efforts to develop a smooth bargaining process and eliminate sources of conflict, the chances are that conflicts are still likely to emerge at various points throughout the negotiation process. Not only are such conflicts often inevitable, they can at times be helpful in forcing both parties to look deeply into what each side is actually trying to accomplish. The important issue is this: when conflicts between partners or prospective partners emerge, what are managers supposed to do? A long tradition of studies on conflict management points to several common strategies for dealing with conflict.[19]

Process strategies for resolving conflicts

To begin with, consider five common process strategies for resolving conflicts, along with some factors that may help managers decide which one fits best the specifics of their unique situation (see Exhibit 7.7). These strategies are accommodation, collaboration, competition, avoidance, and compromise. From a negotiation standpoint, determining which of these strategies may be most suitable is

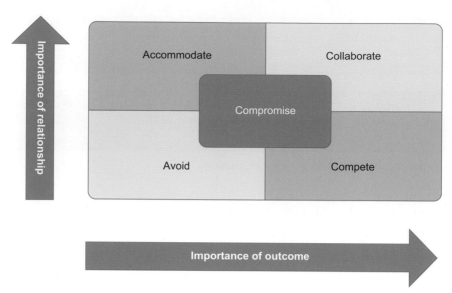

Exhibit 7.7 Conflict resolution strategies

influenced – though not exclusively – by two factors. First, how important is the *relationship*? Is it highly valued (perhaps essential) or just convenient? What would happen if this relationship were broken? Second, how important is the *outcome*? Is this contract or partnership essential for your organization's goals and objectives or are there alternative ways to accomplish them?

Think about the options. First, in some situations, developing and nurturing a relationship may be more important than the specific outcome of a particular issue of conflict. In these cases, strong assertive strategies may be counterproductive, and accommodating the other party may be the best strategy. Small losses may represent big wins later on, as they will strengthen a relationship that is critical for success. Second, at other times the relationship is important, but so too is the outcome of the particular issue on the table. In such cases, perhaps the most successful strategy is to look for ways of collaborating: jointly looking for a solution to the problem that represents a win–win for all involved. Third, there are times when the relationship is not that important, yet the outcome may be critical. These are occasions when competition is most appropriate. Fourth, there are times when a conflict is just not worth bringing forward. The issue itself may not be that important and the relationship may not be critical. At such times the advice is "Don't sweat the small stuff," and avoid the conflict altogether. Finally, in situations in which both the relationship and the outcome are reasonably important, but time does not allow negotiators to engage in a collaborative problem-solving exercise, parties may decide to compromise, or split the difference in a solution that is acceptable all round.

Obviously, these five strategies are not always as clear-cut as they might at first appear, and other approaches may combine a variety of strategies to work more effectively. Moreover, several contingency factors can also enter into decisions concerning the most appropriate conflict resolution strategy. These include the following.

1. How crucial is a particular solution to one or more team members? If this is the case, a short-term imposition of a solution or long-term educational efforts are likely to make more sense than avoidance, negotiation, and accommodation. Of course, experienced global managers also need to understand that taking actions such as the unilateral imposition of a solution can have adverse consequences. For example, causing someone to lose face in many Asian countries presents very real risks for the long-term viability of the team.
2. How much power does each party have vis-à-vis the others? Stronger team members, for instance, can afford competitive strategies to which weaker members may have to acquiesce and be accommodating, while similarly powerful members may need to engage in collaborative forms of negotiation.
3. The viability of a given strategy is also dependent on the timing with which a solution needs to happen. Urgent action may be easily compatible with avoidance and accommodation strategies, but less so with collaboration or compromise, which can be more time-consuming.
4. It is also important to think about any precedents that may be created by negotiators looking for expediency. For example, accommodation by a negotiator in order to secure a contract or partnership quickly may limit approaches that managers wish to take in the future. Expectations would have been created that may be difficult to modify.

People strategies for resolving conflicts

Taking a somewhat more applied viewpoint, conflict resolution expert Nick Carstarphen suggests several people strategies to consider when dealing with conflicts during the negotiation process.[20]

1. Prepare people. Preparing successfu negotiators includes fostering a positive and open attitude towards dialogue, focusing on commonalities, not differences. People are central to any conflict, and in order to find common ground "we" must replace the attitude of "us-versus-them."
2. Assess the situation. Preparing the negotiation process means fully assessing the situation, identifying the parties that should be present and the appropriate interventions to deal with the conflict. For instance, is it necessary to ask for outside help or can the conflict be solved with the people at the table? Is the conflict widespread or concentrated on a particular person?

3. Explore past and present. Exploring the past and the present, the origins of the conflict and its current dynamic, helps uncover cultural assumptions and meanings that may be obstructing collaboration. Giving negotiators an opportunity to explore how things were in previous meetings and what frustrates them now may make it possible to identify the real issues causing the conflict.

4. Envision the future. By asking negotiators to imagine a common future, creativity and imagination may help to find solutions to the conflict. By envisioning a future together, common values and needs are likely to become salient, and a common solution may emerge.

5. Create solutions. Resolving conflicts is not just about envisioning possibilities; it is also about taking action. Here, negotiators must identify concrete actions to be taken to ease the conflict, and then take those actions, evaluating their effectiveness along the way and adjusting them if necessary.

6. Rejuvenate and reflect. Dealing with conflicts is an intensive, energy-consuming endeavor. It is important to pause from time to time, to reflect, regroup, and recover energies before the process can continue. It is also important to take time to celebrate successes and give a boost to morale.

7. Don't forget relationships. Finally, conflicts are often about relationships between individuals or groups. It is the very interdependence among people that can create conflict, and no solution will be found if this interdependence is not acknowledged and fostered.

Managing agreements and contracts

If countries often approach negotiating strategies so differently, it is not surprising that other aspects of building and managing partnerships can also be quite different. Consider contracts. In most Western countries, a contract – especially a written contract – represents a company's most effective tool against uncertainty and risk. This is not surprising in view of the largely monochromic orientation of these countries, where message content is often far more important than message context. Every dictionary in the world gives roughly the same definition of a contract: an agreement between two or more parties that establishes rules governing their business transactions.[21] Contracts typically spell out levels of investment, areas of responsibility and accountability, cost data when appropriate, control over proprietary technology, and procedures for sharing the benefits (and losses) of the enterprise. As such, most managers from most countries believe that written contracts are far superior to the proverbial handshake among honorable people. Or, as legendary MGM co-founder Louis B. Mayer observed long ago about negotiating with screen actors, "A handshake is only as good as the paper it's written on."[22]

Mutual trust and contract interpretation

In many regions of the world, much of the business is conducted on the basis of personal relationships and mutual trust, as in the case of *guānxi* in China (see Chapter 4). In these regions, prospective partners often see written contracts as a sign of distrust; contracts are unnecessary among trusted friends. It is very easy for this divergence across cultures to create a dilemma for global managers. What do they do when trying to develop a secure business relationship in countries where written securities are not commonplace? Again, how much can you trust a handshake?

In theory, a contract is a legally binding instrument that guarantees for all parties to the contract what will happen and when (e.g., what each item or product will cost, when materials will be delivered, the costs of technology transfer, etc.). Also, in theory, certain penalties are stipulated for noncompliance with the contract (e.g., financial penalties for late payments, criminal penalties for fraud or theft, etc.). Good negotiators are adept at capturing the essence, as well as the details, of contracts in clearly understandable wording. Moreover, experienced negotiators typically use specialized attorneys to ensure that contracts are internally consistent (i.e., there are no vague or conflicting clauses within the contract) and comply with local and international laws. They will also often have contracts translated into all the languages of the parties to it, so that the details and provisions are clear to everyone.

Unfortunately, most experienced managers also know that there can be a sharp difference between what a contract says and what it actually means. At times local governments will refuse to implement a contract for various reasons or will support the local partner to an agreement. As a result, there is a critical need for all parties to a contract to trust each other's personal integrity and corporate intentions. This is when culturally based practices such as *guānxi* come into play. A written contract between strangers represents a conflict waiting to happen in much of the world. This is why successful global negotiators invest so much time in getting to know their partners and nurturing this relationship after the contract is signed and implemented. As a result, the importance of doing business with long-term and trusted partners should not be underestimated.

Doctrine of changed circumstances

One of the principal reasons for contract disputes around the world is the cultural variation in the meaning of a contract. To many Westerners (e.g., people in the United Kingdom, Australia, Germany, Canada, the United States), a contract is a

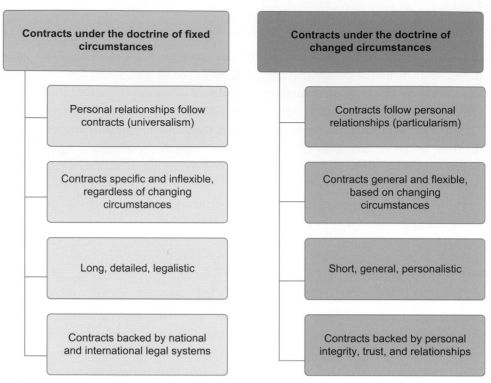

Exhibit 7.8 Contracts and the doctrine of changed circumstances

legal document that spells out the obligations of all the parties. It is the culmination of a successful negotiation process. In the West, where people tend to have an internal locus of control (i.e., they believe that they largely control their own fate), a contract is a contract. It can be renegotiated upon expiration, but not until then unless otherwise specified in advance. As a result, Western negotiators have to anticipate and prepare for every conceivable future problem, leading to rather lengthy business contracts.

Elsewhere in the world, where people tend to have a more external locus of control (i.e., they believe that the future is largely influenced by fate or karma), many businesses accept something called the doctrine of changed circumstances (see Exhibit 7.8). This doctrine holds that, when circumstances beyond the control of a business partner change (e.g., hurricane damage, changes in government policies, price increases for raw materials), both partners are obliged to renegotiate the original contract so that neither party loses materially. Under this doctrine, which can be found throughout much of Asia, Africa, and Latin America, a contract is thought of as a written recognition of a personal relationship between the two parties. As such, it is the beginning, not the end, of the process of mutual benefit as a result of working together.

APPLICATION 7.5 **Changed circumstances at Cosco**

It is not unusual for companies that charter ships to fail to pay their owners, and for the owners to have these vessels and their cargoes impounded. Normally, though, this is either because the company is in financial trouble or because of disputes over delays. It is rare for a charter company to insist that it could pay but won't, simply because shipping rates have gone down since it signed the contract. That is what Cosco did, however.[23] Cosco, China's largest shipping firm, is a major owner as well as a charterer of the huge dry-bulk vessels that feed China's appetite for raw materials. In recent years it has signed numerous long-term contracts to carry goods around the world. When contract rates dropped, however, the company sent word to its partners that it needed to renegotiate their contracts. When partners balked, Cosco began withholding payments on the contracts, describing this as a normal "market-based" approach for the company. The company, owned by the Chinese government, clearly had an ability to pay. Instead, however, it used its market position and refusal to meet its financial obligations to exact revised contracts that were more favorable to the company. In the West, such behavior borders on the illegal or unethical; in this case, apparently, it represents sound business practices. The logic is simple: conditions have changed, so we must renegotiate the contract.

Think about it . . .

(1) Are Cosco's actions illegal or unethical or simply the way business is done today?
(2) What recourse do Cosco's partners have in this dispute?
(3) What are the long-term consequences of Cosco's actions?

An experienced diplomat once observed about his negotiating experiences in China, "The Chinese think in terms of a process that has no culmination. Westerners think in terms of concrete solutions to specific problems."[24] Indeed, many Asian, African, and Latin American companies prefer to have only very brief general contracts (perhaps two or three pages in length), in the belief that it is impossible to anticipate all future circumstances that may affect the contract. As circumstances change, it is often expected that the contract will be modified to fit the new situation. After all, an honorable person would not take advantage of his or her partner if changes occur that were not caused by the two partners. Honorable people look after the interests of each other.

In the East, the doctrine of changed circumstances is supposedly designed to maintain harmony among partners; in the West, it violates the pursuit of mastery over one's environment. This fundamental difference underlying both contract negotiations and contract implementations between global partners often represents a major threat to the long-term prospects of global partnerships. Consider: if written (or even unwritten) contracts in one part of the world frequently mean something very different in another part, and two parties are negotiating an international joint venture, how can either side have confidence, predictability, and trust in their agreements? And what happens to the rookie manager who fails to understand this?

MANAGER'S NOTEBOOK

Negotiating global partnerships

What did we learn here? Some experts have suggested that the most important skills that will be needed in the organizations of the future will be an ability to win friends and influence people on a personal level, to structure partnerships, and to negotiate and find compromises when possible. Business will be much more about finding the right people in the right places and negotiating the right deals. To the extent that this is correct, negotiating skills and skills in building long-term and mutually beneficial relationships will certainly be placed highly in the set of the most important management skills.

People do business with partners they know and trust. As such, many international negotiations begin with both sides trying to establish a personal bond. This does not necessarily mean that they plan to become lifelong friends but, rather, that each side needs to determine if the other party is sufficiently trustworthy to conclude an agreement and stick with it.

Successful negotiators are comfortable in multicultural environments and are skilled in building and maintaining interpersonal relationships. Successes come slowly and failures are common. Nonetheless, it is possible to identify a number of personal factors that can differentiate between successful and unsuccessful negotiators: a tolerance for ambiguity; patience, patience, patience; flexibility and creativity; a good sense of humor; solid physical and mental stamina; cultural empathy; curiosity and a willingness to learn new things; and a knowledge of foreign languages.

In most Western countries, a contract – especially a written contract – represents a company's most effective tool against uncertainty and risk. This is not surprising, in view of the largely monochromic orientation of these countries, where message content is often far more important than message context. Even so, in many regions of the world, much of the business is conducted on the basis of personal relationships and mutual trust, as in the case of *guānxi* in China. In these regions, prospective partners often see written contracts as a sign of distrust; the view is that contracts are unnecessary among trusted friends.

1. Manage preparations	2. Manage negotiations	3. Manage agreements
• Select a suitable partner with complementary goals and objectives • Develop a negotiation strategy • Prepare to manage the negotiation process	• Build initial relationships • Exchange information (competitive or problem-solving) • Bargain in good faith • Make concessions (sequential or holistic) • Finalize agreement	• Build mutual trust • Interpret the contract • Determine contract flexibility (e.g., changed circumstances) • Manage the partnership

Exhibit 7.9 Strategies for negotiating global partnerships

Throughout the negotiation process, several types of environmental constraints help determine the choices or options that managers have available. Remember, factors found in the cultural, organizational, and situational contexts can all influence managerial choices. For example, a culture based on harmony or rules will likely require different managerial behavior from one based on mastery or relationships. Similarly, managerial behavior in the field can be influenced by the degree of centralization in one or more organizations (e.g., who makes the decisions?), as well as whether the organizations in question – and their managers – are risk-averse or risk-oriented. Finally, managerial action can be constrained by such situational factors as the degree to which the negotiating partners have mutual or competing goals, where the negotiations are taking place, and the time pressures involved (i.e., do negotiators have sufficient time to build a personal relationship or not?).

With these demands and constraints in mind, managers face three key issues as they approach bargaining and negotiations with other parties: preparations, negotiations, and agreements (see Exhibit 7.9). These may be considered as three strategies for action. Once again, the interplay between understanding the environment in which these negotiations take place and taking well-considered actions at the table should serve to clarify both what managers attempt to do and how well they accomplish their task.

1. Manage preparations

First, we have already discussed several preparation issues, including selecting a partner, developing a negotiation strategy, and preparing to the extent possible to manage the negotiation process. This last requirement suggests that managers should consider multiple options or negotiation scenarios prior to actual negotiation, so that they can move quickly as circumstances or positions change. Since negotiations are dynamic by nature, experienced managers typically view them much like a chess game. It is usually advantageous to have several moves identified in advance. It is also wise to look for subtle or even silent moves that may help explain future actions (see Chapter 5).

2. Manage negotiations

The second issue involves the negotiation process itself. Various aspects of this process have been discussed in detail in the chapter, including management strategies and tactics. Two key points should be made here. The first involves the importance of building relationships prior to serious negotiation. Getting to know one's prospective partners can avoid considerable problems either later in the negotiation process or after an agreement has been signed. The second involves ethical behavior. Definitions of acceptable ethical behavior often vary by culture. The problem is that many managers don't realize this, and insist on applying their own standards to situations around the globe. One could suggest that this is naïve. Worse, one could suggest that this is dangerous, in that such managers may be impervious to subtle suggestions or actions that can become problematic later. This reality suggests that managers would be well advised to avoid anyone who talks or acts in ways that give rise to questions about his or her ethical standards. Working with such individuals – or companies – is much like the proverbial "playing with fire." It is simply not worth the risk, either to your reputation or the reputation of your company.

3. Manage agreements

A third and final issue also emerges that people tend to ignore. Once a formal contract or agreement has been signed, it is not the end of the process; it is actually only the beginning. Contracts are living documents. As noted earlier, while some cultures believe a written and signed contract represents a permanent document, others believe it remains flexible. Understanding this in advance is crucial. Beyond this, research discussed above has demonstrated that relationships are ever changing, and global agreements are no exception. They must be nurtured and managed through time if they are to succeed. Indeed, one of the principal responsibilities of many frequent flyers is to visit partners on a regular basis to renew the relationship and resolve disagreements before they get out of hand and cause genuine harm.

All this clearly requires considerable time, and suggests a straightforward conclusion: global partnerships should be pursued only when and if all parties to the agreement see genuine mutual advantage. If corporate goals are compatible and trust can be developed, partnerships can be fruitful for all parties. Lacking this, they become risky propositions that should, more often than not, be avoided.

KEY TERMS

accommodation (conflict resolution) • *aisatsu* (Japanese) • avoidance (conflict resolution) • collaboration (conflict resolution) • competition (conflict resolution) • competitive negotiation • compromise (conflict resolution) • contract • doctrine of changed circumstances • holistic approach (to negotiation) • implementation mindset • people strategies (resolving conflicts) • problem-solving negotiation • process strategies (resolving conflicts) • sequential approach (to negotiation)

DISCUSSION QUESTIONS

1. Carlos Slim has sufficient funds to create businesses in any format he likes. Why do you think he believes so strongly in alliances and partnerships where he may lose some control over business activities?

2. Both the Pfizer example at the beginning of the chapter and the GE–Mitsubishi case at the end of the chapter illustrate what appear to be very poor partnering decisions and actions by corporate leaders. What might account for this? Are there lessons here for managers and executives trying to build productive partnerships? Explain.

3. Are there any special management skills required for companies that make heavy use of global alliances and partnerships? If so, what are these skills?

4. Management consultant Charles Handy suggests that the most important skills that will be needed in the organizations of the future will be an ability to win friends and influence people at a personal level, an ability to structure partnerships, and an ability to negotiate and to find compromises. In today's highly competitive and, some would say, destructive business environment, do you agree with his assertion? Why or why not?

5. Exhibit 7.2 outlines a process for preparing for cross-cultural negotiations. This process obviously takes time and considerable effort. In today's fast-paced business environment, can companies streamline or bypass some of these suggested processes? Explain.

6. How would you train junior managers to follow the suggestions of an implementation mindset discussed in this chapter? Explain.

7. If most joint ventures fail within five years and business and technology change so quickly, why is it important to manage the negotiation process so tightly?

8. Is a problem-solving bargaining strategy always preferable to a competitive strategy or are there times when a competitive approach to bargaining is more useful? Explain.

9. Information exchange is an important part of the negotiation process. What can managers do when they realize that their prospective partners are using a different standard of information exchange? What are the long-term effects of this on building a mutually beneficial partnership?

10. Is it always necessary for both parties to an agreement to believe that the agreement is equitable? Are there circumstances when inequitable agreements may be the best solution for both parties?

11. If two parties to a negotiation use different bargaining strategies from each other (e.g., sequential vs. holistic) or have different concepts of how an agreement should be implemented (e.g., doctrine of changed circumstances), how can negotiations continue? What might be appropriate managerial strategies when such a situation occurs?

CASE: PERILS OF BEING A JUNIOR MANAGER

While General Electric had long dominated the market for basic electrical supplies, recent competition from Asia and Europe had begun to seriously erode its market share and the company was determined to reestablish itself in this lucrative global market.[25] In its Asian markets, GE had a long-standing partnership with Japan's Fuji Electric Corporation, but this alliance failed to produce the results GE sought. Perhaps it was time to find a new partner. Jeff Depew, an aspiring young manager at GE, was assigned the task of laying the groundwork to make this happen. Fluent in Japanese, he was sent to Japan with instructions to cultivate a new relationship with Mitsubishi Electric, one of Japan's premier electrical equipment manufacturers and a possible partner for GE's new strategy. It was made clear to him by his boss that success in this assignment would position him well for continued career progression upon his return to the United States.

As Depew tells the story, upon his arrival in Tokyo he began a carefully orchestrated effort to nurture relationships with his counterparts at Mitsubishi and over time won their respect and trust. What he envisioned was a quantum leap of the sort that would catch the attention of GE's then-CEO Jack Welch. Welch valued managers who could take control and make deals happen. He wasted little time on the niceties of negotiation and preferred to work with people who thought as big as he did. To Depew, a possible alliance between GE and Mitsubishi was just such a venture. The partnership would catapult them into a position of dominance in the global market with combined annual sales of $3.5 billion. As Depew saw it, the partnership made strategic and economic sense for both partners. The combined company would be the world leader in six of its eight product lines and would allow GE to establish a working relationship with a leading Japanese conglomerate.

After lengthy and promising discussions with Mitsubishi, Depew was finally ready to invite GE's CEO to come to Japan to meet Moriya Shiki, Welch's counterpart at Mitsubishi. The visit (called an *aisatsu*, or formal ceremonial greeting) would be a brief get-acquainted meeting to demonstrate GE's commitment to the project and begin to establish a working relationship between the two CEOs.[26] A date was set for the official meeting.

When Welch arrived, Depew briefed him on the progress that had been made, as well as the tasks that remained to be done. While many details of the agreement remained to be negotiated, everything looked good to Depew and he estimated that a deal could be reached after approximately five months of further cultivation and negotiation. Welch was obviously pleased and excited about the prospects. A meeting was scheduled for the next morning with Mitsubishi.

The official meeting between the two companies was a standard protocol session – a mating dance that preceded most major alliances. Not only did Welch understand this, he had participated in several such rituals in the past. In these initial meetings, specific discussions about business were studiously avoided. Instead, only general issues were discussed, such as the state of the US electronics industry and Japanese competition. It was only later in private meetings that the details of any partnership would be discussed. The meeting between Welch and Shiki would proceed along a similar path. The two CEOs would exchange pleasantries, declare their mutual respect for one another, and withdraw. It was too early to discuss details; subordinates would handle this later.

When Jack Welch and his colleagues arrived at the Mitsubishi building for the scheduled meeting, he was both well prepared and enthusiastic. He was ushered into the conference room and formally introduced to Mr. Shiki and his subordinates. To Depew, both executives were impressive. Shiki was the epitome of the Japanese executive: dignified, elegant, smooth, and very much in control. As they exchanged business cards, both executives began with a profuse exchange of thanks along with the expected expressions of mutual admiration.

But then without notice, Welch quickly ended the pleasantries and launched into a discussion of why a deal was attractive to GE: the product lines were impressive, the cultures could work well together, and everything seemed to be a good fit. The venture would be a powerful force in the marketplace, one that would allow both Mitsubishi and GE to smash the competition. Mr. Shiki nodded his head quietly while Welch went on to point out that in the past, GE had tried to do deals with other big Japanese companies, but had always had troubles. Maybe this time would be different, he observed. He noted that both firms had large bureaucracies, but that this should not get in the way. Then he surprised everyone by suggesting that the two companies should agree to a deal then and there.

Depew was surprised, but couldn't betray his emotions in the meeting. He sat quietly but nervously. GE had crossed the protocol line. Perhaps they could have gotten away with this in the United States, but not in Japan where protocol was religiously observed. It was highly inappropriate to press for an immediate commitment when negotiating with the Japanese – especially when Mitsubishi had already agreed to GE's proposed five-month timetable for closure of the deal. Shiki looked over at Depew as if to say, "What's going on here?" but Depew didn't have the slightest idea. After a long period of silence, Shiki reiterated his desire to go ahead with the plan – a subtle yet significant indication of how badly his company wanted to finalize the agreement. However, he was not about to conclude a final agreement on the spot.

It was well understood by both parties, although not discussed, that Mitsubishi Electric was trying to extricate itself from a long-standing agreement with GE rival Westinghouse. Mitsubishi was aware that Westinghouse was quietly preparing to abandon its business in Japan, and Shiki needed a new US partner on whom he could depend for the foreseeable future. GE suited his goals perfectly. However, Japanese etiquette required Mitsubishi to inform Westinghouse of its intentions to change partners before signing a formal agreement with GE. But when Shiki mentioned this obligation to Welch, Welch questioned why this was necessary. Shiki tried without success to explain the nature of the relationship, but Welch concluded that his counterpart was trying to play him off GE against Westinghouse. He reiterated that he didn't want to move forward unless Mitsubishi was unequivocally committed to the partnership. Shiki assured him that this was the case and that the agreement would be completed in due time.

With that, the meeting broke up amicably and Welch and his colleagues returned to their hotel. Later that evening, Welch observed that he had pressed Shiki because he concluded that if the agreement was not completed quickly, it would not be accomplished at all. He was convinced that Shiki's reluctance to quickly agree to the proposal meant that he was not serious about it. The next morning, while Welch made a courtesy call on the Ministry of Trade and Industry, Depew returned to Mitsubishi. This meeting went better than the previous one, and a consensus was soon reached concerning how negotiations should proceed and how the agreement should be structured. The deal was back on track. Welch returned to New York and Depew was assigned the task of moving things forward.

Several weeks later, however, Depew received a call from his boss in New York telling him that Welch was leaning against signing the agreement. He felt he had been sandbagged and embarrassed by one of the most prominent leaders of the Japanese business community. The only way to save the deal now, Depew was told, was for Shiki to write a personal letter of apology to Welch in which he stated unequivocally that he would agree to the proposal. Depew dutifully approached

Mitsubishi with his orders. After some negotiation, it appeared that Mitsubishi was on the verge of complying with Welch's demand when Depew received another call from his boss notifying him to break off all negotiations with Mitsubishi. Instead, he was to return to GE's former partner, Fuji Electric, and attempt to rebuild relationships so a new joint venture could be developed.

Two months later, Jeff Depew was recalled to New York headquarters. His boss explained that GE had decided to take a different approach to the Asia/Pacific region, focusing more on sales than business development. As a result of the change, GE was eliminating his position.

Shortly after the failure, Fuji Electric dissolved its partnership with GE. In accordance with the dissolution agreement, Fuji then began selling products in North, Central, and South America under its own brand name. At the same time, the Mitsubishi–Westinghouse partnership not only survived, it expanded and is thriving today. Jeff Depew now works in the high-tech world of Silicon Valley and is doing well.

CASE QUESTIONS

1. There are three principal actors in this case, two CEOs and a junior manager. How does each of them view the situation facing them? What, if any, are the principal differences in their views of the situation?
2. Does it look like either partner prepared sufficiently for their negotiation sessions (see Exhibit 7.2 for a guide)? Why or why not? Did they have the best possible implementation mindset? What could have been done better?
3. How would you describe the negotiation strategies of each prospective partner (see, for example Exhibits 7.4 and 7.7)?
4. How did the parties handle conflicts as they arose? In your view, how could these have been better managed?
5. What could Jeff Depew have done differently to achieve a more positive outcome in terms of a potential partnership between the two companies?
6. What could Depew have done differently to protect his own job?
7. This case tells Jeff Depew's side of the story. Most stories have multiple sides, however, and there can be several versions of the "truth." What questions might you ask people if you were interested in discovering the "full story" of Depew's misadventure? Explain.
8. In Depew's version of events, the American CEO looks either naïve or arbitrary; there is an apparent rush to judgment that is inconsistent with the reputation of this very successful executive. What might account for the image of this CEO that has been created?
9. What are the principal lessons for junior managers from the situation discussed in this case?

10. (*Optional research question*) Identify a different example of two companies or organizations from different cultures that tried, either successfully or unsuccessfully, to create a strategic partnership. What happened, and to what do you attribute the success or failure of the venture? In particular, what situational factors helped or hindered these two endeavors?

NOTES

1. Dolia Estevez, "Mexican billionaire Carlos Slim's top 10 business principles," *Forbes*, April 29, 2014.
2. Based on Randall Schuler, Susan Jackson, and Yadong Lou, *Managing Human Resources in Cross-Border Alliances*. London: Routledge, 2004, pp. 92–3.
3. Schuler et al., *Managing Human Resources*, p. 93.
4. Schuler et al., *Managing Human Resources*, p. 93.
5. Schuler et al.'s, *Managing Human Resources* is an excellent resource for people interested in the human resource management implications of global partnerships.
6. Peter Drucker, "The next society," *The Economist*, November 3, 2001, p. 5.
7. Sarah Kessler, "No Internet, no credit cards, no problem: how Airbnb launched in Cuba," Fast Company.com, April 13, 2015.
8. Schuler et al., *Managing Human Resources*.
9. Andrew Kupfer, "How to be a global manager," *Fortune*, March 14, 1988, pp. 52–8.
10. Jeremy Main, "Making a global alliance work," *Fortune*, December 17, 1990, pp. 121–6.
11. Adam Ewing, "Ericsson sues Apple in Europe over phone patent royalties," Bloomberg.com, May 7, 2015.
12. Charles Handy, *Business: The Ultimate Resource*. London: Bloomsbury, 2002, p. 75.
13. Schuler et al., *Managing Human Resources*, p. 44.
14. John Stoll, "GM, SAIC set to plan to share design," *Wall Street Journal*, July 28, 2015, p. B2.
15. Danny Ertel, "Getting past yes: negotiating as if implementation mattered," *Harvard Business Review*, 82(11) (2004), pp. 60–8.
16. Personal communication
17. Gary Ferraro, *Cultural Dimensions of International Business*, 4th edn. Upper Saddle River, NJ: Prentice-Hall, 2002.
18. Nancy J. Adler and John L. Graham, "Cross-cultural interaction: the international comparison fallacy?," *Journal of International Business Studies*, 20(3) (1989), pp. 515–37.
19. We rely here on the work of Paul F. Buller, John J. Kohls, and Kenneth S. Anderson, "When ethics collide: managing conflict across cultures," *Organizational Dynamics*, 28 (4) (2000), pp. 52–66.
20. Nick Carstarphen, "A map through rough terrain: a guide for intercultural conflict resolution," in Michelle LeBaron and Venashri Pillay (eds.), *Conflict across Cultures: A Unique Experience of Bridging Differences*. Yarmouth, ME: Intercultural Press, 2006, pp. 137–201.

21. Helen Deresky, *International Management: Managing across Borders and Cultures*, 2nd edn. Upper Saddle River, NJ: Pearson/Prentice-Hall, 2008.

22. Gerardo Ungson, Richard M. Steers, and Seung-ho Park, *Korean Enterprise: The Quest for Globalization*. Cambridge, MA: Harvard Business School Press, 1997.

23. "Can pay, won't," *The Economist*, August 27, 2011, p. 57.

24. Wendu.baidu.com, March 12, 2012.

25. Thomas O'Boyle, *At any Cost: Jack Welch, General Electric, and the Pursuit of Profit*. New York: Alfred Knopf, 1998.

26. *Aisatsu* is a Japanese word for greetings or giving a brief speech. It is formed from two *kanji* characters, both of which have the same literal meaning: to come up close to someone. Like anywhere else, greetings in Japan are considered polite, but like most social interactions in Japan are more ritualized than in the West.

8 Managing ethical conflicts

CHAPTER OUTLINE

- Conflicts over beliefs and values   *page* 230
- Conflicts between beliefs and institutional requirements   233
- The ethical global leader   236
- Ethical guidelines for global managers   239
- MANAGER'S NOTEBOOK: Managing ethical conflicts   252
- Key terms   257
- Discussion questions   257
- Case: Energy contracts in Nigeria   258

APPLICATIONS

8.1 IKEA in Saudi Arabia   *page* 232

8.2 Russian *biznez*   235

8.3 What would you do?   238

8.4 Bribery and corruption at FIFA   244

8.5 Labor exploitation in Bangladesh   247

8.6 BMW's environmental stewardship   251

What is an ethical conflict? And what happens when our view of ethics is different from someone else's? Consider three short examples:

- In Mexico City, a small package arrived from the US by air express and was sent to local customs for clearance. Nothing happened. After repeated unsuccessful attempts to complete the delivery, it was suggested to the intended recipient of the package that a bribe to a customs agent would likely resolve the problem. She refused and requested that the package be returned to its original sender. Again, nothing happened. Then it was suggested that a bribe might be necessary to have customs release the package so it could be returned to its original sender.[2] Is this an example of unethical behavior? Why or why not?
- In London, a bank trader who worked for both UBS and Citigroup was indicted for trying to rig a global benchmark interest rate that underpins everything from mortgage rates to giant corporate loans.[3] While several banks had pleaded guilty to similar charges, none of the executives were sent to jail and this was the first criminal indictment of an individual. In his defense, the bank trader argued that his behavior was in line with industry standards, his bosses knew about and condoned what he was doing, and he never realized his behavior was improper. He was convicted and sentenced to fourteen years in prison. Is this an example of unethical behavior? Why or why not?
- In the United States, the average pay of CEOs of large companies was 38 times the average for all US workers thirty years ago. Today it is 224 times. Put another way, the average pay for American workers has grown by three times over the past thirty years, while that of CEOs has grown by seventeen times.[4] Is this an example of unethical behavior? Why or why not?

Do any or all of these examples involve unethical behavior or are they just practices with which we may or may not agree or for which others are responsible? How do you decide which answer is correct?

Ethical standards reside within people, not organizations. In fact, organizations have no ethical standards; it is only their members – executives, managers, and rank-and-file employees – who determine whether or not a particular company will act ethically or responsibly at any given point in time, and even this determination lies in the eye of the beholder. Ethical standards are oftentimes amorphous, conflicting, and transitory, but their impact on local communities around the world can be profound. Unfortunately, the topic of ethical behavior is often explored through personal experiences and random examples. We hear people say, for instance, that some countries are more "corrupt" than others or that some countries conduct business in a more "transparent" fashion than others. Such examples become the touchstone for generalizing about others, as well as for subsequent actions. Comparisons are superficial and frequently undocumented, and efforts at systematic understanding are largely absent.

The seemingly inescapable implication here is that ethical standards in business are "higher" in one country than the other. Simplistic examples such as these are commonplace among people, and everyone seems to have his or her favorite stories about ethical misconduct. However, while such stories may serve a purpose in alerting managers to potential problems abroad, they seldom enhance our level of conceptual understanding of the problem itself. That is, *people's explanations of ethical behavior in business are more often focused on what rather than on why.* While this practice may serve people in search of shortcuts, it fails to help develop a long-term understanding of ethical processes across cultures. Indeed, in the long run, it even fails to help the people themselves to develop more sophisticated approaches to cross-cultural management.

Conflicts over beliefs and values

As we just saw, individuals and groups can at times see the same "facts on the ground" very differently from one another. We can either interpret this conflict in terms of who is right or wrong, or we can dig deeper and try to understand the bases for each point of view. In a nutshell, this is the primary tension underlying most cross-cultural conflicts: how to tease out the "real" facts and discover the "truth" as we are willing to accept it. When we discuss conflicts, it is important to note that conflicts across borders most often involve one of two fundamental issues: (1) conflicts between different beliefs and values; and (2) conflicts between ethical imperatives and institutional requirements (see Exhibit 8.1). Both of these issues deserve attention, not only because they relate to appropriate managerial behavior, but also because, at the very least, they can get managers and their firms into deep trouble very quickly.

Many managers see conflicts between *core beliefs and values* as almost natural and unavoidable in cross-cultural encounters. People disagree based on how they were raised. One way to get to the heart of such conflicts is to ask a simple question: *What is truth?* What do people believe to be correct and true, beyond question, in

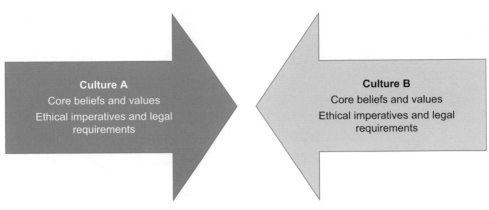

Exhibit 8.1 Sources of ethical conflicts across cultures

this world? While we can easily see different responses to this question within a particular culture, imagine the differences we can see between cultures. Every day, managers are faced with moral or ethical dilemmas relating to conflicting personal and societal beliefs and values. This arena includes both societal norms in general, about right and wrong, and religious beliefs about what people "should" or "must" do.

Complicating this issue is the degree to which people believe that truth is a universal fact or situational. This is really the difference between universalism and particularism discussed in Chapter 3. Some people believe that what they hold to be true is universally correct and true, and that people who disagree with their beliefs are simply wrong, misguided, or heretics. Others believe that truth is in the eye of the beholder, and that peoples in different cultures may have different beliefs (see Exhibit 8.2) about enduring truths.

Communications consultant Richard Lewis has suggested, only partly in jest, "For a German and a Finn, the truth is the truth. In Japan and Britain, it is all right to tell the truth if it doesn't rock the boat. In China, there is no absolute truth. And in Italy, the truth is negotiable."[5] And British actor Peter Ustinov has observed, again only partly in jest, "In order to reach the truth the Germans add, the French subtract, and the British change the subject. I did not include the Americans, since they often give the impression that they already have the truth."[6] To the extent that these observations have merit, it would appear that truth is clearly in the eye of the beholder. That is, the "truth" is not always the "truth."

Thus, universalists tend to emphasize norms, values, and predictability, while particularists tend to favor relationships, flexibility, and sometimes ambiguity. There is nothing intrinsically ethical or unethical about either of these preferences, even if they obviously lead to contrasting, even contradictory, behaviors towards others. Performance appraisal in organizations, for instance, can be practiced through objective, preestablished standards that will be equally applied to each

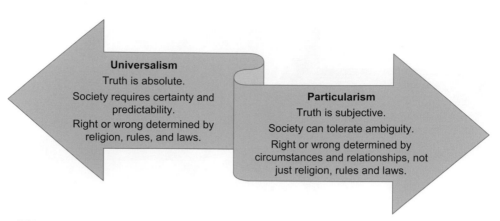

Universalism
Truth is absolute.
Society requires certainty and predictability.
Right or wrong determined by religion, rules, and laws.

Particularism
Truth is subjective.
Society can tolerate ambiguity.
Right or wrong determined by circumstances and relationships, not just religion, rules and laws.

Exhibit 8.2 Universalism, particularism, and ethical beliefs

employee. Not coincidentally, this is the preferred method in mostly universalistic Western countries, as well as in most HR management books. In other more particularistic cultures, the specific circumstances regarding each employee may be given a more salient role in assessing performance and behavior. As a result, we see questions such as this: Why is it inherently wrong to award greater recognition and rewards to those who have worked harder to achieve the same results as their more able peers? The issue, then, is not so much who is right or wrong, but rather what frames of reference are used in making the assessment. Hence, from a purely objective standpoint, treating people "equally" regardless of who they are (as universalists propose) or "differently" based on group memberships (as particularists defend) is, strictly speaking, neutral in ethical terms. It only becomes correct or incorrect when we interject our own value systems into the picture.

APPLICATION 8.1 **IKEA in Saudi Arabia**

Swedish global retailer IKEA prides itself on its Scandinavian flair, with simple and clean lines throughout its product lines and its avant-garde advertising campaigns. But when the company entered the conservative Islamic Saudi market recently, it faced a new market reality. In a country where women dress in conventional black Saudi attire, IKEA wanted to avoid antagonizing the local population – and government regulators – and deleted images of women from their advertisements used in that country.[7] But while the Saudi market was apparently satisfied, IKEA came under strong criticism from its home country – and the Swedish government – for "selling out" its traditional Swedish commitment to gender equality. IKEA's strong egalitarian corporate culture was called into question.

Think about it . . .

(1) IKEA seems to be trapped between two institutional environments. What options does IKEA have to ameliorate the Swedish government's criticisms while protecting its Saudi market?

(2) What would you recommend that IKEA do? What are the likely consequences of your recommendation?

(3) Can you identify another example where companies and their managers are trapped in a conflict between two distinct institutional environments? What might they do to ameliorate the situation? Explain.

Conflicts between beliefs and institutional requirements

Conflicts can also occur between what a person or group thinks is *ethical* and what they think is *legal*. People must often make a decision between following their conscience or following prevailing laws and regulations. One has spiritual or moral implications; the other has enforcement or punishment implications.

Ethical conflicts represent disagreements that arise when two or more people (or groups) disagree on what is morally or philosophically ethically correct. This disagreement is often posed in terms of right and wrong, moral and immoral, and each group gets to decide its own version of these two polar opposites. In this sense, *ethics, conflict, and culture are three of the most intractable words in the English language.* Each concept is by itself both clear and fuzzy, dynamic and static, emotional and objective. Put them together and confusion and disagreements reign. And if ethical questions within a single homogeneous society are complicated, imagine how these challenges multiply when we look at the intersection of two or more cultures.

By contrast, institutional conflicts represent differences over what is legal or consistent with legitimately determined public policy. The fundamental difference here is that, while ethical conflicts focus on what is moral, institutional conflicts focus on what is legal. For example, many governments adopt strong consumer protection laws to protect their citizens from unhealthy, unsafe, or poorly constructed products. Other governments take a more laissez-faire approach (or *caveat emptor* – let the buyer beware). And still others have laws on the books, but seldom enforce them. In addition to laws, governments and public agencies also sanction a number of public policies, policies that are designed for the common good. For example, many governmental organizations issue edicts, recommendations, or targets on

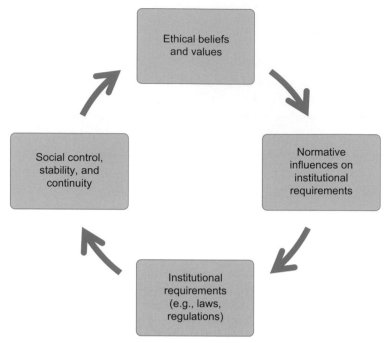

Exhibit 8.3 Ethical beliefs, institutional requirements, and social control

issues relating to social policy (e.g., automobile emissions, greenhouse gases, and sustainable development). Some of these public policies have various means of (usually mild) enforcement, while others are enforced only by social pressure.

What is interesting here is that many institutional requirements (laws, regulations) are implemented to reinforce a society's normative (moral) beliefs (see Exhibit 8.3). For example, if social norms or religious beliefs forbid theft, laws are often enacted to back this up by making such actions illegal. As a result, normative beliefs and institutional regulations tend to correlate highly with one another in most societies, particularly those that are relatively homogeneous. Moreover, in some cultures, legal requirements are directly integrated into religious beliefs (e.g., Islam's *sharia*, often defined as a system of divine law governing beliefs and practices[8]). Even so, what is moral or legal in one society may not necessarily be so in another. For example, while some Western countries consider insider trading (where corporate officers and others close to the executive wing use confidential information that is not publicly available to general stockholders to purchase or sell shares before adverse or unexpected news becomes public) to be both unethical and illegal, others see such behavior as inevitable (i.e., how can society expect executives not to act on future knowledge about their firms?) and do not attempt to proscribe it.

The major practical implication of this separation of the ethical and the legal is that only the most fundamental parameters of human behavior (e.g., major crimes against society) are mandated by the law and oftentimes punished, while ethical misbehavior is often seen as being largely self- or group-regulating and mostly excluded from direct government intervention.

Now we come to an interesting question: What should people (including managers) do, then, when confronted with a conflict between their ethical beliefs, on the one hand, and local laws and regulations, on the other? When all reasonable efforts to reconcile these conflicting forces fail, research shows that in most cultures precedence is more often given to the ethical over the legal. That is, people will follow their conscience before they follow the law. This obviously does not suggest that doing so will be easy. In many cases, following one's moral conscience risks the penalties that breaking the law entails. Even so, most cultures most of the time reinforce the importance of doing what is right over doing what is legal. Indeed, this is how many local heroes are born. Moreover, many companies encourage their employees to adhere to this doctrine.

For example, in-house training programs at Motorola advise their global managers to check out whether the consequences of applying the law in various countries may violate basic principles of human rights or environmental protection prior to taking action. Motorola's reasoning seems to be attractive to many people, yet it assumes implicitly that instances of conflict between ethical and legal prescriptions will take place only in foreign lands, not inside the United States. Far less training in this area is provided to many of its local managers.

Thus, people frequently become more apprehensive when what is at stake is the law of their home country than when it is that of a foreign nation. For example, business travelers to Iran will often lie to Iranian authorities about ever having visited Israel, since this would automatically prohibit their entry. But when these same travelers are asked how they feel about similarly violating the immigration laws of their own country, their responses frequently become much more nuanced and they typically show a clear reluctance to break the law. The question for global managers, then, is when and where to place personal convictions above the law. Not an easy question.

APPLICATION 8.2 Russian *biznez*

Management ethicist Eileen Morgan points out that one of the principal problems when discussing ethics and corruption is that such terms sometimes have different meanings – and different means of implementation – across borders.[9] Think about it: what is the difference between a bribe, a gratuity, and a commission? Are there fundamental ethical differences or is everything in the eye of the beholder?

In Russia, for example, "business" is not a concept that comes naturally in the Russian language. There is no original Russian word for it. *Biznez*, as it is incorporated into the language, carries with it strong cultural baggage dating from Communist times, and it is still associated with ideas such as exploitation and corruption. Unlike some Westerners, Russians differentiate between ethics and corruption. **Corruption** is seen as institutionalized, hierarchical behavior that falls out of the control of individuals. **Ethics**, on the other hand, is seen as the set of principles that should guide one-on-one relationships between individuals. Corruption, then, refers more to the institutional environment in which individuals, like it or not, must operate. It is neither good nor bad; it is just necessary, and individual behavior is not commensurate with the presence or absence of corruption. If one partner steals from another partner, there is a breach in ethical behavior, but not an incidence of corruption.

The implications here are important. If institutions systematically behave in a certain "corrupt" manner, alternative behaviors from individuals may become extremely unsustainable. Even more, when corruption becomes part of the business environment, concepts like guilt and shame lose some of their saliency because free will by individuals regarding corrupt behavior may have disappeared altogether. When corruption becomes part of the institutional fabric, it becomes something to be expected in the normal course of events. The only problem here is that all parties to a deal or partnership should understand how this works and, not surprisingly, many global managers with little or no experience in this region can easily be taken in.

Think about it . . .

(1) In your view, is there a morally correct position on ethical behavior, or is it situationally determined? That is, do you fundamentally believe in universalism or particularism as a basis for ethical behavior? Why?
(2) Does the Russian concept of "ethics" and "corruption" differ from the prevailing views in your own country? If so, in which ways are they different? Explain.
(3) Finally, in your opinion, what is the difference between a bribe, a gratuity, and a commission?

The ethical global leader

Researchers in the GLOBE project, discussed in Chapters 3 and 6, examined the endorsement of ethical leadership practices across cultures by surveying the

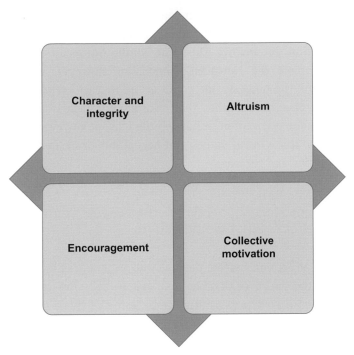

Exhibit 8.4 GLOBE attributes of ethical leaders

research literature to find several key attributes that characterize ethical behaviors.[10] These attributes included: character and integrity; ethical awareness; community and people orientation; motivating, encouraging, and empowering people; and managing ethical accountability. Using the GLOBE data, the researchers identified four factors that matched closely four of the six attributes from the literature review, which they named "character and integrity," "altruism," "collective motivation," and "encouragement" (see Exhibit 8.4).

The study results showed that the endorsement of each of the four dimensions of ethical management differed significantly across the countries used in their study. Because the average endorsement of the attributes was beyond the midpoint average for all dimensions, however, the authors concluded that some degree of common agreement existed in the endorsement of the components of ethical behavior. This research suggests that the four dimensions of ethical leadership represent a fairly universal principle, according to which, while all cultures appreciate and value some common ethical leadership dimensions, they also allow for significant differences in their enactment. In other words, the GLOBE researchers struck a balance between universalistic and particularistic principles.

To illustrate this situation, take, for instance, the "character and integrity" factor in the GLOBE study. This dimension received the highest endorsement by societies in the Nordic European cluster, and the lowest among the Middle Eastern cluster.

Nordic and Middle Eastern countries, the authors pointed out, both value character and integrity in their leaders, but consistently rank very differently in international indexes of corruption (see below). The same Nordic European countries show the lowest endorsement of the "altruism" dimension, however, which societies in Southeast Asia rank the highest. One could argue that this relates to the fact that Southeast Asians also rank higher than Nordic Europeans on in-group pride, loyalty, and a humane orientation. Whatever the reason, however, a logical conclusion here would be that ethical values and acceptable or desired managerial roles vary across countries and regions.

APPLICATION 8.3 What would you do?

Management is all around us. We have all had experiences in which we either led or followed the directives of some manager to get a job done. Perhaps this was at work or in a college project or club. Some of these experiences were probably positive; others were probably not. In some cases, the manager worked hard for the good of the group; in others, he or she may have put his or her own interests ahead of the group's. Throughout at least some of these experiences, moreover, ethical issues may have arisen that forced group members to choose between their perceptions of right and wrong. The problem during such choices is that there are seldom any clear-cut boundaries between the two. As a manager, choices must be made, but options can often be cloudy.

Think about it . . .

(1) Consider Control Data chairman William Norris' predicament: "The computer is on the dock, it's raining, and you have to pay a bribe to get it picked up and delivered." Would you pay the bribe? Why or why not?

(2) A former CEO of Citigroup observed, "We must never lose sight of the fact that we are guests in foreign countries and must conduct ourselves accordingly. Local governments can pass any kind of legislation and, whether we like it or not, we must conform to it." Should global managers follow local laws if they believe they are unethical or socially or environmentally irresponsible? Why or why not?

(3) Recent history has witnessed several major environmental crises caused by oil spills, air and water pollution, and radiation hazards. Realistically, what is a company's responsibility when such a crisis occurs? And why?

Ethical guidelines for global managers

French existential writer Albert Camus once said, "Integrity has no need of rules."[11] While this may be true on an abstract level, it leaves something to be desired in more practical terms. In fact, bribery and corruption are rampant across the globe and numerous groups and organizations have worked hard to reduce the prevalence of such. One of these organizations is the Paris-based Organisation for Economic Co-operation and Development (OECD). The OECD's goal is to promote market-oriented economic growth and development around the world.[12] The organization has thirty-four member states and an additional fifty global partners (semi-official members). As part of its activities, and because of its moral force in the economic community, the OECD has long promoted ethical and socially responsible behavior by companies of its member states. The principal means through which this objective is pursued is through the promulgation and support of the OECD Guidelines for Multinational Enterprises. These guidelines represent a set of normative, yet voluntary, guidelines for global managers and their firms that are aimed simultaneously at developing the economies of less developed nations while protecting them from exploitation by large and rich companies from the industrialized world. They are distinctly universalistic in nature. These guidelines aim to ensure that the operations of these enterprises operate in harmony with local government policies, to strengthen the basis of mutual confidence between global firms and the societies in which they operate, to help improve the foreign investment climate, and to enhance the contribution to sustainable development made by global companies.[13]

The OECD guidelines are divided into five categories: (1) bribery and corruption; (2) employment relations; (3) environmental stewardship; (4) technology transfer; and (5) general business practices (see Exhibit 8.5). We will discuss the first three categories here. These three issues highlight the challenges faced every day by global managers.[14] Here is the problem: Most moral philosophers, business ethicists, business instructors, and other writers on the subject of management ethics send a clear message that violations of ethical standards and fair practices such as those embodied in the OECD guidelines represent a breach of moral integrity for which there is little or no excuse. That is, ethical doctrines are to be followed, period. However, as noted by twentieth-century British philosopher Alfred North Whitehead, "people think in generalities, but they live in detail."[15] That is, the writers on managerial and corporate ethics have seldom been faced with the ethical dilemmas they write about. Instead, such challenges fall to on-site managers who often find themselves in isolated locations and cultures and face-to-face with a conflict of needs, demands, expectations, and laws. This is not abstract or theoretical to them; it is very real and jobs can depend on it.

Exhibit 8.5 OECD guidelines for ethical managerial behavior

OECD guidelines	Principal emphasis
Bribery and corruption	Encourages companies to take a public position against bribery and corruption and discourage such activities in securing or operating a firm.
Employment practices	Encourages fair treatment of all local employees consistent with prevailing local conditions.
Environmental stewardship	Encourages protection of the local environment from unsafe products and practices and helps mitigation of any damage where it occurs.
Technology transfer	Encourages technology diffusion and local licensing of technological processes and technology-based products and services.
General business practices	
Competition	Encourages open and fair competition, particularly involving local firms; supports local government attempts to open markets.
Consumer protection	Encourages fair business, marketing, and advertising practices; promotes product safety and quality.

Moreover, experienced travelers note that ethical standards can vary from one culture to another, as discussed above. This raises an interesting question: Who gets to determine what is ethical? The fact that the OECD guidelines were approved by a group of industrialized (and mostly wealthy) nations may help to illustrate this. Nigeria is not a co-signer, possibly because it loses more than it gains by agreement. In short, implementing these guidelines can be more difficult than it seems. Indeed, there are numerous pressures for both supporting and opposing these guidelines. And the global manager is caught in the middle. This is not to suggest that the guidelines are not a sign of progress in international trade and management. Rather, it is to highlight the difficulty of doing business in multiple and often conflicting environments.

Finally, there is the issue of enforcement. The lax enforcement of these guidelines only adds to the managerial dilemma of what to do. With few penalties, and ongoing corporate competitive pressures for results, it is little wonder that graft and corruption – however defined – is so prevalent. With these issues in mind, let us begin with a look at bribery and corruption.

Bribery and corruption

As noted earlier, we do not live in a perfect world, and ethical challenges like bribery and corruption are a fact of organizational life. In recent years, several organizations have tried to classify countries according to the degree to which corruption

Exhibit 8.6 Global Corruption Index

Country	Corruption index	Country	Corruption index	Country	Corruption index
Argentina	2.8	Hungary	4.9	Portugal	6.3
Australia	8.6	India	2.7	Russia	2.7
Austria	7.8	Indonesia	3.1	Singapore	9.3
Azerbaijan	1.4	Ireland	7.1	Slovakia	3.7
Belgium	7.1	Israel	7.3	South Africa	4.8
Brazil	4.0	Italy	5.2	South Korea	4.5
Canada	9.0	Japan	7.1	Spain	7.1
Chile	7.5	Luxembourg	9.0	Sweden	9.3
China	3.5	Malaysia	4.9	Switzerland	8.5
Colombia	3.6	Mexico	3.6	Taiwan	5.6
Czech Republic	3.7	Netherlands	9.0	Thailand	3.2
Denmark	9.5	New Zealand	9.5	Turkey	3.2
Finland	9.7	Nigeria	1.2	United Kingdom	8.7
France	6.3	Norway	8.5	United States	7.7
Germany	7.3	Philippines	2.6	Venezuela	2.5
Greece	4.2	Poland	4.0		

Note: This scale runs from 1.0 to 10.0, with 10.0 representing high incorruptibility and highly ethical behavior.
Source: Data compiled from The Economist, *The Economist Pocket World in Figures* (London: Profile Books, 2014).

represents a major problem in international business. One such effort is *The Economist*'s Corruption Index, shown in Exhibit 8.6. Using this index, corruption is more likely to be found in Nigeria, Azerbaijan, and Venezuela (with scores of less than 2.5 on a scale going from 1.0 to 10.0) than in Finland, Denmark, and New Zealand (with scores of around 8.6). As with any index, however, rankings of corruption can be imprecise, and they are meant only to highlight the need for further investigation before making investment decisions. Moreover, such ratings can sometimes be surprising. For example, while many people repeatedly point to commonalities between Canada and the United States, note that their ratings on corruption are significantly different.

The existence of underground economies around the world complicates this picture further. The underground economy involves business transactions that are essentially off the books or unrecorded. No public records are kept, no taxes are paid, and applicable laws are frequently ignored. Underground economic activities vary widely from paying under the table for a nanny or someone to mow the lawn to purchasing supplies for one's business outside of governmental regulations or oversight. Underground economies exist everywhere, but are more prevalent in certain countries. According to *The Economist*, the underground economy in the

United States accounts for less than 10 percent of the total GDP.[16] By contrast, in Brazil it is estimated that 40 million people out of a total population of 170 million are employed in the underground economy. Such differences have very clear implications for the conduct of business.

The OECD has been particularly active with respect to ethical behavior in negotiations, contracting, and related business affairs. Here, OECD guidelines place considerable emphasis on fighting corruption and bribery both in the negotiation process and in subsequent multinational partnerships. In this regard, these guidelines proscribe the following:

- Bribes. Managers are not allowed to offer, nor give in to demands, to pay any portion of a contract payment to public officials or the employees of business partners. Nor should they use subcontracts, purchase orders, or consulting agreements as means of channeling payments to public officials, to employees of business partners, or to their relatives or business associates.
- Remuneration. Managers should ensure that the remuneration of agents is appropriate and for legitimate services only. When relevant, a list of agents employed in connection with transactions with public bodies and state-owned enterprises should be kept and made available to competent authorities.
- Transparency. Managers should enhance the transparency of their activities in the fight against bribery and extortion. Measures could include making public commitments against bribery and extortion and disclosing the management systems the company has adopted in order to honor these commitments. The manager should also foster openness and dialogue with the public so as to promote its awareness of and cooperation with the fight against bribery and extortion.
- Advocacy. Managers should promote employee awareness of and compliance with company policies against bribery and extortion through appropriate dissemination of these policies and through training programs and disciplinary procedures.
- Controls. Managers should adopt management control systems that discourage bribery and corrupt practices, and adopt financial and tax accounting and auditing practices that prevent the establishment of off-the-book or secret accounts or the creation of documents that do not properly and fairly record the transactions to which they relate.
- Contributions. Managers should not make illegal contributions to candidates for public office or to political parties or to other political organizations. Contributions should fully comply with public disclosure requirements and should be reported to senior management.

If these guidelines were universally followed, many believe we would move towards a more perfect world. However – and unfortunately – in many circumstances managers face a series of countervailing forces that make a clear picture fuzzy. That is, at times, questions of ethical behavior vary depending on how people

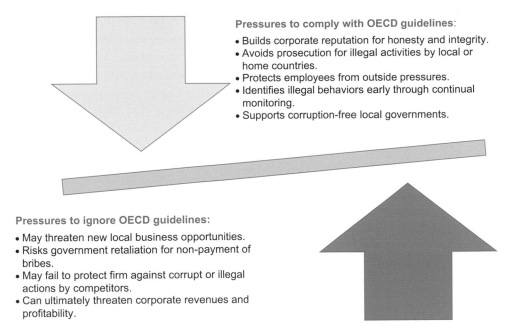

Pressures to comply with OECD guidelines:

- Builds corporate reputation for honesty and integrity.
- Avoids prosecution for illegal activities by local or home countries.
- Protects employees from outside pressures.
- Identifies illegal behaviors early through continual monitoring.
- Supports corruption-free local governments.

Pressures to ignore OECD guidelines:

- May threaten new local business opportunities.
- Risks government retaliation for non-payment of bribes.
- May fail to protect firm against corrupt or illegal actions by competitors.
- Can ultimately threaten corporate revenues and profitability.

Exhibit 8.7 Pressures for and against OECD guideline compliance on bribery and corruption

understand the circumstances surrounding a potential dilemma. One way to understand this is through the use of a force field analysis, a mechanism that simply identifies pressures for and against a value, belief, attitude, or action.[17] Such an analysis can be used productively to understand the dilemmas frequently faced by global managers involving bribery and corruption. As shown in Exhibit 8.7, the decision to remain ethical (as defined by one's culture) is at times challenged by several reasons not to be ethical. Herein is one of the major challenges facing global managers.

To see how this works, suppose you work for a company that wants to build a stronger business presence in a country with a fast-growing consumer market. Suppose also that your promotion and future career with this company is heavily dependent upon your success in securing this deal. Suppose you are aware that the foreign government has lax oversight regulations, poor inspections, and only minimal enforcement procedures across a wide range of the products it makes or sells. Finally, suppose that your own government consistently turns a blind eye to such consumer abuses because it does not want to risk alienating an important trading partner. Question: How would you approach your company's objective – and your personal responsibility – to secure a new business deal? Where do you draw the line? What is an acceptable risk here? And would you be willing to jeopardize your job and take a strong position against any such deals?

In the final analysis, managers should remember two things about this ethical challenge. First, with different names and in different forms, bribery and corruption can be found throughout the global political and business environment; it is not the exclusive province of poor countries. Second, managers typically have a choice in how they respond to corruption. In some cases, governments can help to minimize such practices. When this is not the case, companies can choose not to reinforce such behavior and hold their ground or do business elsewhere. While this may at times lead to short-term losses, it typically leads to long-term gains. The bottom line for managers and their companies is understanding what they stand for and not sacrificing principle for short-term promises.

APPLICATION 8.4 Bribery and corruption at FIFA

International football is often called "the beautiful game," but its worldwide governing body, FIFA, is nothing short of ugly in the way it operates.[18] Even before the US and Swiss governments indicted several current and former FIFA officials on corruption charges, the world had abundant evidence that the Swiss-based international organization governed the world's most popular sport in the manner of a kleptocracy.

In a forty-seven-count indictment of fourteen individuals, the US Justice Department said that FIFA officials had collected a staggering $150 million in bribes and kickbacks from sports-marketing firms for media and marketing rights to international football tournaments. The payoffs involved money that exchanged hands over the selection of South Africa to host the 2010 Men's World Cup (including $10 million paid to three members of the FIFA selection committee) and kickbacks in exchange for votes in FIFA's 2011 presidential elections. Officials from Concacaf, the FIFA-affiliated governing body for North and Central America and the Caribbean, also allegedly took bribes in exchange for the rights to World Cup qualifying events, the Gold Cup tournament, and the Concacaf Champions League, a competition among franchises selected from professional leagues in member nations. The indictments cover activities stretching back more than two decades.

Earlier efforts by various well-intentioned national associations to fix FIFA's pervasive culture of corruption failed because FIFA is organized to resist change and is fiercely defended. But the court-based bribery and corruption charges beginning in 2015 may actually force some change at the top. National football teams are threatening to withdraw from the association, as are some key sponsors.

Think about it ...

(1) Is there any reason to think of bribery and corruption in international sports differently than in the manufacturing or services industries? Why or why not?

(2) Conduct a short force field analysis of the pressures for and against encouraging or supporting a corrupt environment at FIFA. What does this tell you?

(3) If you were brought in as a consultant to help resolve these corruption issues at FIFA, what recommended changes would you offer?

Fair employment practices

A major reason global firms build facilities overseas is to reduce operating costs. This typically takes the form of significantly lowering labor costs. Beyond this, however, do global firms have any obligations to provide these local workers with employee rights and benefits that are similar to those provided to their employees back home? Which employee rights and benefits, if any, are inviolate and universal for all workers regardless of their location and which are situationally determined by the various cultures and locations of the facilities? This question is addressed in the OECD guidelines focusing on the employment relationship.

These HR guidelines focus heavily on company responsibilities to local employees. Towards this end, they suggest that, within the framework of law, regulations, and prevailing labor relations and employment practices, global firms should do the following:

- **Employee representation.** Respect the right of their employees to be represented by trade unions and other bona fide organizations of employees, and engage in constructive negotiations, either individually or through employers' associations, with such employee organizations with a view to reaching agreements on employment conditions, which should include provisions for dealing with disputes arising over the interpretation of such agreements, and for ensuring mutually respected rights and responsibilities; provide such facilities to representatives of the employees as may be necessary to assist in the development of effective collective agreements; provide to representatives of employees information which is needed for meaningful negotiations on conditions of employment; provide to representatives of employees where this accords with local law and practice, information which enables them to obtain a true and fair view of the performance of the entity or, where appropriate, the enterprise as a whole.

- **Employment standards.** Observe standards of employment and industrial relations not less favorable than those observed by comparable employers in the host country.

- **Employee training and development.** In their operations, to the greatest extent practicable, utilize, train, and prepare for upgrading members of the local labor force in cooperation with representatives of their employees and, where appropriate, the relevant governmental authorities.

- Lay-offs and dismissals. In considering changes in their operations which would have major effects upon the livelihood of their employees, in particular in the case of the closure of an entity involving collective lay-offs or dismissals, provide reasonable notice of such changes to representatives of their employees, and where appropriate to the relevant governmental authorities and cooperate with the employee representatives and appropriate governmental authorities so as to mitigate to the maximum extent practicable adverse effects.
- Equal employment opportunity. Implement employment policies including hiring, discharge, pay, promotion, and training without discrimination unless selectivity in respect of employee characteristics is in furtherance of established governmental policies which specifically promote greater equality of employment opportunity.
- Freedom from coercion. In the context of bona fide negotiations with representatives of employees on conditions of employment, or while employees are exercising a right to organize, not threaten to utilize a capacity to transfer the whole or part of an operating unit from the country concerned nor transfer employees from the enterprises' component entities in other countries in order to influence unfairly those negotiations or to hinder the exercise of a right to organize.
- Right of collective bargaining. Enable authorized representatives of their employees to conduct negotiations on collective bargaining or labor–management relations issues with representatives of management who are authorized to make decisions on the matters under negotiation.

As with bribery and corruption, there are a number of forces at work both for and against heeding these guidelines. As such, we can see the managerial challenge. Pressures exist both to adhere to and ignore such guidelines and, as is typical, managers and their companies are faced with a juggling act in an uncertain and competitive environment. What happens, for example, if a company follows these guidelines but the competitors do not? How do they compete? What is also interesting here, however, is the decision point where HR policies are determined. Are these policies set in Berlin, Santiago, or Singapore by executives in corporate headquarters or by local and regional managers who are more sensitive to local conditions and requirements?

A good example of this issue can be found in the HR policies of Sony and Samsung in their electronic assembly plants in Thailand.[19] While Sony applies HR policies dictated largely from Tokyo and treats local employees largely as outsourced workers, Samsung takes a more local approach that is largely determined within Thailand and treats local employees more as members of the Samsung Group. Data suggest that subsequent employee commitment, job attitudes, and productivity are higher in the Samsung facilities. This is not to say that there is a universal conclusion here, since it is not always the case that higher adherence to ethical standards will necessarily lead to higher performance; rather, it highlights the need for local managers to monitor the impact of corporate HR policies as they relate to local conditions.

APPLICATION 8.5 Labor exploitation in Bangladesh

Most people don't know or care who makes the clothes they wear.[20] Nor for that matter do many retailers. According to a recent study, many retailers have no idea what factories made the products they sell in their high-end shops and boutiques around the world. That's because manufacturers often farm out work to local factories in the poorest nations that aren't registered with trade associations or the local government and that operate away from the eyes of regulators. As a result, many retailers don't know whether the garments they sell were stitched together by workers earning rock-bottom wages in some of the world's most decrepit, ramshackle factories. Or whether they were made by child labor. Or even if there are cracks in the factory's walls that could trigger a catastrophe like the recent collapse of the Rana Plaza factory complex in Bangladesh that killed more than 1,100 people.

"We're hiding," said the owner of one small unregistered factory in Bangladesh, the world's second-largest exporter of ready-made garments. "Customers don't want to see my factory because it's a tin shed." He and his wife employ 110 laborers who spend their days jammed into a little concrete edifice in front of their house, surrounded by heaps of fabric. The finished clothes carry the labels of major European brands. The factory is one of up to 2,000 unregistered garment facilities in Bangladesh.

Why is it so difficult to track manufacturing logistics? When retailers place orders for clothes, production doesn't always go smoothly. Factories end up pressed to get their shipments out on time, or risk losing future jobs. Rather than open extra lines at the factory, forcing workers to work extra hours or trying to negotiate a later delivery date, garment-makers often subcontract the goods to other factories in their business networks. Such subcontractors often work in grimy factories outside the reach of any regulatory systems put in place by the government. The subcontractors use a system of informal handshake agreements, in which factory managers simply call a friend who runs an unregistered operation, and they agree to terms verbally. Then, it's a simple system of bills and receipts where cash is exchanged for garments.

To take a closer look, *CBS News* recently went inside the Monde Apparels factory in Dhaka, which employs 1,400 workers making shirts for Wrangler and ics sportswear

Asics sportswear. Monde's manager said the factory has not been approved by Wal-Mart for production, but they still had an order for a million Wal-Mart boxer shorts, subcontracted to them by another factory.

A common problem in Bangladesh's garment industry is factory fires. The manager at Monde Apparels showed the journalists an evacuation map marking the location of thirteen fire extinguishers, but nearly all of them were missing. There are several hundred workers on one floor of the factory, covering 100,000 square feet, but there were only two fire extinguishers. And if there were a fire, the workers would find emergency exit doors blocked by boxes.

The manager also was adamant that his company does not allow child labor. "Until they turn 18, we cannot employ them," he said. To the visitors, however, some workers looked much younger. However, when the journalists spoke to a woman and her daughter, both employed at Monde Apparels, they claimed they earned about $50 a month each. They spoke confidentially; afraid they would lose their jobs for speaking out. The daughter said she was just 12 years old – and one of many children working at the factory. She gave the factory a fake birth certificate showing her age as 18, dodging the rules on child labor because her family needed the money. Asked if she thinks the factory managers suspect her daughter is still a child, the mother said they must know that her daughter is underage.

The mother also said Monde Apparels does not give workers a pay slip to confirm the wages they are paid. "Last month, I worked 20 days, but they only paid me for 11," she said. "If I question them, they yell at me." But she feels lucky to have a job, and things are improving a bit. "Nowadays, when we make a mistake, at least the supervisors don't beat us like they used to," she said. Wrangler told the journalists that an unspecified independent labor group had approved Monde for use, but after *CBS News* contacted the company, it said it sent its own inspector and has now fired the supervisor. Wal-Mart told the journalists it will also investigate, and if unauthorized production or child labor is found, Monde will be barred permanently.

For years, global retailers have tried to improve conditions in Bangladesh; they tell customers they only do business with factories that follow the rules. But some of these claims ring hollow. And even if they do know which factory they're using and inspect it, there can still be problems, because the factories are often tipped off and cleaned up ahead of the inspection and workers are coached on what to say. Following their investigation, the journalists took their findings to Asics, Wrangler, and Wal-Mart. Asics responded that it had been told by its suppliers that they don't do business with the Monde Apparels factory, so it is now investigating whether the Asics clothes may have been counterfeit.

Think about it . . .

(1) Is labor exploitation simply one of the costs nations and their peoples must pay in order to develop their economies and modernize their countries? Why or why not?

(2) Why is it so difficult for local governments (e.g., Bangladesh) to protect workers such as these from unsafe working conditions or exploitation?

(3) Why is it difficult for global institutions (e.g., World Trade Organization, World Bank) to crack down on factories that have unsafe or exploitative working conditions?

(4) What responsibilities, if any, do retailers such as Wrangler or Wal-Mart have to provide safe working conditions for workers in the factories of their suppliers?

(5) Do you know where the clothes you are wearing right now were made?

(6) Have you ever refused to buy a garment because it was made in a sweatshop? If so, how did you learn of the working conditions in the factory that produced the garment?

Environmental stewardship

A related issue facing global leaders is environmental stewardship. Specifically, what responsibilities do global companies and their leaders have to the local communities where they do business? What are their responsibilities to help with local economic development? What are their responsibilities with respect to protecting the environment? What are their responsibilities to help facilitate social justice? This general area often falls within the domain of corporate social responsibility and can be addressed in several ways. We begin with a look at how global companies can often impact local economic development for good or ill.

Global companies are often criticized for being insensitive to environmental needs and, indeed, many companies choose to locate factories in countries that have lax pollution and environmental laws. By the same token, however, many other companies spend millions each year in reclaiming environmental lands and reducing air and water pollution. As Unilever CEO Niall FitzGerald notes, "Corporate social responsibility is a hard-edged business decision. Not because it is a nice thing to do or because people are forcing us to do it, but because it is good for our business."[21] Indeed, the list of environmentally responsible companies is longer than many people think or wish to believe.

Research suggests that in many industries it may actually pay to be "green." That is, companies that are good environmental stewards also tend to be more profitable than their competitors, especially in more dynamic industries. Such findings add substance to the assertion that socially responsible managers frequently find ways to support sustainability and environmental quality as part of their corporate strategies, not in spite of them, and that integrating environmental and sustainability perspectives into business practices can lead to improved overall corporate performance.

OECD guidelines here focus on the protection of the local environment from unsafe products and practices and help mitigation of any damage where it occurs. Global enterprises, within the framework of laws, regulations, and administrative practices in the countries in which they operate, are required to take due account of the need to protect the environment and avoid creating environmentally related health problems. In particular, companies, whether multinational or domestic, should address the following:

- Public health risks. Assess, and take into account in decision-making, foreseeable environmental and environmentally related health consequences of their activities, including plant location decisions, impact on indigenous natural resources and foreseeable environmental and environmentally related health risks of products as well as from the generation, transport, and disposal of waste.
- Environmental impact. Cooperate with competent authorities by providing adequate and timely information regarding the potential impacts on the environment and environmentally related health aspects of all their activities and by providing the relevant expertise available in the enterprise as a whole.
- Accident prevention. Take appropriate measures in their operations to minimize the risk of accidents and damage to health and the environment, and to cooperate in mitigating adverse effects, in particular: (1) by selecting and adopting those technologies and practices which are compatible with these objectives; (2) by introducing a system of environmental protection at the level of the enterprise as a whole including, where appropriate, the use of environmental auditing; (3) by enabling their component entities to be adequately equipped, especially by providing them with adequate knowledge and assistance; (4) by implementing education and training programs for their employees; (5) by preparing contingency plans; and (6) by supporting, in an appropriate manner, public information and community awareness programs.

Once again, the ideal of environmental sensitivity and social responsibility is at times threatened by forces outside the control of the firm that can turn good deeds into potential nightmares. One of the principal liabilities here involves increased costs associated with increased regulation and reporting. Here, good intentions by local governments – or their distrust of multinational firms – have caused many global companies to pick and choose their local operating sites based upon who has the lightest regulations. This is not necessarily to say that such firms are socially irresponsible; rather, many firms seek to do the right thing (again, as defined by their own cultures), but see excessive regulations as being too limiting to guarantee the fulfillment of their corporate mission. In other words, the fundamental challenge here is a balancing act that both corporations and local governments must perform to seek mutual benefit: job creation and sustainable economic development vs. corporate returns on their investments. Without both sides securing benefit, it is difficult to imagine a successful partnership.

APPLICATION 8.6 BMW's environmental stewardship

German automaker BMW recently achieved the highest score ever given in the automobile industry in the Carbon Disclosure Project (CDP). Scoring 96 out of a possible 100 points, the company is listed in both the Carbon Disclosure Leadership Index (CDLI) and the Carbon Performance Leadership Index.[22] "Our corporate sustainability strategy is based on three pillars: economics, environment, corporate social responsibility," stated BMW chairman Dr. Norbert Reithofer. "Climate protection serves an important role in this strategy. As part of our focus on climate protection, we continue reducing vehicle and production facility emissions around the world. By protecting the climate, society as a whole also benefits and it just makes good business sense for the BMW Group."

The CDP acknowledgment is one of the most prestigious ratings in the realm of sustainability. The CDLI analyses the 500 international companies in the FTSE Global Equity Index Series, and only the top 10 percent make it onto the list. BMW's rating further emphasized their long-term efforts in climate protection along the entire value chain. This rating also reinforces BMW's decision to embrace sustainability as part of its corporate strategy.

The CDP listing comes on the heels of the designation BMW received as the industry leader in the Dow Jones Sustainability Indexes, making it the world's most sustainable automobile manufacturer for the seventh year running. The company continues to win such recognition as a result of the development of fuel-saving, alternative vehicle concepts, clean production processes, and green recycling practices. They take the concept of sustainability beyond climate concerns extending well beyond their plants. BMW is also involved in promoting education and road safety worldwide, as well as in projects to fight HIV and AIDS.

Think about it . . .

(1) Why do you believe BMW invests so heavily in environmental stewardship and sustainability compared to its rivals?

(2) In your view, what are the limits of responsibility for global firms like BMW (or oil companies or mining companies, etc.) doing business around the world?

(3) What incentives or rewards accrue to companies that step forward and take responsibility for improving the environment? What penalties?

(4) Global companies like BMW typically do business on a country-by-country basis where they have strategic partnerships. How, then, can companies take concrete action to contribute to global issues that transcend national boundaries (e.g., global warming, water pollution)?

MANAGER'S NOTEBOOK

Managing ethical conflicts

Much of what we do and say is related somehow to ideas – and ideals – of right and wrong, good and bad, and win and lose – whether it is in business, social activities, athletics, or our personal lives. Managers are no exception, as was observed above. Examples of exemplary, disappointing, and sometimes downright illegal managerial behaviors can be found throughout the business environment. As a result, many experts in business ethics argue that all firms, but especially global ones, need an ethical compass to guide their organizational actions in ethical ways. Others, however, seem to make the opposite assertion: There is no such thing as right or wrong – they only exist in the eye of the beholder.

This dichotomy of views suggests that either there are universal truths that transcend all cultures or that concepts such as right and wrong are embedded within cultures and, as such, different cultures can define them differently. Where is the educated global manager in all of this? Probably caught somewhere in the middle. This conflict captures the essence of good management, nationally and globally. Managers must frequently act in the absence of concrete information and in the face of uncertain outcomes. Nonetheless, they must act, and they will be judged based on the outcomes. As such, in terms of ethical behavior, managers require a moral compass, but a compass that is neither self-serving nor xenophobic.

This chapter did not focus on the fundamentals of business ethics in general; rather, we focused specifically on some of the particulars of business ethics as they relate to managers and organizations. Unfortunately, many of these discussions of managerial ethics focus on the negative – violations of trust, ethical standards, or the law. Seldom do these discussions take an optimistic tone. By overemphasizing the negative – some would call this the reality – many managers tend to avoid such discussions, not because they are dishonest, but because they see such discussions as emphasizing the wrong thing. That is, for many managers, ethical behavior is not limiting or disempowering, but rather normal and even empowering at times. Ethical behavior represents the best of the human spirit, as well as an opportunity for companies and their managers to contribute in positive ways to "the betterment of the human condition," as Wharton professor Robert House observed.[23]

It should be clear from this discussion that working in diverse cultures allows managers to understand divergent foreign perspectives, as well as practices and behaviors that are not clear when issues are only seen from the home country perspective. For example, Czech sales representatives traveling to Chile may observe how business transactions differ from their home country. They may see behaviors and practices that are unusual – perhaps even illegal or at least unethical – compared to back home. What they may not see, however, is that many of their Chilean counterparts are also seeing strange – and possibly unethical – behaviors when they visit the Czech Republic, or any other country. In fact, the more widely traveled both the Czech and Chilean managers become, the more likely they are to see patterns of questionable – and admirable – behavior that collectively develop their capacity to understand what is just unusual or different and what is truly unethical.

Distinguishing between personal (and organizational) tastes and preferences, ethical and legal mandates, and beliefs and values, is important for understanding both national and international contexts. Within national contexts, however, some of those differences are not seen as clearly as they are when managers cross cultures. For example, Islamic cultures foster the integration of the legal and the ethical – and the religious – spheres. The religious and the secular are often integrated. Managers working in these regions expect this as a context or background for their business enterprise. At the same time, however, many Western managers work in cultures that are rooted in the separation of these spheres (e.g., separation of church and state). As a result, it is quite common for Western managers to forget the historical evolution that led to that separation and that explains how things stand in present times. But a Western manager's visit to Saudi Arabia or Iran will highlight some of these differences, and add to the developmental process of the manager. The same can also be said for the Saudi or Iranian manager traveling to the West. The point here is simple: Travel is a great educator for managers who are willing to look, listen, interact, compare, and learn.

These differences in managerial behaviors across cultures are easier to understand when some of the heuristics discussed above are employed. For example, the meaning and role of universals and particulars are unlikely to come under scrutiny when managers and decision-makers share the same basic cultural outlook (e.g., a group of Polish or Thai managers). Yet an understanding of what is core (or universal) and what is peripheral (or particular) can be critical in guiding ethical decision-making from either the temporal or historical perspective (the idea of ethics across time), as well as from the spatial and cultural perspective, too.

1.   Managing within ethical and moral constraints

With this in mind, we close by examining the managerial lessons that follow from both the ethical and institutional perspectives discussed here. More specifically, what can global managers learn here to enhance their ability to behave responsibly in the world of work? In our view, based on their ethical beliefs, as well as their tolerance for the beliefs of others, global managers and their employers have a responsibility to work to build a consensus regarding how they define ethical behavior across cultures and nations. In this pursuit, the following points may be germane (see Exhibit 8.8):

- Understand the core values of the firm. It seems reasonable to expect that firms operating in different countries, with different tastes, practices, and values, will need to work diligently to preserve both a core set of beliefs that encourages unity and commonality, as well as clearly articulate spheres for variation, pluralism, and diversity in how to operate across countries. They need to know their limits and degrees of flexibility in doing business across borders.
- Understand the limits of universalism. Feelings of unity and commonality across cultures and business partners can (and perhaps should) rest on what and how people see and understand the concept of universal at different times and places. Is there agreement across parties concerning what beliefs and values are indeed universal? And can all parties take a nuanced approach to universalism

Managing within ethical and moral constraints	Managing within legal and institutional constraints
• Understand the core values of the firm. • Understand different types of cultural conflict. • Understand the limits of universalism. • Understand the cultural contexts underlying agreements. • Understand the roles and backgrounds of the parties to a dispute. • Understand the context or basis of the conflict. • Understand different types of cross-cultural conflict.	• Understand the proper role of institutional guidelines. • Understand the limitations of institutional guidelines. • Understand the controversies underlying institutional guidelines. • Understand the tension created by forces both for and against "doing the right thing." • Understand where conflicts need to be settled. • Understand the lack of education or awareness of institutional guidelines in the training of managers.

Exhibit 8.8 Strategies for managing ethical conflicts

that never assumes that the universals have been completely and perfectly defined? To the contrary, what is seen as universal generally evolves (and hopefully improves) over time and space, and managers need to build on universalist principles that are never final but in search of continual improvement. What this means for managers is that flexibility and tolerance are key to success across borders. Managers have to recognize that while all of their partners may oppose company theft as a general principle, for example, their perspectives concerning what constitutes theft may vary. For example, is taking minor office supplies home theft or not? The question for managers is whether this is acceptable or, perhaps more importantly, to what extent it is acceptable.

- **Understand the cultural contexts underlying agreements.** Universal positions are seldom self-sustaining. They do not rest in thin air, and they require continual reinforcement at various points in time and space. As such, universals always need to be grounded in a given culture. Indeed, they cannot be understood, much less acted upon, in isolation from their cultural context. As such, any effort to seek agreement on a set of universal standards or principles first requires an understanding of the various cultures to the proposed agreement. Without this understanding and appreciation, the likelihood of reaching – or enforcing – agreements diminishes rapidly.

- **Understand the roles and backgrounds of the parties to a dispute.** Simply identifying the parties to a dispute is insufficient to move towards conflict resolution. In addition, we must understand something about the other party's roles and backgrounds. What does their company or their society expect from them? How much leeway might they have in bargaining? And what types of conflict resolution strategies may be appropriate or expected? Such knowledge clarifies where the other parties to a dispute are, as well as how to deal effectively with them. This may require an ability on the part of managers to negotiate in a particularistic environment, instead of a universalistic one.

- **Understand the context or basis of the conflict.** The content of an ethical exchange also needs to account for cultural differences even at the initial phase of the interchange when people are trying to discover what is right and wrong. What exactly is the basis of the conflict? Such bases are often masked in the guise of a different – often more superficial – issue. Without such knowledge, time is easily wasted discussing or debating things that really don't matter, while the root cause of the conflict remains.

- **Understand different types of cross-cultural conflict.** Finally, managers must be able to distinguish between different types of cultural conflict in organizations. Conflicts involving tastes and practices, the legal system, and beliefs and values cannot be conflated in a single category. Instead, they can require different approaches to problem-solving.

2. Managing within legal and institutional constraints

Since their publication, the OECD guidelines have proven to be a respected point of reference for many companies. Even though the guidelines are voluntary, they carry the weight of a joint recommendation of OECD governments. Alongside national laws, they form part of a legal or at least quasi-legal infrastructure that promotes responsible behavior by global firms. In addition, the guideline language has influenced other codes of conduct for global firms, such as the International Labour Organization's (ILO's) Tripartite Declaration and the Code of Conduct for Transnational Corporations of the United Nations. Still, there are several issues that global managers should be aware of prior to being placed in situations where such guidelines carry significant weight:

- Understand the proper role of institutional guidelines. There are many guidelines and, taken together, they can serve to seriously constrain the activities of many honest companies. So, too, are there many questions: First, is it proper for national governments to come together to formulate such guidelines or is it better to allow companies to develop their own guidelines within the boundaries of national and international laws? And second, the OECD guidelines are just that: guidelines. They have no legal standing. If these guidelines are important for global business, should they have some type of enforcement provisions behind them? If so, how would such provisions be enforced?

- Understand the limitations of institutional guidelines. We have attempted to overview one approach to encouraging ethical and socially responsible behavior on the part of global firms. As members of the OECD will affirm, it is not a perfect solution, but perhaps it is a major first step in securing responsible action on the part of highly diverse and competitive firms around the world. What remains to be seen is the degree to which the respective governments of OECD member states get behind these guidelines. To date, the response has been encouraging among many European members, but less so among other nation states.

- Understand the controversies underlying institutional guidelines. As with any internationally negotiated instrument, however, these guidelines have sometimes been criticized, either for being too general or too detailed. Some have argued, for example, that they do not go far enough in ensuring that global firms comply with various national laws and practices, while others have suggested that the guidelines go well beyond those standards in some areas so as to restrict legitimate business goals and strategies. Another area of debate involves the follow-up, which some say needs to be made stronger, while others argue that it is too juridical.

- Understand the tension created by forces both for and against "doing the right thing." Indeed, in many situations, how do we know what is the right thing to do? Institutional guidelines attempt to set common rules to guide everyone. However, it is difficult to account for cultural differences and preferences when assembling one set of rules. Moreover, as with legal requirements, guidelines tend to state the specific when flexibility is sometimes needed. Finally, in view of the fact that only thirty-four countries have signed on fully to the OECD guidelines, why should other nations bother with these since they have no bearing on local regulations or behavior?

- Understand where conflicts need to be settled. When guidelines issues arise, the onus of attempting a settlement is placed largely on the country where the "problem company" – a highly debatable term – is headquartered. As such, the effectiveness of the guidelines depends to a large degree on the commitment of the home and host countries to the principles of the OECD, ILO, and so forth. This effectiveness, in turn, obviously differs from country to country.

- Understand the lack of education or awareness of institutional guidelines in the training of managers. A final thought: The OECD guidelines discussed above – and agreed to by thirty-four full member states – are seldom taught or even mentioned in the business schools of many countries. Why is this? What are we teaching future generations of managers about the importance of behaving responsibly in global transactions?

KEY TERMS

biznez (Russian) • bribe • chopping (Nigerian) • corruption • environmental stewardship • ethical conflicts • ethics • force field analysis • institutional conflicts • OECD Guidelines for Multinational Enterprises • Organisation for Economic Co-operation and Development • particularism • social justice • transparency • underground economy • universalism

DISCUSSION QUESTIONS

1. Pascal's observation points out that what some cultures believe to be true others may believe to be false. Can you provide an example of this from the business world?

2. The chapter opens with three examples of potentially unethical behaviors from three different countries. In your view, which of these actually represent unethical (as opposed to illegal) behavior, and why?

3. What do you think are the principal determinants of ethical or unethical behavior in the world of global business? How are you defining the term "unethical"?

4. If you had to choose, would you agree with the concept of universalism or particularism as they relate to determining what constitutes ethical standards? That is, are ethical standards universal or situational? Explain.

5. It was noted that "ethics, conflict, and culture" are three of the most intractable words in the English language. What does this mean for global managers in the field?

6. GLOBE study results suggest that ethical global leaders share certain common characteristics, such as integrity and altruism. Do you agree with this assertion? Why or why not?

7. British philosopher Alfred North Whitehead observed that people think in generalities but live in detail. What is the meaning of this observation for managers working across cultures?

8. What is the difference between a bribe, a performance bonus, and a sales commission?

9. OECD guidelines guarantee employees the right to unionize, freedom of coercion, and equal opportunity. Should such guidelines take precedence over long-standing and deeply held cultural beliefs opposing such guarantees? Explain.

10. What are the pressures both for and against companies taking the lead in being good environmental stewards in areas where they do business? Do firms have an ethical or moral responsibility to be good environmental stewards? Why or why not?

11. OECD guidelines are aimed at providing managers with some clear guidelines for ethical and socially responsible behavior in the global workplace. If this is correct, why have so few countries adopted these guidelines?

12. OECD guidelines – agreed to by thirty-four full member states – are seldom taught or even mentioned in the business schools of many countries. Why is this? What are we teaching future generations of managers about the importance of behaving responsibly in global transactions?

CASE: ENERGY CONTRACTS IN NIGERIA

Everyone seems to enjoy criticizing the oil and gas industry, even though most people drive and fly, use fossil fuel in one way or another to heat their homes and workplaces, and, if truth be told, would likely be highly inconvenienced if this industry were to simply disappear. For many, this is the proverbial love–hate relationship. Regardless of your position on energy or environmental policy, put yourself in the position of the energy companies for a moment and imagine how you would find and secure oil and gas products for your home market. More specifically, consider how you might try to negotiate an oil or gas lease in Nigeria.

Here is both the opportunity and the problem. Nigeria is Africa's biggest oil producer, generating more than 2 million barrels of petroleum a day, accounting for more than 98 percent of the country's export earnings and 83 percent of federal government revenue, as well as generating more than 14 percent of its GDP. It also provides 95 percent of foreign exchange earnings, and about 65 percent of government budgetary revenues.

In view of the profitability of the industry, these numbers should be good news for the Nigerian economy. But competition for the profits that oil produces has created considerable conflict for those living in the country. Nigerian government officials are the majority shareholders in the profits created by the production of Nigerian oil, and average citizens have seen few socio-economic benefits. Many think that foreign oil companies should compensate people.

But there is another problem facing the industry: extensive corruption going up to the top of the power elite of the country. According to *The Economist*, Nigeria is one of the most corrupt nations in the world. Indeed, bribery is so commonplace that they even have their own name for it: chopping. When Nigeria's Central Bank governor accused the national government of stealing over $50 billion from industry operations, suggesting that Nigeria has "a reputation for corruption but the scale of the alleged oil graft is unprecedented" he was suspended from his job for "unrelated financial recklessness and gross misconduct at the central bank." Many observers believe the suspension was politically motivated.

But it is not just official corruption that troubles oil companies. In its annual report, Royal Dutch Shell also blamed the Nigerian government for poor management of the industry. And along with official misconduct comes private theft. Last year, Shell, the largest foreign oil operator in Nigeria, reported some $1 billion worth of oil and natural gas was simply stolen.

The twin accusations of $50 billion in official theft and $1 billion in oil theft were met with the promise of a government audit and a military crackdown on illegal refineries that netted a total of five arrests and no convictions. Meanwhile, meaningful change to the oil industry, the type that would actually benefit Nigeria's 130 million citizens, remains elusive.

At the same time, lack of oversight has left an environmental disaster in the industry's wake. Not long ago, a Chevron gas rig burned for three weeks straight. When the country tried to ban an Occupy video about the industry, it went viral. Shell's point about oil theft is that many Nigerians looking to profit from the oil sector have turned to stealing oil, refining it in illegal highly toxic refineries, and selling it to brokers.

Here is the challenge: Under these conditions, how might you and your employer negotiate access to Nigeria's vast oil reserves to help supply local demand? In this endeavor, companies that refuse to pay bribes to secure oil contracts risk being shut out of this lucrative market which often has implications for both community well-being and national security. At the same time, however, companies – and managers such as you – that pay such bribes risk breaking their home country laws and OECD guidelines against bribery and corruption. You are aware – or you should be – that most of your competitors are paying these bribes as part of the negotiation process. Question: what are you going to do?

CASE QUESTIONS

1. Describe the nature of the conflict here. Who is involved and what are the controversies? Are there any "good guys" in this conflict?
2. If *The Economist* survey is accurate and Nigeria is indeed a relatively corrupt country, what are the responsibilities, if any, of the foreign oil companies doing business there to follow OECD guidelines? How should they go about this?
3. Do foreign oil companies have a moral obligation to be good environmental stewards of the Nigerian oilfields? Why or why not?
4. If you worked for one of the oil companies and were tasked to negotiate an oil contract with the Nigerian government, how would you go about it? What would you recommend your company do? Why?
5. If your company decided to follow common practice and pay the bribes necessary to secure a contract, what would you do *personally*? Really? Why?
6. Why do some industries like energy and construction seem to be characterized by pervasive bribery and corruption, while other industries such as high-tech do not?
7. (*Optional research question*) What does research suggest about a company's ability to train its employees and managers to behave in a more ethical fashion? How are they defining the term "ethical"? What has been tried? Was it successful? And how would you improve on these training techniques?

NOTES

1. Blaise Pascal, *Pensées: Thoughts on Religion and other Subjects* (New York: Washington Square Press, 1965), p. 90. This popular version of Pascal's quotation is a modern interpretation of the original translation from French that reads, "Three degrees of latitude reverse all jurisprudence; a meridian decides the truth ... A strange justice that is bounded by a river! Truth on this side of the Pyrenees, error on the other side."
2. Personal communication to author.
3. David Enrich, "Trader guilty of rigging rates," *Wall Street Journal*, August 4, 2015, p. A1.
4. Robert Wilmers, "Why excessive pay is bad for the economy," *American Banker*, March 14, 2014.
5. Richard Lewis, *When Cultures Collide.* London: Nicholas Brealey Publishing, 1999, p. 8.
6. Peter Ustinov, quoted in Richard Hill, *EuroManagers.* Brussels: Europublications, 1998, p. 230.
7. Ben Quinn, "Ikea apologizes over removal of women from Saudi Arabia catalogue," *The Guardian*, October 10, 2012.
8. Sharia law is the body of Islamic law. The term means "way" or "path," and is the legal framework within which the public and some private aspects of life are regulated for those living in a legal system based on Islam.

9. Eileen Morgan, *Navigating Cross-Cultural Ethics*. London: Routledge, 2011.

10. Robert J. House, Paul J. Hanges, Mansour Javidan, Peter W. Dorfman, and Vipin Gupta, *Culture, Leadership, and Organizations: The GLOBE Study of 62 Societies*. Thousand Oaks, CA: Sage, 2004.

11. Susan Ratcliff (ed.), *Oxford Essential Quotes*. Oxford University Press, online version, 2014.

12. OECD members include Australia, Austria, Belgium, Canada, Czech Republic, Denmark, Finland, France, Germany, Greece, Hungary, Iceland, Ireland, Italy, Japan, Korea, Luxemburg, Mexico, Netherlands, New Zealand, Norway, Poland, Portugal, Slovak Republic, Spain, Sweden, Switzerland, Turkey, United Kingdom, and the United States. In addition, there are a number of affiliate members who agree to support the group's activities and abide by its guidelines, including Argentina, Brazil, Chile, Estonia, Israel, Lithuania, and Slovenia.

13. www.oecd.org/daf/investment/guidelines

14. www.oecd.org/daf/investment/guidelines

15. Alfred North Whitehead, *Process and Reality*. New York: Free Press, 1978.

16. "Blinded by the dark," *The Economist*, April 2, 1998, p. 15.

17. A *force field analysis* is a management technique developed by Kurt Lewin, a pioneer in the field of social sciences, for diagnosing situations. It is useful when looking at the variables involved in planning and implementing a change program, as well as team projects when attempting to overcome resistance to change. Lewin assumes that in any situation there are both driving and restraining forces that influence any change that may occur. *Driving forces* are those forces affecting a situation that are pushing in a particular direction; they tend to initiate a change and keep it going. In terms of improving productivity in a work group, pressure from a supervisor, incentive earnings, and competition may be examples of driving forces. *Restraining forces* are forces acting to restrain or decrease the driving forces. Apathy, hostility, and poor maintenance of equipment may be examples of restraining forces against increased production. Equilibrium is reached when the sum of the driving forces equals the sum of the restraining forces.

18. Steve Malanga, "Give FIFA the book," *City Journal*, May 28, 2015.

19. Won Shul Shim, Hanyang University, personal communication, 2008.

20. Kim Bhasin, "Nobody knows, cares whether your clothes are made in deadly factories," *Huffington Post*, June 4, 2014; Holly Williams, "CBS News goes undercover in Bangladesh clothing factory," *CBS News*, May 22, 2013.

21. Larry Elliott, "Interview: Niall FitzGerald, co-chairman and chief executive, Unilever," *The Guardian*, July 4, 2003.

22. Don Bain, "BMW's environmental stewardship lauded by carbon disclosure project," *Torque News*, September 15, 2011.

23. Robert J. House, "Introduction." In House et al., *Culture, Leadership, and Organizations*, p. 1.

9 Managing work and motivation

> ## MANAGEMENT CHALLENGE
>
> According to global entrepreneur Elon Musk, founder of PayPal, Tesla Motors, and SpaceX, "Starting and growing a business is as much about the innovation, drive, and determination of the people who do it as it is about the product they sell."[1] It has been said that managing and motivating others – taking responsibility for their work and welfare – is one of the most stressful jobs in the world. It is something like being a parent to other adults. In a very real sense, this is the supreme test of managerial effectiveness. If a manager can't supervise others successfully, his or her value to the organization as a whole diminishes significantly. Here is the problem, though. If managing and motivating employees is problematic in one culture, imagine the challenge when trying to supervise employees across cultures: different customs, different languages, and different expectations. How are managers expected to succeed here? In this chapter we explore this challenge. We examine the role of work values in employee behavior, as well as the psychological contracts that exist but are often unseen – particularly by new managers on the ground. We further examine how rewards or incentives that are effective in one culture may fail in another. Throughout, the focus is on how managers can learn to improve their people skills in unique or different environments.

CHAPTER OUTLINE

- The world of work   *page* 264
- Culture and the psychology of work   269
- Managing incentives and rewards   275
- Gender, compensation, and opportunities   280
- MANAGER'S NOTEBOOK: Managing work and motivation   283

- Key terms   286
- Discussion questions   286
- Case: Samsung's *maquiladora* plant   287

APPLICATIONS

9.1 Call centers in the Philippines   *page* 268
9.2 Lincoln Electric in Germany   273
9.3 Lincoln Electric in Mexico   277
9.4 Company cars at Intel, Netherlands   279
9.5 Women in the Chinese workforce   282

Advice about motivating employees in the global workplace is readily available. In Thailand, for example, we are told that the use of individual merit bonus plans runs counter to societal norms about group cooperation and can actually lead to a decline rather than an increase in productivity from employees who refuse to openly compete with each other. In the Netherlands, you can't get the Dutch to compete with one another publicly. In Mexico, everything is a personal matter; but a lot of foreign managers don't get it. To get anything done, the manager has to be more of an instructor, teacher, or parental figure than a boss.

We are further told that to improve managerial performance in the United Kingdom managers should focus more on job content than on job context. British and Canadian companies also motivate their employees primarily through financial incentives, while German and Dutch companies focus on providing employment stability and employee benefits. And at the same time, Indonesian and South Korean companies prefer rigid and often autocratic organizational hierarchies in which everyone knows his or her place, while Swedish and Norwegian companies stress informality, power sharing, and mutual benefit in the workplace. Some countries, such as Germany, even combine formality and rigid hierarchies with power sharing and an emphasis on securing mutual gain for all employees.

Unfortunately, although there are many models of employee motivation, few incorporate serious consideration of differences across borders. What, therefore, should managers do? To start with, they can prepare themselves by expanding their understanding of the local work environment. This includes understanding local work values and goals, as well as the prevailing psychological contract as seen by the local community. Moreover, managers must understand variations in the managerial role – the expectations people have about what managers should or shouldn't do – across cultures, including incentive and reward systems. In this way, they enhance their chances of succeeding in global operations, despite being an "outsider." While many managers assigned to work in other cultures may never become insiders, the simple knowledge of how the local workplace works will likely make their jobs both easier and more productive. We begin this exploration by looking at personal work values and goals.

The world of work

Regardless of who constitutes the global workforce, understanding people at work is a huge topic. It becomes a bit easier to tackle, though, if we can break it down into smaller units. Perhaps the best place to begin is with an understanding of local prevailing values and beliefs. Developing such an understanding may be one of the most effective ways for outsiders to work towards becoming insiders. As a result, in this section, we ask two basic questions: first, what are some of the key differences between people in the global workplace in terms of their work values, and, second, how central is work in the lives of these people? While people within given cultures can obviously differ in many respects, most cultures exhibit core cultural traits that can provide conceptual entry into the work lives of local employees.

Work values and goals

Let us start with a fundamental question: *Why do people work?* This question lies at the heart of the topic of personal work values. What is it about work, if anything, that people genuinely value? What motivates people to go to work? Work values reflect individual beliefs about desirable end states or modes of conduct for pursuing desirable end states. As such, they serve a useful function by providing individuals with guidelines and standards for determining their own behavior and evaluating the behavior of others. Personal work values are important because they signal what individuals and groups of employees see as being most important about their work efforts. They also influence the actual quality and focus of employee endeavors and the ways in which various employees may respond to work motivation strategies and tactics (see Exhibit 9.1). Throughout, the focus here is on understanding how personal values influence employee willingness and preparedness to contribute towards the attainment of organizational goals.

Personal work values have been studied systematically from a cross-cultural perspective for many years. One of the earliest studies was conducted by George England.[2] He and his colleagues focused on the impact of such values on employee behavior and found significant differences across managers in the five countries they studied. US managers tended to be high in pragmatism and achievement orientation and demanded competence. They placed a high value on profit

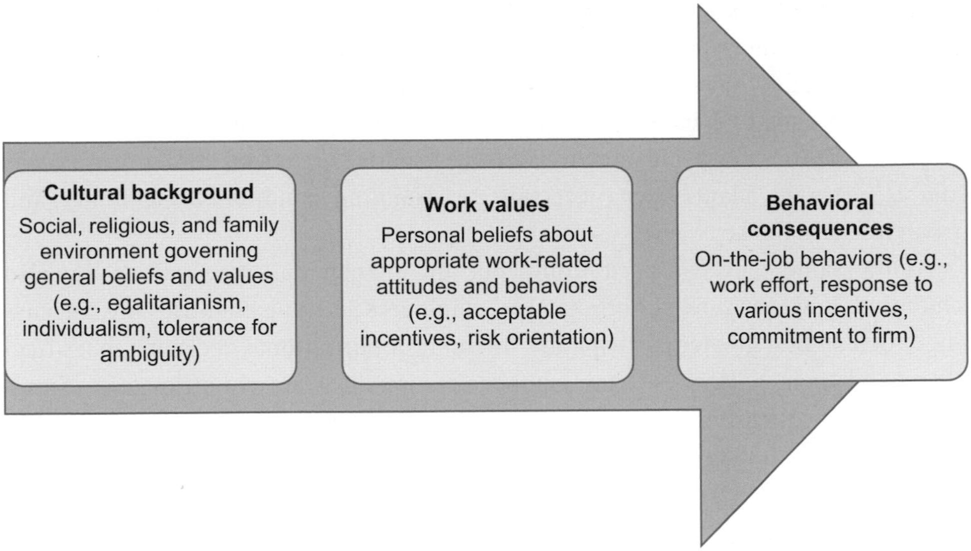

Exhibit 9.1 Culture, work values, and behavior

maximization, organizational efficiency, and productivity. Japanese and South Korean managers also valued pragmatism, competence, and achievement, but emphasized organizational growth instead of profit maximization. Indian managers stressed a moralistic orientation, a desire for stability instead of change, and the importance of status, dignity, prestige, and compliance with organizational directives. Finally, Australian managers tended to emphasize a moralistic and humanistic orientation, an emphasis on both growth and profit maximization, a high value on loyalty and trust, and a low emphasis on individual achievement, success, competition, and risk.

This initial work by England and his colleagues formed the basis for a subsequent international study of managerial values called the Meaning of Work project.[3] This study sought to identify the underlying meanings that individuals and groups attach to work in six industrialized nations: Belgium, Germany, Israel, Japan, the United Kingdom, and the United States. In this study, Japan was found to have a higher number of workers for whom work was their central life interest compared to both Americans and Germans, who placed a higher value on leisure and social interaction. A high proportion of Americans saw work as a duty, an obligation that had to be met. Japanese workers showed less interest in individual economic outcomes from work than their European and American counterparts.

Although personal work values are often discussed in terms of being reasonably stable attributes, they are not set in stone and can evolve over time. We can witness this in recent observations that younger workers in many countries (e.g., Canada, Japan, France, the United States, etc.) are losing their historical work ethic. Instead, they seek more balance between work and family or work and leisure. At times, moreover, they seek simply less work. Their commitment and dedication to their employers have decreased, while their job expectations in terms of compensation and responsibility have increased. Whether these trends are accurate, universal, or reversible is open to debate. The point to be made here is that managers have a dual responsibility both to avoid stereotypes (e.g., "South Koreans are all hard workers") and to learn to adapt when necessary to changing conditions. Flexibility and awareness are the keys here.

At the same time, work environments and managerial expectations are also changing, however slowly. For example, employees in some countries are increasingly demanding greater participation in major organizational decisions that affect them and their colleagues. New labor legislation in some countries (e.g., South Korea) tends to reinforce this trend. At the same time, however, other governments are seen to be moving in the opposite direction by attempting to reduce employee benefits, work rules, and security (e.g., France and the United States).

Work and leisure

A second question we must ask here is how central work is in the lives of employees. Put more bluntly, *do people live to work or work to live?* An example of this comes from a Danish colleague of one of the authors who suggests that the fundamental difference between Danes and Germans is that the Germans live to work while the Danes work to live. (One wonders what the response of Germans might be.) Moreover, we sometimes hear that Americans work harder than Europeans – a comment more likely to be heard in New York than in London or Berlin. We hear, too, that Japanese and South Koreans work harder than anyone else – a comment heard in many places, East and West. Indeed, everyone seems to have an opinion about who works the hardest.

Consider some "facts" as far as they will take us. According to one study, American and Japanese employees work an average of 1,800 hours annually.[4] These data ignore the fact that many employees in both countries often work considerable overtime. In Japan this is called "free overtime" (it is required but not compensated). Indeed, it is estimated that almost one-half of Japanese employees between the ages of thirty and forty work over sixty hours per week but are compensated for just forty hours. Meanwhile, according to this same study, the average German employee works 1,440 hours annually. We also see variations in official vacation policies across countries, ranging from one or two weeks in much of Asia to four or five weeks in much of Europe (see Exhibit 9.2 for examples). The unanswered question throughout this debate, however, is whether working harder than someone else is a badge of honor or a sign of necessity, or, worse still, some deep psychological malfunction.

Exhibit 9.2 Vacation policies in selected countries

Country	Typical annual vacation policy
France	Two and a half days' paid leave for each full month of service during the year.
Germany	Eighteen working days' paid leave following six months of service.
Hong Kong (China)	Seven days' paid leave following twelve months of continuous service with same employer.
Indonesia	Twelve days' paid leave after twelve months of full service.
Italy	Varies according to length of service, but usually between four and six weeks' paid leave.
Japan	Ten days' paid leave following twelve months of continuous service, provided employee has worked at least 80 percent of this time.
Malaysia	Varies according to length of service but usually between eight and sixteen days' paid leave.
Mexico	Six days' paid leave.
Philippines	Five days' paid leave.
Saudi Arabia	Fifteen days' paid leave upon completion of twelve months of continuous service with same employer.
Singapore	Seven days' paid leave following twelve months of continuous employment.
United Kingdom	No statutory requirement. Most salaried staff receive about five weeks' paid leave; paid leave for workers based on individual labor contracts.
United States	No statutory requirement. Typically varies based on length of service and job function; usually between five and fifteen days' paid leave annually.

Source: Based on Arvind Phatak, Rabi S. Bhagat, and Roger Kashlak, *International Management: Managing in a Diverse and Dynamic Global Environment* (New York: McGraw-Hill/Irwin, 2010), p. 125.

A 2015 poll of US workers found that, given a choice between receiving an extra $20,000 a year or an extra four weeks of vacation, 66 percent of those surveyed preferred the extra income.[5] Moreover, consider the effects of work on employee well-being. It might be suggested that, while many Europeans load up on vacation time, many Americans load up on consumer products charged to their credit cards. As the work pace quickens, health-related problems are rising, most notably heart problems among both men and women resulting from increasing job-related stress. The pressure to succeed and concern about the economy and job security frequently lead American workers in the opposite direction, however: towards more work and less play.

Although it is perhaps overly simplistic, the work versus leisure conundrum provides an easy conceptual entry into cultural differences, especially as they relate to the world of work. It indicates how central work is in some people's lives. This debate is only part of a larger debate, however, over the social and economic consequences of increasing globalization. As noted earlier, many people believe – correctly or incorrectly – that the quickening pace of globalization and the competitive intensity of the new global economy are changing how people live in ways not imagined earlier. The open question is whether these changes are for the better or for the worse.

APPLICATION 9.1 Call centers in the Philippines

Electronic outsourcing has been a growing industry for twenty years.[6] For most of this time, India controlled most of the industry, but recently the Philippines has overtaken India as the call-center capital of the world. Experts estimate that the Philippine industry generates about $25 billion in revenues, accounting for about 10 percent of the Philippines' economy and as much as the total amount expected to be sent home by the 11 million Filipino nurses, sailors, musicians, and others working overseas.

Most Filipinos speak excellent English, a real asset. Moreover, "our culture is very similar to most Westerners," said Fred Chua, a lifelong Manila resident who runs a call center. A cousin in San Francisco drums up business for the company, Chua said.

Employee turnover in the industry is high, on average about 60 percent, meaning that a typical worker who starts in January will be gone by July, a sign of how stressful and demanding the jobs can be. Yet the relatively good pay – call-center workers make double the average salary of Manila bank tellers – keeps drawing people into the market. And American and European companies are increasingly outsourcing more sophisticated work that was once largely done by legal secretaries, junior accountants, and medical staff to Filipino technicians.

Despite all of this, customers in North America and Western Europe continually complain about working with overseas call centers. They often feel that it is difficult to communicate and have a hard time resolving their problems. Call center technicians sometimes don't seem to understand their products, rapidly resolve problems, or make decisions.

Think about it . . .

(1) Based on what you have learned here, are employees working in call centers exploited? If so, how?
(2) A recent experience by one of the authors is enlightening. The author needed technical assistance with both some Microsoft computer software and a cable Internet problem with a different company. Both call centers were in Manila. The Microsoft call center provided excellent service; the cable

Internet provider did not. What may account for such differences in the same culture with similar employees?

(3) If salaries are so good at these call centers, why is employee turnover so high? As a manager, what might you do to reduce this turnover?

(4) If you were a manager of a call center, what kind of a management or motivational system would you adopt to achieve good employee performance? Would culture play a role in your actions and plans? Explain.

Culture and the psychology of work

Going one step deeper, it is possible to explore how social psychological processes found both within individuals and within their particular cultural backgrounds can influence attitudes and work behaviors. This can become a highly complex topic, so we focus here on only a few cognitive processes as they influence work behavior across cultures: psychological contracts; expectations, equality, and equity; causal attributions; and risk and uncertainty.

Psychological contracts

A psychological contract is an implicit – that is, unwritten – understanding between people concerning exchange relationships (see Exhibit 9.3). In the workplace, this is most commonly seen in perceived agreements between supervisors and employees over the wage–effort bargain – that is, what benefits are offered to employees in the form of salaries, benefits, job security, and so forth, in exchange for their talents, efforts, commitment, and performance? Such contracts can also be seen in mutual agreements between colleagues, co-workers, and team members, however. Psychological contracts can be tenuous, in the sense that they are mutual understandings between individuals or groups, yet nothing is written down. Perceptions and trust (and sometimes history) play a major role in their mutual acceptance.

Imagine the challenge facing expatriates who sign on as sales or marketing representatives for foreign companies. What does the organization expect of them? What do their fellow sales representatives expect of them? Are they expected to work nights and weekends to secure business, even if they are paid only for working weekdays? Are they expected to meet their sales quota or exceed it? Are they supposed to wait their turn for promotion or overtake senior colleagues if they can? In short, what are the unwritten rules governing their employment and performance?

Manager's perceptions

Organization offers wages, benefits, and job security in varying degrees, influenced by cultural backgrounds, expectations, and interpretations of exchange relationships

Employee's perceptions

Employees offer abilities, skills, and loyalty in varying degrees, influenced by cultural backgrounds, expectations, and interpretations of exchange relationships

Exhibit 9.3 Culture and the psychological contract

The reason psychological contracts become important here, again, is that they contain information that the new manager typically won't have, yet will affect his or her job success. Once more, the admonition remains true to gain as much inside knowledge as possible before beginning new assignments. Although a complete understanding of such contracts may be impossible, a simple awareness of their fundamentals can go a long way towards making an outsider an insider.

Expectations, equality, and equity

Cultural influences on individuals' cognitions and expectations remain a dominant force in the study of organizational behavior today.[7] These theories are based largely on the assumption that people tend to make reasoned choices about their behaviors on the basis of their expectations and culturally based worldviews. These choices, in turn, influence job-related outcomes and work attitudes. While the majority of cognitive theories, as well as much of the empirical work relating to them, derive from North American efforts, a number of studies have also been conducted to test the external validity of these models in other regions of the world.

Research has long demonstrated that people's cultural surroundings can frequently influence their hopes and expectations.[8] Likewise, what people expect or prefer as reward for hard work is also culturally based to some degree. Research has identified an equity principle in many Western countries, through which people are motivated to achieve or restore equity (i.e., fairness) between themselves and others they compare themselves to. This principle is different from an equality principle, where people believe everyone should be rewarded equally regardless of effort or productivity. Both principles focus on "fairness" but define it very differently.

Some researchers have suggested that the equity principle may be somewhat culture-bound, however.[9] In Asia and the Middle East, notably, examples abound concerning individuals who apparently readily accept a clearly recognizable state of inequity in order to preserve their view of societal harmony. For instance, men and women frequently receive different pay for doing precisely the same work in countries such as Japan and South Korea.[10] One might think that equity theory would predict that a state of inequity would result for female employees, leading to inequity resolution strategies such as those mentioned above. In many cases, however, no such perceived inequitable state has been found, thereby calling the theory into question. A plausible explanation here may be that women workers view other women as their referent other, not men. As a result, so long as all women are treated the same, a state of perceived equity could exist. This is not to say that such women feel "equal"; rather, compared to their female reference group, they are receiving what the others receive. A state of equity – if not equality – exists.

These cultural idiosyncrasies create at least two cultural limitations on the acceptable actions of managers and employees alike. The first limitation focuses on problem analysis. In other words, cultural drivers can at times affect in no small way how problems are identified and understood by both managers and employees. Indeed, they can even sometimes help determine whether something is seen as a problem at all. For example, while managers in one country (e.g., in Singapore) may focus very seriously on problems of employee absenteeism, managers elsewhere (e.g., in Sweden) may see such behavior as more of a personal employee issue and acceptable within broader limits. The issue in these two cultures is not whether absenteeism is good or bad; rather, it is the magnitude or severity of the problem compared to other behaviors and actions.

In addition, cultural drivers can influence the variety of possible solutions or preferred outcomes that are acceptable on the part of organizations, managers, and employees. Using the employee absenteeism example again, managers in some cultures (e.g., in Singapore) may see strict punitive actions (e.g., financial penalties or termination) as either acceptable or even desirable when employees fail to come to work. In other cultures (e.g., in Sweden), this may seem overly harsh and lacking in understanding of the underlying causes of the absences; such cultures may accept counseling but not termination. In still other cultures (e.g., in Egypt), no action may be taken at all, in the belief that absences are largely beyond the control of individuals and, as such, should not be a legitimate issue for managers.

Causal attributions

A significant area where Western theories of management and motivation are limited involves the role of causal attributions in the process of individual judgment. Attribution theory was largely developed in North America based on laboratory experiments using predominantly Anglo American college undergraduates.[11] This theory focuses on how individuals attempt to understand and interpret events that occur around them. One aspect of this theory that has been repeatedly demonstrated in US studies is the so-called self-serving bias, which asserts that in a group situation leaders will tend to attribute group success to themselves and group failure to others. Hence, a manager might conclude that her work team succeeded because of her leadership skills. Alternatively, this same manager may conclude that her team failed because of group negligence and despite her best efforts.

Evidence from one study, however, suggests that this process may be influenced by cultural differences.[12] In a comparison of Koreans and Americans, this study found support for the self-serving bias among the American sample but not in the Korean sample. Following Confucian tradition, Korean leaders accepted responsibility for group failure and attributed group success to the abilities of the group members – just the opposite of the Americans. Clearly, work motivation theories, regardless of their theoretical foundations, must account for cultural variations before any assertions can be made concerning their external validity across national boundaries.

Risk and uncertainty

Issues related to risk and uncertainty focus on the extent to which people at all levels of an organization either seek to avoid or embrace uncertainty. As noted in Chapter 3, Geert Hofstede identifies uncertainty avoidance, his term for a lack of risk tolerance, as a key variable in differentiating between cultures in an aggregate sense. Like personal work values, expectations, and causal attributions, risk and uncertainty can be influenced – at least to a degree – by cultural differences. For example, cultural differences have been found to affect employee preferences for fixed versus variable compensation. For example, more risk-oriented American managers are frequently prepared to convert 100 percent of their pay to variable compensation, while more risk-averse European managers would seldom commit to more than 10 percent.[13]

Similarly, cultural variations can influence employee preferences for financial or non-financial incentives. Thus, Swedes will typically prefer additional time off for superior performance instead of additional income (due in part to their high tax rates), while if given a choice Japanese workers would prefer financial incentives (with a distinct preference for group-based incentives). Japanese workers tend to take only about half of their sixteen-day holiday entitlement (compared to thirty-five days in

France and Germany) because taking all the time available may show a lack of commitment to the group. Japanese workers who take their full vacations or refuse to work overtime are frequently labeled *wagamama* (selfish).[14] As a result, *karoshi* (death by overwork) is a serious concern in Japan, while Danes, Swedes, and Norwegians see taking time off as part of an inherent right to a healthy and happy life.

APPLICATION 9.2 Lincoln Electric in Germany

Consider the example of Lincoln Electric as it attempted to expand its operations from the United States to Germany. Lincoln Electric is a medium-sized company based in Cleveland, Ohio, that manufactures arc-welding equipment. By any measure, it is a success story.[15] The company's business strategy is simple: sell high-value, high-quality products at competitive prices and provide outstanding customer service. The key to Lincoln Electric's success is its stable, hard-working, and highly skilled workforce. In a country that lavishes sizable executive bonuses on CEOs and other senior managers who can squeeze maximum productivity out of workers, Lincoln was founded – and continues to operate – on the twin principles of self-determination and equal treatment of all employees. Above all, it stresses pay for performance.

Lincoln Electric has an abiding respect for the ability of the individual and believes that, properly motivated, ordinary people can achieve extraordinary results. It also believes firmly that gains in productivity should be shared with consumers in the form of lower prices, with employees in the form of higher pay, and with shareholders in the form of higher dividends. This philosophy has been reinforced by the creation of an incentive system that continues unchanged to this day, more than seventy years after its introduction. All workers at Lincoln are paid on a piece rate system; they are paid for each unit they produce and do not receive either a salary or an hourly wage. There is no paid vacation, no paid sick leave, and no bonuses or job security for seniority. This principle applies to all employees up to and including the company president, with minor adjustments for the nature of managerial work. In addition to receiving piece rate wages, however, workers can earn substantial bonuses on the basis of their individual job performance and company profits. Bonuses are paid twice each year based on performance. Under this system, employee bonuses have been paid each year since 1934, and the company claims that its workers are the highest-paid blue-collar workers in the world. Indeed, employee bonuses often exceed annual wages, thereby more than doubling their income. There have been no lay-offs in the company's long history, and absenteeism and turnover rates are the lowest in the industry. Indeed, it is said that, when a severe snowstorm shuts Cleveland down, Lincoln employees make it to work. Moreover, despite its high employee compensation, Lincoln Electric's workers are so productive that the company has a lower cost structure than any of its competitors.

In recent years Lincoln Electric decided to expand its operations internationally and become a bigger player in the emerging global economy. It set its sights on Germany, buying a small German arc-welding equipment manufacturer. None of the US executives involved in the acquisition decision had any international experience, but they believed that, because they had been so successful in the United States, success would likewise follow elsewhere. One of their first decisions was to retain the local German managers, on the grounds that they best understood local customs and work practices. It was assumed that the Lincoln Electric compensation system would be adapted to fit local conditions, leading to increased productivity through heightened individual motivation. It quickly became apparent, however, that the local German managers were either unable or unwilling to introduce Lincoln Electric's individualistic incentive plan among workers used to a somewhat more collectivistic work culture. Finally, out of exasperation, US headquarters ordered it to be implemented. The response of the employees was quick and decisive. Employee grievances and even lawsuits arose challenging the newly imposed system, which was seen by many as being exploitative and even inhumane. Workers were being asked to work ever harder with little consideration for their quality of living. Many workers rejected the piece rate concept on principle, while others preferred extra leisure time over higher wages and were not prepared to work as hard as their US counterparts.

After a visit to the German facility, Lincoln Electric's president observed:

Even though German factory workers are highly skilled and, in general, solid workers, they do not work nearly as hard or as long as the people in our Cleveland factory. In Germany, the average factory workweek is thirty-five hours. In contrast, the average workweek in Lincoln's US plants is between forty-three and fifty-eight hours, and the company can ask people to work longer hours on short notice – a flexibility that is essential for our system to work. The lack of such flexibility was one of the reasons why our approach would not work in Europe.[16]

Looking back over their German misadventure, Lincoln Electric executives drew what for them was a surprising conclusion: "We had long boasted that our unique culture and incentive system – along with the dedicated, skilled workforce that the company had built over the decades – were the main sources of Lincoln's competitive advantage. We had assumed that the incentive system and culture could be transferred abroad and that the workforce could be quickly replicated."[17]

Think about it . . .

(1) How would you describe the psychological contract in this example?
(2) How did the job and reward expectations, and perceptions of equity, differ between the US company and its German employees?
(3) What could the US (and German) managers have done to improve the motivational environment in their German operation? How successful do you think such attempts might be?

Managing incentives and rewards

What do people expect to happen – and, indeed, what do they wish to happen – as a result of their work efforts? Performance consequences can vary widely, as can reward structures. In general, when people are offered incentives to perform or rewards for good performance (or even punishment for poor performance), such actions are viewed and evaluated by employees as being appropriate or inappropriate, acceptable or unacceptable, with corresponding attitudinal and behavioral consequences. If these positive or negative consequences are important to managers, then, clearly, care must be taken in developing incentives and reward systems.

Consider the variety of outcomes and rewards offered to employees in exchange for their efforts on behalf of the organization. Generally, we refer to two types of incentives and rewards.

- Extrinsic rewards are rewards (or punishments) that are provided to employees as a result of good (or poor) performance, and usually include such items as salaries, bonuses, benefits, and job security. They are largely "administered" by the firm, not the employee, as a consequence of his or her performance.
- Intrinsic rewards are rewards that arise from doing one's job in a satisfactory way. They are largely "self-administered"; in other words, employees may feel pride or satisfaction from a job well done or they may enjoy the holiday time they receive as a consequence of hard work.

Looking across cultures, it readily becomes apparent that reward preferences are, to a degree, culture-bound. Some cultures emphasize security, while others emphasize harmony and congenial interpersonal relationships, and still others emphasize individual status and respect. For example, a study examined the employees of a large multinational electrical equipment manufacturer operating in forty countries around the world and found important similarities, as well as differences, in what rewards employees wanted in exchange for good performance.[18] Interestingly, in all countries, the most important rewards that were sought involved recognition and achievement. Second in importance were improvements in the immediate work environment and employment conditions such as pay and work hours.

Beyond this, however, a number of differences emerged in terms of preferred rewards. Some countries, such as the United Kingdom and the United States, placed a low value on job security compared to workers in many nations, while French and Italian workers placed a high value on security and good fringe benefits and a low value on challenging work. Scandinavian workers de-emphasized "getting ahead" and instead stressed greater concern for others on the job and for personal freedom and autonomy. Germans placed high value on security, fringe benefits, and "getting ahead," while Japanese ranked low on personal advancement and high on having good working conditions and a congenial work environment.

Financial incentives and distributive justice

Many merit-based, or pay-for-performance, incentive systems that are in use around the world (particularly in the West) attempt to link financial compensation and promotional opportunities directly to individual, group, or even corporate performance. Managers employing such systems view them as a statement of equity, if not equality. In other words, the higher one's performance, the greater the rewards – a simple performance–reward contingency. Other cultures believe compensation should be based on group membership or group effort, thereby emphasizing equality. Everyone is deserving of more or less the same rewards. To understand the logic underlying such differences, it is helpful to understand the concept of distributive justice across cultures, especially as it relates to individualism or collectivism. One example of this can be seen in an effort by a US multinational corporation to institute an individually based bonus system for its sales representatives in a Danish subsidiary. The sales force rejected the proposal because it favored one group over another. The Danish employees felt that all employees should receive the same amount of bonus instead of being given a percentage of their salary, reflecting a strong sense of egalitarianism.[19]

Similar results were found for Indonesian oil workers; individually based incentive systems created more controversy than results. As one manager commented: "Indonesians manage their culture by a group process, and everybody is linked together as a team. Distributing money differently amongst the team did not go over that well; so, we've come to the conclusion that pay for performance is not suitable for Indonesia."[20] Similar results were reported in studies comparing Americans with Chinese, Russians, and Indians. In all three cases, Americans expressed greater preference than their counterparts for rewards to be based on performance instead of equality or need.[21]

It is interesting to note that the basis for some incentive systems has evolved over time in response to political and economic changes. China is frequently cited as an example of a country that is attempting to blend quasi-capitalistic economic reforms with a reasonably static socialist political state. China's economy has demonstrated considerable growth, as entrepreneurs are increasingly allowed to initiate their own enterprises largely free from government control. Within existing and former state-owned enterprises, moreover, some movement can be seen towards what is called a reform model of incentives and motivation. In this regard, a distinction can be made between the traditional Chinese incentive model, in which egalitarianism is stressed and rewards tend to be based on age, loyalty, and gender, and the new reform model, in which merit and achievement receive greater emphasis and rewards tend to be based on qualifications, training, level of responsibility, and performance. Some researchers have suggested, however, that the rhetoric in support of the reform model far surpasses actual implementation to date.

In Japan, meanwhile, efforts to introduce Western-style merit pay systems have often led to an increase in overall labor costs. Since the companies that adopted the merit-based reward system could not simultaneously reduce the pay of less productive workers for fear of causing them to lose face and disturb group harmony (*wa*), everyone's salary tended to increase.

Similar results concerning the manner in which culture can influence reward systems as well as other personnel practices emerged from a study among banking employees in South Korea.[22] The two South Korean banks studied were owned and operated as joint ventures with banks in other countries, one from Japan and one from the United States. In the American joint venture, US personnel policies dominated management practice in the South Korean bank, while in the Japanese joint venture, a blend of Japanese and South Korean HRM policies prevailed. Employees in the joint venture with the Japanese bank were significantly more committed to the organization than employees in the US joint venture. Moreover, the Japanese-affiliated bank also demonstrated significantly higher financial performance. However you look at it, employees do not always seek the same rewards and outcomes for job performance.

APPLICATION 9.3 Lincoln Electric in Mexico

Let's return to our example of Lincoln Electric. Lincoln Electric's disappointment in Germany was soon replaced with optimism following its experience with a Mexican subsidiary that occurred about the same time.[23] The company had purchased a unionized manufacturing plant in Mexico City. Despite the fact that piece rate systems are generally rejected by Mexican workers (like their German counterparts), Lincoln introduced its system gradually and only following discussions with workers in the plant. Initially, when employees expressed reservations about the Lincoln plan, executives asked for two Mexican volunteers to test-drive the system. They were guaranteed that they would not lose money under the system during the trial period, but could keep any additional income they earned. Two employees reluctantly agreed to try the system. Soon, as the two workers began making more than their colleagues, other employees asked to join the plan. Over the next two years everyone in the plant gradually asked to join. Today, the Mexican facility continues to prosper under the Lincoln incentive system.

From its experience in Germany and Mexico, Lincoln Electric concluded that moving across borders must be done slowly and only after gaining a thorough understanding of local cultures. Moreover, they learned that transplanting ideas – whether they relate to incentive systems, management practices, or anything else – would succeed only after a thorough dialog with the workers who are directly involved. As we look back on this example, one wonders why the Lincoln Electric incentive program that had worked so well for decades in the United States was so soundly rejected in these two other countries. Could this rejection be attributed exclusively to cultural differences, or were there other factors in play here? If so, what are these other factors?

Think about it . . .

(1) Why was Lincoln Electric more successful in Mexico than in Germany? Explain.
(2) What are the lessons here for other companies and managers who are faced with the challenge of motivating employees in their overseas facilities?

Employee benefits

As HRM executives know all too well, employee benefits and prerequisites represent a sizable portion of overall labor costs for any operation. These costs typically range from 33 to 50 percent of salaries. These same executives also understand that such benefits can vary significantly across cultures, not just in their magnitude but also in their nature. As expatriate packages decline and global growth increasingly seeks to attract local talent from around the world, employers who ignore local quirks and customs do so at their own risk. Companies that extend their stock options plans abroad often discover that the local tax systems substantially reduce any income – or motivational – advantages. The trick for managers here is to study local customs and work to match corporate benefits to local conditions. To understand the extent to which these customs can vary, consider several examples.

- In many parts of the world, past financial crises mean that employees aren't very interested in deferred compensation plans such as 401(k) plans, which are commonly used in the United States as one way to save for retirement. Why be rewarded in stocks and bonds that could collapse?
- Indian firms frequently pay the expenses for the aging parents of employees.
- Companies in China are often required to chip into housing funds, usually on a matching basis, so that employees can buy their own houses.
- Likewise, companies in India and Russia often arrange for home mortgages for their employees and sometimes even pay part of the monthly mortgage expenses.
- Employers in both Japan and the Philippines traditionally receive a monthly family allowance (called a *rice allowance* in the Philippines and *kazoku teiate* in Japan) in addition to their wages.
- Many Mexican firms offer *pollution escape trips* to allow employees to escape from polluted Mexico City and other cities to holidays in either the Pacific or Gulf of Mexico coasts. In Mexico as well, Mother's Day is on a weekday, and employees often receive the entire day off to take their mothers to lunch.
- Executives in both Brazil and Mexico are often given chauffeur-driven cars with bulletproof windows to protect them against kidnapping.
- As if the high number of days off were not enough, some French employers offer the use of company-owned ski chalets and beach houses to employees for a nominal fee. Such perks are also occasionally seen in Germany.
- In recognition of the litigious nature of American society, many US companies pay for employee legal services insurance just as they do employee healthcare insurance.

These are significant – and at times very expensive – benefit differences. Not receiving them can anger local employees and even lead to more drastic behavior. It is more a question of local, rather than global, equity.

APPLICATION 9.4 Company cars at Intel, Netherlands

A small Dutch high-tech firm was recently acquired by US electronics giant Intel. Consistent with Dutch tradition, the small company had long provided many of its middle managers with company cars to offset the country's high tax rate on personal incomes. In the eyes of its employees, this was part of their compensation package. To many outsiders, however, the proliferation of new BMWs among the managers of the small start-up seemed a bit excessive. After the acquisition of the company by Intel Corporation, Intel's HRM executives sought to rescind the Dutch company's car policy, since it was far more generous than that of the parent company back in the United States. Following a number of complaints and several key resignations, however, the parent company policy change was dropped. This example illustrates the conflicts and challenges faced by many of today's global managers. From their standpoint, the Intel executives were seeking equality in their employee personnel policies across the two countries, but from the Dutch standpoint the company cars were part of this equality, since their income tax rate on salaries is substantially higher than that for their US counterparts.

Think about it . . .

(1) Should reward systems within one company be the same across the globe or tailored to each country? What problems may each of these approaches create?
(2) Faced with a disparity of benefit and reward systems across borders, as in the case of Intel, what can global organizations and their managers do?
(3) Sitting in the corporate headquarters of a multinational firm, how can a manager discover what level of compensation and benefits is both fair and functional in other regions of the world? What would you do?

Finally, it is important for managers to remember that no culture or country has an absolute preference for one incentive system over the other. In other words, almost all cultures make use of a combination of extrinsic and intrinsic incentives. What does differ, however, is the relative balance between the two. Some cultures place greater emphasis on concrete, typically financially based, incentives, in the belief that, at the end of the day, money matters. Others obviously recognize the importance of money as a motivator but prefer to emphasize and support improvements in such areas as work design and employee involvement, in the belief that challenging and interesting work will maximize individual and collective contributions to organizational goal attainment. In any case, managers must discover, understand, and respond to work environments as they are influenced by cultural differences.

Gender, compensation, and opportunities

In many countries, significant differences can be found in pay levels between men and women. This can be a difficult topic to explore, because it can very quickly turn

Exhibit 9.4 Gender wage gaps across nations

Country	Wage gap (%)	Country	Wage gap (%)	Country	Wage gap (%)
New Zealand	6	Sweden	15	Finland	20
Belgium	9	Spain	17	United States	21
Poland	11	OECD average	18	Canada	22
Greece	12	Czech Republic	19	Switzerland	22
France	12	Portugal	19	Germany	24
Hungary	12	Ireland	20	Japan	32
Denmark	14	United Kingdom	20	South Korea	40
Australia	15				

Note: Numbers indicate the percentage difference between the average wage of men and women by country, expressed in terms of men's wages.
Source: Data derived from OECD, *Women and Men in OECD Countries* (Paris: OECD, 2013), pp. 15–18.

into disagreement over beliefs and values irrespective of cultural differences. Put another way, should this discussion focus on what companies across borders do in their compensation policies or on what they should do? Moreover, in making pay comparisons between genders, are we discussing disparities between the pay of men and women in similar jobs (e.g., assembly line workers, marketing representatives, healthcare providers, etc.) or in different jobs that someone has determined to be on a par with each other in terms of the skills or qualifications required (e.g., a teacher and a manager) – the issue of comparable worth?

Our focus here is on basic statistical differences between what men and women make by job category in different countries. To accomplish this, we turn to a recent OECD study of gender wage gaps, as summarized in Exhibit 9.4. As can be seen, gender-based wage gaps can be found in all the countries studied, ranging from a low of 6 percent wage disparity in New Zealand to a high of 40 percent disparity in South Korea. Some of these disparities can be explained by the fact that women are more likely to be found in contingent labor categories, which typically pay less than permanent job status. Other disparities can be explained by differing sex role expectations and norms in some countries. Some can be explained by simple job discrimination. In this regard, it is interesting to note that in no country do men on average make less than women, disputing the notion that such wage differences are random in nature.

From both a managerial and a motivational standpoint, this issue can become intractable for the following reason. When global managers are assigned abroad, what is (or should be) their philosophy on compensation policies? Should they abide by prevailing local wage patterns (e.g., paying women lower salaries than men doing similar work) or should they apply the equal-pay-for-equal-work policies that may prevail in their home countries? Simply put, should global managers strive to play by local rules as defined by local cultures (particularism) or be agents of change as defined by their home-country beliefs and values (universalism)? This value conflict illustrates another challenge facing managers who work in foreign assignments.

APPLICATION 9.5 Women in the Chinese workforce

Women make up 46 percent of China's labor force, a higher proportion than in most Western countries. In large part, this can be traced back to Mao Zedong's efforts to get more women into the workforce with his famous dictum "Women hold up half the sky." In recent years China has been generally recognized as being more open to women than other East Asian countries. If women expect to be taken seriously, as one Chinese female investment banker in Beijing puts it, "We must not come across as deferential."[24] Young Chinese women have been moving away from the countryside in droves and piling into the electronics factories in the booming coastal belt, leading dreary lives but earning more money than their parents ever dreamed of. Others have been pouring into universities, at home and abroad, and graduating in almost the same numbers as men. Once they have negotiated China's highly competitive education system, they want to get on a career ladder and start climbing. Here are just two examples.

Pully Chau spent eight years working for the Chinese office of a big international advertising agency and never got a pay rise; there was always some excuse. "It was stupid of me not to ask," she says. "If I had been a Caucasian man, I would have done better." She stuck around because she liked the idea of working for an outfit that was well known in China and hoped to learn something. Eventually she got fed up and took a job with another Western agency, Draftfcb, for which she is now chairman and CEO for Greater China, based in Shanghai. Highly confident and with boundless energy, today she could pick and choose from any number of jobs. There are lots of opportunities for women in China, she says – but, in business, life is still easier for men.

A second example is Iris Kang, who heads the business unit for emerging markets at Pfizer. Kang was trained to be a doctor in a state-owned hospital, but soon changed careers for the global pharmaceutical industry. She says there is less sex discrimination in multinationals than in Chinese companies, and the number of women in senior posts in her firm is rising rapidly. Hers is another tale of relentless self-improvement. Soon after she joined the private sector she took an executive MBA at one of China's leading business schools, the CEIBS in

Shanghai. Last year she added a Master's degree in pharmaceutical medicine, all the while heading a team of 120 people in her job with Pfizer.

Think about it . . .

(1) Statistics suggest that women in China have greater opportunities on the executive ladder than their counterparts in other Asian countries. What might explain this difference?
(2) The examples of Pully Chau and Iris Kang illustrate highly successful women executives. In the realm of speculation, why do you think these two women succeeded whereas others have not?
(3) In general, do you think women in various countries are largely motivated by the same factors as their male counterparts? Explain.

MANAGER'S NOTEBOOK

Managing work and motivation

So what have we learned? To begin with, whether a manager's assignment is to supervise local employees in an overseas operation, build or manage a global partnership, or simply fly in to check on the progress of a team project, the challenge basically remains the same: he or she is immersed in a foreign environment with unfamiliar or uncomfortable norms and then expected to perform. In many cases, moreover, it is the responsibility of the singular outsider – the global manager – and not the multitude of insiders to make adjustments.

We also learned that personal work values reflect individual beliefs about desirable end states or modes of conduct for pursuing desirable end states. They provide individuals with guidelines and standards for determining their own behavior and evaluating the behavior of others. They are important because they signal what individuals and groups of employees see as being most important about their work efforts. They also influence the actual quality and focus of employee endeavors and the ways in which various employees may respond to work motivation strategies and tactics.

A psychological contract represents an implicit understanding between people concerning exchange relationships. In the workplace, this is most commonly seen in perceived agreements between supervisors and employees over the wage–effort bargain. What benefits are offered to employees in the form of salaries, benefits, and job security in exchange for their talents, efforts, commitment, and performance? These contracts can also be seen in mutual agreements between colleagues, co-workers, and team members. They can be tenuous, in the sense that they are mutual understandings between individuals or groups, yet nothing is written down. Perceptions and trust play a major role in their mutual acceptance. The reason psychological contracts become important for new managers is that they contain information that they typically won't have, but will affect their job success.

We also learned that people's cultural surroundings often influence their hopes and expectations. Likewise, people's expectations or preferences as rewards for work are also culturally based to some degree. Research has identified an equity principle in many Western countries whereby people are motivated to achieve or restore equity (i.e., fairness) between themselves and others they compare themselves to. Some international researchers have suggested that the equity principle may be somewhat culture-bound, however. Notably in Asia and the Middle East, examples abound concerning individuals who on the face of it readily accept a clearly recognizable state of inequity in order to preserve their view of societal harmony.

Without a highly motivated workforce that uses its brains, not just its backs, competitive advantage becomes highly problematic. This is particularly true as we move further into an era in which technology and knowledge often determine winners and losers. Simply put, competitive organizations need all their employees striving on behalf of the organization's goals and objectives, not just the people at the top. The challenge for global managers is to accomplish this within a work context in which behavior is often determined by cultural variations beyond their control.

Finally, we learned that different countries often use different motivational and managerial strategies to get work done. The organizational goals may be similar, but the psychology and concomitant behaviors can be very different. If employee behavior is critical for the success of an organization, and if culture influences such behavior, then it represents a major influence on the ultimate competitiveness of the firm. Knowledge of this fact, as well as an understanding of how culture influences employee behavior and performance, represents a critical strategic asset for global managers in a highly competitive world.

Based on these lessons, a number of motivational tools exist that managers can draw upon to help shape their local incentive and reward systems. These include the following.

1.   Understand the local work environment

As discussed in this chapter, work values, incentives, and rewards often vary widely across cultures. Individuals assigned to work or manage in foreign cultures need to understand the local work environment in order to succeed (see Exhibit 9.5). This entails advance preparation, when possible, including reading and discussions with people from the local culture. It also requires clear observations and a willingness to learn and adapt upon arrival. Simply put, the more that

1. Understand local work environments	2. Understand corporate constraints on rewards	3. Manage employee expectations and rewards
• Understand local work environment, including personal work values and psychological contracts. • Understand local work–life balance. • Build productive working relationships with subordinates and others.	• Understand company expectations and resources regarding performance expectations and rewards. • Develop long-range incentive and compensation program. • Develop managerial flexibility to fit local situations.	• Create realistic employee expectations regarding wage–effort bargain. • Develop and reinforce a psychological contract that is mutually understood and accepted. • Manage fair and equitable distribution of rewards as seen locally, not just organizationally.

Exhibit 9.5 Strategies for managing work and motivation

managers know and understand about a new place of work prior to their arrival, the greater the chances of success.

2. Understand corporate constraints on rewards

Organizations face equity pressures from two fronts. On the one hand, employees frequently compare themselves with others in similar positions in the country where they operate. On the other hand, individuals in the same position in different countries may be paid very differently but work side by side in on-site or virtual environments. For example, many international air carriers pay flight attendants according to their local wage environments (that is, the country in which they were hired and officially posted), even though they are working side by side in the cabin. What is fair here? Consider the example of company cars discussed above. Is it fair to offer employees the same rewards that their colleagues in similar companies in the same country receive or the same rewards they would receive in the same position within their firm but in different countries? What happens to expatriates moving from one country to another?

To get around these issues, organizations often come up with corporate policies that leave some leeway to accommodate local conditions – such as the availability and quality of a health program – but at the same time establish a set of parameters to guide incentives and rewards across locations. In many cases, individual managers have limited discretion in how much they can offer in terms of rewards. As such, they need to understand what the home- and host-country constraints are that they have to deal with as they work to motivate the workforce.

3. Manage expectations and rewards

Finally, managers can work hard to create realistic job expectations. This includes being candid about what jobs entail and what is expected of local employees. This seems obvious, but people are frequently surprised how often managers are ambiguous (and sometimes less than truthful) about specific job requirements. In addition, managers can also be transparent concerning what specific rewards are realistically available in exchange for employee work effort. It also includes being candid with employees concerning the available rewards for superior performance, as well as the potential consequences of poor performance.

A famous illustration of this from several years ago involves an auto company that asked its employees to work doubly hard during the coming year to improve the company's productivity and balance sheet. One year later company executives announced that, due to productivity increases, it was laying off many of its employees because they were no longer needed. Once again, trust issues become salient when managers pursue such shortsighted strategies.

In summary, managers have a responsibility to balance – and manage – long-term expectations with outcomes and rewards. While gamesmanship or ambiguity may be a common strategy in the world of compensation, it is not usually a successful one.

KEY TERMS

causal attributions • distributive justice • equality principle • equity principle • extrinsic rewards • intrinsic rewards • *karoshi* (Japanese) • *maquiladora* (Spanish) • *patron* (Spanish) • psychological contract • self-serving bias • *simpatico* (Spanish) • *wagamama* (Japanese) • *wa* (Japanese) • work values

DISCUSSION QUESTIONS

1. Entrepreneur Elon Musk suggests that success in industry, especially in the technology sector, is as much about the drive and innovation of a company's people as it is about its products. If you were launching a new start-up, what criteria would you use to hire your people? Would these criteria change if your company were to be located in various parts of the globe? Explain.

2. Introductory examples in this chapter suggest that work motivation in different countries can be influenced by very different factors. Again, if you were launching a new start-up, how would you accommodate these differences in your incentive and rewards strategies?

3. Some countries (e.g., France, Sweden) seem to adopt more of a work–life balance than other countries (e.g., Korea, Japan). In an increasingly competitive global business environment, how will companies in these cultures compete over the long term?

4. Individual differences both within and between cultures have been discussed throughout this book. Is there an ethical concern if companies require their employees to adopt the work values of their leaders or leave the company?

5. Psychological contracts are based fundamentally on trust. For a company entering a new foreign market, what steps can it take to begin building such trust with its new local employees?

6. Employee motivation is often influenced by a combination of extrinsic and intrinsic rewards. While companies and managers have considerable control over extrinsic incentives what, if anything, can they do to help build intrinsic incentives? Explain. Are global companies able to adjust intrinsic incentives between locations to accommodate local values and work practices? If so, how?

7. Why is knowledge of distributive justice important for managers to understand as they work across cultures?

8. A study of Indonesian oil workers found that individually based incentive systems created more controversy than results. "Indonesians manage their culture by a group process, and everybody is linked together as a team. Distributing money differently amongst the team did not go over that well; so, we've come to the conclusion that pay for performance is not suitable for Indonesia." In a competitive global economy, what can global managers do to motivate Indonesian (and other) workers who reject pay-for-performance rewards systems?

9. A number of societies hold strong beliefs that women should stop working and stay home when they have children. Raising children is thought to be more important for a society than the added income. Particularly in poorer countries where daycare may be less available, do you agree or disagree with this belief. Why?

10. When global managers are assigned abroad, what should be their philosophy on compensation policies? For example, should they abide by prevailing local wage patterns that pay women lower salaries than men doing similar work or should they apply the equal-pay-for-equal-work policies that may prevail in their home countries but not locally? That is, should global managers strive to play by local rules as defined by local cultures (i.e., particularism) or be agents of change as defined by their home-country beliefs and values (i.e., universalism)?

11. The strategies for managing work and motivation suggested in Exhibit 9.5 present managers with some difficult choices – even conflicts. What are these conflicts for managers and what would you do as a manager if you were caught in such potential conflicts? Explain.

CASE: SAMSUNG'S *MAQUILADORA* PLANT

Cultural anthropologists describe the Mexican culture as being collectivistic, hierarchical, polychronic, paternalistic, group-centered, security-oriented, somewhat formal, and at times fatalistic.[25] This certainly does not apply to all Mexicans; indeed, it doesn't even recognize that Mexico is a multicultural society with both European, Asian, and native influences. Even so, foreign visitors frequently observe that Mexicans will at times go to great lengths to protect their dignity, uphold their honor, and maintain their good name. The uniqueness of the individual is honored in Mexico, and people are judged on their individual achievements, demeanor, trustworthiness, and character. Personal respect is a very important element in any relationship. Even a relatively insignificant comment or action can be interpreted in a negative or deprecating manner and can destroy the trust between two people.

Foreign observers also suggest that management in Mexico tends to be autocratic. However, while a manager in Mexico must be respected by his or her subordinates for being tough and decisive, he or she must also be seen as *simpatico*, or understanding. Managers in Mexico tend to exhibit a strong sense of paternalism, a caring for the personal side of their employees that is often absent and at times even resented north of the border. They must act like a *patron* and treat their subordinates like an extended family. Along with this, managers must also treat their employees with a strong sense of respect; personal slights frequently bring strong resentment. Mexican workers often need more communication, relationship-building, and reassurance than their counterparts in some "Western" countries.

Enter Samsung Electronics. Founded in 1938, the Samsung Group is the largest corporate entity in South Korea, with $300 billion in revenues and 315,000 employees worldwide. Best known for its flagship, Samsung Electronics – producer of semiconductors, cell phones, TVs, and LCD panels – the group's highly diversified businesses span a wide range of industries, including financial services, information technology services, machinery, shipbuilding, and chemicals. When Lee Kun-Hee succeeded his father as only the second chairman in the company's history, Samsung was the leader in Korea in most of its markets. But its overseas position as a low-cost producer was becoming untenable in the face of intensifying competition from Japanese electronics makers, which were setting up manufacturing plants in various parts of the globe, and rising domestic wages in South Korea's newly liberalizing economy.

But Lee spotted an opportunity in the reluctance of Japanese companies to adopt digital technology, which consumers were flocking to in cameras, audio equipment, and other electronic products. This opened the door for Samsung to surpass its rivals if it developed the agility, innovativeness, and creativity to succeed in the new digital market. Samsung moved quickly and decisively and began to increase its market share. A key part of its global strategy was the establishment of overseas plants to manufacture its products inexpensively but with a standard of excellence required for a global technology leader. As part of this strategy, Samsung Electronics established a *maquiladora* manufacturing plant in Mexico; that is, a plant that operates in a free trade zone (FTZ), where factories import material and equipment on a duty-free and tariff-free basis for assembly, processing, or manufacturing and then export the assembled, processed and/or manufactured products, sometimes back to the raw materials' country of origin.

In the Samsung facility, the Mexican assembly workers were supervised by South Korean managers.[26] Value conflicts began almost as soon as the plant opened, and grew more intense over time. The Korean managers tended to believe that Mexicans viewed work not as a sacred duty, as in South Korea, but as a means to an end, or even a necessary evil. In their view, their Mexican subordinates routinely made commitments they had little intention of keeping. They also failed to distinguish between work and play. They played loud music and talked excessively during work, wasting time. The Korean managers were dumbfounded by such a lack of commitment.

Needless to say, the Mexican workers had a different point of view. To many of them, the South Korean managers evaluated all people and work situations using their own "Confucian" values and standards. The workers often felt that the managers should not use Korean cultural values as a criterion when comparing work ethics between countries. To the Mexicans, their managers established unrealistic goals and then blamed the workers for being lazy when these goals were not achieved. Moreover, although the Korean managers might have been willing to work fifteen hours a day, this was Mexico, not South Korea. Finally, first-line Mexican supervisors in these plants suggested that the reason for poor plant performance had less to do with work ethics and more to do to with unwillingness on the part of the Korean managers to allow Mexican participation in the production-planning process. Who is right in this conflict may depend more on where you live than on what you believe.

CASE QUESTIONS

1. Briefly summarize the Korean managers' view of the conflict in this case. What do they want to happen? Briefly summarize the Mexican workers' view of this conflict. What do they want to happen?
2. Does the concept of psychological contracts help in understanding this conflict? If so, in what ways?
3. What are the motivational bases of each group? That is, what factors motivate each side to perform well or poorly?
4. What are the constraints on both managers and workers in resolving this issue?
5. If you were an outside consultant, what would you recommend to resolve, or at least reduce, this conflict? Why do you think your recommendation might work?
6. What would be your challenges in selling your proposed solution to each side? Explain.

7. (*Optional research question*) Instead of Mexico, assume you have just been assigned to manage a small pharmaceutical firm in Uganda making vaccines for local doctors and healthcare professionals. This local firm is an NGO. Salaries are low and working conditions are generally poor. Your job is to work with local administrators and employees to ramp up production of needed vaccines without losing product quality. How would you prepare yourself for this new assignment? What would you try and learn about motivating local employees prior to your departure?

NOTES

1. John Brandon, "Elon Musk on how to innovate," *Inc Magazine*, July 14, 2015.
2. George England, *The Manager and His Values: An International Perspective from the United States, Japan, Korea, India, and Australia.* Cambridge, MA: Ballinger, 1975.
3. George England, *National Work Meanings and Patterns: Constraints on Management Action.* Norman, OK: Center for Economic and Management Research, 1986; David Thomas, *International Management: A Cross-Cultural Perspective.* Thousand Oaks, CA: Sage, 2002, pp. 210–12.
4. "Jobs for life," *The Economist*, December 22, 2007, pp. 68–9.
5. "Poll watch," *This Week*, July 24, 2015, p. 15.
6. Don Lee, "The Philippines has become the call center capital of the world," *Los Angeles Times*, February 1, 2015, p. 1.
7. Terrence R. Mitchell and Denise Daniels, "Motivation," in Walter C. Borman, Daniel R. Ilgen, and Richard J. Klimoski (eds.), *Comprehensive Handbook of Psychology, vol. 12: Industrial and Organizational Psychology*, 5th edn. New York: Wiley, 2002, pp. 225–54; Wendelien Van Eerde and Henk Thierry, "VIE functions, self-set goals, and performance: an experiment," in Miriam Erez, Uwe Kleinbeck, and Henk Thierry (eds.), *Work Motivation in the Context of a Globalizing Economy.* Mahwah, NJ: Lawrence Erlbaum, 2001, pp. 131–47; Lyman W. Porter, Gregory A. Bigley, and Richard M. Steers, *Motivation and Work Behavior.* New York: McGraw-Hill, 2003.
8. Porter, Bigley, and Steers, *Motivation and Work Behavior.*
9. Geert Hofstede, *Culture's Consequences: International Differences in Work-Related Values.* Beverly Hills, CA: Sage, 2001; Carl F. Fey, "Opening the black box of motivation: a cross-cultural comparison of Sweden and Russia," *International Business Journal*, 14(3) (2005), pp. 345–67.
10. James Abegglen and George Stalk, *Kaisha: The Japanese Corporation.* New York: Basic Books, 1985; Kae H. Chung, Hak Chong Lee, and Ku Hyun Jung, *Korean Management: Global Strategy and Cultural Transformation.* Berlin: Walter de Gruyter, 1997.
11. H. Kelley, "The process of causal attributions," *American Psychologist*, 28 (1973), pp. 107–29; Barnard Weiner, *Human Motivation.* New York: Holt, Rinehart & Winston, 1980.
12. Sang Nam, "Culture, control, and commitment in an international joint venture," *International Journal of Human Resource Management*, 6 (1995), pp. 553–67.

13. Richard M. Steers and Carlos Sanchez-Runde, "Culture, motivation, and work behavior," in Martin J. Gannon and Karen L. Newman (eds.), *The Blackwell Handbook of Cross-Cultural Management*. Oxford: Blackwell, 2002, pp. 190–216.

14. "Jobs for life," *The Economist*, December 22, 2007, pp. 68–9.

15. Donald F. Hastings, "Lincoln Electric's harsh lessons from international expansion," *Harvard Business Review*, 77(3) (1999), pp. 163–78 (p. 164).

16. Hastings, "Lincoln Electric's harsh lessons," p. 174.

17. Hastings, "Lincoln Electric's harsh lessons," p. 178.

18. Steers and Sanchez-Runde, "Culture, motivation, and work behavior."

19. Steers and Sanchez-Runde, "Culture, motivation, and work behavior."

20. Steers and Sanchez-Runde, "Culture, motivation, and work behavior."

21. Steers and Sanchez-Runde, "Culture, motivation, and work behavior."

22. Nam, "Culture, control, and commitment."

23. Hastings, "Lincoln Electric's harsh lessons."

24. "Women in China: the sky's the limit," *The Economist*, November 28, 2011, pp. 14–16.

25. Christopher Engholm and Scott Grimes, *Doing Business in Mexico*. Upper Saddle River, NJ: Prentice-Hall, 1997; Eva Kras, *Management in Two Cultures: Bridging the Gap between U.S. and Mexican Managers*. Yarmouth, ME: Intercultural Press, 1989.

26. Yongsun Paik and Yong Suhk Pak, "The changing face of Korean management of overseas affiliates," in Chris Rowley and Yongsun Paik (eds.), *The Changing Face of Korean Management*. London: Routledge, 2009, pp. 165–88; Yongsun Paik, Praveen Parboteeach, and Won Shul Shim, "The relationship between perceived compensation, organizational commitment, and job satisfaction: the case of Mexican workers in the Korean maquiladoras," *Journal of Human Resources Management*, 18(10) (2007), pp. 1768–81.

10 Managing global teams

MANAGEMENT CHALLENGE

So far we have considered five competencies designed to improve global management techniques: communication, leadership, negotiation, ethical management, and work motivation. We now come to the sixth competence: managing global teams. If one-on-one relationships can be complicated, imagine how much more difficult it can be to create or work in a cohesive, collaborative work team consisting of multiple individuals from around the world. The challenges here include understanding the strengths and weaknesses of various types of work teams, knowing how to build and lead global teams, and understanding how to build trust among team members. Clearly, this is no easy task, but in today's highly competitive environment managers have little choice but to learn how to get the best out of the people around them. As an ancient African saying goes, "If you want to walk fast, walk alone; if you want to walk far, walk together."[1] The challenge for many global managers – and companies – is that both are important and difficult decisions must be made.

CHAPTER OUTLINE

- Global teams   *page* 294
- Co-located and dispersed global teams   299
- Special challenges of dispersed global teams   300
- Managing dispersed global teams   306
- Managing tasks and team processes   308
- Leadership and global team-building   312
- MANAGER'S NOTEBOOK: Managing global teams   317
- Key terms   321

- Discussion questions   321
- Case: IBM Cloud Labs   322

APPLICATIONS

10.1 Culture and global teams   *page* 296

10.2 Dispersed teams at Dow Chemical   299

10.3 Working together, working apart   305

10.4 Face time for dispersed teams   310

10.5 Developing collaborative skills at Accenture   313

One of the earliest recorded experiments with global teams in an industrial setting occurred in the 1990s and involved Siemens, Toshiba, and IBM. The three companies created a partnership to jointly develop new state-of-the-art chips for the next generation of computing. To accomplish this, all three companies decided to bring their best people together, share their knowledge, and leapfrog the competition. Scientists from all three companies were brought to a state-of-the-art research facility in New York. Unfortunately, each group of scientists quickly identified problems with the joint venture. German scientists from Siemens were shocked to find their Toshiba colleagues closing their eyes and appearing to sleep during meetings. They failed to understand that such behavior is a common practice in Japan for concentrating on what is being said. At the same time, the Japanese scientists from Toshiba, who were used to working in groups, found it uncomfortable to sit in small individual offices all day and speak English. And the US scientists from IBM complained that the Germans planned too much and the Japanese wouldn't make clear and decisive decisions. Inter-group trust evaporated as suspicions began to circulate that some researchers were withholding their best information from the group. Over time, the well-intentioned alliance simply melted away.[2]

Now fast-forward to the present, and we see the same three companies in the forefront of global strategic alliances – including with each other. Not only have all three companies learned the strategic importance of global teams in both R&D and marketing, but they have also seen to it that their global teams are now less insular and more multicultural by design. All three companies now have extensive training programs aimed at improving managers' abilities to work across cultures, including not only cross-cultural communication but also cross-cultural conflict resolution. Moreover, much of their multi-company work is now done virtually instead of face-to-face. Each company has learned from its past mistakes and now works to face the global economy as a partner instead of a competitor whenever possible. Global teams have come a long way, but numerous roadblocks remain.

International success once meant having employees and factories on the ground from São Paulo to Singapore to Stuttgart. Coordinating their activities was a deliberately planned effort managed from corporate headquarters. Today the challenge is very different, and includes building sizable and globally dispersed workforces into superfast, efficient organizations. Given the conflicting needs of global staff and the swiftly shifting nature of competition brought about by the Internet, some think that this has become an almost impossible task. Meanwhile, getting global employees to collaborate instantly – not tomorrow or next week, but now – requires nothing less than a management revolution. Complicating matters even further is the fact that the very idea of a company is evolving from a single outfit with full-time employees and a recognizable hierarchy to something much more fluid, with a classic corporation at the center of an ever-shifting network of suppliers and outsourcers, some of which join the team only for the duration of a single project.

In order to adapt, global firms are hiring sociologists to unlock the secrets of teamwork among colleagues who have never met one another. They are arming staff with an arsenal of new-tech tools to keep them perpetually connected. They include software that helps engineers co-develop three-dimensional prototypes in virtual worlds and services that promote social networking and that track employees and outsiders who have the skills needed to nail a job. Using Global Positioning System locators has become commonplace. Corporations are investing lavishly in posh campuses, crafting leadership training centers, and offering thousands of online courses to develop pipelines of talent.

While the experiment at Siemens, Toshiba, and IBM may have been ahead of the learning curve, most firms now make some use of co-located or dispersed teams to manage and operate various aspects of their global operations. They have to in order to compete. Sometimes these teams consist of groups of employees from one country or culture who join forces to work on an issue of local or global nature (e.g., developing a business strategy for the Baltic region, launching a new product or service in Southeast Asia, etc.). At other times, teams are made up of individuals from different parts of the world that work together to achieve a common goal. In this chapter, we focus on the latter – that is, teams consisting of sometimes highly diverse members from different countries or cultures working together either co-located or virtually.

Global teams

The term global team has many meanings, so it is important to deal with definitions up front. We use global team to identify a group of heterogeneous employees from two or more countries, and sometimes two or more companies, who work together to coordinate, develop, or manage some aspect of a firm's global operations.[3]

Companies usually turn to global teams either when they need specific cross-cultural expertise on some aspect of the business (e.g., developing a new product marketing strategy for a particular geographic region) or when they partner with a foreign firm (e.g., form a strategic alliance or international joint venture). Many firms prefer using such teams because they can often do a better job than homogeneous teams consisting exclusively of either home- or host-country nationals. Global teams can provide an opportunity to incorporate widely differing social, cultural, and business perspectives into key decisions affecting the success of international operations, as discussed below.

Despite their name, most multinational corporations typically have more national (or single-nation) teams than global teams. This is not surprising, since, in many ways, multinationals are collections of multiple companies with multiple local operations. For example, if we look at marketing teams within Velux America, a division of the Danish manufacturer of skylights and solar water heaters, it is not surprising that most of these teams are comprised exclusively of Americans. The same can be said for Velux Company Ltd., the division covering the United Kingdom and Ireland. Team members are almost exclusively English, Irish, Scottish, or Welsh. Indeed, within this sphere, all the local marketing teams in Ireland are specifically Irish. This practice makes sense in terms of understanding and serving local markets. Within the larger Velux operations, however, headquartered in Denmark, *global* marketing strategies and coordination across various local divisions require teams composed of people from across the company's marketing regions.

Advantages and drawbacks of global teams

Global teams come in a variety of shapes, forms, and sizes. Some companies use multicultural or transnational development teams or product launch teams to help develop or refine products that are aimed at multiple international markets. Other firms use multicultural functional business teams in such areas as international marketing or core R&D technology development. Global teams bring cultural diversity to help solve specific challenges, and exist naturally in both the regional and the global headquarters of many multicultural firms, and in various international strategic alliances and joint ventures. Global teams also bring international expertise to decision-making and managerial actions that can otherwise be missing in less diverse teams. These benefits – and some disadvantages – are summarized in Exhibit 10.1.

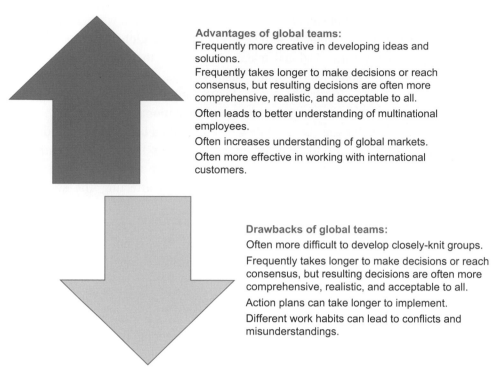

Advantages of global teams:
Frequently more creative in developing ideas and solutions.
Frequently takes longer to make decisions or reach consensus, but resulting decisions are often more comprehensive, realistic, and acceptable to all.
Often leads to better understanding of multinational employees.
Often increases understanding of global markets.
Often more effective in working with international customers.

Drawbacks of global teams:
Often more difficult to develop closely-knit groups.
Frequently takes longer to make decisions or reach consensus, but resulting decisions are often more comprehensive, realistic, and acceptable to all.
Action plans can take longer to implement.
Different work habits can lead to conflicts and misunderstandings.

Exhibit 10.1 Advantages and drawbacks of global teams

APPLICATION 10.1 Culture and global teams

According to INSEAD professor Erin Meyer, culture plays a major role in how teams function. In Sweden, for example, teams learn to make decisions through lengthy consensus-building, which can span many meetings but eventually leads to strong buy-in and rapid implementation.[4] In France, the Descartes-inspired education system teaches that debate and confrontation are necessary elements of any decision-making process. In the United States, managers are trained to solicit input from a team, choose a direction quickly, and make adjustments as the project moves forward. And in Japan, decisions tend to be made in informal one-on-one discussions before a formal group meeting.

Now what happens if we put these groups together in multicultural teams? Based on his experience managing both Americans and Japanese at Panasonic, Atsushi Kagayama observed, "Getting Americans and Japanese to work together is like mixing hamburger with sushi."[5] And former Swiss-based ABB CEO Percy Barnevik notes, "When we sit together as Germans, Swiss, Americans, and Swedes, with many of us living, working, and traveling in different places, the insights can be remarkable. But you have to force people into these situations."[6]

Think about it . . .

(1) To the extent that these observations are accurate, what are the implications for global managers?
(2) To the extent that these observations are accurate, what are the implications for "global subordinates" – that is, the people working under such managers?
(3) Regarding Percy Barnevik's comment that people prefer to sit and work with others from their own cultures and that you must "force" them into cross-cultural interactions, what strategies might you use as a team leader to get these individuals to cross cultural lines and work together?
(4) How might the observations here change how you personally would approach working in multicultural teams?

Global team synergy

As Alibaba founder and CEO Ma Yun (Jack Ma) notes, "If we are a good team and know what we want to do, one of us can defeat ten of them."[7] Working with global teams can bring important advantages. They are usually more creative and innovative than less diverse teams, and can draw on different sources of information as members bring understanding of both different locales and relationships with different stakeholders. Making such teams work effectively is not an easy task, however. It is often more difficult and requires more time to develop group cohesiveness when team members' backgrounds are highly diverse. Moreover, it often takes more time both to reach decisions and to implement them, again because of differences in how decision-making processes are viewed. Finally, people's work habits – the way they approach even simple tasks at work – not only differ significantly across cultures but can also lead to considerable misunderstandings, conflict, and mistrust.

McGill professor Nancy Adler argues that cultural diversity in work teams provides the biggest asset for teams when members are engaged in difficult discretionary tasks requiring innovation.[8] Under such circumstances, the differing perspectives provided by having people from different cultures around the table frequently leads to greater insights and a wider array of possible problem solutions. According to Adler, however, when teams are working on simple tasks or are working on implementation problems as opposed to creative or strategic problems, global teams may be of less value. Indeed, they may slow the process. Thus, a global team's greatest asset appears to be during the planning and development (or analysis) stage, not the implementation (or action) stage.

 University of Michigan professor Paula Caproni suggests that teams in general achieve global team synergy by building on five foundations or facilitators: purpose, performance measures, people, process, and practice.[9] These same facilitators apply to a wide variety of global teams, as described in Exhibit 10.2. Global teams that make use of such techniques to manage both tasks and processes typically have an easier time completing their assigned responsibilities in a creative and productive manner. Group objectives, responsibility tasking, and ground rules

Exhibit 10.2 Influences on global team synergy

Goals	Influences on global team synergy
Clear, engaging purpose	Provide direction, inspiration, and motivation to team members. A clear purpose keeps the team together in difficult situations.
	A powerful purpose should be consistent with organizational values and missions, create a sense of urgency, be positive and inspiring, be easily understood and remembered, be performance-based, and be flexible, attainable, but challenging.
Performance goals and measures	Provide specific and measurable performance goals to evaluate the team's progress, focus the team's efforts on results, enable team members to see how they contribute to the team's goals, and create milestones that build team commitment, confidence, and competence.
People	Team members need to have complementary skills and together have all the skills needed to accomplish a task.
	Team members should also be committed to the team's purpose, have a specific expertise or skill set to contribute to the team, and possess problem-solving, decision-making, and implementation skills. They should also have relationship skills, including the ability to develop trust, deal with conflict, and communicate effectively, be adaptive, and be aware of their own strengths and weaknesses.
Results-driven processes	To accomplish complex tasks, teams need processes in place to identify problems and opportunities, generate solutions, make trade-offs, agree on decisions, implement solutions, evaluate the consequences of their decisions, and coordinate their efforts.
	Teams also need relationship processes to help them deal with conflict and develop trust, a sense of cohesiveness, and commitment.
	These processes rest on norms of behaviors that can be implicit and well assimilated in the team's culture or explicit and well documented in a team contract.
Preparation and practice	One of the most critical aspects of team success – and one frequently neglected – is preparation and disciplined practice.
	High-performing teams routinely reflect on their performance, identify skills they need to succeed, and make efforts to acquire them.

are clearly understood by members. By contrast, groups that fail to manage these activities tend to do less well, because they spend needless time assessing and reassessing goals and objectives and reinventing solutions to recurring problems that could have been dealt with more easily had a structure and a process been squarely in place to guide behavior.

Co-located and dispersed global teams

Not only do teams vary in their degree of heterogeneity and tasks, but they also vary regarding the location of their team members. At one extreme, members of co-located global teams are all located in the same place and meet face-to-face to accomplish most of the tasks. At the other extreme, members of dispersed global teams are dispersed around the globe and seldom – or never – meet face-to-face. Instead, tasks are accomplished largely virtually, with greater use of information and communication technology, such as video conferencing, Skype, text messaging, and e-mails. Each approach has its own unique advantages and challenges.

In real life, however, teams may not always fit neatly into these boxes. For instance, co-located teams may meet face-to-face periodically but accomplish a significant amount of tasks independently and communicate primarily through e-mail and telephone, even though they are working in the same building. Likewise, most dispersed teams meet face-to-face at various times for coordination and relationship-building. Still, general differences can be identified, leading to some differences in how these two groups are managed (see Exhibit 10.3).

APPLICATION 10.2   Dispersed teams at Dow Chemical

Consider the example of Dow Chemical as it tries to navigate in the new world.[10] Dow expects 30 percent of its 20,000 workers to retire in the next five years. Meanwhile, enrollment in US chemical engineering schools is declining, forcing Dow to fight against deep-pocketed oil and gas companies for scarce talent. Recruitment is only the beginning of its challenges, though. The hard part is getting people to work well together, especially given that day-and-night collaboration across the globe is growing. Over the past decade many companies rushed to spread key functions, such as product development, to the far corners of the earth. The idea was to save time and money. Corporations are finding that running these new operations requires much more effort than connecting staff by phone and e-mail, however. "One problem with distributing work is that you lose the intimacy of talking things through at a local café," observes Forrester

Research network innovation specialist Navi Radjou. In her view, dispersed global teams can be a real struggle.

Think about it . . .

(1) For companies such as Dow Chemical that have historically used co-located global teams effectively, how can they make the jump to using dispersed global teams? In other words, do such companies need to make preparations before launching dispersed teams, and, if so, what should these preparations consist of?
(2) In view of the lack of transparency of many dispersed global teams, how can a manager know when the team is working effectively or when it could be more productive? Explain.

Special challenges of dispersed global teams

An increasingly popular approach to global teams today is the dispersed global team. These teams take advantage of technology to draw knowledge and resources from different parts of the organization and different geographical locations without relocating workers. Dispersed global teams are typically characterized by a collaborative network of people dispersed across spatial, temporal, cultural, and organizational boundaries, and working together to achieve common goals. In other words, while co-located teams emphasize time, dispersed teams emphasize space.

Although culture does play a role in the acceptance and use of technologies and work arrangements, technology also influences culture and norms of behavior in a reciprocal fashion. As people incorporate technologies into their lives, they develop new ways of dealing with and relating to tasks and people. For example, a few years ago, when people needed information, they went to the nearest library. Today most people go first to Google or some other Internet search engine. The way, and the frequency with which, we get information has changed. Similarly, the persistent use of technology may very well shape the way individuals work and relate, changing the way cultures interact.

For managers, this means great opportunities, but also challenges. As technology changes the way work is organized, managers need to help members to make sense of new ways of working and relating to the organization. Not only is our relationship with technology likely to change, but our relationship with work and with each other will also have to be adjusted. Managers will be in charge of keeping it

Exhibit 10.3 Characteristics of co-located and dispersed global teams

Global team characteristics	Co-located global teams	Dispersed global teams
Team location and working patterns	Team members work regularly in close proximity; considerable reliance on face-to-face interactions.	Team members work separately from various locations; considerable reliance on virtual communication.
Principal uses	When face-to-face discussions are important and possible, building trust and relationships are important, and decision time horizons can vary.	When key players are unable to co-locate, when contextual information from different locations is important, when tasks are well defined and can be accomplished independently, when ambiguity is low.
Principal team challenges	Communicating, making decisions, and taking actions in a largely face-to-face environment, in which interpersonal styles can differ significantly (e.g., nonverbal communication; language subtleties, preserving or losing face).	Communicating, making decisions, and taking actions in a largely dispersed and often computer-mediated environment, in which interpersonal style, communication, and body language may be largely unseen. Developing cross-cultural understanding and sensitivity from a distance. Developing productive working relationships from a distance. Understanding communications and reaching decisions in a largely computer-mediated environment.
Required skills for interaction	Emphasis on interpersonal and intercultural skills.	Emphasis on interpersonal, intercultural, and technical skills.
Principal leadership challenges	Sensitivity to cross-cultural differences. Accommodate divergent viewpoints. Coordinate interpersonal group dynamics and keep members on-task. Master intercultural communications by listening for contextual messages behind content messages. Lead group efforts to achieve targeted objectives.	Sensitivity to cross-cultural differences. Accommodate divergent viewpoints. Coordinate computer-mediated group dynamics and keep members on-task. Master intercultural communications by reading between the lines on written messages and video conferencing. Lead group efforts to achieve targeted objectives.

together, preventing dispersed forces from pulling organizations apart, and holding the organization together through effective communication and the enunciation of clear goals and shared meaning.

Successful global managers understand that technology alone will not do the trick. It does not matter how good the technology is, and how effectively the task may get done; it is important to remember that individuals are behind the computer. As such, human dynamics and relational issues are just as important as – or more so than – the technology and the task-related issues at hand.[11] In other words, the leader in a dispersed team is a social problem solver and needs to create the conditions for workers to succeed in a dispersed environment.

Perhaps the biggest challenge of working with dispersed teams is that the members, spread as they are across different boundaries, have to learn a completely different way of interacting, overriding age-old human preferences for social interaction. Many of these changes can be beneficial for communication and team performance, but some negative consequences also exist. Three such limitations can be identified that lead to a lack of shared understanding.[12]

Lack of mutual knowledge and context

First, consider the lack of mutual knowledge. When team members are dispersed across a distance, they typically work in different contexts, live in different time zones, and have access to different information.[13] Geographically dispersed teams are able to take advantage of these differences to obtain and use knowledge from multiple contexts. Whereas co-located teams must search for and may miss important market, cultural, and contextual information, teams with greater geographic reach have access to diverse knowledge. While greater geographic reach provides access to more diverse information, dispersed team members lack mutual knowledge, which can lead to an obstruction of information flow. Also known as "common ground," mutual knowledge is the knowledge that individuals have in common and are aware that they share. In other words, mutual knowledge refers to the common basis of information that does not have to be repeated when communicating.

Relatedly, when communicating across distances, people also have a tendency to omit context or contextual information from their messages and discussions, erroneously assuming similarities between locales. For example, one individual reported that, when he was working on a project with a team member in another country, he repeatedly asked for copies of a document to be mailed to HQ, but never received any response. After some time he discovered that there was no photocopier easily available to the foreign team member.

To make matters worse, when contextual information is communicated, it is frequently ignored or forgotten. It is difficult to imagine remote partners' contexts, and even harder to update our mental picture of their contexts as their situation changes. This difficulty in understanding the other's situation also hinders our ability to identify which aspects of our own situation need to be explained. This lack of mutual knowledge frequently creates conflict, as remote partners fail to understand why others fail to honor deadlines, insist on particular points, or drop out of communication without warning. For example, if we have an on-site meeting at 8:00 a.m. on a particularly bad weather day and a colleague is late, we quickly assume that our colleague must be stuck in traffic or is having difficulties arriving because of the weather. When our online colleague does not show up at the scheduled time and has no way of contacting us, however, we do not have any contextual information to make sense of the absence, and may erroneously attribute his or her absence to a lack of interest or responsibility. Similarly, while we do not expect an answer during an important local holiday, we may not be aware of other countries' holidays and may misinterpret the other side's silence.

Global dispersed teams are also likely to face important cultural differences. Although a wealth of academic and practitioner literature recognizes and discusses the challenges of working abroad and working with people from different cultures (see Chapter 3), much less is known about how we deal with other cultures without the benefit of "seeing" how different things are abroad. In face-to-face cross-cultural situations, managers are advised to rely on contextual information in order to make sense of the communication. In dispersed communications, however, such contextual information is not available, and we may not be looking for it, despite the fact that it is still there.

For example, if we arrive by plane in, say, South Africa, we quickly notice that it is not home. The architecture, the smells, the way the people dress and talk, the accents, and the gestures all remind us that we are in a foreign environment and therefore should suspend judgment, pay attention, and assume nothing. When we receive an e-mail from someone in South Africa, however, we are likely to be in the comfort of our own environment, we do not hear any accent, we do not see anything different, and we may fail to realize that we are in a cross-cultural situation. The chances are that our South African counterpart has been influenced by his or her culture while writing the e-mail and has embedded meaning in his or her communication that we may be unable to uncover.

Overdependence on technology

Second, an overdependence on technology can often create problems. Technology brings both beneficial and detrimental influences to dispersed teams. Information technology has made dispersed teams possible by allowing instantaneous information exchange regardless of geographic location. Teams transmitting information electronically may benefit from the fact that information is recorded prior to transmission, providing a record of transactions. Additionally, the ability to hand off work to teammates across time zones allows work to continue around the clock. Technological dependence for communication may lead to some problems, however, and these shortcomings curtail understanding, experimentation, and creative problem-solving.

Unfortunately for all of us, electronic messages sometimes fail to reach their final destinations, attachments may not go through, and different versions of documents may be erroneously circulated. Sometimes members send information to one team member but assume that everyone had access to that information. Even when messages get through, members can't control how the others will read or interpret their messages.

When communicating face-to-face, we indicate what we consider to be important through changes in the tone of voice, facial expressions, and nonverbal gestures. Likewise, receivers signal their understanding by nodding their heads, gesticulating, or making brief verbalizations such as "Yeah" and "M-hmmm." These signaling activities are more time- and energy-consuming in technology-mediated communication, and emoticons are sometimes of little help. Most of the time people do not write e-mails checking their understanding of message context, saying something to the effect of "I read your text, and this is what I understood. Is that what you meant?"[14]

Loss of useful details

Third, dispersed teams often entail a loss of useful detail. When communicating via text-based media, such as e-mail, electronic chat, and text messaging, not only is less information richness transmitted (e.g., body language or facial expressions), but less is explained as well. Writing down details tends to be laborious, so individuals do not write as much as they would say, hence oversimplifying communication and omitting important information. For example, consider how much information you would provide a colleague who missed an important meeting if the request for the information came in person, a telephone call, or a text message. And even when someone takes the time to write all the details into a coherent e-mail or message, chances are many details will be missed as the receiver skims for critical context or simply erases the message entirely.

For instance, one study found that, in similar circumstances, individuals communicating via text-based e-mail technology exchanged an average of 740 words, while individuals communicating verbally exchanged an average of 1,702 words.[15] Text messaging and Facebook obviously lead to even shorter messages. This, of course, is understandable, as it is very difficult to know what information is important, and it takes a lot of work to write down details of our everyday reality, not knowing which parts of it may be relevant to our dispersed team members.

APPLICATION 10.3 Working together, working apart

Sometimes, global project teams evolve from co-located to dispersed, depending on the situation. One example of this concerns the three authors of this book, an American, a Brazilian now living in Canada, and a Spaniard. This "global team" began as a co-located project team and grew out of necessity into a dispersed project team. At the beginning of the project, two members of the team each knew the third author, but did not know each other. Electronic communications were used to bring the three team members together. Soon all three members were living in separate countries, increasing the reliance on electronics. This dispersion, in our view, led to a better outcome, not unlike project teams in the business world. It opened numerous opportunities for taking multiple, and not necessarily congruent, perspectives on various topics.

The lessons were many. First and foremost, we learned that facts and realities often have transient meanings, and can change both across time and borders. We learned that neither individualism nor collectivism is inherently good; that mastery and harmony can at times work in tandem; and that time has many different definitions and applications. Calendars and stopwatches do not necessarily lead to meaningful progress. Goal-directed behavior is often complemented, not displaced, by the more jumbled intersections of multiple simultaneous activities. We learned that rules and relationships can both create a vibrant and committed global team that works closely together in a spirit of flexibility and goal orientation. We learned that nonlinear systems can often trump linearity in both quality and completeness. We learned that cultural friction between partners is often a desirable quality, not something to be avoided. In our case, it led to greater creativity and a more realistic view of the world of work. We learned that assuming a leadership role can be both loud and assertive or quiet and subtle, but both approaches involve disagreements and debates. Finally, we learned that working in a global team can be a great deal of fun, and can create an environment in which much can be learned and shared.

Think about it . . .

(1) This project team involved people from three countries writing a book (this book). How might an academic team like this differ from a business project

team? Are these differences significant for purposes of team management or team success? Explain.

(2) If you were assigned the responsibility of recruiting a global team in your company, how would you go about finding and securing the services of the best team members possible?

(3) If you were assigned the responsibility of managing a global team, what kind of introduction would you give at the beginning of your first meeting?

(4) What do you think your own personal strengths are in managing a global team? What would you be good at? At the same time, what possible weaknesses might you have in such an assignment?

Managing dispersed global teams

Working with – or, indeed, managing – a dispersed global team with workers dispersed around the globe suggests a need to select members carefully with the right skills, abilities, and motivation to work in a highly complex and often ambiguous environment. It also suggests a need to provide these individuals with extensive training in technology use, virtual communication, virtual work, and cultural sensitivity. In addition, expectations and reward systems ought to be consistent with the goals and nature of virtual or distributed work. Managers can't control the behavior of dispersed team members and members are not "seen" while at work. Clear expectations, and measurable goals, are a better way of judging employees' performance and assigning rewards.

Not all tasks can be accomplished virtually, and successful dispersed managers understand this. Some tasks are very difficult to accomplish using traditional media and may require members to meet face-to-face, at least for an initial phase, so that participants can get to know each other and negotiate ways to interact. As a rule of thumb, the higher the level of decision process or the more complex the message, the richer the communication medium required.[16] In other words, simpler tasks can easily be accomplished through lean media, while some tasks are better saved for co-located teams. In cases when insights from several regions are required, global teams may be assigned temporarily to a common location to work on a task.

Once managers have identified the right tasks, the right people, the right technology, and the right reward systems, they must work on processes to enable coordination, shared understanding, and trust. Managers can ease the challenges caused by a lack of common context by actively working in disseminating information. For example, periodic face-to-face meetings may be arranged when possible. If it is impossible or too costly to have all members visit each other, one member of each location may visit remote locations and share information. Additionally, video- and teleconferences should be utilized for information sharing, at which each member is invited to tell how he or she is doing. This will create the conditions for contextual information to emerge, as members have the opportunity to mention things that are important parts of their reality, such as other projects or pressures they are facing.[17]

Managers also have to facilitate communication among members. They can help members' communication by making communication norms explicit, providing intercultural communication training, and developing team-building interventions that help participants to develop communication rules and build mutual understanding.[18] Managers also need to make sure that individual members do not feel isolated in remote locations. The key word here is communicate. Frequent short messages may go a long way to making members feel valued and feel they belong to the team. Exhibit 10.4 summarizes the key issues managers must take into consideration when managing dispersed teams.

Exhibit 10.4 Strategies for managing dispersed global teams

Team components	Management strategies
People	Selection of members with right skills, abilities, and motivation.
	Provide training on technology use, virtual communication, and cultural sensitivity.
	Align reward systems with nature of dispersed work.
	Set clear expectations and measurable goals for performance appraisal purposes.
Tasks	Select tasks that are appropriate for virtual work.
	Use richer media for more complex problems.
Processes	Disseminate information among team members.
	Arrange periodic face-to-face meetings when possible.
	Allow time for information sharing in video- and teleconferences.
	Make communication norms explicit.
	Provide intercultural communication training.
	Develop team-building interventions.
	Make sure individuals do not feel isolated.
	Communicate frequently with all members.

Source: Based on Martha L. Maznevski and Nicholas Athanassiou, "Designing the knowledge-management infrastructure for virtual teams," in Cristina B. Gibson and Susan G. Cohen (eds.), *Virtual Teams that Work: Creating Conditions for Virtual Team Effectiveness* (San Francisco, CA: Jossey-Bass, 2003), pp. 196–213.

Working virtually requires learning a new way of relating and interacting. Success in working virtually as a manager or collaborator requires learning to communicate information that maybe we would not have communicated in a face-to-face interaction. Members must communicate task-related information (details about what has to be done), social-related information (the personality, styles, and reputation of those directly or indirectly involved in the task), and context-related information (the type of support available, equipment, competing responsibilities, cultural norms, holiday schedules, office layouts, local rules, expectations, and regulations).

The conundrum facing dispersed teams is that, while they often need more information than co-located teams, they usually share less, because members do not realize what information is important, take their own context for granted, assume similarity between locations, and have a difficult time imagining what is different for other members, and because it takes a lot of time and effort to write down or communicate everything. Nonetheless, context affects behavior in ways we may not anticipate. For example, one member may feel pressured to finish a task quickly because he or she is under pressure to tackle another task. Another member may be experiencing technological problems, however, that may be slowing him or her down. In summary, succeeding in a virtual environment requires taking the time to communicate in a variety of ways all the elements that may be affecting the work and work environment. It may include details about progress on the task, how you and other team members work, upcoming holidays, the planned construction on your building, or server shutdowns. In short, everything you know that helps you to do your job is likely to help your counterpart to do his or her job as well.

As technology continues to evolve and globalization pressures increase, it is likely that organizations around the world will continue experimenting with new work arrangements and new ways to take advantage of resources available in different locations. The challenge for global managers is to keep up with these changes and adapt their management styles accordingly.

Managing tasks and team processes

A critical issue that comes to the forefront in any discussion of global teams is how they can best be organized and managed. Two factors are important here. First, managers must recognize the principal challenges facing such teams, including how to manage both tasks and processes. Second, managers need to understand what they can do to facilitate team performance. In other words, what are the key success factors here? In this endeavor, getting global teams off to a good start emerges as an essential requirement.

Recruiting and staffing global teams is only the first challenge faced by global firms. Beyond this, strategies and mechanisms must be developed to create truly

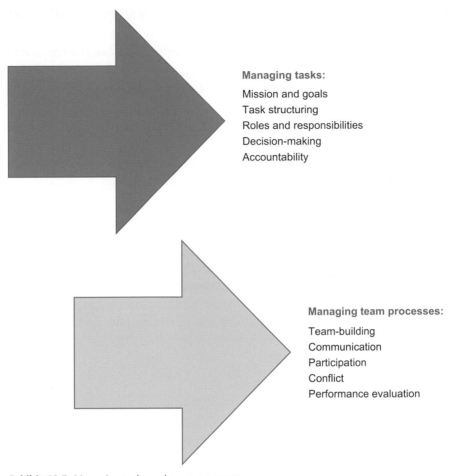

Managing tasks:

Mission and goals
Task structuring
Roles and responsibilities
Decision-making
Accountability

Managing team processes:

Team-building
Communication
Participation
Conflict
Performance evaluation

Exhibit 10.5 Managing tasks and team processes

effective work teams – to get members from divergent cultures to actually work together as a team. Global teams face two fundamental challenges in order to accomplish their mission: managing tasks and managing processes (see Exhibit 10.5).

Managing team tasks

First, global teams must identify their areas of responsibilities and organize their members. Managing tasks involves making sure that all team members understand why the group was formed. This includes clarifying the mission and goals of the team, setting a clear agenda and operating rules for team management, clarifying individual roles and responsibilities, clarifying how decisions will be made, and identifying who is responsible for task accomplishment.

- Mission and goal setting. Identifying team mission, goals, and objectives; identifying performance expectations.
- Task structuring. Agenda setting; creating operating rules and procedures; time management procedures.
- Roles and responsibilities. Division of labor; responsibility charting; team interdependencies; role of leader.
- Decision-making. Delegation of authority; selection and role of a leader; how decisions should be made.
- Accountability. Identifying who is responsible for task accomplishment.

Managing team processes

Second, global teams must develop productive group processes to facilitate collective efforts towards goal attainment. Managing group processes includes developing and completing team-building activities, understanding communication flows and patterns among group members, facilitating participation across team members, specifying methods of conflict resolution, and clarifying how and when performance will be assessed.[19]

- Team-building. Team-building activities; trust building; cross-cultural understanding; opportunities for social interaction.
- Communication patterns. Selection of a working language; challenges of language fluency; appropriate use of information technologies.
- Participation. Guaranteeing everyone a voice; balancing quiet and more vocal members; getting the best from everyone.
- Conflict resolution. Accommodating legitimate differences of opinion; managing constructive conflict; eliminating destructive conflict; strategies for compromise.
- Performance evaluation. How and when to evaluate performance; one-way versus two-way evaluations; role of feedback; who evaluates performance.

APPLICATION 10.4 Face time for dispersed teams

As businesses expect more managers to both oversee more far-flung teams and spend more time with distant clients, face time has become a precious commodity – and a source of professional stress.[20] Technologies like video conferencing and enterprise social networks claim to enable true connection over great distances, but the reality is often far from perfect. When it comes down to it, there is still no good substitute for being in the same room with a direct report or a high-level boss, many executives say.

Yet there is little consensus about how much face time it takes to manage effectively. Ramesh Tainwala, CEO of Samonite International, says that after advancing into the top job in October, he quickly replaced its head of Latin America because the man ran the region from the United States and spent only forty days a year in Latin America. "Unless you are in the field with your people, it's difficult for you to manage it," he adds.

The new head of Latin America is based in Chile, but is almost constantly on the road. Tainwala told him, "You need to be traveling twenty to twenty-five days a month" in the new role.

Tainwala himself travels twenty-five days a month for Samsonite from his base in Hong Kong. Since becoming CEO last fall, he has held four face-to-face sessions with his senior management team, stationed in four regions worldwide. "A conference call cannot substitute for face-to-face interactions. When we meet in person, we almost hear each other's thoughts."

Yet a distant boss with a sudden desire for face time may encounter resistance from subordinates. This happened to a senior manager at an environmental consulting firm. The manager realized she had been too hands-off with her team, missing meetings due to conflicting client demands. She began scheduling half-hour sessions with each team member. Several staffers bristled at the sudden outreach, complaining that she was micromanaging them. She then convened a meeting to explain how her increased engagement could be helpful. "I want you to help me help you," she said. Her team adjusted over time.

Think about it . . .

(1) How can a dispersed team leader balance the need for control and coordination of team efforts with the need to provide team members with sufficient autonomy to do their jobs?

(2) In view of the distance between managers and dispersed teams, how does a manager know when he or she is hovering too closely over team members?

(3) Are special skills required to be a successful dispersed team leader, as opposed to a successful co-located team leader? Explain.

(4) When dispersed global team members want to be "left alone to do their jobs," what can team leaders do to convince them of the need for closer face-to-face coordination?

(5) When face-to-face meetings are simply impossible, identify several specific actions managers can easily take to keep in contact with their dispersed team members.

Leadership and global team-building

Leading successful global – or any – teams includes knowing how to build them. This is no easy task if concrete results and ultimate success are important. Successful teams are not generally constructed from whomever in the organization or division is not busy or is otherwise available. Nor are they typically constructed through a "Noah's ark" approach of appointing a member or two from every country represented. Rather, creating effective teams requires considerable thought, attention to detail, and, above all, an understanding of purpose. What is the principal goal of this team? Who can best facilitate this goal? Who is best qualified to organize and supervise this team through goal accomplishment? These are not simple questions, nor can they be resolved in an expedient way.

Team leader responsibilities

The role of a team leader or coordinator is critical in helping global teams develop the foundations for high group cohesion and job performance. As might be expected, managers need to create the right context for teams to succeed, rather than try to intervene and manage group behavior. To this end, managers and coordinators may productively focus their efforts on the following areas (Exhibit 10.6).

- Select members on the basis of skills. Select members for their skills and invest in global team members' development: teams need the skills to accomplish their tasks and to work together. Team members should be carefully selected to make sure all necessary skills are available, or, if not, are developed.
- Provide clear direction. Provide global teams with direction, purpose, and clear performance goals: team members must believe they have a worthwhile purpose to accomplish and have common expectations regarding their performance goals.
- Build a positive team culture. Help nurture a positive team culture. As discussed above, groups develop cultures on the basis of their first experiences and the solutions they find to the problems they encounter. For this reason, the creation of a global team must be carefully managed, as members are monitoring each other and the leader's behavior carefully to infer rules that will inform future behavior. Clear rules of behavior need to be developed at the outset of team formation, with the team purpose in mind.
- Build team camaraderie. Encourage global teams to take time to get to know one another. Teams need to develop a sense of trust and camaraderie that will facilitate creative exchanges. Teams need to spend time together, not only on-task but also building relationships and getting to know each other.
- Tie rewards to performance. Develop milestones and provide feedback and rewards throughout the project duration, and not just at the end of it. It will help

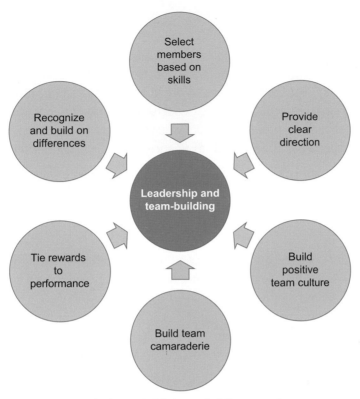

Exhibit 10.6 Leadership and global team building strategies

global teams to reflect on their performance, celebrate small wins, and take action to deal with shortcomings.

- **Recognize and build on differences.** Heterogeneity of cultures and points of view may be a fundamental source of advantage (more knowledge, different perspectives, better problem-solving) if used properly but a major challenge if not managed (conflicts and misunderstandings). Teams that recognize their differences and use the difference to their benefit will perform better than homogeneous teams.[21]

APPLICATION 10.5 Developing collaborative skills at Accenture

It is much easier to identify leadership and team-building skills than to actually develop them. Considerable leadership training is involved. One company that does a lot of this type of training is Accenture. Accenture is a global management consulting, technology services, and outsourcing company, with approximately

236,000 people serving clients in more than 120 countries. As a global firm, it is intent primarily on making employees globally minded. It spends millions of dollars each year on employee education, mostly focused on developing collaboration skills with offshore colleagues. In addition, Accenture puts 400 of its most promising managers through a special leadership development program annually. They are assigned to groups that can include Irish, Chinese, Belgians, and Filipinos, and specialists in fields such as finance, marketing, and technology. Over ten months teams meet in different international locations. As part of the program, they select a new project and learn how to tap the company's worldwide talent pool to complete it.

Think about it . . .

(1) Accenture goes to great lengths and spends a considerable sum to train its managers and consultants to work across cultures. How does such a company carry out a cost–benefit analysis of such expenditures?
(2) Team-building strategies include selecting members on the basis of their skills, building a positive team culture, and building team camaraderie. What can managers do concretely to ensure that these strategies are implemented effectively in global teams?

Building mutual trust

Trust among the members of global teams is both important and elusive. Experience tells us that, without trust between members, the likelihood of long-term team success is significantly reduced. Indeed, a review of the research on successful teams reveals clearly that trust represents one of the key success factors.[22] Exhibit 10.7 compares trust levels by country. As can be seen, the belief that people can be trusted varies somewhat by region. Latin American countries in this study ranged from 7 percent for Brazil to a high of 34 percent for Mexico, while most – but not all – European countries were above this (between 23 and 68 percent). This was particularly true in the Scandinavian countries, where trust levels ranged from 58 to 68 percent. Canada and the United States were in the third quartile, fairly trusting but also cautious.

Now consider another comparison of trust levels, this time within the European Union. This study found that nearly half the people in the European Union trusted citizens from their own countries, but only 20 percent trusted citizens of other EU countries.[23] In one example of this, German farmers and politicians quickly blamed

Country	Agreement (%)	Country	Agreement (%)	Country	Agreement (%)
Brazil	7	Austria	32	United Kingdom	44
Turkey	10	Mexico	34	Ireland	44
Romania	16	South Korea	35	United States	47
Slovenia	17	Spain	35	Canada	52
Latvia	18	India	35	Netherlands	54
Portugal	23	Russia	37	Denmark	58
Chile	24	Germany	38	China	60
Nigeria	24	Japan	42	Finland	64
Argentina	24	Switzerland	43	Norway	67
France	24	Iceland	44	Sweden	68

Exhibit 10.7 Can people be trusted?

Source: World Values Survey, University of Michigan, Institute for Social Research, reported in Nancy R. Buchan, "The complexity of trust: understanding the influence of cultural environment on the nature of trust and trust development," in Rabi S. Bhagat and Richard M. Steers (eds.), *Cambridge Handbook of Culture, Organizations, and Work* (Cambridge University Press, 2009), pp. 373–417.

Spanish farmers for selling them diseased cucumbers, even though it was later found that the problem originated in Germany. Another example can be seen in the recent finger-pointing across the EU concerning who is really to blame for the ongoing economic crisis.

Considering the disparity across countries and regions in general trust levels, the issue of trust in global teams raises two questions. First, what is the process by which trust between team members is developed? Second, what can team members do to facilitate or enhance this trust over time? To answer the first question, consider a simplified model of trust development as shown in Exhibit 10.8. As shown here, a principal ingredient in the development of trust is the foundation upon which it is based. In this regard, three trust expectations can be identified: competence-based trust – the degree to which members believe the others can deliver on their commitments; incentive-based trust – the extent to which each member believes the others are sufficiently motivated to deliver on their commitments; and benevolence-based trust – the extent to which each member believes the others are making a good-faith effort to meet their commitments.[24]

Following the model, team members weigh each of these three expectations and calculate an overall expectation that the other members of the team can be trusted. This trust judgment leads to trust behaviors (e.g., increased openness with members, fewer demands for costly control systems or oversight, etc.) and subsequent trust-related outcomes (e.g., increased efficiency, cost reductions, goal attainment, etc.). While no model can capture the entirety of a complex process

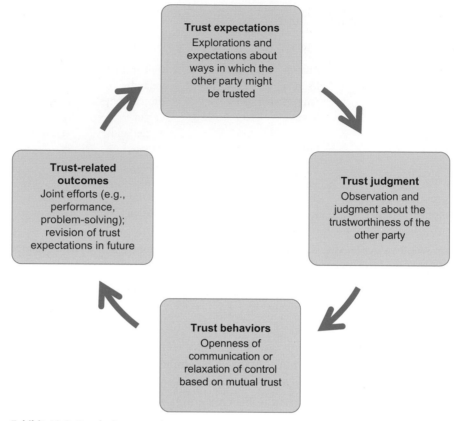

Exhibit 10.8 Developing mutual trust

Source: Based on Nancy R. Buchan, "The complexity of trust: understanding the influence of cultural environment on the nature of trust and trust development," in Rabi S. Bhagat and Richard M. Steers (eds.), *Cambridge Handbook of Culture, Organizations, and Work* (Cambridge University Press, 2009), pp. 373–417.

such as the development of trust, this model does serve to highlight several of the key factors in the process.

As might be expected, when trust development has to occur between team members from significantly different countries and cultures, the challenges of working can increase exponentially. In point of fact, a number of strategies can be identified that, though simple, can nonetheless be effective. To start, team members must be open and candid in their communications with the other members. One misrepresentation of the facts can destroy months of stability and success. This is not to say that all proprietary information (e.g., trade secrets) must be shared; rather, it suggests that other members must know when and why information is proprietary. If such information has little to do with the goals of the team project, there is little reason for honest members to push for answers in these confidential areas. On the other hand, when one member keeps to him- or herself confidential information relating to the operation and success of the team, the commitment of other members will likely decline.

Finally, successful teams are universally characterized by mutual benefit for the various individual members. No one likes to remain willingly in an inequitable relationship. When members see others working diligently on behalf of the collective good, however, and not just for their own personal goals, openness and trust will logically follow.

MANAGER'S NOTEBOOK

Managing global teams

The use of teams – both co-located and dispersed – has increased significantly in recent years as a result of two pressures. First, the move towards increasing globalization has required companies and their managers to work more closely with people from different regions or the world in order to accomplish their goals and objectives. Second, major changes in communications and computer technologies have created new environments in which global teams can operate and new tools for them to use. It only seems logical that these two changes will continue. As such, an understanding of how global teams work, as well as how they can be successfully managed, probably represents one of the most important tools in a manager's repertoire of skills.

By way of summary, a global team was defined here as a group of employees selected from two or more countries who work together to coordinate, develop, or manage some aspect of a firm's global operations. Companies usually turn to such teams either when they need specific cross-cultural expertise on some aspect of the business or when they partner with a foreign firm. Many firms prefer using global teams because they can often do a better job than homogeneous teams consisting exclusively of either home- or host-country nationals.

To be effective, global teams must identify their areas of responsibilities and organize their members. Managing tasks involves making sure that all the team members understand why the group was formed. This includes clarifying the mission and goals of the team, setting a clear agenda and operating rules for team management, clarifying individual roles and responsibilities, clarifying how decisions will be made, and identifying who is responsible for task accomplishment. Second, global teams must develop productive group processes to facilitate collective efforts towards goal attainment. Managing group processes includes developing and completing team-building activities, understanding communication flows and patterns among group members, facilitating participation across team members, specifying methods of conflict resolution, and clarifying how and when performance will be assessed.

While cultural differences can play a role in the acceptance and use of technologies and work arrangements, technology also influences culture and norms of behavior in a reciprocal fashion. As people incorporate technologies into their lives, they develop new ways of dealing and relating to tasks and people. The way, and the frequency with which, we receive information has changed. Similarly, the persistent use of technology may well shape the way individuals work and relate, changing the way cultures interact. For managers, this means great opportunities, but also challenges. Working virtually requires learning a new way of relating and interacting. Success as a manager or team member requires learning to communicate information that maybe we would not have communicated in a face-to-face interaction. Members have to communicate task-related information, social-related information, and context-related information.

Trust among the members of global teams is both important and elusive. Without trust between members, the likelihood of long-term team success is significantly reduced. Indeed, a review of the research on successful teams reveals clearly that trust represents one of the key success factors. Several trust-building strategies, though simple, can nonetheless be effective. Teams must be open and candid in their communications with the other members. A misrepresentation of the facts can destroy months of stability and success. This is not to say that all proprietary information must be shared; rather, it suggests that other members must know when and why information is proprietary. If such information has little to do with the goals of the team project, there is little reason for honest members to push for answers in these confidential areas. On the other hand, when one member keeps to him- or herself confidential information relating to the operation and success of the team, the commitment of other members will likely decline.

Once again, looking at – or trying to build – teams without reference to the environment in which they operate is clearly a suboptimal management strategy. Differences in local cultures, such as individualism or collectivism or polychronic or monochronic approaches to work and time, often impact the work habits of team members. When the members come from highly diverse cultures, these differences are only exacerbated. Likewise, differences in the organizational environment, such as management style or organizational culture, help shape how teams view their jobs, as well as the extent to which they might be willing to collaborate openly with one another – or with other teams. Finally, situational differences, such as variations in personal characteristics, the location of the team, or differences in personal or subunit goals, or available technologies, can often create significant limitations on managerial action.

Within this constraint set, managers clearly have considerable room to maneuver. Their choices must be carefully considered, however. Although a number of management actions have been suggested throughout this chapter, we can distill these down to three key items (see Exhibit 10.9).

1. Build and develop multicultural teams	2. Manage on-site multicultural teams	3. Manage virtual multicultural teams
• Mapping: Engage differences among team members, and understand their implications. • Bridging: Build effective cross-cultural communication. • Integrating: Use cultural differences to create new ideas, build participation, and resolve conflicts.	• Recognize the importance of managing both team goals and tasks and team progresses. • Build leadership skills in working with global teams. • Build trust among team members. • Understand and utilize conflict resolution strategies.	• Recognize the advantages and drawbacks of virtual teams compared to on-site teams. • Manage the special circumstances under which virtual teams operate (e.g., asynchronous time). • Match communication styles to the virtual team environment.

Exhibit 10.9 Strategies for managing global teams

1. Create and develop global teams

Leadership and team-building were discussed above. By way of summary, IMD professor Martha Maznevski has suggested three very useful strategies for getting the most out of team efforts.[25] These are called mapping, bridging, and integrating.

Mapping is engaging the differences between people. It is literally drawing a picture of the similarities and differences in the team, and then working to understand what implications these differences have. There are several different dimensions that can be mapped by managers and team members alike. For example, we might want to map the differences in cultures among different team members. We might want to map differences in personality, in function, in different business units – all the different perspectives that people bring to the team that can be used with the team. It may appear to be somewhat odd to sit down with a team and literally put their names, strengths, and weaknesses on paper, but research has shown that teams that do this actually perform better, because they end up being able to use their whole selves in bringing every aspect of the team and the team members into the team, and using it for performance. Mapping – drawing a picture of the different dimensions of diversity in the team – is the first step to using it to get high performance.

The second strategy is bridging. In essence, bridging is communicating effectively, taking differences into account, speaking and listening from the other person's point of view. There are three steps to bridging. The first step is *approaching* or preparing, really being motivated and wanting to understand other people from their points of view. The second step is *decentering*, or putting ourselves in the other person's place and speaking and listening from their point of view. The third step is *recentering*, or finding commonalities, and developing common norms, common definitions of the situation, and common objectives.

The third strategy suggested by Maznevski is integrating. This involves using the differences between team members to create new ideas, build participation, resolve conflicts, and create a more innovative work environment. Taken together, these three strategies help build well-integrated teams committed both to team cohesiveness and to team performance.

2.   Manage co-located global teams

As noted above, working with co-located global teams can potentially add value to corporate objectives. Such teams are often more creative and innovative than less diverse teams, and are often able to draw from a wider array of sources of opinion and information. Co-located working can help facilitate trust and the sharing of information. Building such teams can be more difficult than building monocultural teams, however, and it requires more time to develop group cohesiveness. In addition, it can take more time both to reach decisions and to implement them, on account of variations in decision-making processes. Finally, people's work habits – the way they approach even simple tasks at work – not only differ significantly across cultures but can lead to considerable misunderstanding, conflict, and mistrust. As a result, managers are advised to be sensitive to changing levels of team trust, as well as any conflicts that arise.

There are specific action strategies that managers can initiate in this regard. First, they need to recognize the importance of managing both team goals and tasks and team progress. In addition, they can work to build their leadership skills in working with global teams. They should also work to build trust among team members. Finally, managers need to develop their skills in understanding and utilizing conflict resolution strategies where needed.

3.   Manage dispersed global teams

Emerging electronic technologies have led to an explosion of virtual work, including dispersed teams. Although such teams promise improved productivity, this can occur only when such teams are well managed and well led. Opportunities for problems proliferate. Building cohesive dispersed teams is problematic in the absence of face-to-face interactions. Social loafing can be a problem, as can overwork (working 24/7). The manager's challenge is to find a productive and sustainable medium. The role of the manager is to understand when and under what circumstances dispersed teams have advantages – or, potentially, disadvantages – compared to co-located teams. In many cases there is no choice, as the people we want for our team may reside in different locations.

Beyond this, as discussed above, managers must have sufficient tools to manage effectively regardless of location or technology. This includes recognizing both the advantages and the drawbacks of dispersed teams compared to co-located teams. It also includes managing the special circumstances under which dispersed teams operate (e.g., asynchronous time). Finally, it includes matching communication technologies to the dispersed team environment. This is no easy task, but it is becoming increasingly important as we move with both speed and determination towards a more electronically based work environment.

KEY TERMS

bridging (model) • co-located global team • dispersed global team • global team • global team synergy • innovation portal • integrating (model) • managing tasks (characteristics) • managing team processes (characteristics) • mapping (model) • team-building strategies • trust behaviors • trust expectations • trust judgment • trust-related outcomes

DISCUSSION QUESTIONS

1. How does a manager know when he or she has an effective global team? What are the indicators?
2. Alibaba CEO Ma Yun says that if we are a good team and know what we want to do, one of us can defeat ten of them. Do you agree or disagree with this assertion? Why or why not?
3. Research demonstrates that a global team's greatest asset is typically during the planning and development stage, not the implementation or action stage. What are the implications for a company creating global marketing teams to advertise, market, and distribute its various products around the world? Explain.
4. In what ways can global team synergy be developed and sustained over the long run?
5. What criteria influence whether a global team should be co-located or dispersed in order to be most effective?
6. Three special challenges for dispersed global teams were discussed in the chapter (lack of mutual knowledge and context, overdependence on technology, and loss of useful details). What actions can team leaders or more senior managers do to alleviate some of these challenges? Explain.
7. "The conundrum facing dispersed teams is that, while they often need more information than co-located teams, they usually share less . . ." Can you think of two examples of why this assertion from the chapter may be accurate?
8. If your boss asked you to develop a two-day team-building workshop for members of several new dispersed global teams, how would you structure the program? What would you include, and why?
9. In your view, what are the principal qualities for a global team leader? Are these leadership qualities the same or different for co-located and dispersed teams? Why?

10. Consider: You have just been assigned to create and then lead a small dispersed global team. What specific actions would you take to build trust among the new members of this team? How might your strategy differ if you were leading a new co-located global team?

11. What are the strengths and possible drawbacks of the mapping–bridging–integrating approach to building high-performance global teams?

CASE: IBM CLOUD LABS

Willy Chiu was parked outside a Palo Alto, California, Seven-Eleven store early one evening when he heard the ping of an instant message arriving.[26] It was the Tokyo-based head of IBM's Asia operations, with urgent news: a major competitor was homing in on a pivotal project IBM had been chasing. The job, to develop a new IT system for a South Korean bank, could be worth up to $100 million. Chiu, who runs IBM's worldwide network of elite cloud labs, was needed to help develop a pilot product. The plea ignited a flurry of online, Galaxy, and iPhone conversations across four continents. Within minutes Chiu had eighteen chat windows open simultaneously on his laptop (see Exhibit 10.10). "How do we mobilize resources

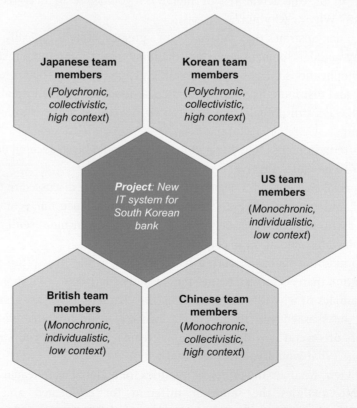

Exhibit 10.10 IBM's dispersed global development team for South Korean bank

worldwide?" he typed in one message to the head of worldwide operations in San Jose. "I'll take the lead," responded IBM's country manager in Seoul. Chiu dashed off a note asking a team in Beijing to free up staff and quickly received confirmation that they were on the case. Then a banking specialist from England chimed in: "Our team can provide reference cases from Spain." Chiu to his administrative assistant: "Stella, please change my flight to a later time tonight. Also, looks like I may go to Korea again in a few weeks." Chiu to his wife: "Will be working late."

IBM aims to set itself apart, with a spate of Web-based services that make it easier for its 360,000-member staff to "work as one dispersed team," says Chiu. The company has launched what it calls an innovation portal, whereby any employee with a product idea can use online chat boxes to organize a team, line up resources, and gain access to market research. Developers in IBM cloud labs around the world can then collaborate on prototypes and testing. This way, enterprising staff can build a global team in as little as half an hour and cut the time to start a business from at least six months to around thirty days.

To see how this works, IBM organized a twenty-member group including staff from Japan, Brazil, and the United Kingdom for a major US telecom client that needed a Web-based tool to launch new services, such as video streaming for cellphones. IBM staff experts built a working prototype in two weeks and delivered a finished product in two months.

CASE QUESTIONS

1. In the case of IBM Cloud Labs, is being dispersed an advantage or a drawback over collecting people at a single location? Why?
2. What special qualities as a manager, if any, must people like Willie Chiu possess to carry out their responsibilities?
3. If your company had technically competent people like Willie Chiu, how would you help them develop the global managerial talents required to succeed? Explain.
4. What is your opinion of IBM's innovation portal as a means of encouraging and supporting productivity among global teams?
5. (*Optional research question*) Explore what various companies do to build, develop, and manage effective global teams. What are some of the best practices from global firms to accomplish this?

NOTES

1. Rajesh Kurup, "Ratan says 'tata' to Mumbai shareholders," *The Hindu Business Line*, August 29, 2012.
2. E. S. Browning, "Side by side: computer chip project brings rivals together, but the cultures clash," *Wall Street Journal*, May 3, 1994, p. A1.

3. Anil Gupta and Vijay Govindarajan, *Global Strategy and Organization*. New York: Wiley, 2004.

4. Erin Meyer, *The Culture Map*. New York: Public Affairs, 2014.

5. Personal communication, Atsushi Kagayama, Panasonic Corporation, Osaka.

6. Cited in Richard M. Steers and Luciara Nardon, *Managing in the Global Economy*. Armonk, NY: M. E. Sharpe, 2006.

7. Preetisha Sen, "Four things we learned from the Alibaba documentary," *Fortune*, August 13, 2014.

8. Nancy J. Adler, *International Dimensions of Organizational Behavior*, 3rd edn. Cincinnati: South-Western College Publishing, 1997.

9. Paula Caproni, *Management Skills for Everyday Life: The Practical Coach*. Upper Saddle River, NJ: Prentice-Hall, 2005, pp. 316–20.

10. Jon R. Katzenbach and Douglas K. Smith, "The discipline of teams," *Harvard Business Review*, 83(7/8) (2005), pp. 162–71.

11. Martha L. Maznevski and Nicholas Athanassiou, "Designing the knowledge-management infrastructure for virtual teams," in Cristina B. Gibson and Susan G. Cohen (eds.), *Virtual Teams that Work: Creating Conditions for Virtual Team Effectiveness*. San Francisco, CA: Jossey-Bass, 2003, pp. 196–213.

12. Pamela J. Hinds and Suzanne P. Weisband, "Knowledge sharing and shared understanding in virtual teams," in Gibson and Cohen, *Virtual Teams that Work*, pp. 21–36.

13. Catherine D. Cramton, "The mutual knowledge problem and its consequences for dispersed collaboration," *Organization Science*, 12(3) (2001), pp. 346–71.

14. Cramton, "The mutual knowledge problem."

15. Susan G. Strauss, "Getting a clue: the effects of communication media and information distribution on participation and performance in computer mediated and face-to-face groups," *Small Group Research*, 27(1) (1996), pp. 115–42.

16. Martha L. Maznevski and Katherine M. Chudoba, "Bridging space over time: global virtual team dynamics and effectiveness,"*Organization Science*, 11(5) (2000), pp. 473–92.

17. Catherine D. Cramton and Kara L. Orvis, "Overcoming barriers to information sharing in virtual teams," in Gibson and Cohen, *Virtual Teams that Work*, pp. 214–30 (p. 229).

18. Cramton and Orvis, "Overcoming barriers to information sharing."

19. Susan Schneider and Jean-Louis Barsoux, *Managing across Cultures*, 2nd edn. London: Prentice-Hall, 2003.

20. Joann Lublin, "Managers need to make time for face time," *Wall Street Journal*, March 17, 2015.

21. Martha L. Maznevski, *IMD: Leading Diverse Teams*, Financial Times video, available at http://video.ft.com/v/62063401001/IMD-Leading-diverse-teams (accessed October 7, 2011).

22. Nancy R. Buchan, "The complexity of trust: understanding the influence of cultural environment on the nature of trust and trust development," in Rabi S. Bhagat and Richard M. Steers (eds.), *Cambridge Handbook of Culture, Organizations, and Work*. Cambridge University Press, 2009, pp. 373–417.

23. Pankaj Ghemawat, "Why can't Europeans get along?," *Fortune*, December 26, 2011, p. 22.

24. Ghemawat, "Why can't Europeans get along?," p. 32; Mark E. Mendenhall, Joyce S. Osland, Allan Bird, Gary R. Oddou, and Martha L. Maznevski, *Global Leadership: Research, Practice and Development*. London: Routledge, 2008.

25. Martha L. Maznevski, *IMD: Leading Diverse Teams*, Financial Times video, available at http://video.ft.com/v/62063401001/IMD-Leading-diverse-teams (accessed October 7, 2011).

26. Charles Babcock, "IBM talks up cloud computing," *Information Week*, June 26, 2009.

11 Managing global assignments

MANAGEMENT CHALLENGE

British author Robert Louis Stevenson once observed, "There are no foreign lands. It is the traveler only who is foreign."[1] Living and working globally is both exciting and routine. It is both easy and difficult. Why? Because some people initially bring more skills to global assignments than others – that is, some have less to learn – and because some foreign locations are more comfortable or familiar than others. For example, a manager from Singapore would likely have an easier time moving to Canada or the United Kingdom than to Ecuador or Peru, because more Singaporeans speak English than Spanish. This does not suggest that they should avoid South America; they just have to work harder, as the territory is less familiar. Moving overseas brings with it a number of challenges, including both psychological and socio-cultural adjustments. In addition, there are personal, time, family, and career considerations. There is also the problem of returning home following the assignment. All of this is doable, of course, but it is made much easier to the extent that managers can develop and enhance their multicultural competence.

CHAPTER OUTLINE

- Global assignments — *page* 329
- Challenges of living and working globally — 336
- Finding your way: coping with culture shock — 341
- Finding your place: acculturation strategies — 350
- Managing repatriation — 353
- MANAGER'S NOTEBOOK: Managing global assignments — 356
- Key terms — 361
- Discussion questions — 361
- Case: Global assignment, Myanmar — 362

APPLICATIONS

11.1 Global assignments at Shell   *page* 333

11.2 Wei Hopeman, Citi Ventures   337

11.3 Peter Hessler, Luogang   343

11.4 Andrea Walker, Belize   355

During a recent voyage through the Caribbean on the *Allure of the Seas*, one of the largest cruise ships ever built, two passengers discussed how much they had enjoyed the voyage. As they rode the glass elevator to the top of the ship's massive eleven-story atrium, one turned to the other and said, "I've been on this voyage for two days, and I haven't even seen the ocean yet."[2] This observation raises an interesting question: what was the purpose of the cruise? Relaxation? Adventure? A similar question can be asked about managers who seek global assignments in their companies, particularly those who want to live and work abroad. What is their motivation? What do they seek to gain from their experience? What will they actually see and learn as a result of their assignment? Is it to be a voyage of discovery, a "life experience," or a serious career move? What will their employer gain from the experience and expense, come to that? Then there is a very different question: what if the assignment abroad is the company's idea, not yours? How should you evaluate this? And must you say, "yes"?

Many managers see an international assignment as a great opportunity. It may be an opportunity to advance one's career, make more money, or learn new things. It may represent a personal challenge or a way to a more interesting life. Managers who take such global assignments report learning new managerial skills, increasing their tolerance for ambiguity, learning new ways of seeing things, and improving their ability to work with others.[3] Exciting though it may be, however, living and working abroad is also challenging, and many people fail. In most cases, it implies immersing oneself in a different environment, learning new cultural norms and rules, developing new skills and behaviors, and adjusting to unexpected situations. Clearly, foreign assignments are different and vary in how challenging they are. In some cases host and home countries share many similarities, and differences are often subtle and apparent only after careful observation or experience. In other cases differences may be overwhelming and apparent at first sight (for example, compare how different the experience would be for an Irish manager moving to Romania or Chile). Either way, living in a foreign culture requires adjusting to a different cultural system.

Expatriates and frequent flyers who travel regularly to work in global operations often express the same frustration: on foreign assignments, they often feel decidedly like outsiders, yet they must find ways to "break into" the local culture simply to do

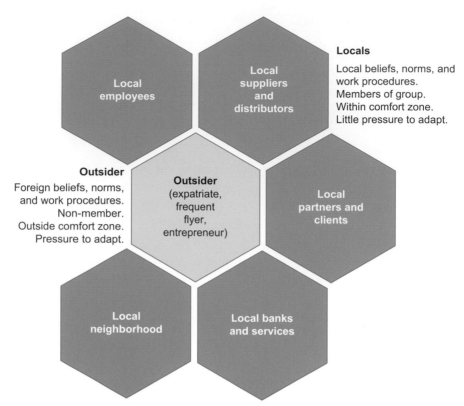

Exhibit 11.1 Key relationships in living and working globally

their job. This is clearly no easy task, since local environments can be highly variable, often secretive, and occasionally hostile. They are, quite literally, surrounded (see Exhibit 11.1). Outsiders are often seen as having "foreign" beliefs, norms, and values. They are not members of the local society, or, in many cases, the local organization. From their standpoint, moreover, outsiders are often outside their own comfort zone. All the same, they have to adjust. Whether their assignment is to supervise local employees in an overseas operation, build or manage a global partnership, or simply fly in to check on the progress of a team project, the challenge is basically the same, although in different degrees: they are immersed in a foreign environment with unfamiliar or uncomfortable norms, and they are expected to perform. In most cases, furthermore, it is the responsibility of the single outsider, not the multitude of insiders, to make adjustments. Hence the question: *how can outsiders live, work, and prosper when surrounded by insiders?* This is the fundamental expatriate challenge.

In this chapter, we look at the process of adaptation to a new cultural environment and discuss strategies to prepare for foreign assignments. While previous chapters dealt with management realities on the ground – how we communicate or negotiate a contract – this chapter is more personal. Certainly, managers require social and technical skills to succeed in foreign environments, but they also need *emotional* skills. This balance – the technical and the emotional – is the topic of this chapter.

Global assignments

To begin with, let us talk briefly about how global managers become "global" in the first place. In other words, how do they get into their new "foreign" assignments or jobs? The variety among these people is probably too large to identify any commonalities or central tendencies. They are all simply too different. Some people are assigned (or requested) by their employers to move abroad for a particular job assignment; others initiate the move themselves by accepting employment with overseas companies that offer them opportunities; and still others move abroad without a job or any concrete idea of how they will make a living. Some want to join established firms; others start their own businesses. Some go abroad for a month; others for several years; and still others emigrate permanently. Each unique combination of location, reasons for the relocation, length of assignment, and other individual characteristics creates constraints and opportunities for the individual worker and his or her family, as well as the local organization employing him or her.

Employer- and self-initiated global assignments

A topic that is often overlooked in discussions concerning foreign assignments is how they begin. We sometimes fail to recognize that there can be major differences between employer-initiated or self-initiated assignments. People's motivations and expectations may be different, as well as their commitment to being away from their home culture for long periods of time (see Exhibit 11.2). Business organizations have long relied on employer–initiated global assignments to develop and control organizations, divisions, and subsidiaries in different regions and countries of the world, transfer knowledge and skills across subsidiaries, and develop globally experienced managers. Such assignments vary in terms of their difficulty, complexity, opportunity, and duration.

Recently, large numbers of people have been choosing to pursue international careers and move across borders without the support of a home organization or employer – self-initiated global assignments. On their own accord, they relocate to a foreign country in search of new career opportunities or a more satisfying life. These are a new breed of international workers, and they vary widely in skill sets and motivations, from adventurous travelers who perform low-level jobs in exotic countries to those at the higher end of the job market, particularly coming from

Exhibit 11.2 Implications of employer-initiated and self-initiated global assignments	
Employer-initiated global assignment	Self-initiated global assignment
Implications for individual (managers, entrepreneurs, global workers)	
Employee may not want the assignment, but feel pressured to accept in order not to jeopardize future career advancements.	Individual can choose where and when to relocate.
Employee may not be able to select location of new assignment.	Individual takes the responsibility for finding a job and relocating the family.
Employee should have relative job security while abroad.	Individual may take a long time to establish local relationships and credentials.
Employee may negotiate financially interesting expatriate package, including trips home, foreign living allowances, support for partner and family.	Individual may need to take a job below what he or she was used to in home country.
Employee may negotiate terms of repatriation.	In many cases, limited expatriate support is provided.
Employers vary widely in the amount of support they provide and how well they manage the expatriation process.	At times individual may negotiate attractive packages when organization can't find local talent, but most times must accept local standards – or less.
Employer is typically responsible for legal arrangements, such as visas and licenses.	Individual may need to deal with work visa and other legal requirements on his or her own.
Implications for employer (companies, NGOs)	
Employer needs to manage the expatriation and repatriation.	Employer may have difficulty evaluating credentials of individual from foreign country.
Costly and potentially high-risk for employer.	Employer needs to manage multicultural workforce.
Employer can select employees with knowledge of the company and technical skills.	Employer may need to accommodate difficulties experienced by the worker due to his or her foreign status (e.g., visa restrictions, local knowledge, lack of family support).

developing countries, in search of better career opportunities. Many are highly educated and experienced; many others are not. Most end up working in organizations of different sizes in the host country, bringing such organizations many advantages and challenges.

By their nature, self-initiated assignments are unique to each individual and circumstances, and the reasons for engaging in each of them and the length of the assignment vary widely. Employer-initiated assignments also vary widely, but share some important commonalities. In the remainder of this chapter we focus on organization-initiated assignments, but in many cases the challenges identified here also apply to self-initiated assignments.

Long- and short-term global assignments

Business organizations routinely rely on global work assignments to develop and control organizations, divisions, and subsidiaries in different regions and countries of the world, transfer knowledge and skills across subsidiaries, and develop globally experienced managers. Such assignments come in a variety of degrees of difficulty, complexity, opportunity, and duration. On a general level, however, they can be categorized into two groupings: those managers who live overseas on relatively permanent, or long-term, assignments; and those who travel overseas on relatively short-term assignments. As shown in Exhibit 11.3, the characteristics (and developmental goals) of each of these sets of managers can be quite different. While long-term assignments require deep knowledge of a particular country or region, shorter assignments typically require broad knowledge of cultural diversity and flexibility. One needs to be a specialist; the other a generalist. One leads a somewhat stable life, albeit in a foreign country; the other leads a highly mobile existence. This is not to say that one approach is superior to the other, only that they are different and that each plays an important role in global commerce.

Long-term global assignments. Traditionally, the most common type of foreign duty involves long-term assignments of parent-company managers to various countries in which the parent firm does, or wants to do, business. Firms often prefer to use expatriate managers for a number of reasons, especially when they feel that they need parent-company representation in a distant location, when they want to provide developmental opportunities for parent-company managers, or when they need to fill skill gaps when locals do not have the skills to do the job themselves (see Exhibit 11.4).[4]

Although the advantages of expatriate assignments are fairly obvious, finding people who can actually succeed in expatriate assignments can be problematic. While traveling abroad (perhaps on a vacation or business trip) is often seen by people as an enjoyable experience, actually living abroad can be frustrating and stressful, and sometimes very unpleasant. For many, staying in a four-star hotel, eating in fine restaurants, seeing new sights, and knowing that soon you will be

Exhibit 11.3 Long- and short-term global assignments

Exhibit 11.4 Long-term global assignments

Principal roles	Advantages	Disadvantages
Integrate local operations into parent company's global strategy.	Provides ongoing opportunities for close scrutiny and control of local operations.	Costly for parent company to pay for expatriate and family.
Enhance parent-company management and control over local operations.	Easier to instill parent-company business values and management philosophy in local operations.	Cultural similarities, friendships, and connections between expatriates and their parent company may serve to reduce any trust or confidence in local (foreign) managers by parent company (e.g., local voices may not be heard).
Fill positions or skill gaps caused by a lack of local talent (e.g., technology transfer).	Local problems can often be more easily identified and reported back to headquarters for resolution.	Local managerial talent is often developed only to the extent that expatriate managers wish, impeding local training and development efforts.
Develop experienced parent-company managers for more challenging foreign assignments or promotion to parent company HQ.	Can facilitate more direct communications and reporting (e.g., same language, same customs) when communicating with HQ.	Expatriate assignments can be used by parent company to remove less effective managers from the home office.
Develop experienced local managers for more challenging global assignments or promotion to parent-company HQ.	Useful when local talent is in short supply. Provides good training ground for expatriates for promotion to future parent-company executive positions. Can facilitate on-the-ground mentoring of local employees and managers for future executive responsibility.	Global assignments can cause considerable family stress, both between spouses (e.g., career conflicts) and with children. Work permit and taxation issues can be problematic in some locations. Repatriation problems for expatriates and/or their families.

back in your own bed is far preferable to setting up a household in a strange neighborhood where few people speak your language, where schools for the kids have to be found, and where one faces the challenges of shopping in local markets stocked with foods one can't identify, and using public transportation. For others, these same experiences provide a sense of adventure and learning. The challenge for managers – and their companies – is to discover which type of person they are before getting on the airplane.

Many people see an international assignment as a great opportunity. It may be an opportunity to advance one's career, to make more money, or to learn new things. It may represent a personal challenge or a way to a more interesting life. Managers who take international assignments report learning new managerial skills, increasing their tolerance for ambiguity, learning new ways of seeing things, and improving their ability to work with others.[5] Living and working abroad is not easy, however. Long-term international assignments are particularly challenging for managers with a family, when a partner may need to give up a career at home and not find suitable employment in the host country, and when children require special attention such as international schooling. A recent survey found that 81 percent of workers declining an expatriate assignment cited family reasons.[6]

APPLICATION 11.1 Global assignments at Shell

Royal Dutch Shell is a global petroleum company with joint headquarters in London and The Hague. The company employs over 100,000 people, approximately 5,500 of whom live and work abroad at any given point in time. Shell's expatriate managers are a highly diverse group, representing over seventy nationalities and working in more than 100 countries. The company supports this because it realizes that, as a global company, success requires the international mobility of its workforce.

Over time, however, Shell found it increasingly difficult to recruit key personnel for overseas assignments. To understand the problem, Shell interviewed 200 expatriate employees and their spouses to uncover their biggest concerns. These data were then used to create a survey, which was sent to 17,000 current and former expatriate managers, expatriates' spouses, and employees who had declined international assignments. Surprisingly, the response rate for the survey was 70 percent, clearly suggesting that many employees believed this to be an important issue. According to the survey results, five key issues had the greatest influence on the willingness of employees to accept an international assignment. In order of importance, these were: (1) separation from children during their secondary education (the children were often sent to boarding schools in their home countries while their parents were away); (2) harm done to a spouse's career and employment; (3) failure to recognize and involve spouses in the relocation decision; (4) failure to provide adequate information and assistance regarding relocation; and (5) health-related issues, such as access to good hospitals, or the ongoing ailment of a family member.

As a result of these findings, Shell implemented a number of programs designed to make it easier for employees to go abroad. To help with the education of children, Shell built elementary schools for employees in locations with heavy expatriate concentrations. For secondary education, they worked with local schools, often providing grants to help upgrade their facilities and educational offerings. They also offered employees an educational supplement for parents wanting to send their children to private schools in the host country. Helping spouses find suitable employment proved to be a more vexing problem. According to the survey, one-half of the spouses were employed when the international assignment was made, but only 12 percent were able to find suitable work after arriving in their new location. Shell established a spouse employment center to address the problem. The center provides career counseling and support in locating employment opportunities both during and immediately following the overseas assignment. The company also agreed to reimburse up to 80 percent of the costs associated with vocational training or reaccreditation.

Finally, Shell established a global information and advice network, known as "the Outpost," to provide support for families contemplating overseas assignments. The Outpost is headquartered in The Hague and now runs forty information centers in more than thirty countries. Staffed by spouses and fully supported by Shell, this global network has helped more than 1,000 families prepare for overseas assignments. The center recommends schools and medical facilities and provides housing advice and up-to-date information on employment, overseas study, self-employment, and volunteer work. Clearly, Shell is working hard to provide a supportive work environment for its global employees in a way that also facilitates the long-term objectives of the company.

Think about it . . .

(1) How would you evaluate the actions taken by Shell to make lives easier for expatriate employees and their families?
(2) What other actions might Shell take to improve the overseas environment for their employees?

Short-term global assignments. In the past, the most popular international assignments involved expatriation, or individuals moving residence from the home country to a foreign location for a significant period of time, usually between one and five years. Today, due to the increased availability of local talent in host countries, increasing cost pressures, a higher incidence of dual-career couples, and the ease of transportation and communication across countries,

Exhibit 11.5 Short-term global assignments

Principal roles	Advantages	Disadvantages
Initiate, monitor, or complete new projects in diverse locations.	Provides parent company with greater flexibility in matching specific managers with specific global plans or problems.	Sometimes difficult for short-term visitors to develop working relationships with local managers due to brevity of visits.
Coordinate ongoing operations and plans across multiple locations.	Flexibility; travel to overseas locations often requires little advance planning.	Parent company can lose strategic benefits on long-term on-site observations and connections.
Send troubleshooters to various locations as needed.	Frequently more cost-effective than supporting "permanent" overseas staff.	Short-term visitors may be less well equipped in terms of linguistic skills than expatriates.
Retain highly skilled talent that may wish to remain in home country (for lifestyle, dual career, etc.).	Managers can more easily maintain connections and friendships at parent company.	Scheduling conflicts with managers who are continually on the go.
Expand talent pool available for various global assignments.	Provides global developmental experience for broad array of parent-company managers.	Physical strain on managers and their families resulting from continual travel.

various forms of alternative international work arrangements, including short-term overseas assignments, are becoming popular.

Global assignments of shorter duration are usually focused on a specific task or project and, as such, provide easier-to-measure results (see Exhibit 11.5).[7] Additionally, there are many workers who would not consider uprooting the family for a long-term expatriate assignment but would be interested in a shorter international opportunity. This increases the pool of talent available for such postings, which is a major plus point, as the demand for international assignees is considerably higher than the supply.[8] It is also the case that short-term assignments are easier on employees, who feel it is easier to remain connected to the home country and career opportunities.

The main challenge facing short-term assignees is that they find themselves in a foreign country without family and friends, and with a very short time to develop relationships and get adjusted.[9] Since assignees are usually sent abroad for a short period to solve a specific problem or perform a specific task, they are not given the time to learn the ropes and adjust to the new locale, as would be the case with traditional long-term expatriate assignments. Instead, short-term assignees are expected to perform as soon as they hit the ground, which increases the challenges of the assignment. Strong pressures to perform – quickly – coupled with a limited social and family life, frequently lead assignees to work long hours and endure high levels of stress. The resulting unsatisfactory work–life balance and high stress levels may lead to unwelcome side effects, such as alcoholism and other destructive behavior.

Challenges of living and working globally

Working abroad poses a number of challenges that can affect people in very different ways depending upon their personal and organizational circumstances. These challenges emerge both prior to departure (e.g., suitability for such assignment, family considerations) and afterwards (duration of assignment, family considerations again). The nature of some of these challenges can evolve with time, while others are ever-present. We explore three of these challenges: personal considerations, family considerations, and career considerations (see Exhibit 11.6).

Personal considerations

An important question for all companies is who to select for global assignments. While many people are interested in such assignments, far fewer are usually qualified. As such, successful companies approach overseas assignments in a

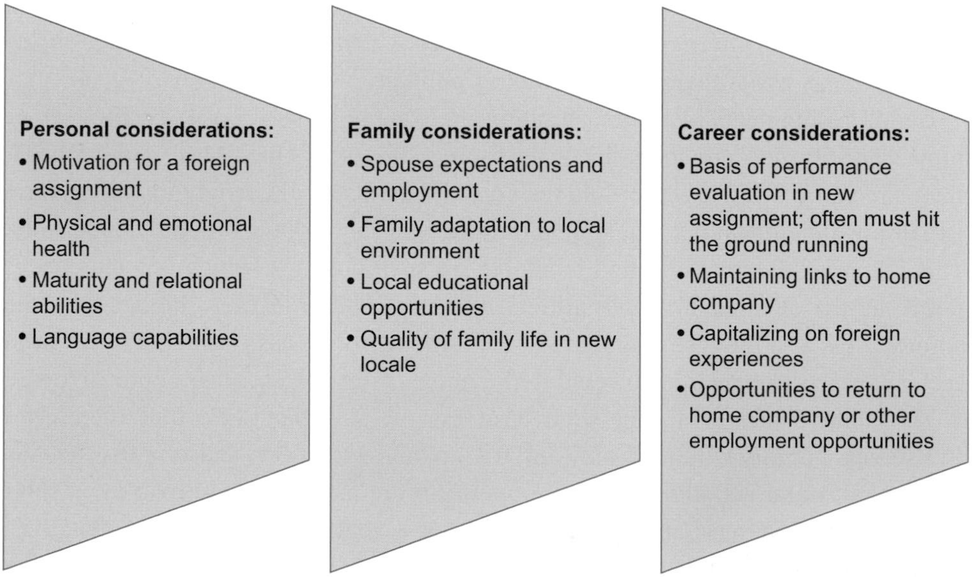

Personal considerations:
- Motivation for a foreign assignment
- Physical and emotional health
- Maturity and relational abilities
- Language capabilities

Family considerations:
- Spouse expectations and employment
- Family adaptation to local environment
- Local educational opportunities
- Quality of family life in new locale

Career considerations:
- Basis of performance evaluation in new assignment; often must hit the ground running
- Maintaining links to home company
- Capitalizing on foreign experiences
- Opportunities to return to home company or other employment opportunities

Exhibit 11.6 Challenges of living and working globally

systematic way, beginning with employee selection and progressing to cultural adaptation programs for those finally selected. The first issue to be addressed is what qualifications candidates for overseas positions should possess. To ensure that those selected have a reasonable chance of success, companies look for certain characteristics in job applicants.[10] Although professional and technical competencies remain prerequisites for most international assignments, other key success factors should also be considered, including the following:

1. **Motivation for a foreign assignment.** Is the manager really interested in going abroad or was he or she talked into it? Why does he or she want to go? Is he or she motivated by career concerns, company commitment, or personal goals?
2. **Physical and emotional health.** Many overseas assignments can be exhausting, with business meetings during the day and social obligations at night. Such assignments are not for the weak of mind or body. Companies must ensure that managers sent overseas are physically up to the challenge. They should also ensure that managers do not carry with them undue emotional baggage that could escalate out of control in a stressful foreign environment.
3. **Maturity and relational abilities.** Can the manager work independently, accept setbacks gracefully, and adapt to new and strange situations? Does the manager have good interpersonal and cross-cultural skills? Can the manager accept other people as they are or must he or she try and change them to fit a predetermined mold?
4. **Language capabilities.** Learning local languages facilitates learning local cultures. It also helps develop close personal and business relationships abroad. Does the manager speak the local language? Is he or she willing to learn?

These key factors do not guarantee success in an overseas assignment, but they enhance the likelihood of success. What expatriate managers really need to succeed is a combination of these skills, a supportive family, and a supportive company. With these three mutually supportive factors, expatriate managers can focus their energies and talents on running the business for the benefit of all.

APPLICATION 11.2 **Wei Hopeman, Citi Ventures**

What is it like being a Chinese-American working for a US financial services company in Shanghai? Ask Wei Hopeman of Citi Ventures, a division of Citigroup.[11] As managing director for the Shanghai office of Citi Ventures, Hopeman leads a very busy life. By day, she works with entrepreneurs throughout Asia to identify their operational and financial needs. By night, she turns her focus to the other side of the world, working a full shift with her American colleagues connecting those start-ups with Citi business units. After eight years of dealing with the thirteen-hour time difference and the fifteen-hour flights between Shanghai and New York – not to mention numerous trips across China to India, Hong Kong, Singapore, and Palo Alto – she has learned to adapt.

Along the way, Hopeman has picked up a few tricks concerning the life of an on-the-go global executive. She calls them her "survival skills." First, since her working day is so long and opportunities for jet lag so frequent, she simply ignores the clock; she has learned to sleep in three-hour chunks of time. Second, she prefers to stay in hotels near her current projects instead of commuting from her home; it is easier to be close to her customers. Third, she blends her work and private life. In much of Asia, the boundary between professional and personal space is much more blurred and she must make herself available 24/7. "I make myself available. It's how business gets done."[12] Fourth, she does not ask what she is eating at business dinners, since this can be seen as rude. Finally, she uses long flights as relaxation time; they have become her sanctuary away from the never-ending demands of her job.

Think about it . . .

(1) Would you like to have Wei Hopeman's job? Why or why not?
(2) What is your opinion about her "survival skills"? Would these skills work for you?
(3) What other survival skills can you identify that global managers might make good use of?

Family considerations

Family considerations are at least as important as personal considerations when deciding whether to accept a global assignment. Long- and short-term assignments carry both risks and challenges, although often of a different nature. For long-term assignments, spouses typically relocate with expatriate partner, and dual-career challenges can be accentuated. The spouse may lose contact with his or her extended family, friends, and support group. While family may reside together, considerable stress can still result from raising children in unfamiliar settings. Children typically relocate with one or both of their parents. Although they can have numerous opportunities to learn about other cultures, make new friends, learn new languages, experience new cuisine, etc., they can also experience culture shock (see below), requiring significant adjustments to the new location and changed circumstances (e.g., missing old friends, dislike of local foods, etc.). Parents who are responsible for their own parents – an increasingly common phenomenon – also face challenges. Thus, everyone in the family is affected. In view of the complexities of interpersonal relationships – even within a single family – decisions to move should not be taken lightly.

Family challenges exist for short-term assignments too. Being away from the family also places a burden on family life. On the one hand, the global manager is immersed in a foreign location experiencing situations that are unfamiliar to his or her family, and it may be difficult for them to comprehend. As discussed above, the manager is likely to be working long hours under pressure, and may be subject to high levels of stress, straining communication. Frequently the manager retains some responsibilities back home, and after a long day at work may spend hours in an empty hotel or apartment room, answering e-mails and on the phone with the home country in a different time zone. On the other hand, the spouse at home is left with the sole responsibility for the house and family, and must pick up the slack left by the partner and assume new roles. As the family settles into a new routine it may be difficult to adapt back, creating resentments on both sides. All this may weaken family ties, and a high divorce rate is associated with this type of assignment. Of course, if the personal life of the manager crumbles, it may also jeopardize the success of the assignment (see Exhibit 11.7). The two are typically highly intertwined.

An additional problem facing short-term assignees and companies alike is that often the original assignment was conceived for a short period and a specific project, but, as the project develops, it is enriched and enlarged, or unforeseen problems can emerge, resulting in extensions of the assignment. It is estimated that more than one-half of short-term assignments get extended to eighteen months or longer,[13] and once the employee is involved in the project and in the foreign location it may be difficult to go back home. This creates a difficult situation in which the manager may feel stuck in a foreign country, and may have family problems. From the company point of view it is not necessarily better, as the costs of the position may rise quickly. Common concerns in this regard are taxes, social security payments, and work permits – issues that are frequently overlooked by managers making a decision to extend an assignment, but ones that should be taken seriously by both the assignee and the company.

Career considerations

Finally, the implications of global assignments – both long- and short-term – on careers should be considered. As illustrated in Exhibit 11.8, long-term assignments often cause managers to lose touch with their home base and home connections.

Exhibit 11.7 Family considerations in global assignments

	Long-term assignments	Short-term assignments
Managers	Some companies prefer managers with overseas experience for promotion consideration.	High levels of stress due to combined pressures from home and abroad and limited social support while abroad.
	Manager may lose friends and connections, both at parent company and in local community.	
Spouses	Spouse typically relocates with expatriate partner. Dual-career challenges can be accentuated significantly.	Spouse typically remains at home, while manager-partner is continually on the road.
	Spouse may lose contact with extended family, friends, and support group.	Ongoing stress between partners can result from continual separations.
	While family may reside together, considerable stress can still result from raising children in unfamiliar settings.	
Children	Children frequently relocate with parents; keeps family together.	Children typically remain at home with one parent, friends, and extended family, but without traveling parent.
	Children have numerous opportunities to learn about other cultures, make new friends, learn new languages, experience new cuisine, etc.	Less change and potential turmoil for children.
	Like parents, children often go through culture shock, requiring significant adjustments to new location and changed circumstances (e.g., missing old friends, dislike of local foods, etc.).	No culture shock or reentry problems for children.
	Also like parents, children often go through stresses of repatriation (e.g., readjusting to old school, old friends, etc.).	May damage relationship with or lose influence over children due to repeated absences.

Simply put, they might become forgotten. This is true whether people work for global corporations or on their own as entrepreneurs. Even so, such assignments can lead to learning and skills development that may prove to be an asset back home.

At the same time, short-term assignments also have pluses and minuses. As already noted, many managers sent on short-term assignments carry part of their home job assignments with them, causing additional work and dividing their focus and attention. Moreover, there is little time to adjust to the new culture (or cultures, in the case of frequent fliers). Short-term assignments often allow managers to experience foreign countries and meet new people without actually moving overseas, however. There are many good opportunities for personal and professional development, as well as networking. Perhaps the critical issue here is the extent to which global managers make use of their assignments for the benefit of the various parties concerned, personal and organizational alike.

Exhibit 11.8 Career considerations in global assignments

Long-term assignments	Short-term assignments
Difficult to maintain connections, possibly making it more difficult to return.	Need to fulfill responsibilities and maintain relationships with home office while abroad, leading to a double workload.
Difficult to keep up with home-office changes (e.g. changes in processes or technology), possibly making it more difficult to return.	Need to hit the ground running; no time to learn about the new country; must get down to work quickly.
Out of sight, out of mind. May miss out on important promotion or other opportunities.	Limited time to learn and adjust and high pressures to perform can lead to high stress and possible failure.
International experience may be an important asset for future career advancement.	Good way to gain international experience without unsettling the family or making long-term commitments.
Have more time to learn and adjust to foreign culture, but need to adjust is more acute as success depends on establishing local connections.	Breadth of knowledge acquired from various short-term international assignments may be an asset back home.

Finding your way: coping with culture shock

Living in a foreign country suggests that individuals are caught between two cultures. On the one hand, there is the individual's culture of origin, which has provided him or her with assumptions, skills, behavioral preferences, and ways of thinking that have contributed to his or her actual position in life. For example, a manager selected for a foreign assignment is often perceived as a successful manager at home and has achieved this position by doing things in a particular way. On the other hand, there is the foreign culture, which may have different values, assumptions, and ways of thinking and require different behaviors. Behaviors that have contributed to success at home may not be appreciated – and may not be successful – in a foreign country. When two or more cultures come into contact, cultural friction (see Chapter 3) can be experienced, and a process of adjustment may be required in which new ways of relating need to be crafted.

Most people naturally and unconsciously adapt their behavior in order to adjust to new external environments. This adaptation may or may not improve the fit between individuals and their environment, however. Despite the widespread belief that given enough time people will "go native," this is not necessarily true. While most people change as a product of living in a foreign country, it does not necessarily mean that they change to be more like the people in the host culture.[14] Indeed, some people may become more attached to their original culture than they were beforehand. Expatriate and ethnic enclaves are not uncommon, and some people spend many years in a foreign country without ever assimilating local values or even learning the local language. For this reason, it is often helpful to separate the process of adaptation to a foreign culture into two related but quite different processes.[15]

- Psychological adjustment: the process of developing a way of life in the new country that is personally satisfying.
- Socio-cultural adjustment: an individual's ability to interact competently with the host culture.

Both processes are related, but they do not necessarily occur simultaneously, and in some cases only one type of adjustment may be achieved. For example, an expatriate with little cultural competence may be happy living in an enclave excluded from the local culture, while a culturally competent person may be unhappy in the foreign environment. Separating psychological and cultural adjustment helps us see why people may use different strategies to deal with foreign environments depending upon their identification with home and host cultures, their ability and willingness to modify their behavior, and the outside pressures they face. Below, we discuss the challenges associated with each type of adjustment, and strategies to deal with them.

Psychological adjustment

The challenge of psychological adjustment is pervasive among global residents. Immersing oneself in a new environment often results in some level of stress resulting from information overload, a breakdown in one's capacity to make sense of the environment, and the need to learn a new approach to everyday tasks. When in a foreign environment, people frequently cannot use their past experiences to interpret and respond to cues, and their behavior may not produce the expected results, causing heightened anxiety and frustration. In addition, seemingly minor things, such as an inability to find one's favorite food or perform simple tasks such as making a phone call, using public transportation, or mailing a letter, can cause confusion and a feeling of loss of control. Individuals can face a state of internal disequilibrium created by the realities imposed by the new culture and the expectations based on the old. This disequilibrium often forces them to question their behavioral habits and can lead to feelings of anxiety, stress, and confusion that are often referred to as culture shock.[16]

Culture shock can take many forms, from a psychological sense of frustration, anxiety, and disappointment to full-fledged chronic depression. Some individuals may experience physiological responses such as insomnia, headaches, or other psychosomatic symptoms. Even so, culture shock is not a disease. Rather, it signifies that an individual is trying to come to terms with his or her new environment – a good starting point for psychological adjustment. As such, the question is not how to avoid culture shock, but how to manage it.

APPLICATION 11.3 Peter Hessler, Luogang

When American journalist Peter Hessler was invited for lunch in the rural Chinese village of Luogang in Guangdong province he was in for a surprise.[17] After sitting down at a table in the Highest Ranking Wild Flavor Restaurant, the waitress asked him bluntly, "Do you want a big rat or a small rat?" Unsure of what to do, Hessler asked the waitress what the difference was, and was informed that the big rats eat grass while the small rats eat fruit. Both tasted good, he was assured. As he contemplated his choice, Hessler looked at the people sitting at the next table. A young boy was gnawing on a rat drumstick, but he couldn't tell whether it was from a big rat or a small one. After asking himself how he got into this predicament, he finally made a decision: a small rat. He chose an item from the menu called Simmered Mountain Rat with Black Beans. He selected this over other possibilities, including Mountain Rat Soup, Steamed Mountain Rat, Simmered Mountain Rat, Roasted Mountain Rat, Mountain Rat Curry, and Spicy and Salty Mountain Rat.

The Chinese say that people in Guangdong will eat anything. Besides rat, people at the Highest Ranking Wild Flavor Restaurant can order turtle dove, fox, cat, python, and an assortment of strange-looking local animals whose names don't translate into English. Selecting a menu item involves considerations beyond flavor and texture. You order cat not just because you enjoy the taste but also because cats are believed to impart a lively *jingshen* (or spirit). You order a snake because it makes you stronger. You order the private parts of a deer to make you more virile. Why would you eat a rat? Because it will keep you from going bald and make your white hair turn black.

After a few minutes the waitress asked Hessler to come back to the kitchen and select his rat. In the back of the kitchen, he saw several cages stacked on top of one another. Each cage contained about thirty rats. "How about this one?" the waitress asked. "Fine," Hessler replied. The waitress then put on a white glove (presumably for hygiene purposes) and grabbed the chosen rat. "Are you sure this is the one?" she asked. The rat gazed at Hessler with its little beady eyes. He nodded his approval. Then the waitress grabbed the rat by its tail and flipped her wrist, thereby launching the rat through the air until it landed on its head on the concrete floor with a soft thud. There was little blood. Hessler was told that he could return to his table; lunch would arrive shortly.

Waiting for his meal to come, Hessler had an opportunity to speak with the owner of the restaurant. The first thing he noticed was the owner's full head of thick black hair. The owner said that local people have been eating rat for more than 1,000 years. His customers insist on eating rats from the mountains, however, because they are clean; they won't eat city rats, he insisted. He assured Hessler that the government hygiene department came by regularly to inspect his rats and had never found anything wrong. Before walking away, the owner smiled and said that you couldn't find food like this in America.

When lunch was finally served, Hessler tried to think of this as a new experience. He tried the beans first, and they tasted fine. Then he poked around at the rat meat. It was clearly well done and attractively garnished with onions, leeks, and ginger. Nestled in a light sauce were skinny rat thighs, short strips of rat flank, and delicate tiny rat ribs. He hesitantly took his first bite, and found the meat to be lean and white without a hint of gaminess. It didn't taste like anything he had had previously. It tasted like rat. Fortunately, he had lots of beer to wash it down with.

Think about it . . .

(1) What would you do if you were faced with the situation that Peter Hessler experienced at the Luogang restaurant, especially if an important Chinese client had invited you to the restaurant?

(2) Have you ever had a similar experience in another culture when you were pressured to eat or do something that was acceptable – or even required – in the local culture but that you found uncomfortable? What did you do?

(3) Are there aspects of your own home culture that foreign visitors might find offensive or uncomfortable for some reason? What might you do to put your foreign guests at ease in this situation?

(4) Think about your eating habits and food preferences. How easy would it be for you to live in a foreign country with drastically different cuisine?

Stages of psychological adaptation

The process of psychological adjustment to a new culture can be quite personal and can vary widely depending on individual characteristics, the cultures involved, and the particulars of the situation. Nevertheless, knowledge of common stages in the process of adaptation is helpful in coping and understanding one's feelings while abroad. One of the most popular models of adaptation to

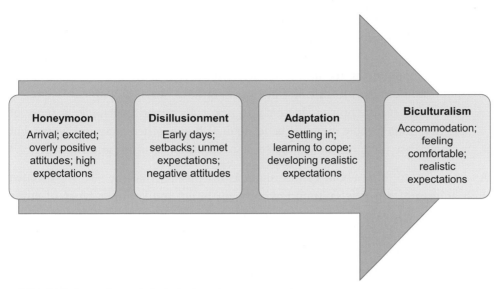

Exhibit 11.9 Stages in psychological adaptation to a new culture

a foreign culture suggests four distinct stages: honeymoon, disillusionment, initial adaptation, and adaptation (see Exhibit 11.9).[18]

1. Honeymoon. Upon first arriving at a foreign location, expatriates may experience a great deal of excitement. Things are interesting, sometimes beautiful, and often amusing. The fascination with new things makes the difficulties and differences encountered seem relatively minor, and people often overestimate the ease of adjustment to the foreign culture. This period can last from only a few days to several months, depending on the person, the nature of the assignment, and the degree of similarity between the home and host countries. Many expatriates report that the honeymoon happened before arrival at the foreign location or not at all. Some suggest that, while many individuals experience excitement upon arrival at the foreign location, these feelings may be overwhelmed by the stresses associated with settling in and coping with the differences in lifestyle.[19]

2. Disillusionment. After the honeymoon period is over and the initial euphoria or excitement has faded, the differences in lifestyles, lack of comfortable food, and difficulties coping with the uncertainties of the new environment cease to be amusing and become irritating. These difficulties become magnified, and people often feel overwhelmed and psychologically exhausted. This is the most difficult stage in the cultural adaptation process. Many individuals give up at this stage and return home, while others remain in the foreign surroundings but withdraw emotionally, refusing to speak the local language or interact with locals. Some may even adopt dysfunctional coping behaviors, such as excessive drinking or drug use.

3. Initial adaptation. During the third stage of initial adaptation, people begin to understand the new culture and adjust to everyday living. This stage can still be characterized by mood swings, but their magnitude or intensity is less pronounced than during the disillusionment stage.

4. Adaptation and biculturalism. Finally, expatriates begin to gain confidence in their ability to function productively in new culture and experience a sense of stability. Some people may feel better than at home, others may feel worse, but in either case there is a newfound sense of stability, comfort, and competence.

Another way to think about culture shock is to consider that the stress associated with adjusting to a new cultural environment is not unlike other types of stress caused by a mismatch between our internal capabilities and new demands of the environment (e.g., starting a new job, starting college, or having a child). As is the case with other types of stress, adapting to a new cultural environment offers a unique opportunity to change and recreate ourselves. As we strive to maintain a functional relationship with our surroundings, we make internal changes and adjustments. This process of adaptation and growth is cyclical and continual: each stressful experience leads to some adaptation on the part of the individual, which will often lead to internal growth. The stress–adaptation–growth process continues as long as there are new environmental challenges, but tends to be less severe over time as the major changes are likely to be experienced in the early stages of the foreign assignment (just as the first semester at university may be more emotionally challenging than later years, even if courses become harder and workload increases).

The degree and pace of adjustment to the foreign culture will vary person by person depending on many variables, including individual expectations, personal characteristics and circumstances, and the characteristics of the host environment.

First, disillusionment is often magnified by individuals' unrealistic expectations about what the experience in the foreign country is likely to be. Many people find the prospects of living in an exotic location appealing, but fail to prepare for easy-to-know realities of life such as the traffic, weather, and other features of daily life. For example, a manager may find it appealing to live surrounded by lush tropical vegetation, but fail to consider the mosquitoes that invariably come with it. Individuals may also underestimate the cultural differences or overestimate their own abilities to cope, adjust, and learn a new language or ways to live in a new environment.

Second, people are different in how readily they adapt to new situations, how easily they develop new relationships, and how comfortable they are with ambiguity and temporary loss of control. Likewise, individual circumstances vary widely and may help or hinder adaptation. For example, individuals moving with family may have higher emotional support, but face more challenges in settling in a spouse and children than someone moving alone. Individuals with prior experience in the country and knowledge of the language may find it easier to adapt than someone with no knowledge of the language or experience in the culture. The expected length of the assignment may also influence how culture shock is experienced. For instance, the difficulties in practicing a favorite sport or hobby may not bring much frustration in a three-month assignment but may be a major source of concern in a permanent relocation.

Third, the external environment in which the expatriate is immersed has an important role in shaping the process and degree of adjustment. For example, some countries are more open to foreigners than others and have developed an infrastructure to support foreigners, in the form of language training, information centers, and support groups. There may also be important variation within the same country. For example, it may be relatively easy to speak English to get around in large or tourist cities, but not in smaller towns. Cultures also vary in the extent to which they tolerate difference and embrace multiculturalism. In some cultures differences are valued and appreciated and it is not expected that people will let go of their own cultures, while in others a strong emphasis is placed on fitting in. The organization hosting the expatriate also plays an important role. If a Canadian manager is in Thailand working for a Canadian organization the experience is likely to be different from the situation if the same manager were working for a Thai firm.

A key question surrounding the ease of adaptation is whether expatriates can improve their adaptation skills after multiple assignments. On the one hand, experience is helpful, because individuals learn how to cope with culture shock, gain confidence, and may not feel as stressed by the prospects of settling in a foreign environment. On the other hand, however, overconfidence may be a hindrance, because one overlooks important details and may fail to prepare appropriately. Additionally, some expatriates report fatigue after several international assignments, and lose interest in learning yet another language and culture and taking the time to develop relationships in a foreign country they expect to leave soon.

Coping with culture shock

Culture shock cannot be avoided, but it can be alleviated to some degree through proper advance preparation.[20] This preparation includes aligning expectations by understanding both the host environment and oneself. The more that expatriates understand about the local environment, including the local culture and organizational demands, the easier the transition is likely to be. Likewise, the more that expatriates understand about the challenges posed by their own personal preferences, the more prepared they will be to address those needs. Below we offer some suggestions to better prepare for an international assignment (see Exhibit 11.10).

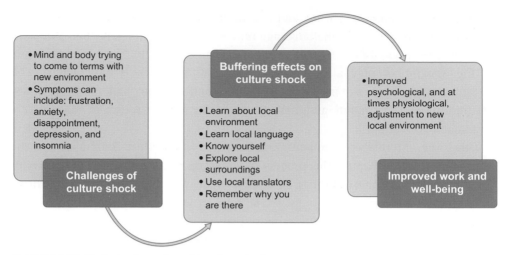

Exhibit 11.10 Strategies for coping with culture shock

1. Learn about the local environment. Cultures are complex, fragmented, dynamic, and idiosyncratic. Cultural knowledge is often useful to explain behavior but seldom to predict it. Each situation is unique, and it is impossible to predict the cultural conflicts that one is likely to experience. In spite of these challenges, learning about the local culture, history, and geography can help people make sense of the new environment and situations they encounter and will facilitate conversations with locals. At a minimum, it helps expatriates to know what to look for. When possible, it is often a good idea to visit the host country for a short period prior to moving there. A quick visit goes a long way to shape expectations and help expatriates to be better prepared psychologically for what is to come. If nothing else, expatriates get a feel for what the immediate challenges will be – traffic, pollution, language, or food. Indeed, many firms send expatriates and their families to the worksite for a brief visit prior to the assignment, so that they can decide if the assignment is suitable for themselves and their families. Talking with previous expatriates or others with experience in the foreign country is also helpful in knowing what to expect. It is important not to rely excessively on others' accounts, however. People and situations are unique, and it is likely that your experience will be different.

2. Learn the local language. As discussed in Chapter 5, language is a key channel of cultural information. Learning the local language can facilitate the process of cultural adaptation immensely. Learning the host language can provide a sense of being in control and facilitate communication with locals. In addition, locals are often more receptive to foreign visitors if they speak the local language, even if only in a rudimentary way. Interestingly, research has shown that learning new languages facilitates cognitive flexibility – a critical asset for managers who work and move around the globe.[21] One should not underestimate the challenges involved in learning a new language, however. Particularly for short-term

assignments, learning the language may not be possible given the short time available and the high work demands. Some managers have several expatriate assignments throughout their careers; how many languages can one realistically master?

3. **Know yourself.** Given the challenges of getting to know the host country, the best knowledge expatriates can take on a foreign assignment is knowledge about their own culture and themselves. First, foreigners are likely to ask you questions about your country and culture you may have never thought about. Many expatriates report learning about their own country when they were abroad. Second, knowing how your own culture has influenced you will help you to look at situations more neutrally. When we recognize that our ways of thinking are a product of our culture just as someone else's ways of thinking are a product of his or her culture, it is easier to look at conflict neutrally and not expect that everyone will agree with our notions of what should be a universally agreed best way of doing things. When we know our culturally imposed limitations (e.g., believing that meetings should start promptly) we are also better able to look for information and deal with situations. Finally, knowing yourself also helps with the more practical aspects of the relocation. It may sound silly, but packing some goods "you can't live without" may go a long way to making your first days abroad go more smoothly. For example, one student reported an "addiction to peanut butter" and how helpful it was to take some on her journey to Europe (no, peanut butter is not available everywhere).

4. **Explore the local surroundings.** Upon arrival in a foreign location it is possible to take measures that will ease the process of culture shock. As a starting point, it is important to get to know your environment quickly and establish a sense of control over your surroundings. Simple things such as making your place feel comfortable and walking around the neighborhood will help to establish some confidence and reduce anxiety. Venturing out is the only way to learn about the foreign environment and start a process of adjustment. While at a distance this may seem non-problematic, it can be more challenging than it seems. As one exchange student summarized it: "It is very tempting to stay home watching YouTube videos rather than venturing out feeling lost when you don't know anyone and do not have a particular place to go to."[22]

5. **Use cultural translators.** After getting settled in a new country, it is often a good idea to look for mentors or **cultural translators**. These are individuals who have a good understanding of both cultures and can help new arrivals make sense of what they are experiencing. The best cultural translators usually have international experience of their own, allowing them to recognize and interpret cultural differences as well as the reasons behind them. They may also prove an important source of basic information locals may not realize you need to know (e.g., not being allowed to throw toilet paper into the toilet). It also helps to join clubs or social groups in different areas of interest, as this is

a good way to integrate into the community and know people who may become an important source of support.

6. Remember why you are there. It also helps not to lose track of your reasons for embarking on the foreign assignment in the first place. Whether it was a professional opportunity, a lifestyle choice, or just an adventure, keeping in mind how the experience will help you grow may make things a little more bearable. Some individuals report benefiting from writing a personal journal (or blog) as a way of keeping track of their experiences and observing their progress.

A key point to keep in mind is that the process of adjustment is about finding ways to resolve conflicts about internal and external demands in ways that are both comfortable and helpful. In some cases, it may mean recreating aspects of the home culture in the foreign environment (e.g., cooking your favorite meal) and making choices about how involved one becomes with the new surroundings (e.g., avoiding religious ceremonies). There are many options between "going native" and "not changing at all." Dealing with culture shock is about finding the balance that works for each individual.

Finding your place: acculturation strategies

A second major challenge to global residents is called socio-cultural adjustment. This is the point when global travelers begin to feel at home and better integrated into the local community. The process of adapting to a new cultural environment may involve both acculturation (the acquisition of new cultural practices in wide-ranging areas, including the learning of a new language) and deculturation (the unlearning of at least some of one's old cultural practices, at least in the sense that new responses are needed in situations that previously would have evoked old ones).[23] Through trial and error, people adjust their behaviors so as to fit the new environment better, either by learning how to behave like the locals or finding an alternative behavior that is both comfortable and acceptable. For example, at home the individual may be used to speaking bluntly, but the culture of the new environment may be one that praises subtle and indirect communication. Although he or she may find it difficult to speak indirectly, he or she may learn to look for contexts within the foreign environment in which direct comments are more appropriate, such as outside the office environment or in one-on-one conversations.

Acculturation strategies

Acculturation is seldom absolute. Even after many years people may incorporate practices of the host culture and fit in perfectly in the work environment and public

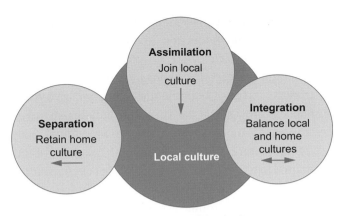

Exhibit 11.11 Acculturation strategies in local cultures

spheres but retain social values and/or assumptions from their own culture in more private realms. For example, it is not uncommon that perfectly adjusted professionals will choose to marry within their own culture and retain some aspects of their original culture at home. As discussed previously, culture has many components, and, while adjusting superficial behaviors at the public level is relatively unproblematic and mastered by most (e.g., bowing, kissing, or shaking hands), some assumptions are hard to accept or let go of (e.g., accepting polygamy). In situations in which cultural conflict becomes unavoidable because the new behavior or assumption is neither acceptable to the individual nor possible to replicate, alternative acculturation strategies are in order.

For the purposes of simplicity, we identify three main types of strategies of acculturation available to managers (see Exhibit 11.11). In reality, individuals probably navigate between those strategies depending on specific situations.[24] At the one extreme, *separation*, managers can try to hold on to their home culture and refuse to adopt practices and interact with the local culture, limiting their interaction with locals to the minimum necessary. These are expatriates who prefer to live in expatriate enclaves, do not learn the local language, and reconstruct a life that resembles the life they would have at home. Managers adopting this strategy may have a difficult time building rapport with the local workforce and community. Depending on their job requirements, however, they may very well be able to perform their duties satisfactorily (e.g., an English teacher working for an American college abroad).

At the other extreme, *assimilation*, managers can work to assimilate in the local environment and "go native." They let go of their original cultural habits and assumptions and incorporate the habits and assumptions of the new cultural milieu. Managers moving permanently to a foreign location may find this strategy appealing, as it decreases the opportunities for cross-cultural conflicts. On the other hand, it may prove challenging to return home if needed. Sometimes completely letting go of the home culture may not be possible, and, depending on the reason for the assignment, it may be counterproductive. Often managers are sent abroad to promote changes in the foreign location, and excessive assimilation of the local culture may be seen as an obstacle.

In between assimilation and separation, *integration*, managers employing an integration strategy work to integrate both cultures. They are able to retain important aspects of their home culture while at the same time building successful relationships in the local environment. An undervalued aspect of cultural adaptation is that an individual's original culture can be an important resource. Within each culture, people develop skills and habits that can be useful in other circumstances and constitute an important advantage in the host environment. For example, a Brazilian manager who is used to a polychromic environment in which he or she is expected to perform many tasks simultaneously may prove a useful resource in highly dynamic situations. Integration is only possible, however, with the participation and collaboration of the host culture. If individuals in the host culture are unable to accept and value the behaviors of the foreign culture, integration may be difficult to achieve. Although at first glance it may seem that integration is the best strategy and should be chosen by all managers, host cultures vary in the degree to which it is possible. Some cultures are open to multiculturalism (e.g., that in Canada) and make this option possible, while in other environments the pressures to fit in are higher and managers who fail to assimilate tend to be separated from the environment.

Influences on acculturation success

The process of socio-cultural adaptation depends on several variables, including cultural knowledge, cultural distance, inter-group attitudes (i.e., how the cultural groups involved perceive each other), multicultural competence, and the role one plays in the new environment (see Exhibit 11.12). To begin with, operating successfully within a new cultural environment requires understanding the norms, rules, and expectations of the local culture. Previous exposure to the culture and the availability of cultural translators are likely to speed up the process of adaptation by helping individuals make sense of new situations quickly and minimizing the number of trials and errors needed to identify suitable behaviors (see below for a discussion on acquiring cultural knowledge).

The degree and type of cultural differences between the home and host cultures are important determinants in how difficult or easy it will be to master and accept new cultural elements. In some cases cultural differences are relatively unproblematic and can be mastered easily, while in others the differences are too great and adaptation is very challenging, or even impossible.

The stereotypes and perceptions held by people from home and host cultures about each other may ease or hinder adaptation. For example, if the host culture is

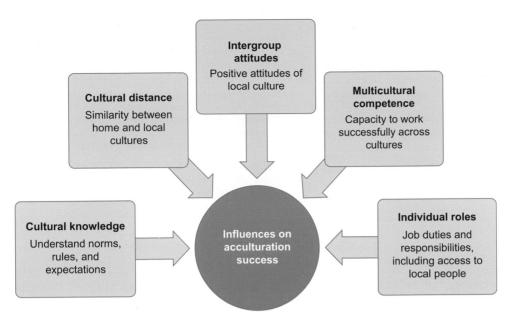

Exhibit 11.12 Influences on acculturation success

admired by the people in the home culture, becoming more like the host culture may be perceived as desirable. On the other hand, if the host culture is perceived as "inferior" or "backward," adapting may be perceived more negatively. At the same time, if one is admired for being from the foreign culture and is granted privileges for belonging to that group, there may be no incentives to let go of the home culture.

Successfully interacting with other cultures is a learnable competence that will help individuals to find a comfortable place within the local environment. As discussed in Chapter 2, multicultural competence represents the capacity to work successfully across cultures by developing a flexible way of thinking and behaving that embraces diversity and accepts complexity.

Finally, the role the foreign individual plays in the host culture will influence not only how important and desirable it is to adapt to the host environment but also how much exposure one has to local individuals and, as a consequence, local cultural knowledge. For example, an expatriate working in a home-based organization primarily with other expatriates may have little exposure to the local culture, and as a consequence experience a very slow process of acculturation.

Managing repatriation

Repatriation refers to the process of returning expatriates to their home countries. Repatriation may occur because the assignment has been completed, family

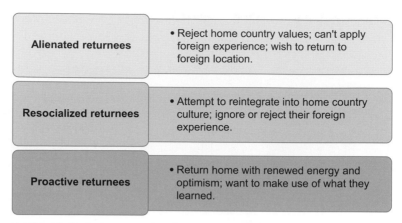

Exhibit 11.13 Coping strategies of returning expatriates

reasons, failure, or dissatisfaction. Even though repatriation can at times cause as much culture shock as expatriation, organizations and managers alike often overlook the effects. When going home, managers can face reverse culture shock.

Reverse culture shock may result from dissatisfaction with the job or old way of life in the home country. The excitement of foreign travel is gone. Sometimes an expatriate returns to his or her previous jobs and feels demoted or bored. At other times the employer may have undergone major changes and the expatriate's skills are no longer useful or valued. In addition, superiors and colleagues may not value the international experience or the skills acquired abroad. Reentry can also be challenging on a personal level. Family and friends may have moved, made new friends, or acquired new interests, and are no longer as available as they were before departure. Finally, sometimes the expatriates themselves have changed. They have incorporated new values, habits, and worldviews that may be at odds with their old friends at home. At the extreme, they can become foreigners in their own land. As one student said after returning to a foreign internship, "the hardest part for me [returning home] was reconciling how much I had experienced and therefore changed with people and things that had remained the same at home."[25]

Returning expatriates tend to adopt one of three coping strategies (see Exhibit 11.13). To begin with, resocialized returnees are people who attempt to fit in back in the home culture by ignoring or rejecting what they learned in their foreign assignment. Such returnees typically failed to assimilate into the foreign culture during their overseas assignment, often living in expat communities and minimizing their interactions with the locals. As a result, they tend to find it relatively easy to return psychologically to their home culture.

Next, alienated returnees are at the other end of the spectrum. While abroad they tended to "go native," and over time began to reject the values of their home country in favor of the values of their host country. When they return home they feel alienated. They find it difficult to apply their foreign experiences in meaningful ways now that they have returned. For many, they simply wish to return to their adopted home.

Finally, proactive returnees represent an optimistic breed of traveler. They return home with a conviction that they can succeed in melding the two cultures in positive or productive ways. They realize that they have changed personally as a result of their overseas assignment and want to make use of what they have learned. They often seek out new friends or colleagues with similar experiences or they launch new projects or adventures. Above all, they want to make use of what they have learned abroad.

To reduce the difficulties associated with reentry, many companies create various mechanisms by which expatriates can keep in touch with their colleagues back home at company headquarters. These mechanisms can include special newsletters, regularly scheduled home visits, special web pages focusing on expatriate concerns, and assigning HRM specialists to oversee both overseas assignments and repatriation activities. The key for most major multinational firms (and most expatriates) is to ensure that expatriates do not get lost or forgotten when they are out of their home country. The old adage "Out of sight, out of mind" is pertinent here, and responsibility often falls on the expatriates themselves to guarantee that this does not occur.

APPLICATION 11.4 Andrea Walker, Belize

Examples like the following have occurred in many companies in many countries. While the details may vary, all these stories have one thing in common: they are all problematic. Consider: after working as an entry-level marketing representative for an Australian kitchen appliance company for three years, Andrea Walker was offered a promotion and an overseas assignment to Belize as the local marketing manager. She readily accepted the opportunity, in order to gain both global business experience and greater corporate recognition. She spent three years in Belize, developing good contacts and building markets for her employer. She learned a lot about culture and work procedures in the region around Belize that she felt would be of use to her employer as a global manufacturer of consumer products.

When she decided that it was time to return home for her daughter's schooling, however, her employer seemed less than enthusiastic. The executive who had originally hired her was no longer with the company, and other managers at the home office preferred to work with their own protégés. Some managers observed that they couldn't remember Andrea except through her periodic market summary reports. Even so, Andrea had a written contract guaranteeing that she could return to corporate headquarters following her three-year assignment.

Think about it . . .

(1) If you were Andrea and concluded that there was little enthusiasm for your return to corporate headquarters, what would you do? Why?
(2) If you were in company management, and recognized that few people were enthusiastic about Andrea's return, what would you do? Why?
(3) What might the company have done differently to take full advantage of Andrea's work experience abroad?
(4) What might Andrea have done differently to retain contacts and communications with the home office?

MANAGER'S NOTEBOOK

Managing global assignments

Wei Hopeman, Peter Hessler, and Andrea Walker share a common experience. They all needed to cope – and, hopefully, prosper – in very different environments from the ones in which they grew up. They were all global travelers. While they may have shared relatively common goals, however, there were sizable differences in the environments to which they had to adapt.

We learned here that working abroad can pose a number of challenges that can affect people in very different ways depending upon their personal and organizational circumstances. These challenges emerge both prior to departure and afterwards. The nature of some of these challenges can evolve with time, while others are ever-present. We have explored three of these challenges: personal considerations, time considerations, and family and career considerations. Although most people change as a result of living in a foreign culture, this does not necessarily mean that they change to be more like the people in the foreign culture. Indeed, some people may become more attached to their original culture than they were beforehand. Expatriate and ethnic enclaves are not uncommon, and some people spend many years in a foreign country without ever assimilating local values or even learning the local language. It is therefore often helpful to separate the process of adaptation to a foreign culture into two related but quite different processes: psychological adjustment refers to the process of developing a way of life in the new country that is personally satisfying; socio-cultural adjustment refers to the individual's ability to interact competently with the host culture.

At the same time, in order to minimize the problems of reentry after working abroad, companies often create various mechanisms by which expatriates can keep in touch with their colleagues back home at company headquarters, including special newsletters, regularly scheduled home visits, special web pages focusing on expatriate concerns, and appointing HRM specialists to oversee both overseas assignments and repatriation activities. The key for most major multinational firms (and most expatriates) is to ensure that expatriates do not get lost or forgotten when they are out of their home country.

As noted throughout this book, one of the first challenges in preparing for new assignments is to understand the cultural, organizational, and situational environments that characterize one's future home and workplace. For example, if a manager is used to an individualistic and egalitarian environment, moving to an environment characterized by collectivism and hierarchy can be a shock. Likewise, moving from an organization characterized by openness to "strangers" and significant corporate support (like the Shell example discussed above) to one characterized by a more closed and perhaps hostile environment with little corporate support can also create tension to would-be travelers (see discussion on culture shock). Finally, situations and the people within them are always different. What are the traveler's goals in a foreign assignment and what are his or her skills, including multicultural competence? What family responsibilities must be considered in such moves? Assessing the living and working environment (both before and after a move) is not an easy task, but it is nevertheless necessary, or at least prudent, in order to prepare adequately for new ventures. As an English football player and coach noted, "To me the bottom line is the more education you can give yourself, and the more preparation you can do, the less chance of failing."[26]

In *Alice's Adventures in Wonderland*, British author Lewis Carroll made an important observation: To paraphrase, "If you don't know where you are going, any road will take you there."[27] So it is with international travel, living, and working. Goals and plans are essential in order to succeed. This requires advance preparation, obviously, but it also requires continual on-the-job skills development and some degree of self-confidence. The challenge for global managers is to find a workable balance betwee task accomplishment on behalf of the company and personal growth and development on behalf of themselves. Ideally, these two goals should be mutually complementary, but this seldom occurs without planning. What, therefore, should managers do? Here are three suggestions (see Exhibit 11.14).

1. Understand your new environment

There are many things that individuals – and families – can do to prepare themselves for an easier transition. Most of these are not difficult, though some can be

1. Understand your new environment	2. Continue to develop multicultural competence	3. Make yourself at home
• Begin learning about your new environment prior to departure. • If you have a spouse or family, get them involved. • Reach out to prospective contacts in the new location prior to departure. • Build a home base of support to retain contacts back home.	• Continue to develop your self-awareness and empathy skills. • Reflect on your new experiences; look for patterns. • Build your capacity for behavioral flexibility • Think before you act.	• Be yourself, with skill. • Find your place or role in new environment. • Facilitate your integration into local environment through information-sharing. • Most cultures are patient with "foreigners." • Don't take yourself too seriously.

Exhibit 11.14 Strategies for living and working globally

challenging (e.g., learning the local language). Nevertheless, the more that people can learn about their new environment prior to arrival, the more prepared they will be to get settled and get down to work. Consider the following strategies.

- Learn about the new location and its culture.
- Search for local contacts.
- Research local associations and clubs and other interests before arriving.
- Plan to have time for enjoyment before work begins.
- If there is something you "must have," take it with you or make arrangements to have it shipped.
- Talk to friends and family and find ways to keep in touch; build a support network at home.
- Think about your goals for the experience abroad.
- Learn the local language.

2. Continue to develop multicultural competence

A second strategy for living and working globally involves continued self-development. In other words, as discussed earlier in this book, successful managers are the ones who can develop *multicultural competence*. This involves ongoing learning – both about oneself and others – and personal and managerial development. Several key strategies are identified here.

- **Develop greater self-awareness.** Self-awareness refers to an understanding of one's identity, values, and beliefs about one's social position and social interactions. It allows one to preserve one's own identity when faced with experiences that contradict existing beliefs and values. Develop awareness of your own culture and how it has shaped your values, beliefs, and worldviews.

- Develop greater empathy. Empathy refers to the ability to identify and understand others' feelings and motives. It allows one to assist the other party in preserving his or her identity. Understand that others are also complex cultural beings whose actions are a product of deep-seated cultural values and beliefs. When misunderstandings occur, search for cultural explanations of confusing or offensive behavior, before judging it.
- Gather and analyze information. Gathering and analyzing information refers to the ability to observe context, body language, facial expressions, and behavioral cues; actively listen and summarize information, and ask questions in a manner and timing that is apposite. Ask questions when appropriate, observe others, test your assumptions, and stretch frames of reference.
- Integrate and transform information. Integrating and transforming information refers to developing a coherent theory of action on the basis of the information collected in the negotiating meaning stage. As this theory is tested and the behaviors are practiced, new rules are created and fine-tuned. Reflect on intercultural experiences and look for patterns. Test your conclusions.
- Develop more behavioral flexibility. Behavioral flexibility refers to the ability to engage in different behaviors, to switch styles, and to accomplish tasks in more than one way. Look for opportunities to increase your behavioral repertoire by engaging in different activities and practicing doing things in different ways. For example, if you are a direct communicator, practice communicating indirectly. In addition, recognize those behaviors that are challenging to you and compensate with other behaviors. For example, preface a direct statement with an apology.
- Develop greater mindfulness. Mindfulness refers to the ability to pay close attention to one's own feelings and actions and others' actions and reactions. Make the effort to focus on your actions and reactions. Think before you act.

3. Make yourself at home

Finally, living and working globally can be a great opportunity to learn new things and advance one's career. Foreign assignments provide a chance to develop new managerial skills, increase tolerance for ambiguity, develop new perspectives and ways of thinking, and improve one's ability to work with others. Taking advantage of this opportunity requires flexibility and high levels of self-awareness, however. In the final analysis, perhaps the principal key to success is a manager's ability to make him- or herself at home in their new environment.

- Be yourself, with skill. While abroad, managers can still can be themselves – but with skill. In other words, they will have to adapt and change, but they do not need to become someone they are not. They do not necessarily have to convert to the local religion or develop an appetite for fried ants (even though they are tasty) to be accepted and have a fruitful experience. They will have to be flexible in some important things, however, and learn to accept that others may not agree with them (or even like them). The key here is balance: what is really important to people and can't be compromised, and what can people live with? Revisit this question often, as the answer may change.

- Find a place or role in the new environment. Even though individuals are the same people, they may need to occupy a different role in the new environment. For example, at home they may be the best manager in their unit and the one helping others to succeed. Abroad, however, these same people may be the ones needing help with their assignments. People working abroad should expect that they will play different roles, and should actively look for roles that will make them feel part of the new environment.

- Actively look for and provide information to facilitate integration. Two communication tools may be helpful here: inquiry and advocacy. *Inquiry* refers to exploring and questioning one's own reasoning and the reasoning of others. In other words, ask yourself the following questions any time you are confronted with a cross-cultural conflict: How do you and I perceive the situation? What do you and I wish to achieve in this situation? Which actions are you and I willing to take to achieve this goal? Inquiry requires suspending judgment, letting go of a previous understanding, and tolerating uncertainty until a new understanding may be created. We like to be right, but in a cross-cultural situation what is right is relative. *Advocacy* refers to expressing and standing for what one thinks and desires. Advocacy suggests stating clearly what you think and want, and explaining the reasoning behind your view. In other words, it requires knowing yourself and understanding what your assumptions and points of view are. It also requires taking responsibility for how you feel about things. For example, if you are frustrated because your counterpart always comes late to meetings – something perhaps acceptable in his or her culture – you may say, "I prefer it when I do not have to wait for you, because for me it is very stressful not knowing what time you will arrive." This is very different from saying, "I am a busy person and it is inconsiderate when you fail to keep your appointments." The first statement is about you and how you feel about the interaction, and opens up the possibility for the other person to understand your point of view and to respond. The second can easily be construed as a specific attack on the individual that is likely to be taken personally. After all, he or she will likely provide a reason for his or her tardiness, and the problem will remain unresolved.

- Do not take yourself too seriously. Remember that culture shock is usually temporary, and that everyone experiences it to one degree or another. People must acknowledge that they do not have to be right all the time, and that making mistakes is part of life. Most cultures are patient with "foreigners." Be patient with yourself and others, and remember to have fun.

KEY TERMS

acculturation • acculturation strategies • alienated returnees • cultural translators • culture shock • deculturation • employer-initiated global assignments • long-term global assignments (advantages and disadvantages) • *jingshen* (Chinese) • proactive returnees • psychological adjustment • resocialized returnees • reverse culture shock • self-initiated global assignments • short-term global assignments (advantages and disadvantages) • socio-cultural adjustment

DISCUSSION QUESTIONS

1. A fundamental challenge for managers on a new global assignment is that they often feel decidedly like outsiders, yet they must find ways to "break into" the local culture simply to do their job (see Exhibit 11.1). What advice would you give to a colleague about to depart on an assignment to facilitate the process of "breaking in"?
2. Many people like to travel, but working globally can be a different experience from a holiday. In this regard, what are some of the risks of taking a global assignment too early in one's career?
3. How can a manager determine when he or she is "ready" for a global assignment?
4. Do gender or age differences influence how managers can or will adapt to a new foreign assignment? Explain.
5. What is the difference between psychological and socio-emotional adjustment to a new setting? Provide an example of each.
6. Have you ever experienced culture shock firsthand? If so, what happened?
7. If you were asked to develop a two-day workshop for minimizing culture shock among a group of employees about to set off on their first global assignment, what would this workshop look like?
8. What are the advantages and drawbacks of each of the three acculturation strategies discussed in this chapter (separation, assimilation, integration)?
9. Why might employees returning from a global assignment have such a difficult time readjusting to a country in which they were born and raised? Explain.
10. A number of strategies are discussed at the end of the chapter (see Manager's Notebook) regarding how to manage global assignments. Which of these strategies are relatively easy for a new manager to master? Which may be very difficult? Why?

CASE: GLOBAL ASSIGNMENT, MYANMAR

Myanmar has had a sad history in recent decades. It has been politically and economically isolated and suppression of dissent has been widespread. Beginning in 2012, however, the country and its leadership initiated several steps to open up the country, allow greater individual freedom, and rejoin the global economy. While most outside observers are cautious – or even skeptical – about whether real political and economic reform is coming, first-mover advantages may exist for foreign companies who enter Myanmar's markets early to meet the demand for new products and services.

Economic development experts have advised the Myanmar government that modernizing its agricultural sector could significantly help with the country's overall economic development plans. While the country has extensive lands devoted to agriculture, production is low and inefficient. To remedy this, the government has discussed importing both technical experts and farm equipment to help build a more efficient system allowing it to increase farm exports and gain foreign capital for future investments.

Wells-Wakefield LLP, your employer and a farm equipment manufacturer from the United Kingdom, hopes to capitalize on this endeavor by establishing a field office in Yangon to assess evolving events in this rapidly changing nation and make recommendations as to whether the country's emerging economy is sufficiently strong and stable to support the establishment of a permanent sales and distribution network to sell Wells-Wakefield farm equipment. If the government takes serious steps to improve its agricultural sector, the company would like to be part of this development.

At this stage, however, everything is exploratory. You have been asked by your employer to move to Yangon to lead this exploration and conduct a full assessment of the economic, political, and social opportunities and limitations associated with such a venture. Your assignment is for three years. You, your spouse, and your two young children will leave for Yangon in ninety days.

CASE QUESTIONS

1. As you prepare for your assignment, what is the most important information you will need to understand before you depart to make this assignment a success? Specifically, what are the most important questions you need answers for prior to your departure?
2. How will you get accurate and useful answers to these questions prior to your departure?
3. What are the principal challenges you will face in moving to Myanmar? Explain.

4. After you arrive in Yangon, what will you do to continue to acculturate yourself, both psychologically and socio-culturally, to your new environment? What will you do for your family?

5. Also after you arrive, what will you do to better understand the local cultural, political, and economic environments to determine whether or not there is a long-term market potential for your company in Myanmar?

6. Finally, what might you do during your assignment to reduce the potential repatriation problems following its completion?

7. (*Optional research question*) In preparation for your move, explore the available housing options and living conditions in Yangon, and prepare a brief proposal for your boss outlining what you believe would be reasonable monthly living expenses there.

NOTES

1. Robert Louis Stevenson, *Travels with a Donkey in the Cévennes*. Oxford University Press, 1993 [1879].

2. Bill Newcott, "Big boat, little boat," *AARP The Magazine*, January 2012, p. 26.

3. Nancy J. Adler, *International Dimensions of Organizational Behavior*, 5th edn. Mason, OH: Thompson, 2008.

4. Marja Tahvanainen, Denice Welch, and Verner Worm, "Implications of short-term international assignments," *European Management Journal*, 23(6) (2005), pp. 663–73.

5. Nancy J. Adler, *International Dimensions of Organizational Behavior*, 3rd edn. Cincinnati, OH: South-Western College Publishing, 1997.

6. Martha J. Frase, "International commuters: are your overseas assignments creating risky 'stealth-pats'?," *HR Magazine*, 52(3) (2007), pp. 91–5.

7. Carla, Joinson, "Cutting down the days: HR can make expat assignments short and sweet," *HR Magazine*, 45(4) (2000), pp. 92–7.

8. "Travelling more lightly," *The Economist*, June 22, 2006, pp. 99–101.

9. Helene Mayerhofer, Linley C. Hartmann, Gabriela Michelitsch-Riedl, and Iris Kollinger, "Flexpatriate assignments: a neglected issue in global staffing," *International Journal of Human Resource Management*, 15(8) (2004), pp. 1371–89.

10. Richard Hodgetts and Fred Luthans, *International Management: Culture, Strategy, and Behavior*, 5th edn. New York: McGraw-Hill-Irwin, 2003.

11. Scott Gummer, "Citigroup's Wei Hopeman transcends time zones," *Fortune*, January 16, 2012, p. 21.

12. Gummer, "Citigroup's Wei Hopeman."

13. Sue Shellenbarger, "Separation anxiety: job transfers create problems for families," *Wall Street Journal*, October 27, 2005, p. D1.

14. John W. Berry, "Acculturation: living successfully in two cultures," *International Journal of Intercultural Relations*, 29(6) (2005), pp. 697–712.

15. Colleen Ward, Yutaka Okura, Antony Kennedy, and Takahiro Kojima, "The U-curve on trial: a longitudinal study of psychological and sociocultural adjustment during

cross-cultural transition," *International Journal of Intercultural Relations*, 22(3) (1998), pp. 277–91; Berry, "Acculturation."

16. Young Yun Kim, "Intercultural personhood: globalization and a way of being," *International Journal of Intercultural Relations*, 32(4) (2008), pp. 359–68.

17. Peter Hessler, "A rat in my soup," *The New Yorker*, July 24, 2000, p. 38.

18. Adapted from Lillian H. Chaney and Jeanette S. Martin, *Intercultural Business Communication*. Upper Saddle River, NJ: Prentice-Hall, 1995.

19. Lorraine Brown and Immy Holloway, "The adjustment journey of international postgraduate students at an English university: an ethnographic study," *Journal of Research in International Education*, 7(2) (2008), pp. 232–49.

20. Kim, "Intercultural personhood."

21. Harry C. Triandis, *Culture and Social Behavior*. New York: McGraw-Hill, 1994.

22. Personal communication.

23. This framework builds on the work of Berry, "Acculturation," on the acculturation strategies of ethno-cultural groups. In the original framework, Berry identified a fourth strategy, marginalization, when ethno-cultural groups let go of their original culture but fail to integrate with dominant groups. We find that this strategy is less likely to be used successfully by managers given their job requirements.

24. Ward et al., "The U-curve on trial"; Berry, "Acculturation."

25. Personal communication.

26. Stuart Pearce, *Wikipedia*, 2012.

27. Lewis Carroll, *Alice's Adventures in Wonderland*. London: Penguin Books, 1960 [1865]. This "quotation" is a paraphrase because, while this is the message Carroll was trying to convey, and while it is often cited as being his, he never actually wrote these words. Instead, he wrote a longer dialog between two characters that yields this conclusion. Moreover, Lewis Carroll is his pen name; his real name was Charles Lutwidge Dodgson, and he was an author, mathematician, logician, Anglican deacon, and photographer.

12 Lessons learned

MANAGEMENT CHALLENGE

Apple founder Steven Jobs cautioned managers about timidity. "Don't be trapped by dogma – living with the results of other people's thinking. Don't let the noise of others' opinions drown out your own inner voice. And most important, have the courage to follow your heart and intuition."[1] This sense of independence of thought and action has guided our exploration of what global managers need to know and do. We have argued here that in today's economy all managers are global managers, and most face similar challenges regardless of where or how they work. We have explored these challenges, examined similarities and dissimilarities across managerial work, and the suggested key skills required for managers to succeed. The challenge for managers, then, is to integrate these lessons into a unified approach to global management. This is a difficult, but nonetheless necessary, task for future success. We close with a summary of our discoveries, as well as several reflective thoughts on the future of management and what global managers might consider as they go forward into uncharted waters.

CHAPTER OUTLINE

- What have we learned?   *page* 366
- Where do we go from here?   372

Futurists and their closely watched predictions abound in these changing times, and nowhere is this trend more prominent than with regard to future economic trends and the future of global business. Some experts predict that past competitors will become future partners, while other experts predict just the opposite. Some predict increased economic integration brought on by globalization, while others predict increased economic fragmentation and turmoil, also brought on by globalization.

Even the opinions of great philosophers of the past apparently disagree. The eleventh-century Persian mathematician, astronomer, and poet Omar Khayyám suggested that, in order to see the future, we must study the past. Learn from history; the past is prologue. At the same time, the fifth-century BCE Hindu prince and founder of Buddhism, Siddhārtha Gautama, suggested that if we want to see the future we need to step forward. Keep your eye on the ball; the future belongs to those who search it out and are prepared to capitalize on it. Two philosophers and two different opinions – again. Once more, our challenge is to learn from such contradictions, past and present.

What have we learned?

For managers, advice is easy to get, but getting good advice is more difficult. We have tried throughout this volume to summarize what we consider to be good advice for managers in the field. Why? As Italian novelist Alberto Moravia has noted, "When facts are lacking, rumors abound."[2] Without facts and good advice, managers are left to sink or swim on their own and substituting unsubstantiated rumors or unsupported opinions hardly improves their chances of survival or success. Our proposed strategy here is to develop sufficient multicultural competence to prosper in an otherwise unfamiliar world.

As introduced in Chapter 1, we approached this topic in three parts, or stages (see Exhibit 12.1). In the first stage, emphasis was placed on better *understanding the challenges facing managers*. In the second stage, emphasis shifted to better *understanding the environments* (cultural, organizational, and situational) in which management occurs. Finally, in the third stage, emphasis was placed on *developing global management skills*, as well as understanding where and how to use these skills. Taken together, we viewed these three stages as a roadmap to developing multicultural competence.

Stage I. Understanding management challenges

The first task of managers is to understand the new global realities, considering the changing nature of both global business and global managers.

- Global challenges. Globalization has become a fact, but it is much more than this. Business changes include increased globalization, a globalized workforce, technological revolutions, political and regulatory volatility, and economic opportunities and turmoil. We need to ask ourselves what this means for contemporary global business. We introduced the concept of multicultural competence in Chapter 1 as a framework for understanding what skills managers must develop in this uncertain global economy.

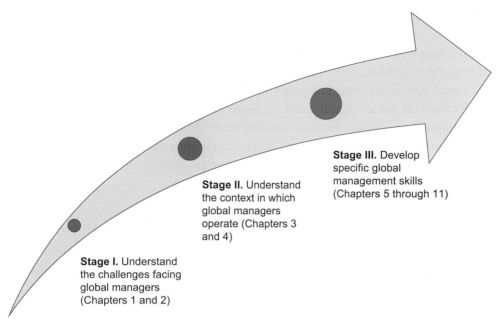

Stage III. Develop specific global management skills (Chapters 5 through 11)

Stage II. Understand the context in which global managers operate (Chapters 3 and 4)

Stage I. Understand the challenges facing global managers (Chapters 1 and 2)

Exhibit 12.1 Stages in developing multicultural competence

- **Global managers.** We also explored how the responsibilities of today's managers differ from those in the past. Global awareness and understanding have become the litmus test of successful managers. We identified three general types of global managers in Chapter 2 – expatriates, frequent flyers, and virtual managers – and how the global responsibilities and qualifications can differ for each. We concluded this chapter by introducing a model for global management to guide readers throughout their reading of the book, discussed below.

Stage II. Developing global understanding

In the second part of the book (Chapters 3 and 4), we focused on better understanding the environment or context in which global managers work. We broke this environment down into three chapters focusing on cultural, organizational, and situational contexts (see Exhibit 12.2).

- **Cultures.** We discussed the various meanings of culture as a concept. We also noted that cultures affect managerial actions through prevailing work values and social normative beliefs. We introduced the concept of core cultural dimensions as a means of building thumbnail portraits of various peoples and cultures. For example, compared to people in individualistic cultures, people working in collectivistic cultures may be more likely to value working in groups, share

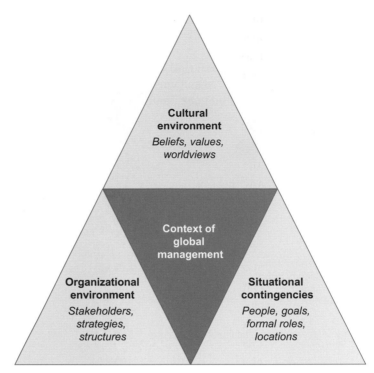

Exhibit 12.2 Cultural, organizational, and situational contexts

information, and strive for group success over individual performance. Like thumbnails, however, these portraits lack details, which need to be fleshed out through further investigation. We also pointed out that all cultures exist in environments characterized by complexities and contradictions. Generalizations are difficult. Finally, we discussed institutional environments as a subset of culture but still an important factor for managers to understand.

- Organizations. People working in organizations with manifestly different structures, values, and processes, such as centralized or collaborative decision-making, may approach negotiation, leadership, and workforce management in very different ways. Because of this, it is important to understand the relationships between global strategy, organization design, and structure. Moreover, when and where are we likely to see autocratic or collaborative decision-making? How do different cultures define the concept of employee participation? How do organizational cultures influence employee and managerial behavior?

- Situational contingencies. Each unique situation that managers find themselves in can influence both behaviors and managerial success. For example, negotiating a contract or managing people in a location where the manager does not understand the local language changes the work environment equation significantly. Interpreters must be used, and considerable information can easily be lost.

This is just one example of how situations can vary. We discussed differences among people as well as roles and responsibilities, locations, and goals and tasks. Understanding factors such as these help frame the managerial task environment in ways that illuminate potential suitable actions.

Stage III. Developing global management skills

Finally, in the third part of the book (Chapters 5–11), we focused specifically on examining the more pragmatic aspects of managing in the global economy, by exploring several global management skills that support managerial efforts to move from understanding to action (see Exhibit 12.3).

- **Communicating across cultures.** A model of cross-cultural communication was introduced and used to analyze how various environmental factors can influence success in interpersonal relations. Cultural screens on interpersonal communication were discussed, including cognitive limitations on communication and communication protocols. Content and context were explored as key factors influencing verbal, as well as nonverbal, behavior. Strategies for understanding and managing first encounters were also discussed.
- **Leading global organizations.** Leadership in a global context is something that everyone agrees is important, but few know how to implement. It remains an

Exhibit 12.3 Global management skills

ambiguous concept largely because its implementation relies heavily on leaders understanding (and being able to leverage) local environments in ways that direct collective energies towards the accomplishment of specific tangible goals. Without understanding cultures, organizations, and variations in situations, this endeavor becomes largely a hopeless task. The GLOBE study was introduced here as one framework for understanding and then applying leadership behaviors within cultural constraints.

- Negotiating global partnerships. Negotiation and bargaining across borders is no easy task, because so many of the variables involved are culture-based. In many cases, they are even hidden from view, leaving managers to work partially blindfolded in a very high-stakes game. The discussion ranged from making preparations for negotiations all the way through to managing final contracts once made. Ethics and the importance of building mutual trust – and even mutual benefit – emerge as key considerations when seeking partners, negotiating agreements, and managing the subsequent partnerships.

- Managing ethical conflicts and social responsibility. Managing in an imperfect world has many challenges, including bribery and corruption, fair employment practices, and environmental stewardship. Finding a way to succeed in business while remaining true to both your core ethical beliefs and institutional or legal requirements is no easy task. This dilemma was explored as we considered why cross-cultural conflicts are so pervasive throughout the world, bases of cross-cultural conflict, ethical and institutional conflicts, universalism and particularism, ethical global leader behavior, and guidelines for ethical managerial behavior.

- Managing work and motivation. Managing and motivating people across borders must be one of the most challenging jobs facing managers. It can also be one of the most stressful. We explored the management and motivational environment. We looked at how work values can affect employee behaviors, and how managerial roles can change with different environments. We examined the psychology of work, as well as psychological contracts. Finally, incentives and rewards were discussed as potential motivational strategies.

- Managing global teams. Working with teams, global or otherwise, can be both exhilarating and threatening for managers. It can be exhilarating to the extent that positive group dynamics leads to creative and collaborative efforts that may have been impossible working individually. It can also be threatening, though, to the extent that the manager and the team are working from different scripts, don't like each other, don't trust each other, or simply have opposing objectives. Accordingly, team management becomes an important skill. In this regard, we explored different types of global teams, as well as key success factors. We explored the role of leadership in team-building and the importance of building mutual trust among members. Finally, we examined strategies for resolving – or at least living with – team conflicts. Throughout, it was suggested that highly diverse teams, including global teams, can bring much to the table and find truly creative solutions to the extent that such endeavors are managed, nurtured, and rewarded.

- Managing global assignments. Finally, we explored the challenges of living and working abroad. We examined the advantages and disadvantages of global assignments, as well as potential differences between self-initiated and organizationally initiated assignments. The two concepts of psychological and socio-cultural adjustment were discussed, as were strategies and techniques for managing the acculturation – and repatriation – processes.

Putting it all together

Finally, as initially introduced in Chapter 2, we followed the path of a model of global management throughout the text that incorporates all three of these stages. This model, illustrated in Exhibit 12.4, suggests that in order to succeed global managers must recognize at least two challenges. First, they must understand their environment. What must they know or do? What must they not do? Where are the opportunities? And how much discretion do they have in making reasoned decisions

Exhibit 12.4 Model for global managers

or taking concrete actions? Second, they must have or develop the requisite skills and abilities to pursue their goals and objectives within the constraints of their immediate environment. Without these skills, opportunities are easily missed.

- Targeted goals and objectives. As suggested in this model, a manager's first task is to develop a coherent set of targeted goals and objectives (box 1). What is he or she trying to accomplish in upcoming global encounters, including contract negotiations, relationship-building, partnership management, managing global work?
- Contextual demands and constraints. Beyond establishing clear goals, strategies, and objectives, the model asks managers to understand various contextual demands and constraints that can enhance or limit managerial actions (box 2). All managerial work is constrained in varying degrees by existing demands (what people must do) and constraints (what people must not do). Demands and constraints are in no small way influenced by local cultures, organizations, and situations: what we refer to as the "context of global management" (discussed above).
- Managerial options and actions. Within these limitations, managers typically have multiple managerial options and actions open to them about what is done and how it is done (box 3). The challenge for managers is to understand the demands and constraints – cultural, organizational, and situational – involved in each unique problem within their environments and then act within these limitations. This may not always be easy, but it is essential to long-term success.
- Global management skills. Finally, none of this can happen unless managers have sufficient global management skills to accomplish their targeted objectives working in a global environment (box 4).

Where do we go from here?

Throughout this volume, an effort has been made to integrate issues of culture with those of management, in the belief that success in the global economy requires a detailed understanding of both. Successful global managers move with ease across international borders and adapt readily to local changes and challenges. They look for a competitive edge wherever they can find it. Most of all, however, they continually learn from their surroundings and apply these lessons to their work.

Learning from the past

In this regard, perhaps a good place to begin this learning process is with history. Spanish philosopher George Santayana once observed, "Those who fail to learn from the mistakes of their predecessors are destined to repeat them."[3] This may be true, but it is equally correct that one of the benefits of studying history – learning from the past – is that it alleviates the need to start from scratch. History provides lessons as building blocks upon which to build our own approach to management, as well as our own careers. In this spirit, we offer three lessons from three very different time periods and involving very different people and circumstances. The first two examples, Christopher Columbus and Mahatma Gandhi, come from earlier generations, while the third comes from the very recent past. All speak to business managers, locally and globally.

Christopher Columbus is widely credited with being the first European explorer to "discover" America. (Many Scandinavians disagree, and point out that the Vikings landed and actually colonized the northeastern tip of Canada centuries earlier. Many Native Americans and Inuits also disagree, and point out that they were actually there first; indeed, some of them met Columbus on the shore of Hispaniola when he arrived in the "New World," and paid a heavy price.) Columbus is also widely, if incorrectly, credited with proving that the world was round instead of flat. The controversies surrounding Columbus aside, what many scholars have over-looked in this story is that Columbus succeeded in his quest of discovery because he was wrong, not because he was right.

Consider: ancient Greek mathematicians demonstrated long before Columbus that the world was round. They even estimated with amazing accuracy that the earth was approximately 25,000 miles in circumference. Columbus and his maritime contemporaries understood this, even if many peasants and less educated people did not. Most explorers of the time reasoned with moderate accuracy that India and the Spice Islands – their targeted objective – were roughly 8,000 miles to the west of Spain. They also reasoned, correctly, that in view of this distance such a voyage was impossible. Given the prevailing technology of the time, no ship could travel so far without running out of water and supplies. Columbus studied available maps and charts of the time and concluded, incorrectly, that his contemporaries were wrong and that India was only about 3,000 miles away – a journey he considered possible, if difficult. Off he sailed in 1492. After his long voyage at sea and, ironically, just over 3,000 miles from Spain, Columbus sailed into the undiscovered Caribbean and concluded, again incorrectly, that he had reached India.

The useful lesson from Columbus' voyage is simple. If Columbus had had more accurate information or had listened to local experts about the true distance to India, he might never have attempted the voyage. He believed he was right, however, and he initiated action on the basis of his belief. As he continued his journey, he adapted his strategies and tried to learn from his mistakes. Indeed, many of today's managers have learned this same lesson: Some of life's greatest successes result from accidents, hunches, or simple luck. All managers make mistakes and miscalculate – some more than others. Managerial success is seldom linear; there are many bumps and detours along the way. What differentiate winners from losers, however, is both their steadfastness and determination and their ability to learn, adapt, and, when possible, capitalize on their mistakes.

The second lesson is more direct, and comes from the nonviolent Indian peace activist of the twentieth century, Mahatma Gandhi. Gandhi was fond of saying: "We must be the change we wish to see in others."[4] In other words, the real challenge for global managers is leadership, not followership. The challenge is how to build both a more prosperous company and a more prosperous world. To accomplish this, successful global managers must bring people together in collaborative and symbiotic ways that create value for the organization and its surroundings. In this endeavor, an understanding of how cultures differ and how they influence organizational and managerial processes alike emerges as an essential ingredient in a successful global manager's toolkit.

A final example comes from the global economic turmoil of the past several years. We have heard much recently about economic downturns, financial exigencies, bankruptcies, corporate bailouts, recessions, and unemployment. We have also seen a number of people and institutions being blamed, including bankers, investors, mortgage lenders, manufacturers, offshore companies, and politicians. We see leaders from entire continents collectively blaming leaders from other continents. The finger of blame is pointing in an almost infinite number of directions. Finally, we have seen individual and collective greed as never before. In the world of business, regardless of geographic location, we have witnessed entrepreneurs and managers alike desperately trying to find a quick fix, a short-term competitive advantage that will allow them to become wealthier than their competitors and colleagues. Wealth is celebrated, even worshipped, in places. Meanwhile, millions of people around the world in both developing and industrialized countries lose their homes, jobs, security, health, and even education for their children.

What has been lost in all this chaos is a fundamental premise of successful global (and local) business: mutual exchange and mutual benefit. Researchers and managers alike see successful global negotiations as being based on people and companies coming together to achieve their common objectives. Even in countries where legal contracts reign supreme, the role of personal relationships is not undervalued. Likewise, successful communication is typically seen as being best facilitated when all parties share a common understanding – and a common cause. Leaders are seen to be more effective when they strive to see that everyone involved wins. Work motivation and performance are best facilitated when employees at all levels see a reason for buy-in. Equity, fairness, and stewardship are seen by most people to be the most effective way to create a more ethical and sustainable world order.

Certainly, these management processes get more complex and challenging when managers and their companies cross borders, yet the fundamental principles hold. The individual and corporate selfishness of the past few years has demonstrated quite clearly that greed is a short-term and non-sustainable strategy for future development and security, both at home and abroad. Breaking faith with one's stakeholders – whether they are customers, investors, or employees – is invariably suboptimal in the long run. Instead, global managers and their firms would be better advised to seek long-term global strategies and partnerships and to incorporate a genuine stakeholder model as part of their business plan: inclusion rather than exclusion; partnerships rather than lethal competition.

Looking to the future

We suggested earlier in this book that culture and cultural differences represented major keys to understanding managerial thought and action, although they are certainly not the only key. We also suggested that a productive way to discover the utility of these keys is to approach intellectual discovery and management development as part of an overall learning strategy (see Exhibit 12.5).[5] By doing so, managers still may not have the power to see into the future, but they do have an ability to prepare themselves for it better. Chung Ju Yung, founder of the Hyundai Business Group, observed "The difference between winners and losers in a highly competitive business environment is the ability both to prepare for upcoming challenges and opportunities and to recognize such opportunities when they emerge."[6] Preparation *and* recognition: both are required. Seeing opportunities for the future without adequate preparation or preparing for the future without adequate study of emerging opportunities are both recipes for coming in second or third place.

Looking backward . . .

Some of our greatest successes result from accidents, hunches, or simple luck. Learn from our mistakes, so we can make better choices in the future.

Successful global managers bring people together in collaborative and symbiotic ways that build on past experiences and create value for the organization and its surroundings.

Global managers must seek long-term global strategies and partnerships and incorporate genuine stakeholders as part of their business plan.

Winning in today's highly competitive environment relies on the ability to both prepare for upcoming challenges and opportunities and recognize them when they emerge.

We must learn from the past as we prepare for the future, understanding all the while that most new opportunities occur somewhere in between.

Education never stops; continue to learn in order to move forward. Seek to ask the new questions that no one else has asked.

Looking forward . . .

Exhibit 12.5 Learning from the past, looking to the future

In the same manner, many have noted that the word *weiji* means "crisis" in Chinese, and is typically expressed using two characters: one for danger and one for opportunity. This interpretation of the concept suggests that crises are often related to two other variables: threats and opportunities. In many cases, threats and opportunities can indeed lead to productive changes in organizations to make them more nimble, quicker to respond, and more competitive. Again, however, this occurs only if and when managers realize what is happening and understand the surrounding environment to the extent that they are in a position to capitalize on the events as they unfold.

When the business environment is viewed in this manner, it may be that Omar Khayyám and Siddhārtha Gautama are actually giving the same advice to global managers in the twenty-first century. Yes, the past is prologue, and we must understand the "how's" and "why's" of how we got to this point; but also, yes, if we believe that we are headed in the right direction (that we can "see" the future, at least metaphorically), all we need to do is to pursue it. Perhaps the focus of our principal attention right now, therefore, should be on the present, so long as we see the present in dynamic or continuous terms: *past > present > future*. Most business opportunities are here now, not in the past and not in the future. Maybe the wisest thing global managers can do is to understand this dynamic. What can we learn from the past that can help us in the future, and what can we do in the present that can help guarantee this success in the future?

To accomplish this, as we have discussed throughout this book, global managers must develop proficiencies in working across cultures, because this is where most future opportunities will be found. They must develop an ability to distinguish between cultural differences and similarities across borders, as well as differences within single countries. They must develop an ability to tease out the subtle contradictions and dualities that are rooted in various cultures, and not look for easy answers when none may exist. They must also develop an ability to adapt traditional management skills, such as leadership, motivation, negotiation, and communication, to fit cross-cultural or multicultural venues. Herein lies the essence of effective global management.

The prospects of dealing with people from different cultural backgrounds can be very challenging, but potentially it can also be very rewarding. For many managers, though, it doesn't happen easily. Remember ABB CEO Percy Barnevik's observation that global managers are made, not born; it is not a natural process.[7] Remember, too, Thomas Stewart's observation that a global manager is set apart by more than a worn suitcase and a dog-eared passport.[8] To the extent that these observations are correct, the onus is clearly on managers to prepare themselves for success in the future. Engaging with managers and entrepreneurs from different cultures opens up considerable opportunities to learn more about ourselves, discover new ways of doing things, and find creative solutions to problems both old and new. It is clearly part of the developmental process for most managers; and, in this pursuit, continual cognitive, analytical, and experiential learning play a significant – and often underappreciated – role.

NOTES

1. Steven Jobs, commencement address, Stanford University, California, June 12, 2005.
2. Alberto Moravia, *The Indifferent Ones*. New York: E. P. Dutton, 1932.
3. George Santayana, *The Life of Reason or the Phases of Human Progress: Reason in Common Sense*. New York: Charles Scribner & Sons, 1924, p. 284.
4. Mohandas Karanchand Gandhi, *Gandhi: An Autobiography*. Boston, MA: Beacon Press, 1993.
5. David A. Kolb, "Management and the learning process,"*California Management Review*, 18(3) (1976), pp. 21–31; David A. Kolb, *Experiential Learning: Experience as the Source of Learning and Development*. Englewood Cliffs, NJ: Prentice-Hall, 1984.
6. Richard M. Steers, *Made in Korea: Chung Ju Yung and the Rise of Hyundai*. London: Routledge, 1999.
7. Percy Barnevik, cited in Philip R. Harris, Robert T. Moran, and Sarah V. Moran, *Managing Cultural Differences: Global Leadership Strategies for the 21st Century*, 6th edn. Amsterdam: Elsevier, 2004, p. 25.
8. Thomas Stewart, cited in Harris, Moran, and Moran, *Managing Cultural Differences*, p. 1.

APPENDIX
Models of national cultures

For many managers, the study of culture often begins with a comparison of different cultures or countries using several cultural dimensions (e.g., individualism/collectivism). For example, if a manager from France is traveling to Prague in the Czech Republic, it can be quite helpful to understand differences in cultural trends between the two locales prior to arrival. While such models clearly do not explain everything managers need to know to succeed, they can be a useful starting point.

A number of such models are available and have been widely adopted. These include the works of Clyde and Florence Kluckhohn and Fred Strodtbeck, Geert Hofstede, Edward T. Hall, Fons Trompenaars, Shalom Schwartz, and Robert House and his GLOBE project associates. Each attempts to capture the essence of cultural differences through the use of multiple dimensions or measures. In doing so, each model highlights different aspects of societal beliefs, norms, and/or values, and, as such, convergence across the models has been seen as being very limited. This may not be the case, however. Below, we briefly summarize each of the six models. This is followed by a brief comparison between the models in search of commonalities.[1]

Models of national cultures

Based on the initial research by Clyde Kluckhohn, cultural anthropologists Florence Kluckhohn and Fred Strodtbeck suggested one of the earliest models of culture, which has served as a principal foundation for several later models.[2] They proposed a theory of culture based on value orientations, arguing that there are a limited number of problems that are common to all human groups and for which there are a limited number of solutions. They further suggested that values in any given society are distributed in a way that creates a dominant value system. They used anthropological theories to identify five value orientations, four of which were later tested in five subcultures of the American southwest: two Native American tribes, a Hispanic village, a Mormon village, and a farming village of Anglo-American homesteaders. The five dimensions are identified in Exhibit A.1. Each dimension is represented on a three-point continuum.

Exhibit A.1 Kluckhohn and Strodtbeck's cultural dimensions

Dimensions	Scale anchors		
Relationship with nature: beliefs about the need or responsibility to control nature	*Mastery:* belief that people have a need or responsibility to control nature	*Harmony:* belief that people should work with nature to maintain harmony or balance	*Subjugation:* belief that individuals must submit to nature
Relationship with people: beliefs about social structure	*Individualistic:* belief that social structure should be arranged on basis of individuals	*Collateral:* belief that social structure should be based on groups of individuals with relatively equal status	*Lineal:* belief that social structure should be based on groups with clear and rigid hierarchical relationships
Human activities: beliefs about appropriate goals	*Being:* belief that people should concentrate on living for the moment	*Becoming:* belief that people should strive to develop themselves into an integrated whole	*Doing:* belief in striving for goals and accomplishments
Relationship with time: extent to which past, present, and future influence decisions	*Past:* in making decisions, people are principally influenced by past events or traditions	*Present:* in making decisions, people are principally influenced by present circumstances	*Future:* in making decisions, people are principally influenced by future prospects
Human nature: beliefs about good, neutral, or evil human nature	*Good:* belief that people are inherently good	*Neutral:* belief that people are inherently neutral	*Evil:* belief that people are inherently evil

Dutch management researcher Geert Hofstede has advanced the most widely used model of cultural differences in the organizations literature.[3] His model was derived from a study of employees from various countries working for major multinational corporations and was based on the assumption that different cultures can be distinguished on the basis of differences in what they value. In other words, some cultures place a high value on equality among individuals, while others place a high value on hierarchies or power distances between people. Likewise, some cultures value certainty in everyday life and have difficulty coping with unanticipated events, while others have a greater tolerance for ambiguity and seem to relish change. Taken together, Hofstede argued that it is possible to gain considerable insight into organized behavior across cultures on the basis of these value dimensions. Initially, Hofstede asserted that cultures could be distinguished along four

Exhibit A.2 Hofstede's cultural dimensions

Dimensions	Scale anchors	
Power distance: beliefs about the appropriate distribution of power in society	*Low power distance:* belief that effective leaders do not need to have substantial amounts of power compared to their subordinates	*High power distance:* belief that people in positions of authority should have considerable power compared to their subordinates
Uncertainty avoidance: degree of uncertainty that can be tolerated and its impact on rule-making	*Low uncertainty avoidance:* tolerance of ambiguity; little need for rules to constrain uncertainty	*High uncertainty avoidance:* intolerance of ambiguity; need for many rules to constrain uncertainty
Individualism/collectivism: relative importance of individual versus group interests	*Collectivism:* group interests generally take precedence over individual interests	*Individualism:* individual interests generally take precedence over group interests
Masculinity/femininity: assertiveness versus passivity; material possessions versus quality of life	*Masculinity:* values material possessions, money, and the pursuit of personal goals	*Femininity:* values strong social relevance, quality of life, and the welfare of others
Long-term versus short-term orientation: outlook on work, life, and relationships	*Short-term orientation:* past and present orientation; values traditions and social obligations	*Long-term orientation:* future orientation; values dedication, hard work, and thrift
Indulgence versus restraint: Relative emphasis on individual happiness, leisure, and personal control	*Indulgence:* Societal emphasis on enjoyment and need gratification	*Restraint:* Strict societal control to suppress or regulate gratification

dimensions, but later he added a fifth dimension based on his research with Hong Kong researcher Michael Bond.[4] A sixth dimension was added in 2010 based on the work of Bulgarian sociologist Yulian Minkov. The final six dimensions are illustrated in Exhibit A.2.

Edward T. Hall, a noted American cultural anthropologist, has proposed a model of culture based on his ethnographic research in several societies, notably Germany, France, the United States, and Japan.[5] His research focused primarily on how cultures vary in interpersonal communication, but also included work on personal space and time. These three cultural dimensions are summarized in Exhibit A.3. Many of the terms used today in the field of cross-cultural management (e.g., monochronic and polychronic) are derived from his work.

Exhibit A.3 Hall's cultural dimensions

Dimensions	Scale anchors	
Context: extent to which the context of a message is as important as the message itself	*Low context:* direct and frank communication; message itself conveys its own meaning	*High context:* much of the meaning in communication is conveyed indirectly through the context surrounding a message
Space: extent to which people are comfortable sharing physical space with others	*Center of power:* territorial; need for clearly delineated personal space between oneself and others	*Center of community:* communal; comfortable sharing personal space with others
Time: extent to which people approach one task at a time or multiple tasks simultaneously	*Monochronic:* sequential attention to individual goals; separation of work and personal life; precise concept of time	*Polychronic:* simultaneous attention to multiple goals; integration of work and personal life; relative concept of time

Building on the work of Hofstede, Dutch management researcher Fons Trompenaars has presented a somewhat different model of culture based on his study of Shell and other managers over a ten-year period.[6] His model is based on the early work of Harvard sociologists Talcott Parsons and Edward Shils and focuses on variations in both values and personal relationships across cultures.[7] It consists of seven dimensions, as shown in Exhibit A.4. The first five dimensions focus on relationships among people, while the last two focus on time management and society's relationship with nature.

Taking a decidedly more psychological view, Shalom Schwartz and his associates asserted that the essential distinction between societal values is the motivational goals they express.[8] He identified ten universal human values that reflect needs, social motives, and social institutional demands.[9] These values are purportedly found in all cultures and represent universal needs of human existence. The human values identified are: power, achievement, hedonism, stimulation, self-direction, universalism, benevolence, tradition, conformity, and security. Schwartz argued that individual and cultural levels of analysis are conceptually independent.[10] Individual-level dimensions reflect the psychological dynamics that individuals experience when acting on their values in their everyday life, while cultural-level dimensions reflect the solutions that societies find to regulate human actions. At the cultural level of analysis, Schwartz identified three dimensions: conservatism versus autonomy, hierarchy versus egalitarianism, and mastery versus harmony, summarized in Exhibit A.5. Based on this model, he studied school teachers and college students in fifty-four countries. His model has been applied to basic areas of social behavior, but its application to organizational studies has been limited.[11]

Exhibit A.4 Trompenaars' cultural dimensions

Dimensions	Scale anchors	
Universalism/particularism: relative importance of applying standardized rules and policies across societal members; role of exceptions in rule enforcement	*Universalism:* reliance on formal rules and policies that are applied equally to everyone	*Particularism:* rules must be tempered by the nature of the situation and the people involved
Individualism/collectivism: extent to which people derive their identity from within themselves or their group	*Individualism:* focus on individual achievement and independence	*Collectivism:* focus on group achievement and welfare
Specific/diffuse: extent to which people's various roles are compartmentalized or integrated	*Specific:* clear separation of a person's various roles	*Diffuse:* clear integration of a person's various roles
Neutral/affective: extent to which people are free to express their emotions in public	*Neutral:* refrain from showing emotions; hide feelings	*Affective:* emotional expressions acceptable or encouraged
Achievement/ascription: manner in which respect and social status are accorded to people	*Achievement:* respect for earned accomplishments	*Ascription:* respect for ascribed or inherited status
Time perspective: relative focus on the past or the future in daily activities	*Past-/present-oriented:* emphasis on past events and glory	*Future-oriented:* emphasis on planning and future possibilities
Relationship with environment: extent to which people believe they control the environment or it controls them	*Inner-directed:* focus on controlling the environment	*Outer-directed:* focus on living in harmony with nature

Finally, in one of the most ambitious efforts to study cultural dimensions, Robert House led an international team of researchers that focused primarily on understanding the influence of cultural differences on leadership processes.[12] Their investigation was called the **GLOBE study** (Global Leadership and Organizational Behavior Effectiveness). In their research, the GLOBE researchers identified nine cultural dimensions, as summarized in Exhibit A.6. While several of these dimensions have been identified previously (e.g., individualism/collectivism, power distance, and uncertainty avoidance), others are unique (e.g., gender egalitarianism and performance orientation).

Based on this assessment, the GLOBE researchers collected data in sixty-two countries and compared the results. Systematic differences were found in leader behavior across the cultures. For example, participatory leadership styles that are often accepted in the individualistic West are of questionable effectiveness in the more collectivistic East. Asian managers place a heavy emphasis on paternalistic

Exhibit A.5 Schwartz's cultural dimensions

Dimensions	Scale anchors	
Conservatism/autonomy: extent to which individuals are integrated in groups	*Conservatism:* individuals are embedded in a collectivity, finding meaning through participation and identification with a group that shares their way of life	*Autonomy:* individuals are autonomous from groups, finding meaning in their own uniqueness. Two types of autonomy: intellectual autonomy (independent pursuit of ideas and rights) and effective autonomy (independent pursuit of affectively positive experiences)
Hierarchy/egalitarianism: extent to which equality is valued and expected	*Hierarchy:* cultures are organized hierarchically; individuals are socialized to comply with their roles and are sanctioned if they do not	*Egalitarianism:* individuals are seen as moral equals who share basic interests as human beings
Mastery/harmony: extent to which people seek to change the natural and social world to advance personal or group interests	*Mastery:* individuals value getting ahead through self-assertion and seek to change the natural and social world to advance personal or group interests	*Harmony:* individuals accept the world as it is and try to preserve it rather than exploit it

leadership and group maintenance activities. Charismatic leaders can be found in most cultures, although they may be highly assertive in some cultures and passive in others. A leader who listens carefully to his or her subordinates is more valued in the United States than in China. Malaysian leaders are expected to behave in a manner that is humble, dignified, and modest, while American leaders seldom behave in this manner. Indians prefer leaders who are assertive, morally principled, ideological, bold, and proactive. Family and tribal norms support highly autocratic leaders in many Arab countries.[13] Clearly, one of the principal contributions of the GLOBE project has been to systematically study not just cultural dimensions but also how variations in such dimensions affect leadership behavior and effectiveness.

Common themes across models

Taken together, these six culture models attempt to accomplish two things. First, each model offers a well-reasoned set of dimensions along which various cultures

Exhibit A.6 GLOBE project's cultural dimensions

Dimensions	Scale anchors	
Power distance: degree to which people expect power to be distributed equally	*High:* society divided into classes; power bases are stable and scarce; power is seen as providing social order; limited upward mobility	*Low:* society has large middle class; power bases are transient and sharable; power often seen as a source of corruption, coercion, and dominance; high upward mobility
Uncertainty avoidance: extent to which people rely on norms, rules, and procedures to reduce the unpredictability of future events	*High:* tendency to formalize social interactions; document agreements in legal contracts; be orderly and maintain meticulous records; rely on rules and formal policies	*Low:* tendency to be more informal in social interactions; reliance on word of people they trust; less concerned with orderliness and record keeping; reliance on informal norms of behavior
Humane orientation: extent to which people reward fairness, altruism, and generosity	*High:* interests of others important; values altruism, benevolence, kindness, and generosity; high need for belonging and affiliation; fewer psychological and pathological problems	*Low:* self-interest important; values pleasure, comfort, and self-enjoyment; high need for power and possessions; more psychological and pathological problems
Institutional collectivism: extent to which society encourages collective distribution of resources and collective action	*High:* individuals integrated into strong cohesive groups; self viewed as interdependent with groups; societal goals often take precedence over individual goals	*Low:* individuals largely responsible for themselves; self viewed as autonomous; individual goals often take precedence over societal or group goals
In-group collectivism: extent to which individuals express pride, loyalty, and cohesiveness in their organizations and families	*High:* members assume they are interdependent and seek to make important personal contributions to the group or organization; long-term employer–employee relationships; organizations assume major responsibility of employee welfare; important decisions made by groups	*Low:* members assume they are independent of the organization and seek to stand out by making individual contributions; short-term employer–employee relationships; organizations primarily interested in the work performed by employees over their personal welfare

Exhibit A.6 (*cont.*)		
Dimensions	Scale anchors	
Assertiveness: degree to which people are assertive, confrontational, and aggressive in relationships with others	*High:* value assertiveness, dominance, and tough behavior for all members of society; sympathy for the strong; value competition; belief in success through hard work; values direct and unambiguous communication	*Low:* prefers modesty and tenderness to assertiveness; sympathy for the weak; values cooperation; often associates competition with defeat and punishment; values face saving in communication and action
Gender egalitarianism: degree to which gender differences are minimized	*High:* high participation of women in the workforce; more women in positions of authority; women accorded equal status in society	*Low:* low participation of women in the workforce; fewer women in positions of authority; women not accorded equal status in society
Future orientation: extent to which people engage in future-oriented behaviors, such as planning, investing, and delayed gratification	*High:* greater emphasis on economic success; propensity to save for the future; values intrinsic motivation; organizations tend to be flexible and adaptive	*Low:* less emphasis on economic success; propensity for instant gratification; values extrinsic motivation; organizations tend to be bureaucratic and inflexible
Performance orientation: degree to which high performance is encouraged and rewarded	*High:* belief that individuals are in control of their destiny; values assertiveness, competitiveness, and materialism; emphasizes performance over people	*Low:* values harmony with environment over control; emphasizes seniority, loyalty, social relationships, and belongingness; values who people are more than what they do

can be compared. In this regard, they offer a form of intellectual shorthand for cultural analysis, allowing researchers to break down assessments of various cultures into power distance, uncertainty avoidance, and so forth, and thus organize their thoughts and focus attention on what otherwise would be a monumental task. Second, four of the models offer numeric scores for rating various cultures. For example, we can use Hofstede's model to say that Germany is a thirty-five while France is a sixty-eight on power distance, suggesting that Germany is more egalitarian than France. Regardless of whether these ratings are highly precise or only generally indicative of these countries, they nonetheless provide one indication of how these countries might vary culturally.

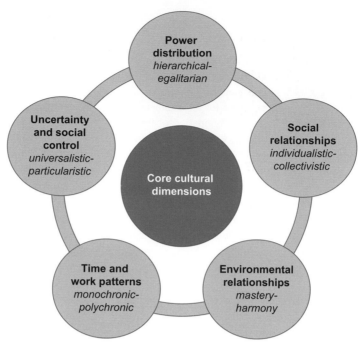

Exhibit A.7 Core cultural dimensions

As is evident from this review, there are many different ways to represent cultural differences. Unfortunately, the six cultural models available frequently focus on different aspects of societal beliefs, norms, or values, and, as such, convergence across the models seems at first glance to be limited. This lack of convergence presents important challenges both for researchers attempting to study cultural influences on management and for managers trying to understand new cultural settings.

Instead of advocating one model over another, we suggest that all the models have important factors to contribute to our understanding of culture as it relates to management practices (see Chapter 3).[14] In order to navigate this culture theory jungle, we argue that the most productive approach is to integrate and adapt the various models on the basis of their utility for better understanding business and management in cross-cultural settings. In doing so, we seek common themes that collectively represent the principal differences between cultures. While no single model can cover all aspects of a culture, we believe it is possible to tease out the principal cultural characteristics through such a comparative analysis.

In our view, five relatively distinct common themes emerge from this comparison (see Exhibit A.7).

- **Power distribution.** How are power and authority distributed in a society? Is this distribution based on concepts of hierarchy or egalitarianism? What are societal beliefs concerning equality or privilege?

- Social organization. What is the fundamental building block of a society: individuals or groups? How does a society organize for collective action?
- Environmental relationships. On a societal level, how do people view the world around them and their relationship with the natural and social environment? Is their goal to control the environment and events around them or to live in harmony with these external realities?
- Time/work patterns. How do people in a society organize and manage their time to carry out their work and non-work activities? Do people approach work in a linear or nonlinear fashion?
- Uncertainty and social control. How do societies try to ensure predictability in the behavior of their members? Do they work to control people through uniformly applied rules, policies, laws, and social norms or do they rely more on personal ties or unique circumstances?

To achieve this clustering, we must recognize that, in a few cases, multiple dimensions in the original models can be merged into a single more general or unifying cultural dimension (e.g., institutional and in-group collectivism in the GLOBE model), as discussed below. In addition, we need to look beyond the simple adjectives often used by the various researchers and seek deeper meaning in the various concepts themselves, also as discussed below.

At first glance, these five themes seem to replicate Hofstede's five dimensions, but closer analysis suggests that the other models serve to amplify, clarify, and, in some cases, reposition dimensions so that they are more relevant for the contemporary workplace. Indeed, we believe the commonality across these models reinforces their utility (and possible validity) as critical evaluative components in better understanding global management and the world of international business. As such, each model thus adds something of value to this endeavor.

Core cultural dimensions

Power distribution: hierarchical versus egalitarian

All societies have normative beliefs governing how power and influence should be distributed and used. Typically, these norms are expressed in terms of whether power should be clustered at or near the top of a hierarchy or distributed in a more egalitarian fashion. In other words, is the culture more *hierarchical* or *egalitarian*? Questions pertaining to this dimension include the following. Should authority ultimately reside in strong centralized governments or in the people themselves? Should organizations be structured vertically (e.g., tall organization structures) or horizontally (e.g., flat organization structures, or even networked structures)? Is decision-making largely autocratic or participatory? Are leaders chosen because they are the most qualified for a job or because they already have standing in the community? Are leaders elected or appointed? Are people willing or reluctant to question authority?

Social relationships: individualistic versus collectivistic

The nature of social organization and perceptions of self-identity have been widely identified in various models of culture as representing a key variable in understanding what differentiates one society from another. This is usually expressed in terms of cultures being more *individualistic* or *collectivistic*. At issue here is whether members of a society see themselves first and foremost as individuals or as members of a group. Do they achieve self-identity through their own efforts or through group endeavors? Are individual goals or group goals more important? Do group sanctions reinforce personal responsibility or conformity to group norms? Is individual or group decision-making preferred? Is business done primarily on the basis of written contracts or personal relationships? Is communication characterized primarily by low context (when the message contains all or almost all the intended message) or by high context (when the context surrounding the message also carries significant information – see Chapter 6)?

An understanding of this dimension is critical for managers to succeed overseas. For example, initiating performance-based incentive systems that reward individual performance will likely have a difficult time succeeding in highly collectivistic cultures. Group-based rewards and incentives will probably be more successful in such circumstances. Likewise, overemphasizing participatory decision-making in a highly individualistic culture may also be problematic (see Chapter 4). Again, the challenge for global managers is to develop administrative practices that support, rather than contradict, local customs and social norms.

Environmental relationships: mastery versus harmony

Most societies have a reasonably widely shared view with respect to their relationship to their surroundings. We refer to this as the distinction between *mastery-oriented* and *harmony-oriented*. This relationship often represents an underlying motive structure or goal for the society. In other words, on a fundamental level some societies seek to control their surrounding environment, while others seek to live in relative harmony with it. Does a society emphasize competition in the pursuit of personal or group goals or striving for social progress, quality of life, and the welfare of others? Does a society attempt to bend nature to its will or conform to nature as much as possible? Is a society assertive, proactive, and "masculine" (to use Hofstede's term) or passive, reactive, and "feminine"? Does a society tend to emphasize extrinsic rewards on the basis of job performance or intrinsic rewards based on seniority or on one's position in the organization? Is there an emphasis on material possessions as symbols of achievement or on economy, harmony, and societal sustainability? Finally, do people tend to engage in conspicuous consumption or do they tend to be more modest and unpretentious?

An understanding of this dimension can help managers determine how to structure work plans and incentive plans, and may even influence leadership style. For example, most employees in a mastery-oriented culture will respond to challenges and personal incentives; they will strive for success. Employees in more harmony-oriented cultures will more likely focus their attention on building or maintaining group welfare, personal relationships, and environmental sustainability. They tend to be more committed to social progress. As such, they will likely be more responsive to participative leadership and be more skeptical of proposed change. Managers who understand this are in a position to tailor their leadership style to fit the situation.

Time and work patterns: monochronic versus polychronic

A fourth major difference across cultures is people's approaches to time and tasks. Here we distinguish between *monochronic* and *polychronic*. People in more monochronic cultures tend to be somewhat methodical in their use of time and their approaches to tasks. They see time as a commodity that can be measured, used, and sometimes sold. They often approach work as a series of tasks or goals that should be tackled sequentially, or one at a time. By contrast, people in more polychronic cultures tend to be more flexible, addressing several problems simultaneously. They are often oblivious to time and resist firm deadlines. They also tend to mix work and personal lives in a more fluid fashion than their monochronic counterparts, who stress a clear separation between work and family.

Logical questions to ask here include the following. Do people have a precise concept of time and tend to be very punctual or do they have a relative concept and tend to be late? Are people more committed to their jobs or to family and friends? Do they separate work and family life or see them as an integrated whole? Do they take a linear or nonlinear approach to planning? Finally, are they focused and impatient or unfocused and patient?

Uncertainty and social control: rules versus relationships

A final dimension used by managers to differentiate across cultures involves the issue of rules versus relationships as a means of reducing uncertainty in society. In other words, how is social behavior best controlled? This distinction is referred to here as *rule-based* and *relationship-based*, although it is also referred to as *universalistic* and *particularistic* (see also Chapter 3).[15] In essence, this issue focuses on the means of social control.

Rule-based (or universalistic) cultures believe that social values and standards take precedence over individual needs or claims by friends and relations; rules are intended to apply equally to the whole "universe" of members. Exceptions serve only to weaken the rule of law. For example, a rule that people should bear truthful witness in a court of law, or give their honest judgment to an insurance company concerning a payment it is about to make, is more important than particular family or friendship ties. This is not to say that "particular" ties are unimportant in universalistic cultures; rather, universal truth as embodied in the law is believed to be more important than these relationships. By contrast, particularistic cultures see the ideal culture in terms of human friendship, extraordinary achievement, unique situations, and close personal relationships. The spirit of the law is deemed to be more important than the letter of the law. Clearly, there are rules and laws in particularistic cultures, but these are designed simply to codify how people relate to one another. Rules are needed (if only to be able to make exceptions to them for particular cases), but people need to be able to count on their friends.

As a result, in rule-based cultures there is a tendency to promulgate a multitude of laws, rules, regulations, bureaucratic procedures, and strict social norms in an attempt to control as many unanticipated events or behaviors as possible. People tend to conform to officially sanctioned constraints because of a moral belief in the virtue of the rule of law, and will often obey directives even if they know violations will not be detected. Waiting for a red light in the absence of any traffic is a good example here. Rules and laws are universally applied (at least in theory), with few exceptions for extenuating circumstances or personal connections. There is a strong belief in the use of formal contracts and rigorous record keeping in business dealings. Things are typically done "by the book," and infractions often bring immediate sanctions or consequences. Finally, decisions tend to be made on the basis of objective criteria to the extent possible. All this is aimed at creating a society with no surprises.

By contrast, relationship-based (or particularistic) cultures tend to use influential people more than abstract or objective rules and regulations as a means of social control.[16] This personal control can come from parents, peers, superiors, supervisors, government officials, and so forth – anyone with influence over the individual. In this sense, relationship-based cultures tend to be particularistic, and individual circumstances often influence the manner in which formal rules are applied. In addition, greater emphasis is placed on developing mutually beneficial interpersonal relationships and trust as a substitute for strict rules and procedures. There is generally less record keeping, and things tend to be done on an informal basis. There is also greater tolerance for non-compliance with bureaucratic rules, in the belief that formal rules cannot cover all contingencies and that some flexibility is often required. Finally, decisions tend to be made on the basis of a combination of objective and subjective criteria and with less formality.

This is not to say that relationship-based cultures do not value laws and official procedures; they do. Rather, laws and procedures are often followed only to the extent that one's social network embraces them and sees either the virtue or necessity of following them, not because of some innate belief in their moral correctness, as is the case with universalistic cultures. When predictability of behavior is important, it is motivated largely through contacts, not contracts, and interpersonal trust and mutual support between partners is critical.

NOTES

1. Luciara Nardon and Richard M. Steers, "The culture theory jungle: divergence and convergence in models of national culture," in Rabi S. Bhagat and Richard M. Steers (eds.), *Cambridge Handbook of Culture, Work, and Organizations.* Cambridge University Press, 2009, pp. 3–22.
2. Clyde Kluckhohn, "Values and value orientations in the theory of action," in Talcott Parsons and Edward A. Shils (eds.), *Towards a General Theory of Action.* Cambridge, MA: Harvard University Press, 1951; Florence Kluckhohn and Fred Strodtbeck, *Variations in Value Orientations.* Evanston, IL: Row, Peterson, 1961.
3. Geert Hofstede, *Culture's Consequences: Comparing Values, Behaviors, Institutions, and Organizations across Nations.* Thousand Oaks, CA: Sage, 1980.
4. Michael Bond and Peter Smith, "Cross-cultural social and organizational psychology," *Annual Review of Psychology*, 47 (1996), pp. 205–35.
5. Edward T. Hall, *The Silent Language.* New York: Doubleday, 1959; Edward T. Hall and Mildred Reed Hall, *Understanding Cultural Differences: Germans, French and Americans.* Yarmouth, ME: Intercultural Press, 2000.
6. Fons Trompenaars, *Riding the Waves of Culture: Understanding Cultural Diversity in Business.* London: Economist Books, 1993; Fons Trompenaars and Charles Hampden-Turner, *Riding the Waves of Culture: Understanding Diversity in Global Business*, 3rd edn. New York: McGraw-Hill, 1998.
7. Parsons and Shils, *Towards a General Theory of Action.*
8. Shalom Schwartz, "Universals in the content and structure of values: theoretical advances and empirical tests in 20 countries," in Mark Zanna (ed.), *Advances in Experimental Social Psychology*, vol. 25. New York: Academic Press, 1992, pp. 1–65.
9. Cigdem Kagitçibasi, "Individualism and collectivism," in Marshall Segal and Cigdem Kagitçibasi (eds.), *Handbook of Cross-Cultural Psychology*, vol. 3. Boston: Allyn & Bacon, 1997, pp. 1–49.
10. Shalom Schwartz, "Beyond individualism/collectivism: new cultural dimensions of values," in Uichol Kim, Harry C. Triandis, Cigdem Kagitçibasi, Sang-Chin Choi, and Gene Yoon (eds.), *Individualism and Collectivism: Theory, Methods and Applications.* Thousand Oaks, CA: Sage, 1994, pp. 85–122.
11. Bond and Smith, "Cross-cultural social and organizational psychology."

12. Robert J. House, Paul J. Hanges, Mansour Javidan, Peter W. Dorfman, and Vipin Gupta, *Culture, Leadership and Organizations: The GLOBE Study of 62 Societies*. Thousand Oaks, CA: Sage, 2004.
13. House et al., *Culture, Leadership and Organizations*.
14. Nardon and Steers, "The culture theory jungle."
15. John Hooker, *Working across Cultures*. Stanford University Press, 2003.
16. Hooker, *Working across Cultures*.

Name Index

Adler, Nancy, 74, 82, 207, 226, 297–8, 363
Aga, Anu, 181
Al-Ghunaim, Maha, 64
Azevedo, Guilherme, 82

Barmanbek, Imre, 64
Barnevik, Percy, 9, 296, 376
Beechler, Schon, 192
Bennett Coleman, 181–2
Bennis, Warren, 161, 192
Bhagat, Rabi S., 58, 93, 95, 104, 267
Boden, Dermot, 33–4
Bond, Michael, 380
Boyacigiller, Nakiye, 192
Brooks, Chad, 179
Buchan, Nancy B., 316

Camus, Albert, 239
Cannon-Brooks, Michael, 17
Caproni, Paula, 298
Carroll, Lewis, 357, 364
Chabria, Vidya, 64
Chau, Pully, 282
Chenneveau, Didier, 33
Chipchase, Jan, 36
Chiu, Willy, 322–3
Chua, Fred, 268
Chung Ju Yung, 375
Columbus, Christopher, 373–4

Dashmalchian, Ali, 192
Davidson-Marley, 203
de Geus, Arie, 12
Deleuze, Gilles, 76
Depew, Jeff, 222–5
Deresky, Helen, 227
Dhawan, Neelam, 182
Dorfman, Peter W., 176
Drucker, Peter, 226

El-Sallab, Sahar, 64
England, George, 264–5
Erez, Miriam, 290
Ericsson, 200–1
Ertel, Danny, 205

Fayol, Henri, 19
Fellini, Federico, 134
Fernandez, Juan, 193
Ferraro, Gary P., 159, 226
FitzGerald, Niall, 249
Follett, Mary Parker, 19

Gandhi, Mahatma, 374
Gates, William, xv
Gautama, Siddhartha, 366, 376
Geertz, Clifford, 49, 81
George, Claude, 19
Ghemawat, Pankaj, 324
Ghosn, Carlos, 166
Govindavajan, Vijay, 324
Graham, John, 207, 226
Gupta, Anil, 324
Gupte, Lalita, 181

Håkansson, Anna, 78–80
Hall, Edward T.
    cultural model, 53–5, 380
    difficulty in understanding culture, 53–5
    mutual benefit model, 103
    silent language, 72, 144
Hall, Mildred Reed, 53, 103
Hampden-Turner, Charles, 27
Handy, Charles, 201, 226
Hanges, Paul J., 192
Harris, Philip, 16
Hayward, Tony, 147
Helú, Carlos Slim, 194
Hessler, Peter, 343–4

Hitt, Michael A., 168, 192
Hofstede, Geert
    cultural dimensions model, 54, 79–80, 379–80
    culture definition, 49
    Culture's Consequences, 81
    German culture, 103
    no universal management solutions, 84
    Swedish culture, 79
    uncertainty avoidance, 272
Holding, Dogan, 64
Hopeman, Wei, 337–8
House, Robert J.
    business ethics, 253
    cultural interconnectedness, 47
    GLOBE cultural model, 56, 81, 175, 382–3

Indu, Jain, 181–2
Ishikawa, Jun, 165, 192
Iyengar, Adhira, 37

Jackson, Susan, 226
Javidan, Mansour, 54, 168, 175–7
Jobs, Steve, 365
Jullien, François, 183

Kagayama, Atsushi, 296
Kang, Iris, 282–3
Khayyám, Omar, 366, 376
Kleinbeck, Uwe, 290
Kluckhohn, Clyde, 49, 378
Kluckhohn, Florence, 378

Lao-Tzu, 49, 81, 161
Laurent, Andre, 26
Lee Kun-Hee, 288–9
Lewis, Richard D., 137, 144, 231
Lindzey, Gardner, 81
Linton, Tom, 33
Liu Shengjun, 193
Luo, Yadong, 75

Ma Yún, 113, 297
Ma, Jack, 113, 297
Mao Zedong, 282
Mayer, Louis B., 214
Maznevski, Martha, 319–20
Mazumdar-Shaw, Kiran, 181

Meyer, Erin, 296
Minkov, Yulian, 380
Mintzberg, Henry, 21
Moran, Robert, 16
Moran, Sarah, 16
Moravia, Alberto, 366
Morgan, Eileen, 235–6
Morparia, Kalpana, 181
Motwani, Sulajja Firodia, 181
Munsterberg, Hugo, 19
Musk, Elon, 262

Nam, Sang Hoon, 290
Nam, Yong, 33
Nardon, Luciara, 391
    core cultural dimensions, 58
    cross-cultural leadership, 165
    cultural screens on communication, 131
    interpersonal communication, 129
    leadership patterns in China, 183
Nicholson, Nigel, 96

Olayan, Lubna, 64
Orly, Levy, 192
Orly, Yeheskel, 75
Osman, Laura, 64

Parikh, Indira, 182
Park, Seung-ho, 227
Pascal, Blaise, 228
Paul, Priya, 181
Perlmutter, Howard, 199
Petursdottir, Kristin, 168–9
Phatak, Arvind, 267

Radjou, Navi, 300
Reithofer, Norbert, 251
Rosen, Lawrence, 62

Samovar, Larry A., 158
Sanchez-Runde, Carlos
    decision-making models, 107
    interpersonal communication, 129
    cultural screens on communication, 131
    cross-cultural leadership, 165
    leadership patterns in China, 183
    regional models of organization, 94, 102, 104

Sandberg, Sheryl, 84
Santayana, George, 372
Schneider, Susan, 324
Schuler, Randall, 226
Schwartz, Shalom, 381
Shenkar, Oded, 75, 82
Shiki, Moriya, 223
Shim, Won-Shul, 261
Shur, Norman, 133
Smith, Peter, 391
Steers, Richard
    core cultural dimensions, 57
    cross-cultural leadership, 165
    cultural screens on communication, 131
    decision-making methods, 105–7
    global mindset, 168
    interpersonal communication, 129
    leadership patterns in China, 183
    regional models of organization, 92, 102, 104
Stevenson, Robert Louis, 326
Stewart, Rosemary, 39
Stewart, Thomas A., 30, 376
Strodtbeck, Fred, 378
Swindler, Ann, 49, 69, 81

Taher, Nahed, 63
Tainwala, Ramesh, 310–11
Tata, Simone, 181
Taylor, Frederick, 19
Taylor, Sully, 192
Thierry, Henk, 290
Thomas, David, 290
Thurow, Lester, 1
Tómasdóttir, Halla, 168–9
Triandis, Harry C., 364
Trompenaars, Fons
    culture definition, 49
    perceptions of managerial roles, 27

Ungson, Garardo, 227
Ustinov, Peter, 231

Walker, Andrea, 355–6
Wang, Yingin, 47, 81
Weber, Max, 20
Welch, Jack, 222–5
Whitehead, Alfred North, 239

Yeheskel, Orly, 75, 82

Subject Index

ABB Group, 296, 376
Accenture, 313–14
accident prevention guidelines, 250
acculturation
 making yourself at home in, 359–61
 strategies, 350–3
adaptation
 and global management, 7, 28–30
 challenges, 341
 stages, 345–6
AIA model. *See* attention–interpretation–action model
Airbnb, 198–9
aisatsu (Japanese), 223, 227
Alibaba, 112–14, 297
alienated returnees, 354
Andur Capital, 168–9
Anglo country decision-making, 105–7
Apeejay Surrendra Group, 181
Apple, 200–1, 365
Arab Bankers Association of North America, 64
Argentina, 156–7, 315
assimilation. *See* acculturation
AT&T, 3
attention–interpretation–action model, 128–30, 149–50
attribution theory, 272
Australia
 gender wage gaps in, 281
 management values in, 265

Baidu.com, 15
Bangladeshi employment practices, 247–8
Bank of America, 59
Bavarian Radio Symphony Orchestra, 3
Belgium wage gaps, 281
beliefs. *See* values
Belize, 355–6
biznez (Russian), 235–6
BMW, 251

Brazil
 cultural logic, 139–40
 employee benefits in, 279
 GLOBE study, 178
 trust levels in, 315
 underground economy in, 242
bribery and ethics, 235–6, 240–4
bridging, 319
British Petroleum, 147
bureaucracy, 20
business culture. *See also* organizational environment, corporate culture
 and cultural differences, 73–7
 and cultural nuances, 63
 and interaction with local work environment, 117–18
 Canada, 96–7
 China, 97–100
 cultural perceptions on managerial roles and practices, 25–8
 Germany, 103–5
 Japan, 100–2, 107–8
 limits of cultural differences on, 65–6
 Scandinavia, 108–9
 Southeast Asia, 237–8
 United Kingdom, 96–7
 United States, 94–6, 105–7
business–government relations, 60
businesswomen. *See also* gender discrimination
 Iceland, 168–9
 India, 181–2
 Middle East, 63–4

call center work values, 268
Canada, 96–7, 139–40
capataz (Spanish), 24
Carbon Disclosure Project, 251
Carbon Performance Leadership Index, 251
career considerations in global assignments, 339–40

causal attributions, 272
centralized decision-making, 105–7
change
    doctrine of changed circumstances, 215–18
    in global business environment, 3–7
Chevron, 259
child labor, 247–8
Chile, 315
China
    centralized decision-making, 106–7
    corporate culture, 15, 112–14
    culture shock in, 190–1, 343–4
    employee incentives in, 267, 277, 279
    family model of organization, 97–100
    gender discrimination in, 282–3
    leadership style, 182–4
    negotiation, 217
    partnerships, 204
    unreliability of commercial law, 94–6
chopping (Nigerian), 259
Citi Ventures, 337–8
clothing factory employment practices, 247–8
Code of Conduct for Transnational Corporations,
    256
codetermination, 104, 121–2
cognition
    cultural logic, 139–40
    definition of, 137
    evaluation, 137–8
    language and linguistic structures, 132–6
collaborative decision-making, 108–9
collectivistic culture, 117, 388
co-located global teams, 301, 320
Commercial International Bank (Egypt), 64
communication
    and cognition, 132, 137–8
    and making apologies, 147
    and native speakers, 135
    challenges, 127–8, 133, 137
    cultural, 139–40, 144–6, 151–4, 156–7
    cultural screens, 130–1
    global team, 300–5
    strategies, 151–4
communication protocols
    acceptable behaviors, 148–9
    appropriate topics for discussion, 141–3
    conversational formalities, 146–7

    interpersonal, 128–30
    message formatting, 144–6
compensation
    and financial incentives, 276–7
    as reward, 280–3
    piece rate pay system, 273–4
competitive negotiation, 208–10
conflict
    ethical, 229–36, 252–7
    in negotiations, 210
    management, 211–14
Confucianism, 34, 97, 123
conservative culture, 232
consultative decision-making, 107–8
context. *See also* environment
    and global management, 255
    in dispersed global teams, 21–4
contingency approach to leadership, 169–71
contracts
    and doctrine of changed circumstances, 215–18
    as legally binding, 215
    definition of, 214–15
core cultural dimensions, 383–91
Corning Incorporated, 203
corporate culture. *See also* business culture
    Alibaba, 112–14
    behavioral norms of, 115
    Dentsu Incorporated, 111–12
    Germany, 103–5
    influences on, 109–11
    Volkswagen, 121–2
corruption. *See* bribery and ethics
Corruption Index, 240–1
Cosco, 217
Cuba, 198–9
cultural contradictions in global business, 2–3,
    66–9
cultural dimensions core concepts, 383–91
cultural dimensions models, 378–83
cultural environments, 47–8
cultural friction, 75
cultural myopia, 32
cultural norms. *See* business culture
cultural screens, 130–1
cultural stereotypes, 73–4
cultural translators, 348–9
culture shock, 341–50

cultures
  and global business environments, 59–62
  and influence on customer service, 51–2
  characteristics of, 50–1
  complexities and contradictions, 63, 65–6
  core dimensions, 57–9
  definition of, 49
  homogeneity limitations, 66–9
  national models of, 53–7, 378–91
customer service and culture, 51–2

decision-making methods
  centralized, 105–7
  collaborative, 108–9
  consultative, 107–8
  global teams, 296
deculturation, 350
Delta Airlines, 69–70
Denmark, 276, 281
Dentsu Incorporated, 111–12
disillusionment stage of psychological
      development, 345
dispersed global team challenges
  lack of mutual knowledge and context in,
      302–3
  loss of details, 304–5
  technology overdependence, 303–4
dispersed global teams
  characteristics of, 301
  Dow Chemical, 300
  management of, 306–8, 320–1
distributive justice, 276–7
doctrine of changed circumstances, 215–18
Dow Chemical, 300
Dow Jones Sustainability Index, 251
Draftfcb, 282
Dutch State Mines (DSM), 200

Ecuador, 142–3
effective management, 25–8
egalitarianism. See also gender discrimination
  and equal opportunity, 63–4
  cultural, 387–8
  Germany, 117
eîdos (Greek), 183
Emerson Electric, 190–1
emotional capital, 168, 337

employee
  induction, 111–14
  OECD guidelines, 245–6
  participation, 117
employee motivation. See also incentives
  benefits, 278–80
  managing, 283–6
employer-initiated global assignments,
      329–30
employment practice fairness, 245–6
environment. See also context
  and expatriate psychological adjustment, 347,
      349
  understanding new, 357–8
environmental impact guidelines, 250
environmental relationships
  as cultural, 388–9
  ethics in, 249–51
environmental types
  cultural, 47–52, 61, 368
  organizational, 114–19, 367–9
  situational, 115–19, 368
equal opportunity, 63–4
equality principle, 270–1
equity principle, 270–1, 284
ethical guidelines
  bribery and corruption, 240–4
  environmental relationships, 249–51
  fair employment practices, 245–8
  in a global environment, 239–40
ethical management attributes, 236–8
ethics
  beliefs and institutional perspective, 233–6
  beliefs and values, 229–32
  conflict management, 252–7
  global leadership, 236–8, 370
  in global business environment, 233–6
  legalities, 256–7
Europe
  managerial risk-taking, 272
  trust levels in, 314–15
exchange relationships, 269–70, 374
expatriates
  cultural challenges, 33–5, 326–9
  varied perceptions of, 42–3
expectations
  creating realistic employee, 285

employee towards work, 270–1
    trust, 315–17
extrinsic rewards, 275

face (Asian concept), 98
Facebook, 5, 84
face-to-face meetings, 306–7, 310–11
fairness
    employment practice, 245–8
    principles based on culture, 270–1
family considerations
    child labor, 247–8
    in global assignments, 338–9
    long-term assignments, 333
family model of organization, 93, 97–100
FIFA bribery scandal, 244
financial incentives, 276–7
Finland, 59
five cardinal virtues (Chinese), 97
force field analysis
    definition of, 243
    OECD guidelines, 242–4
Ford Motor Company, 199
foreign direct investment (FDI), 6
Foundation for Management Education,
    182
Foxconn Technology Group, 200–1
France
    decision-making in, 296
    employee benefits in, 267, 279
    gender wage gaps in, 281
    high value on job security, 276
    trust levels in, 315
free overtime (Japan), 266
free trade zone, 289
Frog Design, 36
Fuji Electric Corporation, 222–5
future of global management, 375–7

gate-keeping leadership, 165
gender discrimination. *See also* egalitarianism,
    businesswomen
    and cultural acceptance, 271
    compensation, 280–3
General Electric Company (GE), 36, 222–5
General Motors, 204
geopolitics, 8–9

Germany
    acceptable behaviors, 148–9
    collaborative decision-making, 108–9
    egalitarian culture, 117
    employee incentives in, 263, 267
    mutual benefit model of organization, 103–5
    success of piece rate pay system in, 273–4
    value on job security, 276
global assignments
    acculturation strategies, 350–3
    challenges of living abroad, 32, 336–40, 362
    culture shock in, 341–50
    employer and self-initiated, 329–30
    key relationships in, 326–9
    long- and short-term, 331–6
    management strategies, 356–61
    repatriation, 353–6
global businesses. *See also* regional models of
    organization
    and relationships between stakeholders,
        strategies, and structures, 115–17
    organization designs, 89
    strategies for, 87–8
    transitioning from national to international
        markets, 88–9
Global Healthcare Argentina, 156–7
Global Leadership and Organizational Behavior
    Effectiveness. *See* GLOBE
global management. *See also* multicultural
    competence, management
    and multicultural competence, 118–19
    definition of, 30–1
    ethical guidelines, 252–7
    targeted goals and objectives, 39
global management model, 38–41, 371–2
global management skills, 369–71
global management strategies
    avoiding cultural stereotypes, 73–4
    preparation for the unexpected, 76–7
    viewing cultural differences in neutral terms,
        74–5
global manager types, 31–7, 367
global matrix design, 89
global mindset, 167–9
global partnerships. *See also* negotiation
    benefits of, 197
    success factors in, 370

global teams
    advantages and disadvantages of, 294–6
    characteristics of, 299
    experiments in corporate, 293–4
    leadership in, 312–17
    management strategies, 319–20, 370
    managing tasks and team processes, 305–8
    synergy, 297–9
    technology advancement and, 300–2
globalization
    and corn ethanol production, 6
    and geopolitics, 8–9
    and global teams, 317–18
    and need for multicultural competence, 9–12,
        366
    magnitude of investments, 6
GLOBE
    cultural model, 54, 56, 382–3
    definition of culture, 49
    ethical leadership practices, 236–8
    leadership project, 170, 174–8
gong-si (Chinese), 99–100, 106
Google, 14–15
Greece, 281
Grupo Carso, 194
guānxi (Chinese), 98, 106, 123
Gulf One Investment Bank, 63

haigui (Chinese), 113
haredim (Hebrew), 69
harmony (Chinese), 98
harmony-oriented cultural dimension, 388–9
Hebrew, 69–70
hierarchical culture dimension, 387–8
Hindustan Lever, 181
holistic bargaining strategy, 211
honeymoon stage of psychological adjustment,
        345
honne (Japanese), 107–8, 124
HSBC Holdings, 43
human resource guidelines, 245–8
Hungary, 281
Hyundai Business Group, 375

Iceland, 168–9
ideographic language, 134
IKEA, 232

illegal contributions guidelines, 242
implementation mindset, 205
incentives. See also rewards, employee motivation
    employee benefits, 278–80
    financial, 276–7
India
    call center outsourcing to, 268
    employee benefits in, 279
    Google in, 14–15
    women leaders in, 181–2
individualistic cultural dimension, 388
Indonesia
    egalitarianism in, 276
    employee incentives in, 263
    vacation policies, 267
Industrial Credit and Investment Corporation
        of India, 181
innovation portal, 323
inpatriates, 23
insider trading ethics, 234
integration
    in acculturation, 352
    of global team management, 319
Intel, 279–80
International Business Machines Corporation
    cloud labs, 322–3
    global teamwork, 293–4
International Labour Organization, 179, 256
Internet penetration rate, 198
intrinsic rewards, 275
investor model of organization, 93–7
Iran, 235
Islamic legal systems, 62, 78–80, 137, 232
Italy, 267, 276

Japan
    acceptable behaviors, 148–9
    Akihabara electronics district, 15
    business culture, 60–2, 111–12, 117
    consultative decision-making, 107–8
    customer service norms, 51–2
    management values in, 265
    network model of organization, 93, 100–2
    Yahoo! Japan, 63–4
Japanese employees
    annual work hours, 266
    benefits, 279

employee incentives in, 277
importance of work in, 265
incentives, 273
vacation policies, 267
value on job security, 276
jeitinho (Brazilian), 68, 178
jiazu gong-si (Chinese), 99–100
jingshen (Chinese), 343
jogode cintura (Brazilian), 178
Jumbo Group, 64

kachou (Japanese), 24
kaisha (Japanese), 101, 107
kao (Japanese), 68
kao o tateru (Japanese), 68
karoshi (Japanese), 273
kazoku teiate (Japanese), 279
keiretsu (Japanese), 101–2
Kinetic Motor, 182
Kirin Holdings Company, Ltd, 102
konzern (German), 103–4

language
    and linguistic structures, 124, 132–5
    importance of learning local, 348–9
    need for skill in, 337
language types
    ideographic, 134
    silent, 144
Latvia, 315
law
    and governmental ethics, 233–6
    Sharia, 260
leadership
    and self-knowledge, 186–8
    as cultural construct, 171–3, 185–6, 369
    dimensions of, 162–4
    Emerson Electric, 190–1
    ethics in, 236–8
    GLOBE, 174–8
    in global teams, 312–17, 370
leadership approaches
    contingency, 169–71
    normative, 167–9
    universal, 164–6
leadership style
    cultural influences on, 56

female, 179–82
transformational, 164
Western versus Eastern traditions, 182–4, 190–1
legal conflict and ethical decision-making, 233–6
legal guidelines, 256–7
leisure conundrum, 266–8
Lenovo, 36
LG Electronics, 33–4
Lincoln Electric
    in Germany, 273–4
    in Mexico, 277–8
lingua franca, 133, 158
long-term assignments, 331–4

Malaysia, 173–4, 267
management. *See also* global management
    centralized decision-making, 105–7
    roles of, 21
    traditional models of, 19–21
mapping global team management, 319–20
maquiladora (Mexican), 287–9
mastery-oriented cultural dimension, 388–9
Mazda Motor Company, 199
Meaning of Work project, 265
medewerkers (Dutch), 172
meister (German), 24, 104
Mexico
    employee benefits in, 279
    Lincoln Electric in, 277–8
    personal nature of business, 263
    rewards and incentives in, 287–9
    vacation policies, 267
Microsoft India, 182
Miksukoshi Department Store, 51–2
Mintzberg's ten managerial roles, 28
mitbestimmung (German), 104
Mitsubishi Corporation, 102
Mitsubishi Electric, 222–5
Mittlestand firms (Germany), 87–8, 122
models
    attention–interpretation–action, 128–30
    cultural dimensions, 54, 79–80, 378–83
    global management, 38–41, 371–2
    GLOBE, 54, 56, 382–3
    national cultural, 53–7, 378–91
    traditional management, 19–21
    Trompenaars cultural, 381

models of organization
    family, 97–100
    investor, 94–7
    mutual benefit, 103–5, 374
    network, 100–2
    regional, 92
Monde Apparels factory, 247–8
monochronic cultural dimension, 389
moral conscience in decision-making, 235
motivation
    and incentives, 276–80
    compensation as, 280–3
    managing, 283–6
    needed for global assignments, 337
Motorola Corporation, 235
multicultural competence
    and acculturation, 353
    and global assignments, 358–9
    development of, 9–12
    need for, 6–9
    stages of, 366–71
multiculturalism
    and cultural diversity, 70–2
    and global management, 72–7
mutual benefit model of organization, 93, 103–5,
    374
mutual knowledge in dispersed global teams, 302
Myanmar, 362

namasté (Hindi, Nepalese), 127
negotiation. *See also* global partnerships
    competitive vs. problem solving strategies,
      208–10
    concessions and bargaining, 210–11
    developing a strategy, 196–8, 204–5
    doctrine of changed circumstances, 215–18
    managing the process, 206–7
    preparation for, 201–3, 222–5
    strategies for, 218–20
nemawashi (Japanese), 107, 124
Netherlands
    business etiquette, 156–7
    collaborative decision-making, 108–9
    employee incentives in, 279–80
    group cooperation norms in, 263
    mutual benefit model of organization,
      103–5

network model of organization, 93, 100–2
New Zealand, 281
Nigeria, 258–60, 315
Nissan Motor Company, 166
Nokia, 36
non-verbal communication, 137, 144
norm of authenticity, 138
normative approach to leadership, 165,
    167–9
normative behavior, 50
norms. *See* values
Norway, 263

objectivist approach, 62
OECD. *See* Organization for Economic
    Cooperation and Development
OECD Guidelines for Multinational Enterprises
    (book), 239
oil and gas industry corruption, 258–60
Olyan Group of Saudi Arabia, 64
organization design, 111–12
Organization for Economic Cooperation and
    Development (OECD)
    environmental guidelines, 250
    ethical guidelines, 239–44
    human resources guidelines, 245–8
    legal guidelines, 256–7
    membership countries, 261
organizational culture. *See* corporate culture,
    business culture
organizational environment. *See also*
    environment
    and global management, 84–5
    evolution of, 114–15
    general management strategies for, 115–19
organizational management, 115–19, *See also*
    management
orgullo (Spanish), 68
outsourcing, 268

Panasonic, 296
particularistic culture
    as cultural dimension, 389–91
    in Brazil, 74–5
    to truth, 231–2
partnerships. *See* global teams
patron (Spanish), 288

Pfizer
    acquiring Pharmacia, 195
    gender issues, 282–3
Pharmacia, 195–6
Philippines
    employee benefits in, 279
    vacation policies, 267
    work values in, 268
piece rate pay system, 273–4, 277–8
pok chow (Malaysian), 173–4
Poland, 281
pollution escape trips (Mexican), 279
polychronic cultural dimension, 389
Portugal, 315
power distribution cultural dimension, 387–8
Prada, 33
proactive returnees, 354
problem solving negotiation. *See* negotiation
psychological adjustment
    in global assignments, 342–4
    stages of, 344–7
psychological contract
    implicit understanding, 283–4
    work, 269–70
psychology
    causal attributions, 272
    expectations in, 270–1
    industrial, 19
    risk, 272–3
public health guidelines, 250

rank (Chinese), 98
regional models of organization
    family model, 97–100
    investor model, 94–7
    mutual benefit model, 103–5
    network model, 100–2
    overview of, 92
relationships. *See also* particularistic culture
    environmental, 249–51, 388–9
    exchange, 269–70, 374
    in global assignments, 326–9
    social, 388
remuneration guidelines, 242
Renault Group, 166
repatriation from global assignment, 353–6
resocialized returnees, 354

restraining forces, 261
returnees. *See* repatriation from global
        assignment
reverse culture shock, 353–4
rewards. *See also* incentives
    compensation, 280–3
    types of, 275–6
rice allowance (Philippines), 279
ringi-sei (Japanese), 107
ringi-sho (Japanese), 108
risk. *See* uncertainty and social control
Royal Dutch Shell (Shell). *See* Shell Oil Company
Rubbermaid, 200
rule-based approach. *See* universal approach
Russia
    employee benefits in, 279
    interpersonal relationships, 236
    perceptions of corruption in, 235–6

Samsonite International, 311
Samsung
    fair employment practices in, 246
    in Mexico, 287–9
Saudi Arabia
    corporate cultural ethics in, 232
    vacation policies, 267
saving face (Japanese), 68
Scandinavia
    attributes of ethical management, 237–8
    collaborative decision-making, 108–9
    employee incentives in, 273
    mutual benefit model of organization, 103–5
    value on job security, 276
scientific management, 19
self-initiated global assignments, 329–30
self-serving bias, 272
separation in acculturation, 351
Shanghai Automotive Industrial Corporation, 204
Sharia law, 79, 260
Shell Oil Company, 259, 333–4
short-term global assignments, 331, 334–6, 341
Siemens, 293–4
silent language, 144
simpatico (Spanish), 288
Singapore, 267
Slovenia, 315
social justice and decision-making, 233–6

social relationships cultural dimension, 388
socio-cultural adjustment, 350–3
sogo shosha (Japanese), 101
Sony Corporation, 246
South Korea
    employee incentives in, 263
    etiquette, 150
    language terms, 134
    management values in, 265
    self-serving bias, 272
Spain, 150
stakeholder impact in organization, 86–7
stereotyping. *See* cultural stereotypes
strategic management cycle, 86
strengths-based organization, 84
Studio D Radiodurans, 36
subjectivist approach, 62
supervisory role across cultures, 24
Sweden
    corporate relations with Islamic countries,
        232
    decision-making methods, 296
    employee incentives in, 263
Swedish Investment Bank, 78
symbolic leadership, 169–71
synergy in global teams, 297–9

Taoism, 81
tatemae (Japanese), 107–8, 124
teamwork. *See* global teams
technik (German), 24, 105
technology advancement
    and dispersed global teams, 300–8
    as driver of globalization, 4–5
    virtual managers, 37–8
    web-based global network designs, 89
télos (Greek), 183
Thailand
    fair employment practices in, 246
    group cooperation norms in, 263
Thermax Group, 181
Thornton International Business Report, 179–82
time and work patterns cultural dimension, 389
Tokyo Electric Power Company (TEPCO),
        169–71
Toshiba, 293–4
Toyota Motor Corporation, 147

transactional leadership, 165
transformational leadership, 164
transparency guidelines, 242
Trompenaars' cultural model, 54, 56, 381
trust among global team members, 314–17
truth interpretations, 231–2
Turkey, 315

Uber Technologies, 91
uncertainty and social control
    as cultural dimension, 389–91
    in a global environment, 2
    in business management, 76–7
underground economies and corruption, 241–2
Unilever, 249
unionization guidelines, 246
United Kingdom
    business culture, 96–7
    employee incentives in, 263
    low value on job security, 276
    vacation policies, 267
United Nations legal guidelines, 256
United States
    business culture, 60–2
    employee benefits in, 279
    low value on job security, 276
    management values in, 264–5
    managerial risk-taking, 272
    self-serving bias, 272
    success of piece rate pay system in, 273–4
    teamwork, 190–1
    vacation policies, 267
universal approach
    as cultural dimension, 389–91
    limits of, 254–5
    to leadership, 164–6
    to truth, 231–2
unwritten rules. *See* psychological contract
Upjohn Corporation, 195–6

vacation policies, 266–8
values
    core, 254
    work, 264–6, 268
Velux, 295
vernacular language, 158
Vietnam, 5

virtual meetings. *See* technology advancement
Volkswagen Group, 121–2
vorstand (German), 103

wa (Japanese), 277
wagamama (Japanese), 273
wages. *See* compensation
Wal-Mart Stores, 43, 247–8
weiji (Chinese), 376
Western countries leadership style, 182–4

Westinghouse Electric Corporation, 224–5
work
    demands and constraints of, 40–1
    importance of, 266–8
    psychology of, 269–74
    values and goals in, 264–6, 283, 285
World Economic Forum, 161
Wrangler, 247–8

yin and *yang* (Chinese), 183